EXPLORING THE NEW TESTAMENT

Volume 2

The Letters and Revelation

Howard Marshall has spent most of his career teaching in the University of Aberdeen, where he is now Emeritus Professor of New Testament. He is a former President of the British New Testament Society and a former Chair of the Tyndale Fellowship for Biblical Research. He has written a book on New Testament theology (*New Testament Theology: Many Witnesses, One Gospel.* Leicester: IVP, 2004), and commentaries on the Greek text of the Gospel of Luke and the Pastoral Epistles as well as on the English text of Acts, 1–2 Thessalonians and 1–3 John. He has a preaching ministry in the North of Scotland Mission Circuit of the Methodist Church and elsewhere. He has four married children.

Stephen Travis is a teacher and writer, formerly Vice-Principal and Lecturer in New Testament at St John's College, Nottingham. He has also enjoyed short spells of teaching (and learning!) in India, Australia and Sri Lanka. He has written at both a scholarly and a popular level on a variety of biblical themes, particularly the Christian hope. A Methodist layman, he has served the church on a number of theological commissions. He is married to Pat, and they have a grown-up daughter.

Ian Paul is Dean of Studies at St John's College, Nottingham, where he teaches New Testament, biblical interpretation and preaching, with a special interest in the Book of Revelation. He is also Chair of the Revelation seminar group at the British New Testament Conference, and is a founding member of the Grove biblical series editorial group. Prior to joining the college, he was for 10 years in parish ministry in Poole, Dorset. His PhD was on how biblical metaphors work, with particular reference to Revelation chapters 12 and 13. He is married to Maggie, who is a GP, and they have three children and one foster daughter.

NEW
TESTAMENT

SECOND EDITION

Exploring the New Testament

A Guide to the Letters & Revelation

I. HOWARD MARSHALL,
STEPHEN TRAVIS & IAN PAUL

Volume
Two

IVP Academic

An imprint of InterVarsity Press
Downers Grove, Illinois

InterVarsity Press
P.O. Box 1400, Downers Grove, IL 60515-1426
World Wide Web: www.ivpress.com
E-mail: email@ivpress.com

Design: Cindy Kiple
Images: The Last Supper, Macip, Vicente Juan (Juan de Juanes) / Prado, Madrid, Spain / Giraudon / The Bridgeman Art Library.

ISBN 978-0-8308-2540-0

Printed in the United States of America ∞

Library of Congress Cataloging-in-Publication Data has been requested.

P	22	21	20	19	18	17	16	15	14	13	12	11	10	9	8	7	6	5	4	3	2	1
Y	30	29	28	27	26	25	24	23	22	21	20	19	18	17	16	15	14	13	12	11		

1   1-3
2   4-5
3   6-8
4   9-12
5   ... 13-14
6   ... 16-17
7   16-20 18-20
8   21

Contents

THE LETTERS AND REVELATION

List of illustrations		x
How to use this book		xi

A. SETTING THE SCENE

1 The world of first-century Christians — 3
How do we know what we know? — 3
The emergence of Roman power — 4
A century of civil conflict — 4
Augustus' successors — 6
The Julio-Claudian dynasty — 6
The Flavian dynasty — 6
Government of the empire — 8
The provinces — 8
Client kingdoms — 9
Cities and colonies — 9
The power of propaganda — 9
The army — 10
The legions — 10
Auxiliaries — 10
The praetorian guard — 10
Roman society — 10
Citizenship — 10
Classes — 11
Women — 12
Patrons and clients — 12
Language and culture — 13
Entertainment — 13
Religion and philosophy — 14
Traditional religion — 14
Healing cults — 15
Mystery religions — 15
Fate, astrology and magic — 16
The imperial cult — 16
Cynics, Stoics and Epicureans — 17
Romans, Jews and Christians — 18
Essay topics — 20
Further reading — 20

B. PAUL AND HIS LETTERS

2 Letters in the New Testament — 23
Ancient letter-writing — 23
The format of letters — 24
The format of Paul's letters — 25
Letters of recommendation or introduction — 28

Other New Testament letters — 28
Further reading — 29

3 Paul, his letters and his life — 31
Where can we learn about Paul? — 31
Material from outside the New Testament — 32
The Acts of the Apostles — 32
The letters of Paul — 34
Difficulties in the Pauline letters — 34
Were the letters all written by Paul? — 34
Do we have the letters in their original form? — 36
Is Paul a reliable informant about himself? — 36
Early days — 36
Paul's call and conversion — 38
Paul as a missionary — 39
Paul the captive — 41
Problems of chronology — 42
Essay topics — 44
Further reading — 44

4 The letter to the Galatians — 47
What led to the writing of the letter? — 47
The structure of the letter — 49
Paul's argument in the letter — 50
'New Perspective' readings of Paul — 52
Was the letter effective? — 53
To whom was the letter sent? — 55
When was the letter written? — 57
Consequences for the date of the letter — 60
For today's Galatians — 60
Essay topics — 61
Further reading — 61

5 The letters to the Thessalonians — 63
Paul and Thessalonica — 63
The contents of 1 Thessalonians — 65
The contents of 2 Thessalonians — 69
Problems in 2 Thessalonians — 72
For today's Thessalonians — 74
Essay topics — 74
Further reading — 74

6 The 'first' letter to the Corinthians 77

Paul's mission 77

The 'previous' letter 78

Getting behind the second (first) letter 79

Continuing immorality 80

Party squabbles in the congregation 80

The rich and the poor 81

'Strong' and 'weak' believers 82

Spiritual superiority and inferiority 83

Questions about the resurrection 84

Surveying 1 Corinthians 84

Party spirit 85

Immorality and litigation 86

Sexual and marital issues 87

Food offered to idols 88

Congregational meetings 90

Spiritual gifts 91

The resurrection 92

In conclusion 92

For today's Corinthians 93

Essay topics 93

Further reading 94

7 The 'second' letter to the Corinthians 95

An overview of the problems 95

The events leading up to 2 Corinthians 1—7 96

Identifying the tearful letter 97

Survey of 2 Corinthians 1—7 99

Thanksgiving (Berakah) 99

The rift with the congregation 100

The nature of apostleship 101

Resuming the story 102

2 Corinthians 8 and 9 103

More fragmentary letters? 104

The problem of 2 Corinthians 10—13 104

The occasion of 2 Corinthians 10—13 107

For today's Corinthians 108

Essay topics 108

Further reading 109

8 The letter to the Romans 111

The purpose of the letter 111

The nature of the argument in the letter 114

An overview of the letter 115

The opening (and the closing)
(Rom. 1:1–15; 15:14—16:27) 115

The text is announced! (Rom. 1:16–17) 116

Universal sin and guilt (Rom. 1:18—3:20) 116

The main proposition (Rom. 3:21–31) 117

Abraham as an example of faith (Rom. 4:1–25) 118

The results of justification (Rom. 5:1–11) 118

Christ contrasted with Adam
(Rom. 5:12–21) 119

No longer under sin and under the law
(Rom. 6:1–23) 120

The law is good – but impotent (Rom. 7:1–25) 121

New life by the Spirit (Rom. 8:1–39) 122

The problem of Jewish unbelief in the gospel
(Rom. 9—11) 123

Practical implications of the new life
(Rom. 12—13) 126

Jews and Gentiles living together in the same
congregation (Rom. 14:1—15:13) 126

Paul's mission – to Rome and beyond
(Rom. 15:14–33) 127

Closing greetings (Rom. 16:1–27) 127

Scribes do strange things 128

Again – the purpose of the letter 130

The composition of Romans 130

The problems of Romans 16 132

Two versions of one letter 132

Two separate letters 133

For today's Romans 134

Essay topics 134

Further reading 135

9 The letter to the Philippians 137

Paul and the congregation at Philippi 137

Paul's situation 138

The situation and needs of the church 141

Attacks on the church 141

Tensions within the church 141

A rival version of the gospel 141

The structure of the letter 142

Philippians as a letter 143

Philippians as an example of rhetoric 143

The development of the message 145

Philippians – one letter or several
fragments? 147

For today's Philippians 148

Essay topics 149

Further reading 149

10 The letter to Philemon 151

Paul, Philemon and Onesimus 151

The structure of the letter 155

The outcome 155

For a twenty-first-century Philemon 156

Essay topics 156

Further reading 157

11 **The letter to the Colossians** 159
The planting of the congregation 159
Why was the letter written? 159
The 'philosophy' 160
The structure of the letter 162
Paul's teaching in the letter 162
Paul's circumstances 166
  Other possible places of origin 166
Did Paul write Colossians? 167
  Arguments against Pauline authorship 167
  Arguments in favour of Pauline authorship 168
For today's Colossians 168
Essay topics 169
Further reading 169

12 **The letter to the Ephesians** 171
To whom was the letter sent? 172
What is the letter? 173
  The unity of the church 174
  'Power' language 174
The structure of the letter 175
A quick survey of the letter 175
Who wrote the letter? 177
  Arguments against Pauline authorship 177
  Arguments for Pauline authorship 179
  Weighing the probabilities 179
For today's Ephesians 180
Essay topics 181
Further reading 181

13 **The letters to Timothy and Titus** 183
Letters that are somehow different 183
The problem of non-Pauline authorship 184
To whom were the letters written? 185
When were the letters written? 186
What are the letters about? 187
The structure of the letter to Titus 187
An overview of Titus 187
The structure of 1 Timothy 188
An overview of 1 Timothy 189
The structure of 2 Timothy 191
An overview of 2 Timothy 191
What is the situation reflected in the letters? 193
  Opposition and heresy 193
  The development of church order 194
  Christian living and pastoral care 195
  Language and style 196
  The theology and the way it is expressed 196

Evaluating the evidence 197
  Not by Paul? 197
  Written or dictated by Paul? 198
  A middle way? 198
For today's congregational leaders 199
Essay topics 199
Further reading 199

14 **Paul – the missionary theologian** 201
Paul as an apostle 201
Humanity and its need 202
  Creation 202
  Human nature 202
  Sin 203
Getting right with God 204
  Justification by works 204
  Covenantal nomism 204
  The marks of belonging 204
  Paul's radical alternative 205
The language of salvation 205
  Sacrifice 205
  Justification 205
  Redemption 206
  Reconciliation 206
  Salvation 206
Faith 206
The new life of believers 207
  God as Father 207
  'In Christ' 208
  The work of the Spirit 210
Theological implications for Paul's
  understanding of God 211
The community of believers 212
Ministry and the functions of the church 213
What principles shape Christian behaviour? 215
  Five general principles 215
  The new way of life 216
Some specific areas of concern 217
  Relations between men and women 217
  Slavery 217
  The state 217
  Money and possessions 217
The future for the world and believers 217
The missionary obligation 219
Essay topics 219
Further reading 219

15 **New Testament letters – interpretation
and authorship** 221
Understanding what we read in
  New Testament letters 221

Two related activities	223
Speeches in the form of letters?	227
Entering into the situation	228
Getting the message	230
Critical methods in the study of the New Testament	232
Historical criticism	232
Form criticism	232
Source criticism	232
Redaction criticism	232
Textual criticism	232
Canonical criticism	233
Literary criticism	233
Socio-rhetorical criticism	233
Reception history and reader-response criticism	233
Ideology criticism	233
The question of pseudonymity	234
The traditional view	235
Alternative suggestions	236
Further reactions	237
Essay topics	238
Further reading	238

C. LETTERS BY OTHER CHURCH LEADERS

16 The letter to the Hebrews	243
Clues about the recipients	243
What kind of a document?	244
The structure and argument of Hebrews	245
Theological themes of Hebrews	250
The high priest and his sacrifice	250
Other perspectives on Jesus	251
Salvation and the Christian hope	251
Discipleship	252
Special issues	252
The author's thought-world	252
Is Hebrews anti-Jewish?	254
Where were the readers located?	254
Who wrote the letter?	256
Some issues for today	257
Essay topics	259
Further reading	260

17 The letter of James	261
The character of the letter of James	261
James as exhortation or 'parenesis'	262
James as wisdom	262
James as a letter	263
The structure of the letter	263
Who wrote the letter?	264

To whom was the letter addressed? Why, and when?	266
Jewish Christians in Palestine?	266
Jewish Christians in the Dispersion?	267
James and the teaching of Jesus	267
James and Paul	268
Themes in James	270
God	270
Jesus	270
Living with integrity	270
The law	271
The testing of faith	271
Poverty and wealth	272
Some issues for today	273
Essay topics	273
Further reading	274

18 The first letter of Peter	277
Outline of the letter	277
The situation of the recipients	278
What was the nature of their suffering?	280
The letter's message to the churches	281
Christian existence in a hostile environment	282
The grace of God in Christ	282
The household of God	282
God's people	282
Facing suffering	284
Christian responsibilities	284
Who wrote 1 Peter?	285
Assessing the arguments	287
Some issues for today	288
Essay topics	289
Further reading	290

19 The second letter of Peter and the letter of Jude	291
What do these letters have in common?	291
The letter of Jude – its purpose	293
The false teachers	293
Jude's strategy for advising his readers	294
Who wrote this letter?	295
2 Peter – genre and outline	296
2 Peter – the problem of authorship	298
The false teachers in 2 Peter	300
The purpose and theology of 2 Peter	301
The hope of Christ's coming	301
Some issues for today	302
Essay topics	303
Further reading	304

20 The letters of John 305

1 John – background and authorship 305
Is the author of 1 John the same as the author of the Fourth Gospel? 306
The location of the author and his readers 307

The circumstances addressed in 1 John 308
The nature of the false teaching 308

John's response to the false teaching 310

The purpose and shape of 1 John 311

Some issues for today 313

2 and 3 John – their relation to 1 John 313

The context and content of 2 John 314
Hospitality to missionaries 314

The context and content of 3 John 315

3 John – evidence of an emerging pattern of church leadership? 316

Essay topics 318

Further reading 318

D. APOCALYPTIC LITERATURE

21 The Revelation to John 323

Language and genre 324

Historical context and dating 326
Dating 326
Authorship 328
Context 328

Theological perspectives 331
God 331
Jesus 331
The Spirit 332
The followers of the Lamb 332

Mythological context and emperor worship 333

Use of the Old Testament 335
Some examples 336

Structure and composition 337

Numbers and their meaning 338
Phrase repetition and word frequencies 338
Numerology 339
Words and their numbers 340
The decoding of 666 (Rev. 13:18) 341

Interpretative issues 342
Traditional approaches 342
Image, symbol and metaphor 342

Some issues for today 344

Essay topics 344

Further reading 345

Glossary 347

Index 351

ILLUSTRATIONS

MAPS AND DIAGRAMS

Roman provinces at the death of
   Claudius (AD 54)   8

Roman empire   39

Roman provinces in Asia Minor   56

The seven churches of Asia   329

CHARTS AND TABLES

Dates and events in Roman history   7

Gods of Greece and Rome mentioned
   in the New Testament   14

A possible chronology of Paul's life   44

Roman leaders/emperors   327

HOW TO USE THIS BOOK

On 17 July AD 180, seven men and five women stood trial in Carthage, North Africa. Boldly professing their faith in Jesus, they were condemned to die by the sword. During the trial the governor asked, 'What do you have there in your bag?' One of the twelve, named Speratus, replied, 'Books, and letters of Paul, a good man.'

Here were twelve people ready to die for the faith expressed in those documents. 'Books' almost certainly refers to the four Gospels, dealt with in *Exploring the New Testament*, volume 1. Volume 2 takes up the letters of Paul, together with those other writings of early Christian leaders which complete the New Testament. It is designed to form the basis of an introductory course on the Letters and Revelation for first- and second-year students in a university, theological college or seminary. This section aims to help you, whether a teacher or a student, to get the most from our book.

OUR AIMS AND OBJECTIVES

We are particularly concerned to get students reading and engaging with the NT documents for themselves, rather than simply learning at second hand what these books say or merely absorbing a lot of interesting theories about them. So we have provided frequent references to the text of the NT and to other relevant ancient literature – excerpts from the latter often being quoted for easy access. In order to give ample space to exploration of the context, purpose and theological message of the books, we have limited the amount of space given to issues such as authorship and date – though of course guidance is given about where such questions can be followed up in more detail.

To aid active learning, we have built into each chapter several sorts of further study for students to pursue, many of which we have used ourselves in the classroom. We do not expect students to have time to do all of them. With the teacher's guidance they will need to select those that are appropriate for the aims of the particular course being taught. And we hope that our suggestions will encourage teachers to add their own ideas.

What do you think? boxes provide questions and issues, which may take 15–30 minutes for a student to work at, and might then be used as the basis of a short class discussion or small group discussion.

Digging deeper boxes suggest a piece of research which may take a rather longer period of private study and could form the basis of a one-hour seminar led by the teacher or by some of the students. Having two or three students lead such a discussion, in our experience, enables the student leaders to engage with the topic at greater length, since they must set the agenda for the seminar, and also enables students to debate views with each other in a way that facilitates learning.

Focus on theology boxes (in most chapters). A new feature of this revised edition, these boxes are varied in content and include summaries of key theological emphases of an NT book or section, reflection on the wider theological interpretation of a theme or topic, consideration of implications for faith and life today based on the NT material being studied, or questions to provoke readers to engage in this kind of reflection. These are designed both to model how the NT can be read theologically, and to encourage our readers to do their own theological reading of the NT.

Essay topics at the end of each chapter (except the brief Chapter 2) provide ideas on topics to research in greater depth, which are to be presented in written form. They are intended to be about 2,000–3,000 words long, although some could be rather longer or shorter if the course being taught required that. Some are identified as 'Introductory' (intended for first-year students), others as 'Intermediate' (for second-year students). Some topics invite students to write for a particular audience or to design material that will relate the biblical text to today's world, rather than writing a traditional academic essay.

Further reading lists at the end of each chapter provide a basis for the research on the essay topics, as well as for further study in greater depth on particular issues within the chapter. We have chosen books that are generally available in British and North American college and university libraries. Within each chapter we have usually referred to books simply by author, or author and date, and full publication details can be found in the 'Further reading' sections.

Many students studying the NT are Christians, as we ourselves are, and will therefore want to ask about the relevance of their studies to living as Christians today. So we have concluded most chapters with a section in which we make suggestions or ask questions designed to stimulate the making of connections between then and now. We hope they will encourage students to reflect further for themselves along these lines.

STRUCTURE OF THE BOOK

The book falls into four sections. First, we sketch the historical, religious and social context in which the writers and first readers of the NT letters lived. We do not repeat here the material in the first chapter of vol. 1, which concentrates on the experience of Jews in Palestine, though some of that is relevant to some of the letters discussed in this volume. The focus here is on the Greco-Roman world in which the church's mission to Gentiles developed.

The second section deals with Paul the apostle and his letters. Between a chapter sketching Paul's life and mission and a chapter summarizing his theology, his letters are studied in their probable chronological order of writing. The section begins with a brief chapter on the nature of ancient letter writing,

Normativity
New perspective
Construct a moral vision of the NT

and ends with a chapter on two questions that have gradually been brought into focus through the study of the letters. These are, first: What problems and methods are involved in the process of understanding and interpreting NT letters for today? And second: How might we react to the proposal that certain letters were not written by the authors to whom they are attributed? Both the first and final chapter in this section of course relate not merely to Pauline letters but to others also, and might therefore have been placed at other points in the book. But it makes practical sense to include them at these points – though readers are of course free to read these and other chapters in any order that suits them!

The third section is devoted to what have traditionally been called the General or Catholic Epistles (because they do not name a specific church as recipients and hence have been thought to be addressed to Christians in general). The title is misleading since most of them do address specific audiences, though in some cases they were in several churches rather than a single community, and it may remain quite unclear to us where they were located.

Finally, we study the book of Revelation, the single example in the NT of 'apocalyptic' literature.

Exam?

A **glossary** at the end provides definitions of certain technical terms, and references to the main places in the book where they are introduced and explained, particularly in boxes within the chapters.

WHO WROTE WHAT?

We have planned this book together (and also with David Wenham and Steve Walton,

authors of the companion volume on the Gospels and Acts), and have commented on each other's drafts of chapters. So while we share responsibility for the whole book, the following chapters/sections were the particular responsibility of each of us:

Howard Marshall: Chapters 3–14, and the section of Chapter 15 on 'interpretation'.

Stephen Travis: Chapters 1–2, 16–20, and the section of Chapter 15 on 'authorship'.

Ian Paul: Chapter 21, and the section on 'Critical methods in the study of the New Testament' in Chapter 15.

Michael B. Thompson, Vice-Principal of Ridley Hall, Cambridge, contributed the feature on 'The New Perspective on Paul' in Chapter 4.

ACKNOWLEDGEMENTS

We are grateful to our students in the University of Aberdeen and St John's College, Nottingham for the encouragement and stimulus they have given to us as teachers. This book is the fruit of our work with them over many years. We have also gained much from our collaboration with David Wenham and Steve Walton on this project, and from their pioneering of the format of the two books in volume 1. We would like also to thank Ruth McCurry, our skilful and supportive editor at SPCK.

Biblical quotations are normally from the New Revised Standard Version. Quotations from Latin and Greek authors are normally from the Loeb Classical Library editions, published by Harvard University Press/Heinemann.

ABBREVIATIONS

Generally, we have used the abbreviations in P. H. Alexander, J. F. Kutsko, J. D. Ernest, S. A. Decker-Kucke and D. L. Petersen, eds, *The SBL Handbook of Style*. Peabody, MA: Hendrickson, 1999, Ch. 8. We list below the main abbreviations used.

ABD	D. N. Freedman, ed., *The Anchor Bible Dictionary* (6 vols). New York: Doubleday, 1992.
Ag. Ap.	Josephus *Against Apion*
Ant.	Josephus *Antiquities of the Jews*
AV	Authorized Version
BJRL	*Bulletin of the John Rylands Library*
CBQ	*Catholic Biblical Quarterly*
DLNTD	R. P. Martin, P. H. Davids, eds, *Dictionary of the Later New Testament and its Developments*. Leicester/Downers Grove: IVP, 1997.
DNTB	C. A. Evans, S. E. Porter, eds, *Dictionary of New Testament Background*. Leicester/Downers Grove: IVP, 2000.
DPL	G. F. Hawthorne, R. P. Martin, D. G. Reid, eds, *Dictionary of Paul and his Letters*. Leicester/Downers Grove: IVP, 1993.
ExpT	*Expository Times*
ESV	English Standard Version
ET	English translation
HCNT	M. E. Boring, K. Berger, C. Colpe, eds, *Hellenistic Commentary to the New Testament*. Nashville: Abingdon, 1995. Annotated collection of about 1,000 parallels from the ancient (mainly Greco-Roman) world to New Testament texts, illustrating similarities and differences.
Hist. eccl.	Eusebius *Ecclesiastical History*
Int	*Interpretation*
JBL	*Journal of Biblical Literature*

JSNT	*Journal for the Study of the New Testament*
JTS ns	*Journal of Theological Studies* (new series)
KJV	King James Version
LCL	Loeb Classical Library
MG.	Marginal note
NDBT	T. D. Alexander, B. S. Rosner, eds, *New Dictionary of Biblical Theology*. Leicester/Downers Grove: IVP, 2000.
NIV	New International Version
NRSV	New Revised Standard Version
NT	New Testament
NTS	*New Testament Studies*
OT	Old Testament
OTP	J. H. Charlesworth, ed., *The Old Testament Pseudepigrapha* (2 vols). Garden City, NY: Doubleday/ London: Darton, Longman & Todd, 1985.
REB	Revised English Bible
RSV	Revised Standard Version
TNIV	Today's New International Version
ZNW	*Zeitschrift für die neutestamentliche Wissenschaft*

A NOTE ON FURTHER READING

A number of standard reference books can be recommended for following up most of the topics covered in this book. As a first step students are encouraged to look up the relevant articles on the New Testament documents in dictionaries such as *ABD*, *DPL* and *DLNTD* (see Abbreviations above). On certain topics *DNTB* and *NDBT* will be useful.

Several reference works published by IVP are also available on a CD-ROM, *The Essential IVP Reference Collection* (separate editions for PC and Mac).

Several one-volume commentaries cover the whole Bible or the NT:

J. Barton, J. Muddiman, eds, *The Oxford Bible Commentary*. Oxford: Oxford University Press, 2001.

J. D. G. Dunn, J. W. Rogerson, eds, *Eerdmans Commentary on the Bible*. Grand Rapids: Eerdmans, 2003. (This and the previous title are two very similar works that attempt to express the state of biblical scholarship at the beginning of the new millennium.)

G. K. Beale, D. A. Carson, eds, *Commentary on the New Testament Use of the Old Testament*. Grand Rapids: Baker Academic/Nottingham: Apollos, 2007. (Very detailed, at times technical, treatment of the quotations from, allusions to and echoes of the OT in the NT.)

D. A. Carson *et al.*, eds, *The New Bible Commentary: 21st Century Edition*. Leicester/Downers Grove: IVP, 1994. (More introductory level with emphasis on explanation of the text than the Eerdmans and Oxford counterparts; unlike them does not include Apocrypha.)

The amount of modern literature on the New Testament letters and Revelation is enormous. This applies especially to commentaries, where there is no way that we can list all the useful works on any of the New Testament books. What we have done is to mention those works that we happen to have found personally helpful without implying that those that we haven't mentioned are somehow inferior. In order to avoid repetition of the same comments it may be helpful here to list a number of commentary series and offer a brief characterisation of each. 'Exegetical' and 'exegesis' refer to trying to understand what the text would have meant to its original readers; 'expository' and 'exposition' refer to trying to explain the

significance that the text might have for readers today.

The descriptions below begin with the abbreviation for each series used in the rest of this book. More specialised, technical works and works that require a knowledge of Greek are marked with an asterisk both here and in the bibliographies.

AB   **Anchor Bible** Ongoing series of full commentaries using Greek in transliteration, generally providing detailed notes followed by explanatory discussion of each passage. Earlier volumes in the series were of unequal quality; more recent ones are very good but some tend to excessive length.

ACCS   **Ancient Christian Commentary on Scripture** Valuable collections of verse-by-verse comment from the early Christian fathers, making their readings of biblical books more easily accessible.

ANTC   **Abingdon New Testament Commentaries** Intended to provide 'compact critical commentaries' catering to the needs of students.

BECNT   **Baker Exegetical Commentary on the NT** Thorough exegesis, with attention to context and theological message.

BNTC   **Black's NT Commentaries** Middle-length, non-technical exegesis of high quality (this series is known in North America as Harper's NT Commentaries).

BST   **The Bible Speaks Today** Expository commentaries with varying amounts of detail; useful for preachers.

EBC   **The Expositor's Bible Commentary** Multi-volume series on the whole Bible originally published some thirty years ago, now appearing in a thoroughly revised new edition with many fresh treatments.

EC **Epworth Commentaries** Short commentaries that have some concern for modern application.

*ECC **Eerdmans Critical Commentary** New series offering detailed exegesis based on the Greek text.

*Herm **Hermeneia** Detailed technical commentaries on the Greek text.

*ICC **International Critical Commentary** Full-scale treatments of the Greek text. Older, nineteenth- and twentieth-century volumes now being replaced by fresh volumes.

Int **Interpretation** Middle-length commentaries specifically designed to be helpful to preachers.

IVPNTC **InterVarsity Press New Testament Commentaries** Similar to BST in bringing out the contemporary relevance of the text, but with a greater emphasis on the basic exegesis.

NAC **The New American Commentary** Multi-volume series. Aiming to be exegetical and expository; largely from a strongly conservative and Baptist background.

NBBC **New Beacon Bible Commentary** Multi-volume series in the Wesleyan/Nazarene tradition with sections on 'Behind the Text', 'In the Text' and 'From the Text'.

NCB **New Century Bible** Very similar to BNTC but generally less detailed.

NCBC **New Cambridge Bible Commentary** Short commentaries using insights of rhetorical, narrative and socio-scientific criticism.

NIB **The New Interpreter's Bible** Vols. VIII–XII cover the New Testament with full-scale treatments providing 'overviews' and both 'commentary' (exegesis) and 'reflections' (help for preachers).

NIBC **New International Biblical Commentary** Entrance-level commentaries, some of which are more useful for out-and-out beginners while others contain good material for students.

NIC **New International Commentary** Middle-length exegesis with technicalities relegated to footnotes. Weaker, earlier volumes now replaced by first-class recent volumes.

*NIGTC **New International Greek Testament Commentary** Detailed commentaries on the Greek text; less technical than ICC.

NIVAC **NIV Application Commentary** Offering a combination of exegesis and application linked together by a 'bridge' between then and now.

NTL **New Testament Library** Good on cultural context and theological exposition.

PNTC **Pillar NT Commentary** Careful blend of exegesis and exposition.

SP **Sacra Pagina** Insightful commentaries by scholars from the Catholic tradition.

THNTC **Two Horizons NT Commentary** Interpretation in relation to concerns of systematic theology.

TNTC **Tyndale New Testament Commentaries** Introductory level commentaries providing the essential exegetical help.

WBC   **Word Biblical Commentary**
Detailed commentaries using
Greek in transliteration; less
technical than ICC.

ONLINE RESOURCES
Since the production of the first edition of this
book web-based resources have mushroomed.
There is a mass of valuable material that can
easily be accessed, as well as some unreliable
material that should be treated with caution.

In our bibliographies there will be reference
to some of the resources available. One of
the most useful sites is Dr Mark Goodacre's
New Testament Gateway, <www.ntgateway.com>.
Resources on Paul which relate to all his
letters are given at the end of Chapter 3.

A large range of resources for biblical studies
is available through
<www.tyndale.cam.ac.uk/online-resources>
and <www.biblegateway.com>.

SETTING
THE SCENE

Chapter 1

THE WORLD OF FIRST-CENTURY CHRISTIANS

In this chapter we shall study:

- how Rome emerged as a world power;
- key characteristics of the early emperors;
- the government of the empire through officials and armies;
- aspects of Greco-Roman society;
- religion and philosophy in the first century;
- the status of Jews and Christians.

Imagine a metalworker in Ephesus, a domestic slave in Rome or a businesswoman in Philippi – people who became Christians in the first century. What kind of a world did they live in and how did it shape their lives? In this chapter we look at some snapshots of this world, which will help to inform our understanding of the letters written to them by Christian leaders.

The whole Mediterranean world was controlled from Rome, a city nestling among seven hills fifteen miles inland from the west coast of Italy. How had the Romans come to dominate the world so completely, and what was it like to be part of that world?

HOW DO WE KNOW WHAT WE KNOW?
We know about the first-century world from various sources:

Greek, Roman and Jewish literature
Historians of the period are described in vol. 1, pp. 3–6. The most important for first-century Roman history are Tacitus (c. AD 56–120) and Suetonius (c. AD 75–150). The earlier period of Rome's history was recorded by Livy (59 BC – AD 17).

Other ancient writers, including Roman poets such as Virgil (70–19 BC) and Horace (65–8 BC), have provided a number of examples of the enthusiasm with which some welcomed the emergence of Augustus as Rome's first emperor. Satirical writers like Petronius (died c. AD 65) and Juvenal (c. AD 65–130) give vivid and comic insights into Italian social life. Philosophers, novelists and poets writing in Latin or Greek convey a sense of what mattered to people. But we should remember that literature was a luxury mostly confined to the wealthy, and as a result it does not necessarily express what ordinary people thought or felt.

When it comes to Jewish literature, the New Testament itself, of course, is a significant source for historians of the ancient world as well as for those more directly interested in Christian thought.

Objects known from ancient times or discovered through archaeology

These include coins, inscriptions carved on stone, documents written on papyrus, public and domestic buildings and all the grand and intimate objects found in them. From these not only historical events but also the habits of daily life can be reconstructed. So we know, for example, the size of the theatre at Ephesus and the details of a woman's jewellery and make-up (compare Acts 19:28–41; 1 Pet. 3:3).

THE EMERGENCE OF ROMAN POWER

According to tradition the city of Rome was founded in 753 BC, the period of Amos and Hosea in Israel. After a period of rule by Etruscan kings, whose main power-base was in Tuscany to the north, it established itself as an independent city-state about 510 BC. The Romans called it their 'republic' (Latin *res publica*, 'commonwealth'). Executive power lay in the hands of two consuls, elected annually by Roman citizens from a Senate of 300 relatively wealthy men belonging to traditional Roman families. Though the Senate had no formal power their regular debates influenced the consuls' decisions. (In the first century BC their number rose to 600 and then briefly to 900.)

At first, Rome was just one of numerous small city-states in central Italy which alternately vied for power with each other and joined together for mutual defence when faced by an external threat. An efficient system for raising an army whenever necessary, from those citizens who owned a certain amount of property, enabled the Romans to gain ascendancy among their neighbours.

By the early third century Rome controlled all Italy. Then a series of threats from outside, and invitations to side with one combatant or another in wars overseas, gradually led to Rome's control of territories overseas. By 200 BC, as a result of wars with the Carthaginians (based in what we call Tunisia), they had annexed Sicily, Sardinia, Corsica, Africa (i.e. Tunisia) and Spain. By 100 BC Greece had been added as the province of Macedonia-Achaia, and the Romans had begun to talk of the Mediterranean as 'our sea'. Acquisition of provinces brought taxes and (from Sicily) grain, and thus fuelled the taste for further expansion.

However, all was not well on the home front. Rome's system of government had a built-in conservatism. New offices of state were gradually created in order to cope with the demands of running a growing state and empire. But not much changed for the ordinary, poor citizens ('plebeians'), even though they outnumbered by ten to one the old aristocratic families ('patricians') from whom the Senate's members came. The patricians could not do without the plebeians because the army was recruited from them. But few plebeians could gain access to power. Attempts at reform were resisted by the Senate, and the period from around 130 to 30 BC was one of violent social conflict.

A CENTURY OF CIVIL CONFLICT

Wars on the edges of the empire, in north Africa and against tribes of Gauls (in France) and Germans (121–101 BC) brought to prominence the general Gaius Marius, who got himself appointed consul for 107 BC and supreme army commander by the popular assembly, against the wishes of the Senate. To recruit sufficient troops he ignored the usual property qualifications for army service, enlisting property-less volunteers.

From then on soldiers who owned nothing began to look to their generals to reward them with land or money on their discharge. This strengthened the bond between soldier and general, but also strengthened a general's sense of his own power and the need to secure land and wealth with which to reward his men.

The following decades were marked by increasing chaos in Italy, inflamed by rival generals using their armies against each other and even against Rome itself. In 60 BC three ambitious politicians who were also successful generals formed a secret pact known as the 'First Triumvirate'. They were Pompey, who had recently cleared the eastern Mediterranean of pirates and had brought Syria and Palestine under Roman control, Julius Caesar who was soon to conquer Gaul, and Crassus, the richest man in Rome. With their prestige and popularity with the army they were more powerful than the Senate.

After Crassus' death in 53 Pompey was persuaded by the Senate to turn against the increasingly powerful Caesar. But Caesar defeated him at Pharsalus in north-eastern Greece in 48 and made his own position apparently unchallengeable. When in 44 BC he was made *dictator* ('absolute ruler') for life, it was the last straw even for some of his friends. In a meeting of the Senate on the Ides (15th) of March his supporters abandoned him and he was stabbed to death.

What now? In 43 Caesar's 19-year-old grandnephew and adopted son Octavian joined with Mark Antony and Lepidus to form the 'Second Triumvirate', dedicated to pursuing Caesar's murderers. The decisive battle was fought at Philippi in Macedonia (42), where Brutus and Cassius, the leaders of the assassins, committed suicide.

The victors divided the empire: Octavian was to rule the west, Antony the east. But intense rivalry between the two now surfaced. There was to be one final showdown. In 31, outside the bay of Actium in north-western Greece, Octavian's admiral Agrippa outmanoeuvred Antony's fleet. Antony himself fled with his lover Cleopatra to Egypt, of which she was queen, where both committed suicide after Egypt fell to Octavian the following year. Octavian made Egypt a Roman province, to be governed by his own appointee because of its strategic role as a major supplier of grain to Rome.

All rivals had been eliminated, and the Roman world was hungry for peace. Octavian delivered it to them. In 27 BC he was granted the title *Augustus* ('revered'), which had religious rather than autocratic overtones, and became the first 'emperor'. His word for this was *princeps*, 'first man'. He was careful to observe Rome's constitutional traditions, and declared 'the transfer of the state to the free disposal of the Senate and people' (Augustus, *Res Gestae* 34). In fact he exercised absolute power by holding one or more of the key offices of state and by controlling the army.

Augustus' tough but far-sighted régime, together with the fact that he ruled more than forty years, ensured that the transition from Republic to empire would be permanent. The *Pax Romana* ('Roman peace'), which he established from Spain to the Black Sea, from Egypt to the English Channel, created conditions under which life could be lived with some security, trade could develop – and the Christian message could be spread far and wide.

5

providence

AUGUSTUS' SUCCESSORS

THE JULIO-CLAUDIAN DYNASTY

After a distinguished military career, Augustus' step-son **Tiberius** (full name Tiberius Claudius Nero) became emperor at the age of fifty-five. His suspicion that opponents were plotting to overthrow him led to numerous treason trials. For the last eleven years of his life he lived in retirement in his luxurious villa on the island of Capri near Naples. Without returning to Rome he controlled affairs through powerful aides and managed to retain the all-important loyalty of the army.

The young **Gaius Caligula** was a popular successor to his dour and distant great-uncle. But, having initially promised constitutional reform, he quickly became a cruel and arbitrary dictator with an extravagant lifestyle. Claiming to be divine he victimized Jews and threatened to set up a statue of himself in the Jerusalem temple. But his own guards assassinated him and the order to set up the statue was revoked.

Caligula's uncle **Claudius**, a scholar who was also physically disabled, proved a more able emperor than anyone had expected. He added five provinces to the empire, including Britain. He developed the imperial civil service, thus further reducing the power of the Senate. He adopted a tough policy towards Jews. For example, in AD 49, after disturbances in Rome 'at the instigation of Chrestus' Claudius decreed that Jews should leave the city (Suetonius, *Claudius*, 25.4, apparently alluding to disturbances caused by disputes between Jews and Christians; see also Acts 18:2). Yet it was during his reign that Paul completed most of his missionary journeys (Acts 13–21).

Claudius' second wife Agrippina fed him poisoned mushrooms so that **Nero**, her son by a previous marriage, could replace him as emperor. At first he managed the empire well, thanks to the guidance of the philosopher Seneca and Burrus, head of the praetorian guard (the emperor's bodyguard). But after AD 62, when Burrus died and Seneca retired, things changed for the worse. In 64, to divert rumours that he had himself started a great fire in Rome in order to make room for his grandiose building schemes, he put the blame on Christians and had many of them executed (Tacitus, *Annals* 15.44 – see text on p. 256). According to early Christian tradition Peter and Paul were martyred in the persecutions that followed.

Nero now ignored the provinces and armies and indulged his love of art and sports. He went to Greece to take part in the Panhellenic Games and was awarded the prize in every event he entered, even when he fell off a chariot. By now, senators and army commanders were increasingly restless and Nero set about ordering the deaths of influential people whom he suspected. There were revolts in Britain (AD 60) and Judea (AD 66). When his own armies, including the praetorian guard, turned against him he had little choice but to commit suicide (AD 68).

For a year there was chaos as rival would-be emperors – **Galba**, **Otho** and **Vitellius** – ruled briefly in turn. Then in summer 69 the legions in Egypt and Judea hailed as emperor **Vespasian**, the general charged by Nero with suppressing the Jewish revolt, and the Senate agreed.

THE FLAVIAN DYNASTY

Vespasian (Titus Flavianus Vespasianus) restored stability to the empire while his son

6

DATES AND EVENTS IN ROMAN HISTORY
(Emperors are in **bold***)*

BC

753	Traditional date of founding of Rome
510	Etruscan kings expelled, Republic begins
264–241	Rome's first war outside Italy, against Carthaginians
241	Sicily annexed as first province
60	First Triumvirate of Pompey, Crassus and Julius Caesar
49–45	Civil War, Caesar's victories
44	Assassination of Caesar
43	Second Triumvirate of Mark Antony, Octavian and Lepidus
42	Death of Brutus and Cassius at Philippi
31	Octavian and Agrippa defeat Antony and Cleopatra at Actium
30	Death of Antony and Cleopatra
27 BC – AD14	**Augustus (Octavian)**
[5?]	Birth of Jesus]

AD

14–37	**Tiberius**
[27–30?	Ministry of Jesus]
[32?	Conversion of Saul]
37–41	**Gaius Caligula**
41–54	**Claudius**
45–57?	Paul's missionary journeys (Acts 13—21)
49	Expulsion of Jews from Rome
54–68	**Nero**
64	Fire in Rome leads to Nero's persecution of Christians
66–70	Jewish Revolt; Vespasian commands Roman forces in Judea
68–69	**Galba**, **Otho**, **Vitellius**. Civil Wars
69–79	**Vespasian**
70	Titus completes siege and destruction of Jerusalem
79–81	**Titus**
81–96	**Domitian**

Titus completed victory over the Jews. The tax, which Jews had previously paid annually to the temple in Jerusalem, was now redirected to the temple of Jupiter in Rome (the *fiscus Judaicus*).

When he died the empire passed briefly to **Titus** and then to Titus' younger brother **Domitian.** Having resented his brother's tenure of power he ruled autocratically, was tough on taxes, boosted the imperial cult and liked to be called *dominus et deus*, 'lord and god' (Suetonius, *Domitian* 13.2). Though his vices were probably exaggerated by Tacitus and Suetonius, he was paranoid about plots against him and put numerous opponents to death. Even in the distant province of Asia he could evoke the kind of apprehension about Rome's power that is reflected in the book of Revelation.

What do you think?

As you read through the next few pages (pp. 8–19) imagine that you are a silversmith in Ephesus (Acts 19:19), a domestic slave in Rome (Rom. 16:14?) or a businesswoman in Philippi (Acts 16:13–15). Then consider the questions listed here.

● What are your hopes and anxieties in life?
● Might you be attracted to any of the religious, philosophical or lifestyle options described in this chapter?
● Do you think that any aspect of the message preached by early Christians might appeal to your outlook or situation?

If you are studying in a group, let each person take a different role and explore the questions in conversation. (If you need extra 'characters', you can find them, e.g., in Acts 14:8; 17:21; 19:19; the centurion in Acts 27:1.)

GOVERNMENT OF THE EMPIRE

THE PROVINCES

Augustus divided the provinces into *senatorial* and *imperial* provinces. Senatorial provinces were generally the older, more stable ones such as Asia and Macedonia. These were governed by 'proconsuls', men of senatorial rank who normally had held office previously in Rome (see Acts 13:7; 18:12; 19:38). Their proconsulship generally lasted for one year only. No legions were stationed in these provinces, though the governor had at his disposal a small number of soldiers under a centurion.

Imperial provinces were mostly those annexed more recently, where legions were stationed because they bordered on as yet unconquered territory or were thought to be places where rebellion might be organized. Governors of these provinces were appointed by the emperor himself, and served for as long as he wanted them there. In the more important provinces, such as Syria, they were of senatorial rank and were called *legati Augusti*, 'delegates of Augustus'. In certain other provinces, for example Judea and Egypt, the governor came from the equestrian class (the class between the senatorial class and the plebeians, so named because they had originally provided cavalry

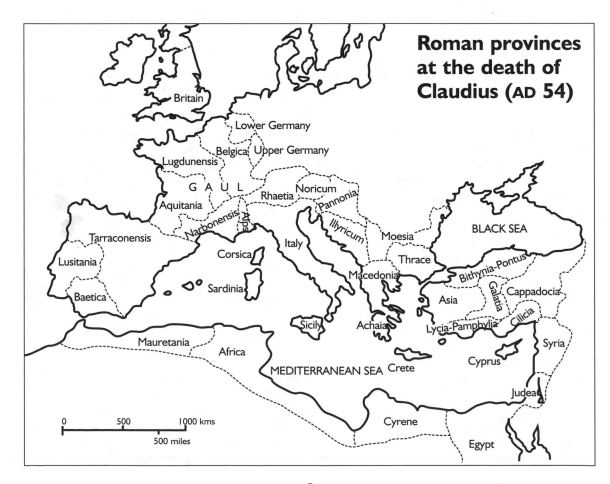

Roman provinces at the death of Claudius (AD 54)

Britain

Lower Germany

Belgica Upper Germany

Lugdunensis

GAUL

Rhaetia Noricum

Aquitania

Pannonia

Narbonensis Alps

Illyricum

Moesia

BLACK SEA

Tarraconensis

Italy

Thrace

Lusitania

Corsica

Macedonia

Bithynia-Pontus

Baetica

Sardinia

Asia

Galatia

Cappadocia

Mauretania

Sicily

Achaia

Lycia-Pamphylia

Cilicia

Africa

Crete

Cyprus

Syria

MEDITERRANEAN SEA

Judea

Cyrene

Egypt

0   500   1000 kms

500 miles

for the army). He was normally called *praefectus*, as on an inscription of Pontius Pilate found in his provincial capital, Caesarea. But by the time of Felix (Acts 23:24) and Festus (Acts 26:30) the title had changed and was no longer *praefectus* but *procurator*.

Essentially, the governor's job was to maintain justice and to raise taxes. He was assisted in these roles by lesser officials. Taxes were of various kinds:
- direct taxes, namely a tax on agricultural land or other property, and a poll tax on every adult, including women and slaves (Matt. 22:17 refers to direct taxes);
- indirect taxes such as customs duties collected at harbours and frontier posts, a general sales tax and a higher sales tax on slaves.

Not all governors could be relied on to act scrupulously in these matters. Josephus says of Albinus, governor of Judea AD 62–64:

Not only did he, in his official capacity, steal and plunder private property and burden the whole nation with extraordinary taxes, but he accepted ransoms from their relatives on behalf of those who had been imprisoned for robbery by the local councils or by former procurators (*Jewish War* 2.14.1 = 2.273; compare Felix's hope of a bribe in Acts 24:26).

CLIENT KINGDOMS

It suited the emperors to maintain good relations with certain kingdoms on the edge of the empire by making special alliances with their rulers. Their rulers were given the title 'king, friend and ally of the Roman people' and they were expected to lead their countries according to policies favoured by Rome. Herod the Great ruled such a kingdom, which was divided on his death

among his sons. In AD 6 the southern part, Judea, became a province ruled by Augustus' own appointee – though it reverted briefly to client kingdom status under Herod Agrippa I (AD 41–44).

CITIES AND COLONIES

Greek cities in the eastern provinces such as Thessalonica and Ephesus retained their traditional patterns of local government (see references to civic officials in Acts 16:6–9; 19:35).

A different type of city was the 'colony', established by Rome to settle army veterans, though they had a substantial local population also. Examples of colonies are Corinth, Philippi and Pisidian Antioch (Acts 13:14). These colonies were seen as 'miniature Romes' and they had a Roman form of government.

THE POWER OF PROPAGANDA

The power of government was underlined by propaganda proclaiming the inevitability of Rome's rule of the world. The poet Virgil (70–19 BC), whose career Augustus promoted, makes Jupiter say, 'For these [Romans] I have set neither boundaries nor periods of empire; I have given them rule without end' (*Aeneid* 1.278–9). And again, 'You, Roman, remember to rule the nations by your empire . . . to crown peace with law, to spare the submissive and subdue the proud' (*Aeneid* 6.851–3). Even then rulers had their spin-doctors! Gradually, all over the empire, imposing architecture in the Roman style and inscriptions in Latin – even in the eastern provinces where Greek was the everyday language – would remind people of Rome's powerful presence. The 'Roman peace' of the expanding empire certainly brought the benefits of stability and increased trade to all but the poorest and the powerless, but the state was ruthless against dissent or rebellion. It was, after all, Rome's goal that 'not individuals merely but countries and nationalities should form one body under the name of Romans' (Tacitus, *Annals* 11.24). Affirmation of the completeness of Rome's dominance even finds expression in a graffito from a private house in Ephesus: 'Rome, ruler of all, your power will never die.'

THE ARMY

THE LEGIONS

At the time of Augustus' death there were 28 legions (of about 5,000 men each, including a few hundred cavalry). They were stationed in the imperial provinces, for example four legions in Syria and two in Egypt. The commander of a legion was assisted by six tribunes. The key tactical officers in a legion were its 60 centurions, each in charge of about 100 men. (These titles are found in Acts 10:1; 21:31–32; 27:1, though there they are Roman officers of auxiliary, non-Roman troops.)

The 50,000 miles of Roman road made possible the efficient movement of legions to other regions if occasion demanded. So, for example, though no legions were initially stationed in the small province of Judea, forces were moved there from Syria at the onset of the Jewish revolt in AD 66.

By the time of Augustus the army had become a volunteer force of professional soldiers, serving for 20 years (25 under Vespasian, emperor 69–79). Though in the western part of the empire legionaries were mostly Italians holding Roman citizenship, in the east they included many provincials, who were granted citizenship unofficially on enlistment.

AUXILIARIES

The legionaries were supported by an equal number of auxiliary soldiers – often specialists such as archers and cavalry – recruited from the provinces. Gradually it became normal to award them citizenship after 25 years. Though no legions were stationed in Judea, an auxiliary force led by Roman officers was there to keep the peace (Mark 15:39; Acts 10:1; 21:31–32; 23:23–6; 27:1).

THE PRAETORIAN GUARD

An élite force served as the emperor's personal bodyguard. Under Augustus about 1,500 soldiers were stationed in Rome for this purpose, with about 3,000 in nearby towns. They enjoyed significantly higher pay and benefits than regular legionaries. Phil. 1:13 (if written from Rome) alludes to the infiltration of Paul's message into the praetorian guard.

ROMAN SOCIETY

CITIZENSHIP

By the death of Augustus there were about six million citizens (including women and children) in an empire of 70–100 million. Under later emperors, for example Claudius, citizenship was greatly extended so that its value became less significant.

Citizenship could be obtained in various ways:

- birth to citizen parents (Acts 22:28). A certificate was issued verifying citizen status. Did Paul carry his around, ready to produce it when in a tight corner? (Acts 22:22–29);
- as a favour for special service to the empire. It has been speculated that Paul's family may have originally obtained citizenship through supplying tents for a military campaign! (compare Acts 18:2 for Paul's trade);

- being freed from slavery to a Roman citizen;
- on enlistment or discharge from army service.

For the privileges of citizenship as Paul experienced them, see p. 40.

CLASSES

A tiny proportion of the Roman population belonged to the wealthy **senatorial** class from whom the leadership of the city and empire were traditionally drawn. Below them in status were the **equestrians**. Emperors increased their influence to counter possible threats from senators. For example, the strategic province of Egypt had an equestrian governor, and an equestrian was head of the praetorian guard. Many found roles in the ever-expanding civil service.

The great majority of Roman citizens were **plebeians**, mostly poor and with little influence on affairs of state. But their sheer numbers made it politically important for rulers to satisfy their basic needs. In the first century more than half of Rome's population were dependent on the regular distribution of free grain.

Slaves made up around a quarter of Rome's population, and a similar proportion of Italy as a whole. Curiously, Roman law acknowledged slavery to be 'contrary to nature' and yet judged it to be legitimate and morally right. People became slaves through getting into debt, through kidnap and sale, through being born into a slave family, and most of all through becoming prisoners of war. Regarded as 'living property', they were sometimes harshly treated. But, for most, their economic value ensured a tolerable level of treatment, and some gained real respect and even friendship from their

owners (see Luke 7:2). Household slaves generally fared better than those who worked in mines or large agricultural enterprises. A runaway slave faced a severe penalty if caught (see Chapter 10). The emperor's household included several thousand slaves with varying degrees of responsibility. Several of the names of Christians mentioned in Romans 16 are common slave names, and it is a plausible guess that 'those in the household of Narcissus' (Rom. 16:11) were slaves in Nero's service.

The Roman philosopher Seneca protests against the usual attitude to slaves:

> I am glad to learn . . . that you live on friendly terms with your slaves. This befits a sensible and well-educated man like yourself. 'They are slaves', people declare. Nay, rather they are men. 'Slaves!' No, companions. 'Slaves!' No, they are unpretentious friends. (*Moral Epistles* 47)

See further Chapter 10; and *DNTB*, pp. 361–6, 1124–7.

Freedmen denotes people who had been freed from slavery (see 1 Cor. 7:21–22). Freedom could be achieved through saving up the meagre pocket money which they received until they could pay their own value to their owner, or through being granted freedom by their owner. Many former slaves remained poor and had less security than in their previous life as slaves. But some who had proved their worth to influential citizens became wealthy and influential themselves. Emperors, particularly Claudius and Nero, gave great power to some freedmen, appointing them as government administrators. Felix, governor of Judea (Acts 23:26) was a freedman of the imperial household.

In the Greek cities of the eastern empire the titles of different social classes might be different and the proportions of slaves and free people different from those in Italy. But society there also had a pyramidal structure, with the majority living at subsistence level. Most of the range of society was represented in the church, at least in some places. Only Sergius Paulus, proconsul of Cyprus (Acts 13:6–12) could be seen as belonging to the highest rank, if indeed Luke intends us to see him as a committed believer. In the church at Corinth there were a few relatively influential people such as Gaius, Erastus and Stephanas (Rom. 16:23; 1 Cor. 16:15), and some like Aquila and Priscilla who had a steady trade but were hardly wealthy (Acts 18:2). But 'not many of you were wise by human standards, not many were powerful, not many were of noble birth' (1 Cor. 1:26).

WOMEN

Women's status was generally inferior to men's, though it varied in different parts of the empire. Baby girls were sometimes 'exposed' (abandoned in a remote place to die) if their parents were too poor to care for them. Girls were often married by the age of fourteen, and few received an education. Greek women were generally confined to the home, living a more restricted life than their Italian counterparts. In Macedonia, however, women had gained greater freedom, and it is interesting to note the names of women associated with the church at Philippi (Acts 16:14–15; Phil. 4:2–3).

Though men played the dominant roles in religion, there were significant functions for women in some religious cults. By the first century AD the temple of Artemis in Ephesus (Acts 19:27) no longer had a high priest but a high priestess. And in the ceremonies of some oriental cults women of all classes found momentary exuberant liberation from the subjection that was their normal experience.

Some women rose above their traditional role to be prominent in commerce. The largest building in the forum at Pompeii on the Bay of Naples was built by Eumachia, a woman with business interests in the wool trade, pottery and brick making.

The opinion of Apollodorus (fourth century BC) was still held by many men in the first century AD:

> We have courtesans (Greek *hetairai*, 'escort girls') for pleasure, handmaidens for the day-to-day care of the body, wives to bear legitimate children and to be a trusted guardian of things in the house. (*Pseudo-Demosthenes* 59.122)

A husband writes home to his wife:

> I urge you, take care of the little one, and as soon as we receive our pay I will send it to you. If by chance you bear a child, if it is a boy, let it be. If it is a girl, expose it. (Papyrus, Egypt, first century BC, Barrett, 1987, p. 40)

PATRONS AND CLIENTS

A basic building block of Greco-Roman society was the patron–client relationship. In an extension of the traditional role of the father in a family, people with some status and wealth became patrons of others who were in a relationship of dependency to them. A patron's standing in society rose as the number of his clients rose. A client relied on his patron to advise and protect him, to bail him out or defend him if he got into trouble. Each morning he would turn up at his patron's doorstep to offer greetings and make requests. In return he would campaign for his patron in elections and boost the crowd at a family funeral. A complex web of social relationships and expectations was built around this basic bond.

A positive value of the patron–client structure was that it ensured a measure of protection for lowly members of society who would otherwise have been more vulnerable to debt and other misfortunes. And it enabled writers such as the poet Horace to gain the security and freedom to get on with his writing. Possibly the historian Luke benefited from a similar relationship, Theophilus being the patron who financed the publication of his books (Luke 1:3; Acts 1:1). Negatively, it strengthened the dependence of the poor on the rich, the weak on the strong, in a way that inhibited the kinds of political change that might genuinely raise the status of the masses.

In the NT the ethos of patronage is reflected in the way householders in the church would host its meetings (Rom. 16:3–5, 23), or an individual would provide some important service for the community (1 Cor. 16:17–18) or would offer hospitality to missionaries and teachers (Phlm. 22; 3 Jn 5–8). Paul calls Phoebe, the deacon at Cenchreae, his 'patron' (NRSV 'benefactor', Rom. 16:2).

LANGUAGE AND CULTURE

Although Rome ruled the world, the cultural legacy of Greece – its art, architecture and literature – continued to dominate. The poet Horace famously observed: 'Greece, the captive, made her savage victor captive' (*Epistles* 2.1.156). While Latin was the language of the west, Greek remained the common language throughout the empire from Italy eastwards. In the early second century the poet Juvenal complained that Italian girls spoke poor Latin and made love in Greek (*Satires* 6.191)! Paul could write his Letter

to the Romans in Greek and expect to be understood. So he and others with a message to proclaim could communicate it over a huge area without having to learn a new language. And, since Greek was the language of a conquered race, the message would not be mistaken for imperial propaganda.

ENTERTAINMENT

In the Greek world there was a long tradition of theatre and athletics. The Isthmian Games were held every two years near Corinth, and occurred when Paul was there in AD 50–52. Though some Jews attended the theatre, it is unlikely that Paul did so, because dramatic productions were dedicated to Greek gods in whom he did not believe. Nor would he attend athletic contests, since the custom of competing naked was contrary to Jewish tradition. But he knows how to use imagery from these contexts to get his point across (1 Cor. 9:24–27; 2 Tim. 2:5).

Though the Romans imitated and developed the Greek enthusiasm for drama and athletics, the Roman masses were most passionate for the amphitheatre and the circus. Whereas the theatre was of semicircular design, traditionally built into the slopes of a hill for acoustic purposes, the amphitheatre was oval. It was the venue for the blood sports with which Romans were obsessed – gladiators fighting to the death, or men fighting against exotic wild animals imported from Africa. In towns that had no amphitheatre, the theatre was often used to stage similar events.

The circus (in Greek, *hippodromos*) was an arena for chariot racing. The Circus Maximus in Rome held 250,000. In Rome under the emperor Tiberius there were 21 race days a year. After him, since financing a day of races was the easiest way for an emperor to make himself popular, their frequency gradually increased. There were usually about 24 races in a day, with professional teams of riders identified by their colour – Reds, Greens, Whites, Blues.

Juvenal comments on the chariot races:

> The people that once bestowed commands, consulships, legions and all else, now meddles no more and longs eagerly for just two things – Bread and the Races. (*Satires* 10.78–81; 'bread' refers to the free hand-outs of grain)

> All Rome today is in the Circus. A roar strikes upon my ear which tells me that the Greens have won . . . Such sights are for the young, whom can cheer and bet at long odds with a smart girl by their side. But let *my* shrivelled skin drink in the mild spring sunshine and escape the toga. (*Satires* 11.197–204)

In the Greek world, as in the West today, the gymnasium was a place where people went for physical exercise and training, and to meet their friends. The Romans developed high-tech public baths, in which bathers could plunge into a warm pool, then take a hot bath, then warm again and finally a cold bath. After this they might have a massage, chat with friends, or have a snack.

> Wine, women and the baths corrupt our bodies. But what makes life worth living? Wine, women and the baths! (Latin inscription)

RELIGION AND PHILOSOPHY

The early Christian movement emerged out of Judaism, in a world where traditional Greek and Roman religion continued alongside more recent developments.

TRADITIONAL RELIGION

The gods of the Greeks and Romans were seen as representing or presiding over various aspects of life, and the function of religious practice was to keep oneself, one's family and one's city or state in favour with the gods. There was no creed that one must believe in, no particular ethical practice to be followed in order to please the gods. What mattered was performing rituals correctly and offering the right sacrifices. These sometimes included grand processions and colourful festivals. And all the skills of Greek

"LEGALISM" OF PHARISEES?

GODS OF GREECE AND ROME MENTIONED IN THE NEW TESTAMENT

Greek name	Roman name	Presided over
Zeus	Jupiter	'Father' of gods and humans (Acts 14:12) Sky and weather god
Hermes	Mercury	Messenger of the gods (see Acts 14:12). He was seen as something of a rogue who embodied the Greek admiration for cleverness
Artemis	Diana	Wild animals, childbirth (Acts 19:24, 34)
Ares	Mars	War (The Areopagus in Athens took its name from Ares, Acts 17:19)

OF DRAW A COMPARISON
BETWEEN Greco/Roma Rel → phic.
+ christia Faith — Explain

USING A REP. SOURCE
PROVIDE ADDITIONAL INFORMATION
on " TOPIC "

THE WORLD OF FIRST-CENTURY CHRISTIANS

and Roman architecture were lavished on impressive temples, each housing a large statue of the god to whom the temple was dedicated. But among the Romans a good deal of the energy of religious officials was focused on the bizarre (to our minds) practice of examining the entrails of an animal or bird to find omens that would disclose the future. More accessible to ordinary Italians was the worship of the *lares* and *penates*, protective spirits who presided over home and family. Both Greek and Roman homes had a small shrine and a family altar, and meals often began and ended with a religious act.

Although Greek and Roman religion had developed along different paths, the Romans had no great difficulty in combining the gods of the two traditions. It could also happen that a 'traditional god' was combined with a local deity worshipped in a particular area and took on the character of the local cult. For example, 'Artemis of the Ephesians' (Acts 19:34) was primarily a 'fertility goddess' whose key role was to ensure the productivity of the earth.

The fact that ethical codes were not closely linked with religious belief and practice does not mean that the gods were indifferent to morality. They were regarded as protectors of the moral order and their disapproval of human wrongdoing could have serious consequences. But there was a paradox, which became the focus of the criticism of traditional religion by Greek dramatists and philosophers: how could gods notorious for their sexual affairs and arbitrary behaviour be the guardians and judges of human morality?

One other important feature of Greek and Roman religion was that it was non-exclusive.

Particular devotion to one god did not exclude worship of others, and acknowledgement of the whole 'family' of Greco-Roman gods did not preclude participation in the cult of a foreign god such as Isis or Mithras. Such tolerance could make life difficult for Jews and Christians, whose exclusive commitment to one God seemed to others strange and subversive.

HEALING CULTS

The shrines of Asclepius, the Greek god of healing (Aesculapius in his Roman form), attracted the hopeful and the desperate from all over the Greek world. Among cities of the NT, Corinth, Athens and Pergamum were centres of his cult. People would go there seeking healing for all kinds of illness. Reflection on the place of healing in the ministry of the early church needs to be set in this wider context.

MYSTERY RELIGIONS

'Mysteries' (Greek *musteria*), in the sense of religious rites kept secret from the uninitiated, had been part of the Greek religious scene for centuries. But in the first century mystery cults from the east gained in popularity across the Mediterranean world. The cults of Isis and Sarapis, for example, came from Egypt, Mithras from Persia. Comparatively little is known about their beliefs and practice because they were reasonably successful at keeping their secrets, though in the second century Apuleius' *Golden Ass* included a moving account of initiation into the cult of Isis, and Plutarch gave details of two cults in his *Isis and Osiris*. Initiation rites typically included much use of ceremony designed to appeal to all the senses. The mysteries proved attractive to many for whom traditional religion did not bring personal meaning, offering:

- personal initiation into the secrets and privileges of the cult, which thereby conveyed a sense of personal significance and belonging to a special group;
- a special relationship with the god;
- assurance of particular benefits, which (with different emphases in different cults) might include overcoming the grip of fate, cleansing from sins and personal immortality.

Though the links between early Christianity and mystery religions have sometimes been overstated by scholars, some in the Greco-Roman world would have seen these two types of religious movement as rivals competing for their allegiance. In Philippians 4:13 Paul is happy to use an image from the mystery cults. Using a verb connected with *musteria*, he says 'I have been initiated into the secret of being content . . .'

FATE, ASTROLOGY AND MAGIC

The fear of fate was very strong in the Greco-Roman world. Many people felt that the course of their lives was predestined and they could do nothing to change it. While some found release from this fear in mystery cults, others turned to astrology. By understanding the movements of the heavenly bodies, which were believed to control human lives, they could at least prepare for what was to come even if they could not change it.

Magic was another way of gaining control. By imposing curses on others you could control them to your own advantage. By a spell appealing to a greater deity over a lesser one you could overcome the destructive power of the lesser. There were spells of sexual attraction whereby you could call up the powers of the underworld to make the object of your desire respond

to you. Acts 19:19 reflects the reputation of Ephesus as a centre of the practice of magic.

The sense of being dominated by fate is something from which the early Christian movement believed there was liberation through Christ. Paul's message that Christ has 'disarmed the powers and authorities' and 'nothing in all creation can separate us from the love of God that is in Christ Jesus our Lord' (Col. 2:15; Rom. 8:39) addresses this issue.

THE IMPERIAL CULT

In Egypt the Pharaoh had been regarded as divine, and since Alexander the Great rulers in the Greek east had been acclaimed as divine. Such language spoke less of religious conviction than of political loyalty. Not surprisingly, it was in the eastern part of the empire that Augustus was first honoured in a similar way. An inscription at Priene in Asia Minor (9 BC) calls Augustus 'Saviour' and adds that 'the birthday of the god has been the beginning of good news brought through him for the whole world' (see Ferguson, p. 193).

Though he resisted being acclaimed as divine, Augustus recognized the political advantages of giving a religious aura to his status by encouraging his subjects throughout the empire to honour him in association with the cult of Rome itself. Several cities in the province of Asia enthusiastically built temples dedicated to 'the goddess Rome and Augustus'. Only on his death was he declared a god.

Among his successors, Tiberius, Claudius and Vespasian similarly declined divine honours in their lifetime. Hence Vespasian's reputed words on his deathbed: 'I think I am becoming a god' (Suetonius, *Vespasian* 23). But Gaius, Nero and Domitian encouraged them. Domitian, for example, expected to be called 'lord and god' and had a large temple built in his honour in Ephesus – part of the background to the expectation of persecution and the negative perception of the Roman state in Revelation.

In each province where a cult of Rome and the emperor was established it was presided over by a high-ranking official generally called 'high priest' in the eastern provinces. He, with other prominent citizens, would take the lead at ceremonies associated with the temple and at other public functions. Since the cult was not something in which ordinary citizens were required to take part, Christians or Jews who felt that to show devotion to the emperor in this way compromised their faith could stay away with impunity. But under the more oppressive emperors they could easily feel vulnerable for taking this stand. And in AD 111 Pliny, governor of Bithynia and Pontus, was reporting to the emperor Trajan that he was requiring those suspected of being Christians to make offerings of incense and wine to Trajan's statue and to insult Christ (*Letters* 10.96).

CYNICS, STOICS AND EPICUREANS

There had been notable thinkers in Greece since the sixth century BC, and in the fourth century Plato and Aristotle had developed sophisticated philosophical systems which have influenced western thought ever since. But three particular approaches were prominent in the first century. The **Cynics** were so called because they lived 'a dog's life' (Greek *kunikos* = 'dog-like'). Their probable founder Diogenes (fourth century BC) was well known for living in a large jar in Corinth and for possessing only a cloak, a staff and a wallet. His motto was, 'Fear nothing, desire nothing, possess nothing'. It was easier to admire his radical lifestyle than to imitate it. There were wandering Cynic teachers in the

first century. Some scholars have compared Jesus' style of teaching with theirs, and to a casual observer missionaries such as Paul and his companions might bear resemblance to them.

Stoics and **Epicureans** are mentioned in Acts 17:18 as the main philosophical schools in Athens. Stoicism was founded by Zeno, who in 304 BC began teaching in the *Stoa Poikile* ('Painted Portico') in Athens. Later exponents in Rome were Seneca (4 BC – AD 65), who served as Nero's chief political adviser for the first few years of his reign, and Epictetus (AD 50–138), who in his youth was a slave of a member of Nero's bodyguard. Key Stoic concepts include:

- pantheism – the belief that God is not distinct from his creation but is immanent within it, permeating it and giving it order;
- use of the term *logos* ('word', 'reason') to describe the creative principle of rationality by which the world is ordered;
- belief that humans themselves, especially their minds, are divine since they are themselves permeated by the divine;
- a sense of human weakness and potential for evil;
- a desire to live in harmony with the universe, finding freedom by resisting self-indulgence and achieving self-sufficiency;
- belief that suicide is the greatest demonstration of human freedom;
- belief that the soul will be reabsorbed into the 'world soul' at the end of the world;
- hence an agnosticism or indifference about personal survival beyond death.

Epicureans took their name from their founder Epicurus (341–270 BC). Believing that though gods may exist they have no interest in human affairs, they were

EPICUREAN BELIEFS

The Roman poet Lucretius, a follower of Epicurus, ridiculed traditional myths about the after-life:

Assuredly whatsoever things are fabled to exist in deep Acheron [the underworld], these all exist for us in this life . . . Cerberus [the watchdog at the entrance to the underworld] and the Furies and the withholding of light, and Tartarus [the place of punishment in the underworld] belching horrible fires from his throat – these neither exist nor in truth can exist. But in this life there is punishment for evil deeds. (*On the Nature of the Universe* 3.978–1023)

A later Christian writer commented:

If any leader of pirates or robbers were exhorting his men to acts of violence, what else would he say except what Epicurus says: that the gods take no notice; . . . that future punishment is not to be feared, because the soul dies after death, and there is no future punishment at all. (Lactantius, *Institutiones Divinae* 3.17)

A common Latin epitaph expressing an Epicurean view is:

I WAS NOT, I WAS, I AM NOT, I DO NOT CARE

consequently called 'atheists' by their contemporaries. The world, they argued, is made up of chance combinations of atoms. No one survives death. Since therefore there can be no punishment after death, the prospect of death holds no fears. People must rid themselves of superstitions and seek the goal of peace or tranquillity of mind.

When Epicurus spoke of pleasure as the goal of life he was not advocating self-indulgence. Working from the basic premise that pleasure is desirable while pain is to be avoided, he explored what gives the purest

pleasure and avoids pain. Thus, for example, getting drunk would not be worth the hangover in the morning. Aiming for political office might bring the pleasure of holding power, but should be avoided because it brings also the pain of conflict and disappointment. As a consequence of such reflections he encouraged his followers to avoid public life and find an alternative community in the circles of 'friends' who formed his philosophical school.

Paper on post - what mode Christian diff

ROMANS, JEWS AND CHRISTIANS

In the 'multi-faith' world of the first century Jews, and then Christians, were distinctive in their exclusive attitude towards other faiths.

Though this could be seen as arrogant or subversive, Judaism was recognized as an ancient religion, and the earliest Christians came under the same protection. Herod the Great through his friendship with the young Augustus had won certain privileges for Jews, such as exemption from army service and permission to observe the sabbath. A daily sacrifice in the Jerusalem temple on behalf of the emperor was accepted as proof of loyalty (Philo, *Embassy to Gaius*, 155–8).

Estimates of the total number of Jews in the first century vary between three and eight million. There were many more outside

Digging deeper

Study in more detail one philosophy *or* one religion popular in the first century, and think about how its appeal was similar to and different from that of early Christianity.

See, e.g., Barrett, Ferguson, *DBNT, DLNTD*

Palestine, known as the Dispersion (Greek *diaspora*), than within it. Since there were sizeable Jewish communities in cities such as Rome, Alexandria and Antioch and smaller groups in many other parts of the empire, people had plenty of opportunity to meet and observe them. Some in the Greco-Roman world respected Judaism for its belief in one God and high moral standards. Some of these became converts to Judaism ('proselytes'), while a greater number were sympathizers who accepted much of Jewish belief and attended synagogue worship but did not take the decisive step (for a man) of submitting to circumcision. These sympathizers were sometimes called 'God-fearers' (e.g., Acts 10:2; 13:16; 17:4).

But most Greeks and Romans appear to have despised the Jews. This was partly because people from the east were generally despised. It was also because they had strange beliefs (only one God, who does not even have a statue of himself in his temple) and strange practices (sabbath, not eating pork), and were a close-knit and therefore suspect community.

Christians at first were seen as a sect within Judaism. Hence they experienced both the protection and the suspicions attached to Jews. When recording Claudius' ejection of Jews from Rome in AD 49 Suetonius gives no indication that at this stage Roman authorities made any sharp distinction between the two groups (*Claudius*, 25.4).

But by AD 64 the situation had changed. When Nero persecuted Christians in 64–65 a distinction was clearly being made between Christians and Jews. Now that such persecution had been originated by an emperor, Christians would feel vulnerable to repetition of such oppression by his successors.

The expectation of persecution by the state forms the background to the book of Revelation. The fact that the imperial cult had been enthusiastically promoted in the province of Asia (where the readers of Revelation lived) ever since its beginnings under Augustus made this a likely location for an eruption of concern about state oppression.

ESSAY TOPICS

INTRODUCTORY

● What differences and similarities would a time-traveller find between first-century Greco-Roman society and your own?

INTERMEDIATE

● Write an account of the roles and status of *either* women *or* slaves in the Greco-Roman world, and reflect briefly on the appeal, or otherwise, which the early Christian message might have had for them.

FURTHER READING

INTRODUCTORY

C. K. Barrett *The New Testament Background: Selected Documents*. London: SPCK, 2nd edition 1987 = *The New Testament Background: Writings from Ancient Greece and the Roman Empire that illustrate Christian Origins*. San Francisco: Harper, 1995.

W. Carter *The Roman Empire and the New Testament: an Essential Guide*. Nashville: Abingdon, 2006.

K. Chisholm and J. Ferguson *Rome, the Augustan Age*. Oxford/New York: Oxford University Press, 1981 (excellent collection of passages from ancient sources shedding light on the early decades of the Roman empire).

E. Ferguson *Backgrounds of Early Christianity*. Grand Rapids: Eerdmans, 2nd edition 1993 (valuable comprehensive survey).

A. R. C. Leaney *The Jewish and Christian World 200 BC to AD 200*. Cambridge/New York: Cambridge University Press, 1984.

A. J. Malherbe 'The Cultural Context of the New Testament: the Greco-Roman World', in L. E. Keck and others, ed., *New Interpreter's Bible*, vol. 8. Nashville: Abingdon Press, 1995, pp. 12–26.

J. E. Stambaugh and D. L. Balch *The Social World of the First Christians*. London: SPCK, 1986 = *The New Testament in its Social Environment*. Philadelphia: Westminster, 1986.

C. Wells, *The Roman Empire*. London: Fontana/Cambridge, Mass.: Harvard University Press, second edition 1992/1995 (very readable account of the empire from Augustus to AD 300).

M. Whittaker *Jews and Christians: Graeco-Roman Views*. Cambridge/New York: Cambridge University Press, 1984.

B. Witherington III *New Testament History: a Narrative Account*. Grand Rapids: Baker, 2001.

G. Woolf, ed., *Cambridge Illustrated History of the Roman World*. Cambridge/New York: Cambridge University Press, 2003 (vivid account of many aspects of Roman life).

INTERMEDIATE

M. Goodman *The Roman World 44 BC – AD 180*. London & New York: Routledge, 1997 (gives insight into many aspects of history and society in NT period).

B. J. Malina *The NT World: Insights from Cultural Anthopology*. Louisville: Westminster/John Knox, 3rd edition 2001 (the standard text on this topic).

See also many excellent articles in *DNTB* on topics summarized in this chapter.

ONLINE

Useful sites dealing with Roman civilization and empire include <www.vroma.org/~bmcmanus/romanpages. html> and <www.pbs.org/empires/romans>. You can take a tour of Rome in AD 320 at <www.earth.google.com/rome>.

PAUL AND HIS LETTERS

Chapter 2

LETTERS IN THE NEW TESTAMENT

This chapter will deal with:

● the practice of ancient letter-writing;
● the format of a first-century letter;
● ways in which NT letter-writers developed this format.

Most NT documents are letters. Although at first glance we may be inclined to group them as 'Paul's letters' and 'the rest', they are in fact of several types:

● letters from an individual to a church (most of Paul's letters; 2 John);
● letters from an individual to other individuals (1–2 Timothy, Titus, 3 John);
● circular letters sent to several churches (Galatians, Ephesians, James, 1–2 Peter, Jude);
● documents which, like a letter, were sent from one place to another, but lack key features of a letter such as identification of the sender (Hebrews, 1 John);
● an apocalypse distributed as a letter (Revelation; see Rev. 1:4–5);
● two letters included in the story of Acts (15:23–29; 23:26–30).

ANCIENT LETTER-WRITING

From ancient times people have written letters when face-to-face communication was impossible, or when a situation demanded that a message should be recorded in writing. Already in the eighteenth century BC rulers and bureaucrats in Mari on the Euphrates were writing diplomatic and administrative letters on clay tablets.

In NT times letter-writing was a necessary role of imperial administrators, and Augustus developed a postal system which enabled official letters to be carried on horseback across the empire at 50 miles a day. Thousands of private and business letters have survived from that period in the ruined buildings and rubbish dumps of Egypt. Writers and philosophers developed the letter form to communicate their ideas. For example, the Roman philosopher Seneca – a contemporary of Paul – wrote 124 letters to his friend Lucilius, which are in effect essays on ethical issues.

Most letters were written on sheets of papyrus, a light and tough material made from stalks of the papyrus plant woven and pressed together. A typical sheet was about the same size as standard American paper, or European A4. For a longer document sheets could be glued side by side to make a roll. The writer used a reed pen and black ink made from soot, gum and water (see 2 John 12; 3 John 13). Since the imperial postal system was not available for the letters of ordinary people, they had to send their letters with a friend, a slave, or a stranger travelling to the desired destination (compare Col. 4:7–9; 1 Pet. 5:12).

Some letter-writers used a secretary (Latin *amanuensis*). The Roman orator and statesman Cicero (106–43 BC) wrote hundreds of letters through his freedman Tiro, who collected them for publication. Julius Caesar was famous for being able to dictate different letters to as many as seven secretaries simultaneously – like a chess grand master playing against several opponents at once, though at a more furious pace! (The elder Pliny, *Natural History* 7.91.)

The secretary's role could vary according to ability and circumstance. There is evidence, mostly from Cicero, for the secretary as:

- recorder, writing at his master's careful dictation, or taking notes in shorthand and then writing them up;
- editor, allowed some freedom to tidy up the style when writing the final text from the rough dictation copy;
- agent or substitute author, writing the letter himself after general instructions from his employer.

This flexibility becomes a significant issue in debates about the authorship of certain NT letters, whose style appears different from what might be expected from the author concerned. We know that Paul used secretaries because Tertius identifies himself

as such in Romans 16:23, and because Paul sometimes draws attention to a change of handwriting when he adds a personal note at the end of a letter: 'I, Paul, write this greeting with my own hand' (1 Cor. 16:21; compare Gal. 6:11; Col. 4:18; 2 Thess. 3:17; Phlm. 19). In cases where the style or thought-pattern seems not quite Paul's (or Peter's – see 1 Pet. 5:12) might it be because the secretary has acted as editor or agent?

We know also from Cicero that an author or secretary would often keep a copy of his letters; hence the collection available for Tiro to publish. This raises an intriguing question about the collection and distribution of Paul's letters. It has often been thought that the letters addressed to individual churches were not generally known outside those churches until someone hit on the idea of travelling round the churches to collect and distribute copies of the letters more widely. But if Paul kept copies of his own letters, maybe his own collection began to be copied and distributed by his associates quite soon after his death?

THE FORMAT OF LETTERS

'Sir Andrew and Lady Marcia Fitzgibbon request the pleasure of your company at . . .'

'Dear Jim,
I was so sorry to hear the sad news of the death of . . .'

'Dear Ms Smith,
Locked in a bonded vault in New York is a number that could be worth $1.6 million to you . . .'

Very often letters begin with standard forms of expression, which indicate instantly the type and purpose of the letter. Standard openings like 'Dear Chris,' 'Dear Sir,' or endings like 'Yours sincerely,' or 'Love from' also help the recipient to 'read' the writer's intention correctly.

Such standard patterns and formulas characterized letters in the NT world, and their essential format remained constant through several centuries. Below is a second-century Greek letter from Egypt (see Lieu 1986, 38–51). I have set it out in a way that highlights the typical letter features of the period.

As in modern letters, the opening and closing sections of the letter are the most stereotyped. The 'body' or central section, which conveys the main message of the letter, is naturally much more varied in length and content. But in this and many other short letters it seems only a brief interlude between the standard opening and closing sections.

What do you think?

Compare Antonios Maximos's letter with 3 John, which is the NT letter most closely conforming to the pattern of a secular private letter.

Which verses of 3 John form the Opening, Thanksgiving and Closing?
In what ways are they similar to and different from Antonios Maximos's letter?

(We will explore the meaning of the Body, verses 5–12, in Chapter 20.)

Then try the same exercise on the shortest of Paul's letters, Philemon.

THE FORMAT OF PAUL'S LETTERS

Although most NT letters are much longer than this, we can see how they follow a

OPENING:	
Sender	'Antonios Maximos
Recipient	to Sabina his sister,
Greeting	very many greetings.
Health-wish	Above all I pray that you are well, as I myself am well.
THANKSGIVING:	
for good news	While I was mentioning you before the gods here I received a letter from
of health	Antoninos, our fellow citizen. When I learnt that you are well I rejoiced greatly.
BODY	I too do not hesitate at every opportunity to write to you concerning my own and my family's welfare.
CLOSING:	
Greetings	Give many greetings to Maximos and to my lord Kopres. My wife Auphidia greets you, as does my son Maximos – his birthday is the thirteenth of Epeip according to the Greek calendar – and so do Elpis and Fortunata. Give greetings to the lord . . . [6 lines missing].
Health-wish	I pray that you are well.'

similar format. And we can notice how their Christian character and purpose provokes certain adaptations. Here is how Paul structured his letters. We shall take 1 Corinthians as an example, and add notes on variations in other letters.

Opening
Read 1 Cor. 1:1–3.

The pattern we have seen in Antonios Maximos's letter and 3 John is clear in Paul, but is expanded in various ways.

To the **sender's name** is added the self-description 'apostle' as in most other letters – but 'servant' in Phil., 'servant and apostle' in Rom., Tit., 'prisoner' in Phlm. In 1 and 2 Thess., 1 and 2 Cor., Phil. and Phlm. he adds the names of his co-workers. Since this is a rare feature of Greek letters, we should assume that it is no mere convention, but that the names are included because they made a real contribution to the creation of the letter.

What do you think?

In Galatians and Romans Paul's self-description is expanded (Gal. 1:1; Rom. 1:1–6). He is extremely anxious and annoyed about the situation in Galatia, and Romans is written to a church he has not yet visited. Why do you think these circumstances would make him want to expand the Opening in these ways?

Look at the way he expands the description of the recipients in some of his letters. What does this suggest about the nature of his relationship with them?

Recipients To the address 'the church in Corinth' is added, as in Paul's other letters except Galatians, a statement about their status as Christians. Is the inclusion of 'all Christians everywhere' Paul's way of reminding the arrogant Corinthians that they are not the only church on the planet?

Greeting In contrast with the Greek letter greeting *chairein* ('greetings') Paul substitutes the similar-sounding *charis* ('grace') and adds the normal Jewish greeting *shalom* ('peace'), as well as expressing the divine source of these blessings. He thus gives new energy and a Christian focus to the traditional formula.

In effect, this wishing of grace and peace to the recipients replaces the health-wish of the secular letter. But the health-wish is also taken up and transformed in the next section, the thanksgiving, where Paul not only thanks God for the spiritual progress of the church, but also expresses a wish or prayer for their continuing development.

Thanksgiving
Read 1 Cor. 1:4–9.

Some Greek letters have a short thanksgiving (e.g., thanks to the gods for deliverance from illness or shipwreck). But this becomes a main feature in Paul's letters. Recurring features of his thanksgiving are:

● it focuses on the faithfulness of the church addressed;
● it may incorporate a 'prayer-report' in which he tells readers about his prayer for them;
● it may lead to affirmation of God's faithfulness to keep them in the faith until Christ's final coming;
● it may act as a brief introduction to themes to be covered in the Body.

It is not always easy to tell where the transition from Thanksgiving to Body occurs. Hence the recurrence of 'thank(s)' in 1 Thess. 1:2; 2:13; 3:9 has led some to argue that the Thanksgiving section continues from 1:2 to 3:10! But it is more likely that Paul has a more flexible view of structure than some scholars and simply merges Thanksgiving and Body together.

In Galatians there is no Thanksgiving: Paul thinks the situation is too serious to spend time on preliminaries. In 2 Corinthians and Ephesians (compare 1 Peter) the Thanksgiving is replaced by a Jewish style of 'blessing' (Hebrew *berakah*).

Body
In 1 Corinthians this runs from 1:10 to 16:18.

The purpose of the Body is to convey the letter's central message. Its structure varies greatly from one letter to another, in the light of the range of issues to be covered. Certain formulas often mark the beginning or a key point of transition within the argument. Examples in 1 Corinthians are:

'I appeal to you' (1:10)
'Now concerning . . .' (7:1; 8:1; 12:1; 16:1)
'I want you to understand' (11:3)
'I do not want you to be uninformed' (12:1)

The end of the Body often includes reference to a forthcoming visit (16:1–11), which reminds us that a key function of a letter was to act as a substitute for personal presence. This in turn points to the fact that the style and content must represent what Paul would have *said* to the recipients if he were with them to preach and teach.

So scholars have often analysed component parts of the Body in terms of the debt they owe to Hellenistic rhetorical practice and moral traditions, and Jewish synagogue sermons. Examples of this are:

- the **diatribe**, a form of speech in which the speaker debates with an imaginary questioner in order to teach his audience (1 Cor. 15:29–41; Rom. 2:1–5; 3:1–9);
- **midrash** (Hebrew for 'inquiry', 'interpretation'), commentary on scriptural texts (1 Cor. 10:1–5; 15:54–55);
- **parenesis** (Greek *parainesis*, 'exhortation', 'advice'), ethical exhortation using traditional patterns. Much of 1 Cor. 5–10 would come under this heading. Some other letters have large sections of parenesis near the end (Rom. 12–14; Eph. 4:1—6:20).

(On rhetorical analysis of letters see further pp. 227–8 below. For fuller discussions of material used in the Body of Paul's letters see Doty 1973, pp. 34–39; Murphy-O'Connor 1995, pp. 64–98; White 1972)

Closing
Read 1 Cor. 16:19–22.

In these four verses Paul includes significant developments from the ordinary Greek letter, while retaining its basic shape. There are:

- various greetings from Christians in Ephesus, where Paul is writing (verses 19–20; compare Rom. 16:3–16, 21–24; 2 Cor. 13:13; Phil. 4:21–22; Col. 4:10–15; 2 Tim. 4:19–21; Tit. 3:15; Phlm. 23–24);
- a final blessing (vv. 23–24; compare all Paul's letters), which performs a parallel function to the 'farewell' (probably in the missing lines) and final health-wish of Antonios Maximos;
- a note in Paul's own hand (v. 21; compare

Gal. 6:11; Col. 4:18; 2 Thess. 3:17; Phlm. 19), adding further material and indicating that he takes responsibility for the letter's contents as written by the secretary – some secular letters had the same feature;

- material of a liturgical nature, reflecting the fact that Paul expected the letter to be read when the church assembled for worship (vv. 20b, 22; the 'holy kiss' also in Rom. 16:16; 2 Cor. 13:12; 1 Thess. 5:26; 1 Pet. 5:14). The Thanksgiving or blessing at the beginning of a letter is also particularly appropriate for a worship context. Some letters have a doxology (expression of praise to God) in addition to the final blessing (Rom. 16:25–27; Phil. 4:20; 2 Tim. 4:18).

Digging deeper

Write a *short* letter from a member of the church in Corinth asking for Paul's opinion about one of the issues to which he is going to respond in 1 Cor. 5—11.

Make sure that your letter conforms to ancient Greek practice, with the various features of Opening, Thanksgiving, Body and Closing.

LETTERS OF RECOMMENDATION OR INTRODUCTION

We normally think of NT letters as written to provide advice or condemnation, instruction or encouragement. But that is not the whole story. Analysers of the letter form between the first and fifth centuries – yes, there were scholars theorizing about letters even then! – identified around forty different types of letters, designed for different purposes.

What do you think?

Look at the openings and closings of the letters from Hebrews to Jude. In the light of your reading in this chapter, what surprises or puzzles you about them?

Note your comments and save them for the time when you study Chapters 16—19.

One type of letter was intended to introduce or recommend the carrier of the letter to the recipient, offering assurance that the carrier was a trustworthy person. Some NT letters include this function alongside others. 3 John 12 recommends Demetrius to Gaius, and in Rom. 16:1–2; 1 Cor. 16:15–18; 2 Cor. 8:16–24; Phil. 2:25–30 Paul recommends various people to those churches. In each of these five instances the persons recommended were no doubt the carriers of the respective letters from Paul to the church. By implication Paul's backing of them is also his way of saying to the churches, 'If you have any questions about my letter ask them. They are authorized to speak on my behalf.'

OTHER NEW TESTAMENT LETTERS

The closest letter to Paul's in form is 1 Peter. The most different are Hebrews and 1 John, and whether they are really letters will be discussed in the appropriate chapters. The variety of NT letters reminds us that, despite certain predictable features, the letter form is almost endlessly adaptable for communicating ideas and information. Church leaders grasped that opportunity so as to fulfil their pastoral responsibility the more effectively.

FURTHER READING

* denotes books assuming knowledge of Greek; most books can be used by all students.

INTRODUCTORY

W. G. Doty *Letters in Primitive Christianity*. Philadelphia: Fortress, 1973

J. Murphy-O'Connor *Paul the Letter-Writer: his World, his Options, his Skills*. Collegeville: Liturgical Press, 1995 (fascinating introduction to the subject).

INTERMEDIATE

J. Lieu *The Second and Third Epistles of John: History and Background*. Edinburgh: T. & T. Clark, 1986.

*J. L. White *The Form and Function of the Body of the Greek Letter*. Missoula: Scholars Press, 1972 (detailed study of the form of Paul's letters in the Greco-Roman context).

ONLINE

See a page from an early third-century manuscript of Paul's letters at <www.katapi.org.uk/BibleMSS/P46.htm>.

Chapter 3

PAUL, HIS LETTERS AND HIS LIFE

In this chapter we shall develop a framework within which we can read Paul's letters by considering:

● the sources for learning about Paul;
● Paul's upbringing and outlook as a Jew;
● his call and conversion;
● his work as a missionary and his imprisonment;
● the chronology of his missionary career.

WHERE CAN WE LEARN ABOUT PAUL?

He saw Paul coming, a man small of stature, with a bald head and crooked legs, in a good state of body, with eyebrows meeting and nose somewhat hooked, full of friendliness; for now he appeared like a man, and now he had the face of an angel.
Acts of Paul and Thecla 3 (a second-century apocryphal account of Paul's missionary journeys) W. Schneemelcher (ed.) *New Testament Apocrypha* Cambridge: James Clarke/Louisville: Westminster/John Knox, 1992 II, p. 239.

What did Paul look like? A friend of mine was once asked to find a suitable picture to go on the cover of his book on Paul's letter to the Galatians. In an illustrated lecture he

shared with us his researches into the early representations of Paul in Christian art. He found that there was a continuous tradition throughout the early centuries of presenting Paul with a dark complexion, a bald head and a beard; this representation (quite different from that of the fair-haired Peter) could be traced back to the earliest pictures that we have of him, and it is not impossible – to put it no more strongly – that it has some basis in historical memory. The tradition gives some credibility to the description in words that we have about him above, although some of this may be pious legend.

Sometimes there may be an element of truth in the exaggerated and libellous comments of opponents and enemies:

‘His letters are weighty and strong, but his bodily presence is weak, and his speech contemptible.’ (2 Cor. 10:10)

Christian writers on the whole were not very interested in details of appearance and character – the Gospels tell us nothing about what Jesus looked like – so it is perhaps not surprising that the evidence about Paul is so scanty. But how do we find out about him in

31

What do you think?

What aspects of what you already know about Paul's teaching or character do you find hard to understand or accept? Make a list and discuss with others.

When you have read more of this book, review your list to see whether it has grown longer or shorter.

the broader sense, about his career as a Christian and a missionary?

There are three possible sources of information.

MATERIAL FROM OUTSIDE THE NEW TESTAMENT

Our opening quotation was from early Christian literature preserved outside the New Testament and written in the second century. The *Acts of Paul*, a compilation of various sources including a shorter work called the *Acts of Paul and Thecla*, is an anecdotal work telling various stories about Paul on his missionary campaigns with a cast of supporting actors, some named in the New Testament and some otherwise unknown, and culminating in the story of his martyrdom. The work is manifestly concerned to present Paul as the great missionary able to work miracles and overcome his opponents and also to encourage asceticism as part of Paul's message. There is complete agreement among scholars that this work is legendary and written to promote a particular interpretation of Paul and that, therefore, we cannot rely on it for any independent accounts of what Paul said and did. We have, therefore, to rely on the New

Testament and on two specific areas, the Acts of the Apostles and the collection of letters ascribed to Paul. Outside these two areas there is a brief reference to Paul in 2 Pet. 3:15–16.

Digging deeper

Read the Acts of Paul, available in W. Schneemelcher (ed.) *New Testament Apocrypha* Cambridge: James Clarke/Louisville: Westminster/John Knox, 1992 II, pp. 213–70; or J. K. Elliott *The Apocryphal New Testament* Oxford: Clarendon/New York: Oxford University Press, 1993, pp. 350–89. Compare the picture of Paul there with that in the Acts of the Apostles. What similarities and differences can you detect? Do you find them interesting or surprising?

THE ACTS OF THE APOSTLES

Paul appears in Acts 9 with the story of his conversion and calling to be a Christian missionary. After some time he is brought by Barnabas to Antioch in Acts 11, and then he shares with Barnabas and other missionaries in a series of missionary campaigns that commence in Acts 13 and last until he is arrested on a visit to Jerusalem in Acts 21; after that he is a prisoner facing judicial enquiries and is eventually sent to Rome where he hopes that his case will be settled before the highest court in the empire. We thus have here a fairly full account of his career as an active Christian missionary, and it would be fair to say that we are told more about the details of his work than about that of any other Christian in the New Testament. If this account is reliable, we are fortunate indeed. But can we trust it?

The debate concerning the historical value of Acts has already been noted in vol. 1 of this book (pp. 302–7), and therefore our comments here can be brief. In essence there are two views of the matter.

From the nineteenth century onwards there has been a tradition, particularly but by no means exclusively in German scholarship (the so-called Tübingen school), to affirm that, like the later legendary material mentioned above, the book of Acts rests on scanty historical sources, fills out the story with legend, and is governed by various tendentious motifs; consequently, its value as a historical source is very dubious, and we cannot rely on it as a source for the story of Paul. This rather broad verdict can be substantiated by reference to specific points.

● The accounts of Paul's early days as related in Galatians 1—2 and in Acts show various discrepancies in detail.
● A good deal of space is devoted to accounts of public speaking by Paul. But these 'speeches' are probably compositions by Luke himself, like the speeches attributed to Peter and Stephen earlier in the book. Their theology differs from that of Paul in various important aspects.

In the light of these discrepancies, it is claimed, we cannot trust the account in Acts in any detail, even though the broad lines of the story may be more or less true to fact. It has been proposed that Acts should be understood as more like historical fiction (in the manner of a Nigel Tranter or Ellis Peters writing on Scottish history and English monasticism respectively) with a good deal of material included and shaped for its entertainment value. Consequently, some scholars would almost entirely ignore Acts. In practice this causes great problems since the historical evidence regarding Paul's career in the letters is so fragmentary and

spasmodic that there is great freedom to speculate in reconstructing the history behind them, and many different, imaginative reconstructions are possible.

On the other side, developing partly as a reaction against nineteenth-century criticism, there has been a strong stream of scholarship which insists on the historical reliability of Acts. The archaeological researches of W. M. Ramsay in Asia Minor led him to a high view of Luke's accuracy in matters of historical and geographical detail, and this approach has been confirmed in the more recent work of Hemer (1989).

Valuable as this work is in showing that the story told by Luke is credibly situated in the world of its time, it does not take us all the way in dealing with the criticisms of him as a historian. One approach has been to attempt to distinguish between what looks like traditional or source material that he has used and what may be attributed to his own writing up of the story. The result of this type of investigation has been to show that time and again there is a historical core to the stories that he tells. But the method is not free from subjectivity, and different critics may estimate the material rather differently. Ultimately there is no substitute for a careful comparison of the material in Acts with that in Paul's letters to determine to what extent there are differences in their recording of the incidents and Paul's teaching and how far such differences are matters of real substance.

It certainly emerges that the story in Acts, as compared with that which can be deduced from the letters, is something of a simplification in matters of detail, and that the picture of Paul's theology, representing almost entirely the kind of things that Paul said to non-Christians (the major exception is in Acts 20:17–38), is lacking in the depth and subtlety found in the letters, which represent what Paul wrote to Christian believers. The story in Acts is very much a story of evangelism and the founding of Christian congregations and ignores almost entirely the pastoral, doctrinal and personal problems that Paul had with his converts. The story is, accordingly, one-sided and partial.

It is probable, therefore, that the extreme attitude to Luke as a poor historian is giving way to a more balanced opinion, and we can use Acts as a proper source for the story of Paul. Some scholars hold that the soundest method is to regard the letters of Paul that stem from his own hand as our primary evidence, always to be preferred to Luke's account, and this approach has obvious plausibility. Nevertheless, there are clearly passages in Acts which rest on eye-witness material (the so-called '"we" passages'; see vol. 1, p. 297), and the historical value of these should not be underestimated. Also it must be remembered that Paul's own comments are isolated, and the letters need to be put into a context; if they fit into the historical context provided by Luke's account without having to distort the evidence, then this is some confirmation that the story in Acts is broadly reliable.

THE LETTERS OF PAUL

In the New Testament there are 13 letters ascribed to Paul, in that each of them names him as the correspondent. (This excludes the Letter to the Hebrews, which later traditions, as exemplified in the AV [KJV], attributed wrongly to Paul.)

We are fortunate in having these letters, which are written (with the possible exception of Ephesians) to specific

congregations and deal to a fair extent with specific situations in their life; they are thus vital sources for our knowledge of the Pauline mission field. At the same time, since they are personal communications from Paul to his friends, they contain a remarkable amount of what is called 'self-disclosure', in which the writer writes about himself, his own situation and his own feelings. Although, then, the letters contain much teaching of a general character, as well as that which is more germane to the immediate needs of the particular congregations, and might be regarded as 'written sermons', they also function powerfully as 'letters of friendship', in which we can find Paul himself.

DIFFICULTIES IN THE PAULINE LETTERS

There are a number of problems that arise in using them in this kind of way.

WERE THE LETTERS ALL WRITTEN BY PAUL?

The first is that there is doubt whether they all actually come from Paul himself. Later on, in post-New Testament times, works were produced, mainly by heretical groups, which were attributed to prominent early Christians in order to gain acceptance for them. Such works are termed 'pseudonymous' or 'pseudepigraphical', i.e. they are wrongly or falsely attributed to the named author, usually with the implication that the aim was to deceive the readers into thinking that they were genuine. Many scholars believe that this practice goes back to the first century, although the extant evidence (which comes from the second century and later) shows that pseudonymity was regarded with disfavour and therefore it is less likely to have been practised by orthodox Christians who stood in the Pauline succession and did not have sectarian axes to grind. Now there are differences in outlook and manner of expression between the various letters attributed to Paul, and there are things said in some of them which might be thought to reflect a later time than that of Paul or to be the kind of things that other people might say about him rather than what he would say about himself. Consequently, it has been claimed that some of the letters are pseudonymous; specifically, some or all of Ephesians, Colossians, 2 Thessalonians, 1 and 2 Timothy and Titus, have been regarded as pseudonymous. If this claim is sound, it follows that these letters cannot be used in the same way as the genuine letters as sources for Paul's life and thought. (On pseudonymity see further pp. 234–8.)

In each and every case, however, this claim has been strongly resisted, and there are scholars who insist on the genuineness of all the thirteen letters. Moreover, scholars who allow the possibility of pseudonymity differ very much in the extent to which this has happened. It would be fair to say that the degree of suspicion is greatest for the Pastoral Epistles (1 and 2 Timothy and Titus), then for Ephesians, then Colossians, and least for 2 Thessalonians. There are also other possibilities to consider.

Digging deeper

'The end justifies the means': if pseudonymity entails deceiving the readers, can it be justified in the light of the greater good achieved by it? Were first-century attitudes different from present-day ones? Evaluate the contrasting opinions in the articles by J. D. G. Dunn, *DLNTD*, pp. 977–84 and D. A. Carson, *DNTB*, pp. 857–64.

One possibility is that during his lifetime Paul shared the authorship of some letters with his colleagues (seven of the letters name Paul and one or more colleagues in the opening greeting), and in some cases it could be that the major work of composition was done by a colleague; the letter would then be authorised by Paul but not composed by him. (How far, for example, did Silvanus and Timothy contribute to the writing of 1 and 2 Thessalonians? Scholars tend to think that Paul was the 'real' author, but this may be too simple an answer.)

Another possibility is that a letter could be based on Pauline material (whether actual letters or fragments of letters or memories of what Paul said) that was written up after his death by friends or colleagues who thus preserved and adapted his teaching for the next generation. This would be something different from pseudonymity in that the intent was not to deceive the recipients by passing off the author's views as if they were Paul's but to present Paul's views as compiled and reworked by friends. (One might compare the way in which the devotional writings of Oswald Chambers, an influential Christian writer in the first part of the twentieth century, were in fact put together posthumously by his wife.) A decision between these various possibilities can be made only by detailed examination of the individual letters.

Because of these uncertainties many attempts to reconstruct Paul's life and teaching rely almost exclusively on the seven letters that are generally accepted as coming directly from him: Romans, 1 and 2 Corinthians, Galatians, Philippians, 1 Thessalonians, Philemon. Such an approach is over-cautious, particularly where the material in the disputed letters coheres with that in the acknowledged letters.

DO WE HAVE THE LETTERS IN THEIR ORIGINAL FORM?

A second problem, which is concerned more with the historical development of Paul's career and teaching, arises from the suspicion that in some cases the letters may be compilations of material from several letters or even contain interpolations from other hands. These problems are most acute in the case of 1 and 2 Corinthians; there are problems with 1 Cor. 14:34–35 which lead some scholars to think that these verses are a later interpolation and do not represent Paul's teaching, and there are some difficulties about regarding 2 Cor. 10–13 with its references to problems in the congregation as part of the same letter as 2 Cor. 1–9, where the problems have been largely solved.

What do you think?

Compare the account of his own actions by the Roman tribune, Claudius Lysias, in his letter to his superior officer (Acts 23:25–30) with Luke's account of what happened in Acts 21:27—23:24. Was Claudius being 'economical with the truth', or did he really see things that way?

IS PAUL A RELIABLE INFORMANT ABOUT HIMSELF?

A third problem is that the letters present matters from the author's own point of view, and we do not learn how the other people involved saw the situation. There can be unconscious bias and conscious tweaking of the story to favour the writer's own agenda.

These problems are simply listed and posed for the time being. We shall have to look in more detail especially at the questions of authenticity and integrity in later chapters.

EARLY DAYS

The man whom we know as Paul was born with the name of Saul in Tarsus in Cilicia. It was a town of perhaps 500,000 inhabitants with a mixed population. Paul was thus by birth a Jew of the Dispersion. When or how his family or ancestors came to Tarsus is not known. Older scholars used to depict the varied influences that would have affected Paul in this environment, the mixture of Jewish, Greek and Roman thought, and so on. This depiction assumed that Paul received his education in Tarsus, perhaps even attending its university. But is this assumption justified?

A decision depends on how we interpret and translate Acts 22:3:

I am a Jew	I am a Jew
(1) born in Tarsus in Cilicia,	(1) born in Tarsus of Cilicia,
(2) but brought up in this city at the feet of Gamaliel, educated strictly according to our ancestral law. (NRSV)	(2) but brought up in this city. (3) Under Gamaliel I was thoroughly trained in the law of our ancestors. (NIV)

According to the NRSV Paul speaks of two stages in his early life: he had his higher education (a narrow sense of 'brought up') in Jerusalem under Gamaliel, and it is implied, or at least possible, that his earlier education was in Tarsus. According to the NIV he speaks of three stages, and his education (in both stages) was in Jerusalem; here 'brought up' refers to his boyhood. If the NRSV translation is correct, Paul *may* have had a broader education in the Hellenistic world; if the NIV is correct, his education was entirely in Jerusalem. The NIV translation, which is based on the assumption that Paul's statement follows a familiar three-stage pattern of upbringing that is known from other writers in the Hellenistic world, is to be preferred, and we can be reasonably confident that Tarsus did not play a significant role in his education.

This conclusion is confirmed by Paul's letters, which do not contain any significant evidence of a Greek education. Rather Paul appears as somebody with a basically Jewish education, and his manner of argumentation is generally thought to reflect a rabbinic training. Nevertheless, this does not mean that he was shut off from the wider influences of Greek civilization, which permeated different sectors of Jewish society to varying extents; at some points, for example, we can detect some possible influences from Stoicism.

According to his own testimony (Phil. 3:5) Paul was a Pharisee (see vol. 1, pp. 39–40). The Pharisees were a religious and political 'party' whose precise identity and nature is now a highly controversial issue. Essentially they were a nationalistic group who laid enormous stress on living according to the ancestral ways handed down from their ancestors; in practice this meant that they

WHAT WAS HIS REAL NAME?

In all his letters Paul uses the name *Paulos*, which was actually a Roman name and would be appropriate for a Roman citizen such as Paul was (Acts 16:37). Romans typically had a set of three names (Gaius Julius Caesar), and Paullus is found as a third name or 'cognomen'. In Acts, however, he is initially introduced with the Jewish name *Saul* (Acts 7:58), and only in Acts 13:9 do we learn that he was also called 'Paul'; thereafter he is consistently called Paul. The change in name is accordingly not associated with his conversion but begins to be used by Luke when Paul is in predominantly non-Jewish society. Such alternations are found elsewhere in the New Testament. Paul sometimes uses the Jewish name 'Cephas' and sometimes the Greek name 'Petros' (both mean 'rock') for the same person. John tells us that 'Thomas' (Jewish) was also called 'Didymus' (Greek; both mean 'twin'; Jn 11:16).

took the traditional laws and explained in meticulous detail how they were to be kept. This task was carried out by the rabbis (otherwise known as scribes or lawyers). One became a rabbi by being taught by a recognized teacher, and Paul's teacher was a well-known Rabbi Gamaliel who figures in Acts 5:33–40. There were two schools of Pharisees at this time, the more conservative one associated with Shammai and the more liberal one associated with Hillel; Gamaliel belonged to the latter party.

As a rabbi Paul had also to follow some manual occupation. He was a tent-maker (Acts 18:3), which is wide enough to include leather work and saddlery. He was, therefore, probably not particularly affluent.

We do not know anything for certain about Paul's family life. Murphy-O'Connor (1997, pp. 62–5), thinks that he would probably have been married, since this was the normal pattern for Jewish men but, if so, there is nothing to suggest that he had a wife during his life as a missionary and in fact 1 Cor. 7:8 rules this out; if he had been married, he was by now either divorced or widowed.

Finally, Paul may have been a member of the Sanhedrin, the Jewish ruling council, if the statement in Acts 26:10 that he gave his vote against the Christians is to be taken literally; but it may be no more than a metaphorical way of saying that he assented to what was going on.

PAUL'S CALL AND CONVERSION

The story of Paul takes on a more definite form some time after the resurrection of Jesus and the beginnings of the Christian church, when Paul appears as an implacable enemy of the Christians, taking a leading role in active attacks on them. The impression that we form is of a person passionately devoted to the Pharisaic interpretation of the Jewish religion. He viewed with intense alarm the rapid development of a heretical movement within Judaism, which committed the twofold blasphemy of elevating an ordinary man to be Messiah and of criticizing the temple worship. These points came to the fore in the teaching of Stephen, in whose lynching Paul had a minor role (Acts 8:1). He joined in the attacks on other Christians, and at this point was halted by a vision of Jesus Christ that completely altered the direction of his life and changed him from being an attacker to an ardent disciple and missionary.

● Read the accounts in Acts 9:1–30; 22:1–21; 26:1–23; Gal. 1:11–24, and identify the key changes which occurred in Paul's experience at this time.

The nature of this event is complex. Essentially it had two sides to it. On the one hand, it was a conversion from one form of religion to another, even though Paul remained a Jew and would have regarded his Christian faith as the true form of Judaism. Central to the experience was the realization that Jesus was the Son of God (Gal. 1:16). Kim (1981) has made out a strong case that Paul realized that Jesus was the image of God and that his subsequent theology flowed out of this experience.

Thus Paul's conversion revealed to him a Messiah whose rule had already begun. The resurrection of Jesus was seen as an anticipation of the general resurrection. The Holy Spirit experienced both in the individual believer's inward consciousness and in the communal life of the church was understood as the gift of the Messiah. This fresh understanding led to a new kind of eschatology (already present in Jesus' own teaching) in which the coming and resurrection of Jesus is the proof of the advent of the new age, but in a way that overlaps with the old age.

What do you think?

What constitutes a religious conversion? Are they right who think that Paul's so-called conversion was simply a development within his understanding and practice of Judaism?

On the other hand, the accounts of the conversion show that it was also an experience of calling to be a missionary (rather similar to that of prophets in the Old Testament; cf. Gal. 1:15 with Jer. 1:5). What Paul emphasizes is that the calling was to proclaim the good news not only to Jews but also to Gentiles in fulfilment of God's plan for the last days. ~~It is pointless to ask whether Paul realized the full implications of his experience at the moment when it happened.~~ Any conversion and call involves a period of preparation and then one of assimilation and fuller realization. When Paul tells us that he went away into Arabia, it may well be that this was a period of reflection as well as one of action.

PAUL AS A MISSIONARY

The evidence of his letters shows that Paul established and worked among congregations of Christian believers in Galatia, Philippi,

THE SO-CALLED 'HIDDEN' YEARS

A period of several years intervenes between Paul's conversion and his activity with Barnabas in Antioch, out of which arose his wider missionary travels. The first three years were spent in Arabia (Gal. 1:17–20). Arabia was the area inland from Judea and Damascus (not modern Saudi-Arabia), and there were people from Arabia present in Jerusalem at Pentecost (Acts 2:11). Despite a long tradition that Paul spent his time in Arabia in quiet reflection and meditation, it is altogether likely that from the start he engaged in Christian mission. The same will be true of his subsequent, longer period back in his home town of Tarsus in the province of Syria (Acts 9:30; Gal. 1:21). It was obviously because of his reputation as a Christian teacher and evangelist that Barnabas took the initiative in bringing him to Antioch.

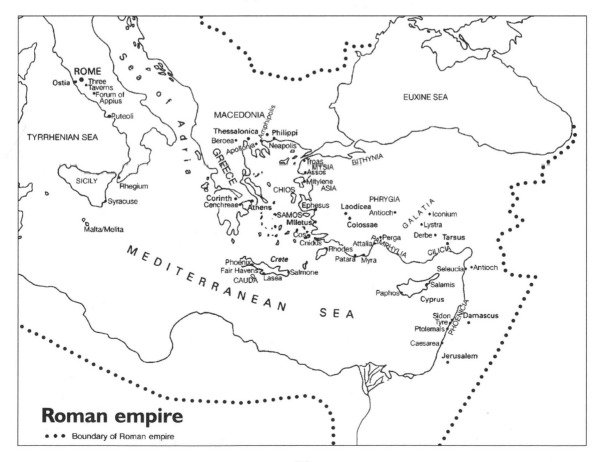

Roman empire
• • • Boundary of Roman empire

Thessalonica, Corinth and Ephesus, and it is reasonable to suppose that these groups carried out further evangelism in their neighbourhoods. It is also clear that Paul had various companions in this work including Barnabas, Silas, Timothy and Titus.

These activities, reflected in the letters, can be put into a coherent framework if we bring in the evidence of Acts. From Galatians 1:21 we learn that after Paul had returned from Arabia he worked in 'Syria and Cilicia'. Acts fills this out by recounting how Paul was active as a Christian in Tarsus, from where Barnabas brought him to assist in the work of the church in Antioch (Acts 11:19–30). Then Barnabas and Paul were sent out by the congregation there to be missionaries in areas where there was as yet no Christianity (Acts 13:1–3). We can distinguish three missionary campaigns.

The *first campaign* in company with Barnabas took Paul to Cyprus and then into the part of central Turkey then known as Galatia (Acts 13—14).

On their return to Antioch, a crisis developed over the important question of whether the non-Jews who had become Christians, both in Antioch and in the new mission areas, were required to accept the key practices of the traditional Jewish religion as well; these included the circumcision of males, the observance of Jewish festivals and the maintenance of Jewish dietary rules concerned with ritual purity. The last of these was particularly important, since orthodox Jews would not eat food prepared by Gentiles because it was 'unclean'. The church at Antioch and its missionaries had not imposed these requirements on the non-Jewish converts. There was a powerful group which was opposed to this, and the matter was taken to a meeting with the leaders of the Christian movement in Jerusalem, where the essential recognition that non-Jewish Christians did not need to be circumcised was accepted (Acts 15; cf. Gal. 2:1–10; see below, pp. 58–60, on the problems of relating these two accounts to each other).

PAUL THE ROMAN CITIZEN

During his travels Paul found it advantageous on occasion to appeal to his status as a Roman citizen (see above on his Roman name, p. 37). Roman citizenship could be inherited at birth or be granted in various circumstances (e.g. to veteran auxiliary soldiers or to whole communities, as a reward for services rendered to the state or for a financial consideration).

According to Acts Paul inherited his citizenship (Acts 22:27f.), but we do not know how his parents obtained it. Some scholars argue that the statement in Acts is fictitious; Paul's Roman citizenship was invented as part of an attempt to depict him as a person of high standing with influential contacts with upper-class people. They claim that this depiction clashes with Paul's failure to appeal to citizen-rights on other occasions when he was threatened with violence and had to endure it (2 Cor. 11:23–25). But there is no good reason to doubt Luke's account, which is based on his sources rather than constructed to suit his alleged agenda. We do not know sufficient about the circumstances and about how a person proved that he was a citizen in critical situations to argue that the presentation is unrealistic. Certainly it was not unknown for magistrates to ignore such appeals, as in the famous case cited by Cicero (see next box). Paul's standing as a citizen gave him a basis for complaining about his ill-treatment in Philippi (Acts 16:37) and forestalling it in Jerusalem (Acts 22:25), and also for his appeal to Caesar (Acts 25:5–12; 26:32); indeed without this background it is difficult to explain why Paul was sent for trial at Rome. See B. M. Rapske in *DNTB*, 215–18.

AN ILLEGAL FLOGGING

Verres was a Roman governor in Sicily who was tried for various crimes (70 BC). In a speech that was not actually delivered his prosecutor, the famous orator Marcus Tullius Cicero, describes how he seized and bound Publius Gavius in the public square in Messana (modern Messina) and gave orders for him to be severely beaten. Finally, the unfortunate victim was crucified:

There in the open marketplace of Messana a Roman citizen, gentlemen, was beaten with rods; and all the while, amid the crack of the falling blows, no groan was heard from the unhappy man, no words came from his lips in his agony except 'I am a Roman citizen.' (Cicero, *In Verrem* II.5.162. LCL)

Thereafter, Paul in company with Silas, set out on his *second campaign*, which took him over some of the territory previously evangelized and on to Macedonia and Achaia (modern Greece), specifically to Philippi, Thessalonica, Athens and Corinth (Acts 16:1—18:21).

The *third campaign* again took Paul through Galatia to Ephesus and then into Macedonia and Achaia (reaching apparently into the area of Illyricum on the west coast of the peninsula; Acts 18:22—20:38; Rom. 15:19). This period included a considerable amount of contact with the church in Corinth where there were internal problems (not recorded in Acts). One particular activity to which Paul devoted energy was the raising of a fund to help the poor in the church at Jerusalem, and he set off back to Jerusalem to take it personally (Acts 21:1—22:17; cf. 24:17).

The resulting picture is of a travelling missionary who visited in turn a number of strategically placed cities and major towns

and stayed as long as was necessary and possible to plant congregations. In this way he laid the foundation for further expansion in the areas where they were situated (cf. Acts 19:10 for this happening in Asia from Ephesus as the centre). At the same time, Paul re-visited these congregations and kept in touch with them through visits by his colleagues and by his extensive correspondence. He was thus not simply an evangelist and planter of congregations but also continued to be responsible for pastoral care of them.

PAUL THE CAPTIVE

Having concluded his work in the east (from Jerusalem and as far round as Illyricum, Rom. 15:19), Paul had it in mind to evangelize elsewhere and he set his sights on Spain, calling at Rome (where there were already Christians) on the way (Rom. 15:28; cf. Acts 19:21). Circumstances intervened, in that he was arrested in Jerusalem as a result of opposition by non-Christian Jews and spent the next few years as a captive, mainly in Caesarea, while the charges against him came before various courts, both Jewish and Roman. Eventually, he appealed to the authority of a higher court than the provincial Roman administration and was taken to Rome (Acts 21—28).

Acts concludes with Paul spending two years under house arrest in Rome, and we do not learn whether his appeal was heard and, if so, what the outcome was. The letters that can be assigned to the period of imprisonment (especially Philippians and Philemon) also leave us in the dark. There are two possibilities.

The first is that Paul died or was put to death. There are hints in Acts that Paul did not survive (Acts 20:25, 38; 21:13), and it is

A MISSIONARY LOOKS BACK

By the time that he wrote Romans (see 15:14–33) Paul could say that he had preached the gospel from Jerusalem right round (through Galatia, Asia, Macedonia and Achaia – the southern part of Greece) to Illyricum (the Dalmatian coast). His mission had thus covered the whole of the north-east of the Roman empire. Judea itself was covered by the mission to the circumcision (Gal. 2:7–8), and Egypt and westwards seem to have been visited by other missionaries. There was already a church in Rome and so Paul, looking for further virgin territories, felt the tug of the west to Spain (a settled Roman province; Gaul [France] was only recently subdued). His comment that there was no more work left for him to do in this area implies that he had planted congregations throughout the area and that the gospel would continue to be propagated through them; it must be remembered that Acts gives only a summary of his work, and it can be assumed that he, his colleagues and the new converts worked outwards from the main cities that Luke mentions into the surrounding areas (as Acts 19:10 implies). From 2 Corinthians 10:12–18 we see that Paul's policy was to refrain from entering what might be considered the territory allotted to other missionaries.

arguable that, since Acts is the story of the progress of the gospel and not a biography of Paul, Luke chose to end with the picture of how the gospel came to Rome through Paul. (There were, to be sure, already Christians in Rome [Acts 28:15], but it was the coming of Paul that was especially significant for Luke.)

The second possibility is that Paul lived on beyond the end of the two-year period. The case against him may have lapsed (though Acts 27:24 probably implies the opposite) or he may have been acquitted, since it is very difficult to see on what grounds he could have been condemned to death. If so, he

may have been able to resume his missionary work. If the letters to Timothy and Titus belong to this period, they suggest that he continued work in the Aegean area. It is also possible that he visited Spain (cf. 1 Clement 5 which says that he reached 'the farthest bounds of the west'). Eventually, he appears to have been re-arrested, tried and executed: this is fairly clear from 2 Tim. 4, but the information here has been thought by some to refer to his first and only arrest and trial.

Either way, it is important to recognize that Paul spent a significant period of his life as a prisoner and not as a travelling missionary.

PROBLEMS OF CHRONOLOGY

Assigning dates to the events in the life of Paul is not easy. There are two problems. First there is the relative chronology, the arranging of events in their chronological order. In particular, there is the problem of assigning the letters that he wrote to the appropriate places in the general outline of his travels and imprisonments. Second, there is the absolute chronology, the establishment of the dates when events happened and the length of the intervals between them. These problems are common to all attempts to establish chronology in the ancient world. As regards the relative chronology, our problem is due to the sparsity of the evidence and the possibility of several different hypothetical reconstructions of what happened. As regards the second, there are very few events for which it is possible to establish exact dates by reference to fixed time points in ancient history. (See also the discussion and chronological table in vol. 1, pp. 303–6. The minor differences between the conclusions reached there and the dates

THE EVIDENCE OF TRADITION

Although the possibility that Paul died a natural death was mentioned above, early Christian tradition is unanimous that both Peter and Paul were put to death; 1 Clement 5 includes them both in a section dealing with people who were persecuted to the point of death:

> Let us set before our eyes the good Apostles. There was Peter, who by reason of unrighteous jealousy endured not one nor two but many labours, and thus having borne his testimony went to his appointed place of glory. By reason of jealousy and strife Paul by his example pointed out the prize of patient endurance. After that he had been seven times in bonds, had been driven into exile, had been stoned, had preached in the East and in the West, he won the noble renown which was the reward of his faith, having taught righteousness unto the whole world and having reached the farthest bounds of the West; and when he had borne his testimony before the rulers, so he departed from the world and went unto the holy place, having been found a notable pattern of patient endurance.

The traditional site where Paul is said to have been beheaded outside Rome is now covered by the basilica of St Paul Outside the Walls; it has strong claims to being the authentic location. It is credible that Paul perished in the general pogrom of Christians instituted by the Emperor Nero c. AD 65 after the great fire in Rome.

offered here illustrate the fact that no chronology can claim to be firmly fixed beyond all doubt!)

There are some half a dozen points where we can try (not always successfully) to establish absolute dates from secular history.

- The 'governor' of Damascus under King Aretas (2 Cor. 11:32). Aretas died in 39 or 40, and this fixes the last possible date for Paul's escape from Damascus. Although some scholars think that the earliest possible date for Aretas to have had a representative in the city is AD 37, we simply do not know and it could have been earlier.
- Death of Herod Agrippa (Acts 12:20–23). This occurred in AD 44.
- The famine in Judea. This was the occasion of Paul's visit to Jerusalem (Acts 11:27–30). Evidence from Josephus (*Antiquities* 20:51, 101) enables us to date this to c. 46–48.
- Aquila and Priscilla move to Corinth. This was a consequence of a decree by Claudius that all Jews must leave Rome (Acts 18:2). The decree is generally dated to AD 49, although some scholars would date it earlier in AD 41. (There are conflicting accounts in ancient sources.)
- Paul's appearance before Gallio, the governor of Achaia (Acts 18:12). An inscription found at Delphi in Greece enables us to date Gallio's governorship with great confidence to AD 51–52 (summer to summer).
- Porcius Festus's governorship in Judea (Acts 24:27). This is debatable. Witherington (1998a, p. 716) argues on the basis of coinage for AD 59 as the year when he entered office.
- The Fast (Acts 27:9). The date of this Jewish festival, the Day of Atonement, varied from year to year dependent on the vagaries of the Jewish lunar calendar. The implication in the story here is that it was late in the year, and the only year in which this was so in the general period in question was AD 59, when it fell on October 5.

We must also take into account the year of the crucifixion of Jesus; sufficient time must be allowed for the events that took place

43

A POSSIBLE CHRONOLOGY

The most recent detailed study by Riesner gives the basis for the following outline. Events dated by Riesner are in lower case type; events in Paul's life that can be fitted into this framework are in upper case type. Possible periods for the composition of the letters have been included in this table, but in several cases these are very uncertain.

30	Crucifixion of Jesus
31–2	Death of Stephen and conversion of Paul
	PAUL IN ARABIA AND TARSUS
	PAUL IN ANTIOCH
45	Visit to Jerusalem to bring famine relief
	FIRST MISSIONARY CAMPAIGN IN GALATIA
	Galatians
	CHURCH COUNCIL IN JERUSALEM
	SECOND MISSIONARY CAMPAIGN IN MACEDONIA AND ACHAIA
50	Paul's arrival in Corinth (for upwards of 18 months)
	1 and 2 Thessalonians
	RETURN TO ANTIOCH
	THIRD MISSIONARY CAMPAIGN IN ASIA
	1 and 2 Corinthians
55	Paul's departure from Ephesus
	VISIT TO MACEDONIA AND ACHAIA
	Romans
	RETURN TO JERUSALEM
	ARREST AND IMPRISONMENTS IN JERUSALEM AND CAESAREA
59	Paul's departure for Rome
60	Paul's arrival in Rome
	TWO YEARS UNDER HOUSE ARREST IN ROME
	Philippians
	Philemon, Colossians
	Ephesians
	1 and 2 Timothy, Titus

between it and the conversion of Paul. Fresh research on the astronomical data regarding the date of the Jewish Passover (the time of the year when Jesus died) appears to limit

the choice to AD 30 and 33. Some recent scholars prefer AD 33 (see vol. 1, p. 162), but this later date does not leave a lot of time for the events in Paul's early years as recorded in Galatians 1:13—2:10, and AD 30 may still be preferable. The box 'A possible chronology' is based on Riesner's detailed discussion (with the crucifixion in AD 30); for alternative chronological schemes which allow for the crucifixion being in AD 33 see L. C. A. Alexander in *DPL*, pp. 115–23.

ESSAY TOPICS

INTRODUCTORY

● What picture of the principles and methods of Christian missionary work in the early church can be derived from a study of Paul's three missionary campaigns in Acts?

INTERMEDIATE

● Is the picture of Paul's life and character presented in Acts compatible with that derived from Paul's own writings?

FURTHER READING

*denotes books assuming knowledge of Greek; most can be used by all students.

INTRODUCTORY

F. F. Bruce 'Paul in Acts and Letters', in *DPL*, pp. 679–92.

B. R. Gaventa *From Darkness to Light: Aspects of Conversion in the New Testament*. Philadelphia: Fortress, 1986 (analyses the different types of conversion and applies to Paul).

R. N. Longenecker *The Ministry and Message of Paul*. Grand Rapids: Zondervan, 1971 (excellent summary of Paul's life and teaching).

D. Wenham *Paul and Jesus: the True Story*. London: SPCK/Grand Rapids: Eerdmans, 2002 (introductory study of Paul's early life and work).

INTERMEDIATE

F. F. Bruce *Paul: Apostle of the Free Spirit*. Exeter: Paternoster, 1977 (= *Paul, apostle of the heart set free*. Grand Rapids: Eerdmans, 1977) (standard detailed survey of Paul's career).

*C. J. Hemer *The Book of Acts in the Setting of Hellenistic History*. Edited by C. Gempf. Tübingen: Mohr (Siebeck), 1989 (technical study of Acts as a document of ancient history).

M. Hengel and A. M. Schwemer *Paul between Damascus and Antioch: The Unknown Years*. Louisville: Westminster John Knox, 1997 (technical study of Paul's early years).

R. Jewett *A Chronology of Paul's Life*. Philadelphia: Fortress, 1979 (= *Dating Paul's Life*. London: SCM Press, 1979) (careful analysis, offering a chronology significantly different from that suggested above).

*S. Kim *The Origin of Paul's Gospel*. Grand Rapids: Eerdmans, 1981; Tübingen: Mohr, 2nd edn 1984 (pioneering research on the way in which Paul's conversion led directly to his new understanding of Jesus).

R. N. Longenecker (ed.) *The Road from Damascus: The Impact of Paul's Conversion on His Life, Thought and Ministry*. Grand Rapids: Eerdmans, 1997 (scholarly, but readable essays on the ways in which Paul's thinking grew out of his conversion).

J. Murphy-O'Connor *Paul: A Critical Life*. Oxford/New York: Oxford University Press, 1997 (carefully argued study, often arriving

at different conclusions from those reached in this chapter).

B. M. Rapske 'Citizenship, Roman', *DNTB*, pp. 215–8.

*R. Riesner *Paul's Early Period: Chronology, Mission Strategy, Theology*. Grand Rapids: Eerdmans, 1998 (full, technical study providing basis for the chronology adopted above).

B. Witherington III *The Acts of the Apostles: A Socio-Rhetorical Commentary*. Grand Rapids: Eerdmans, 1998a (detailed, readable commentary on Acts).

B. Witherington III *The Paul Quest: The Renewed Search for the Jew of Tarsus*. Downers Grove: IVP, 1998b (an attempt to get at an understanding of Paul as a human being and a missionary).

ONLINE

A comprehensive site dealing with Paul is <www.thepaulpage.com>. Some scholars have their own websites that include some of their writings and lectures. One, for example, which includes stimulating material on Paul is <www.ntwrightpage.com>. Good pictures, maps and commentary on Paul's mission and travels can be found at the following sites

- <www.pbs.org/empires/peterandpaul/footsteps/index/html>
- <www.ccel.org/bible/phillips/CN092 MAPS1.htm>
- <www.worshipexcellence.org/PAULS_MISSIONARY_JOURNEYS/0.1WhoIsPaul.html>.

<www.luthersem.edu/ckoester/Paul/Main.htm> has clear maps and pictures of Paul's journeys in Acts.

Chapter 4

THE LETTER TO THE GALATIANS

In this chapter we shall investigate:

● the circumstances leading to the writing of the letter;
● the structure of Paul's argument;
● the way in which Paul develops his argument;
● the success or otherwise of the letter.

We shall also have to discuss matters that are less important for understanding the contents of the letter but are of interest to historians:

● just who were the 'Galatians'?
● was this Paul's first extant letter, or should we place it later?

Paul's letters appear in the New Testament in an order that seems to be determined by three factors: arrangement in descending order of length, so that Romans (the longest letter) comes first; arrangement by identity of destination, so that 1 and 2 Corinthians come together; and arrangement by nature of the addressees, so that letters to congregations precede letters to individuals. This gives us a rather arbitrary order that has no particular merits for studying them. The alternative is to look at them in chronological order. This procedure has its own difficulties, because there is considerable uncertainty about the order of composition and the reader is dependent upon the judgements made by the author of this part of the book. Right at the outset I am assuming that the balance of probability favours the view that Galatians is Paul's earliest surviving letter rather than 1 (and 2) Thessalonians, and in doing so I am siding with what continues to be a minority opinion on the matter. If I am mistaken, the consequences are not too serious. But you will need to consider carefully whether the majority view, that the letter comes from somewhere in the middle of Paul's letter-writing career, may not be the correct one.

WRITTEN ASKN

WHAT LED TO THE WRITING OF THE LETTER?

Galatians is a highly important letter because it is one of the main first-hand testimonies to a serious problem in the early church. The question arose as the Christian outreach began to move out beyond born Jews and Jewish proselytes to include Gentiles who did not follow the Jewish law and way of life. At its beginnings Christianity appeared to be a sectarian group within Judaism. Jesus and his followers were Jews, and Jesus himself had very little contact with Gentiles. To his followers Jesus was the Messiah promised to the Jewish people and through him they were incorporated into a group of people who had received the outpouring of the Spirit promised for the last days. Thus they were essentially Jews for whom the promise of the coming of the Messiah had come true. It was entirely understandable, therefore, that they would continue to keep the Jewish law, even if Jesus' interpretation of it was different from that of the Pharisees, and that any Gentiles who joined their group would thereby become part of the Jewish people and would have to follow the usual steps to do so. But from an early date some Gentiles associated with the followers of Jesus and yet did not take up circumcision and the other requirements of the law. *NOT PROSELYTES*

This caused a double problem. First, there was the obvious inconsistency involved in people accepting Jesus as the Messiah but not accepting the Judaism within which belief in the coming of a Messiah was at home. Second, there was the very practical problem that law-observing Jewish Christians could not eat with Gentile Christians or share their food since it had not been prepared according to Jewish requirements. Consequently there was a difficult period for the Christians as they strove to find the right solution to the problem.

On the one side were the more traditionally minded Jews who insisted on:

● circumcision
● observance of Jewish festivals
● the observance of Jewish food laws.

These three points sum up the main areas of contention. On the face of it they had the stronger case.

On the other side were those who began to question whether believing Gentiles needed to keep the Jewish law. They could point to the way in which various converts had become believers without submitting to Jewish requirements. According to Luke's account in Acts these included: the converts in Samaria (Acts 8:5–25); the official from Ethiopia (Acts 8:26–40); Cornelius (a Roman army officer; Acts 10:1—11:18). Somehow the movement took off in Antioch where there were large numbers of Gentile converts, and it could be that sheer weight of numbers had its effect (Acts 11:19–30).

At some early point Paul became convinced that Gentiles did not need to be circumcised and keep the law of Moses. We cannot reconstruct the process of thought that led him to this conclusion: did he know, for example, about the story of Cornelius (Acts 10—11)? How did he defend it to his own satisfaction? Certainly by the time that he wrote Galatians he had a well thought out position on the matter.

But so too had the other side. Their position was obvious and reasonable. They may have felt threatened by the large numbers of Gentiles who were becoming believers in Jesus and yet continuing to live as Gentiles. Moreover, every Jew knew that Gentile morality was far inferior to their own, and some Gentile converts found it hard to shake off their former way of life (cf. 1 Cor. 6:9–11). How could people live holy lives if they ignored the Jewish law? Added to this there was very probably a strong element of outside pressure on them. At a time of growing nationalist feeling against the Romans and foreigners generally, Christian Jews who consorted with Gentiles were the objects of suspicion, and if their contacts went against the accepted conventions by eating with these 'unclean' people the attacks on them would be all the stronger. It is, therefore, not surprising that there were Christians who felt it to be their duty to urge Gentiles to conform to accepted Jewish practices, and who felt this sufficiently strongly to follow Paul around and pressurize his converts. From the letter it is clear that this was happening even in Galatia and that the pressure was having some success. It may not be too much to think of Paul's opponents (as we must probably call them) as propagators of a missionary campaign with the 'true' version of the gospel.

THE STRUCTURE OF THE LETTER

Galatians is different from the other Pauline letters to churches in that it plunges straight into its subject without the typical thanksgiving to God for the spiritual growth of the readers. Attempts have been made to discern in it the rhetorical structure of a speech designed to persuade the readers of the truth of Paul's argument. In his pioneering application of this approach H. D. Betz analysed the letter as follows, using the Latin terms that were employed by Roman writers on rhetoric:

1:1–5	EPISTOLARY PRESCRIPT	(introduction to letter)
1:6–11	EXORDIUM	(introduction to the argument)
1:12—2:14	NARRATIO	(statement of the facts)
2:15–21	PROPOSITIO	(the point to be defended)
3:1—4:32	PROBATIO	(arguments for the 'proposition')
5:1—6:10	EXHORTATIO	(more emotional appeal to the readers)
6:11–18	EPISTOLARY POSTSCRIPT	(concluding remarks)

This analysis is not altogether persuasive; it is tweaked by more recent commentators who think that Betz has seen the letter too much in terms of forensic (lawcourt) speech making, whereas it is more mixed in character. It is also quite a formal analysis; it does not indicate the content of what Paul is saying at each point, but it does indicate how the letter broadly follows the pattern of a speech in court or a public assembly and uses oratorical devices. It is helpful to recognize the types of argument and persuasion that are employed.

What we also need to understand the letter is some appreciation of the actual content of the argument. A somewhat different type of analysis yields the following outline:

1:1–5	OPENING GREETING
1:6—6:10	BODY OF THE LETTER

  1:6–12 *Theme*
  The message of the Judaizers is not the gospel of Christ.

  1:13—2:14 *Historical sketch*
  Paul's gospel came from God and was approved by the apostles.

  2:15—3:18 *Scriptural argument*
  Experience and Scripture attest that people are saved by grace and not by keeping the law.

  3:23—4:7 *Grace and law*
  The law was a temporary measure until Christ came and brought the possibility of being sons of God rather than slaves.

  4:8—6:10 *Appeal*
  Don't go back to the law, which entails bondage, but enjoy the freedom that the Spirit gives to live a new life.

6:11–18	FINAL PLEA

Paul's autographical concluding comments.

This outline is not entirely satisfactory because it cannot do justice to the subtlety of Paul's thought and to the way in which the different parts of his appeal flow into one another without sharp transitions, but it captures the main divisions in the discourse.

PAUL'S ARGUMENT IN THE LETTER

The broad lines of the argument and the way in which Paul develops his case can now be discerned.

What do you think?

Before you read my attempt to analyse what Paul is saying, read through the letter for yourself; try to identify what Paul's opponents must have been saying and then how Paul's reply can be understood as a response to their arguments. In a classroom situation set up a debate with different speakers taking the role of Paul's opponents and his sympathizers so that both sides of the argument are given a full and fair hearing.

1. Paul argues that the message of his opponents cannot be another 'gospel' with divine authority (1:6–10). His own message has more than human authority; it came by a revelation of Jesus to him and not from any human body. This is seen from the fact that after his conversion he did not discuss his calling with the apostles. Only after three years did he briefly visit Jerusalem (1:11–24). Only after another long period did he revisit Jerusalem, and this time in order to see whether the leaders accepted his work among the Gentiles – which they did, without qualification (2:1–10). On the basis of this recognition Paul felt able to oppose Peter when he refused to have fellowship with uncircumcised Gentiles in Antioch (2:11–14).

SOME PUZZLING TERMS

- **Justification** (2:16–17; 3:8, 11, 24; 5:4) is Paul's term for the action of God in not reckoning up sins against those who have committed them but rather forgiving them and entering into a positive relationship with them.

- **Flesh** (3:3) is Paul's term that is used widely to cover the perishable material of which human beings are made, hence to refer to them on a physical level (2:16, 20). It also refers to them in their human weakness and inability to resist temptation, and thus comes to refer to the sinful state from which they cannot escape by their own power (5:13, 16–19, 24; 6:8). Modern translations tend to substitute other terms such as 'lower nature' or 'human effort' to bring out the varying significance of a term which can be misleading when literally translated into English.

- **Law** (2:16; 3:10–13; 4:4–5) refers normally to the system of commandments given to the Jews through Moses (3:10, 17; 5:14), with a focus on males being circumcised (5:3), and all Jews observing various religious festivals and dietary rules that marked them out as different from other people (4:10). These laws had been considerably elaborated by the Pharisees. Paul could also speak about a 'law of Christ' (6:2).

- **Elemental spirits** (Gk. *stoicheia*; 4:3, 9) can refer to elemental units (such as the letters that make up words) or to the physical elements out of which the world is made (earth, fire, air and water) or to the heavenly bodies that were often associated with spiritual powers (as in astrology). Paul appears to regard the commandments of the Jewish law as being used by these powers to keep people under their control. For Gentiles to accept the law, then, would be to come under a fresh bondage to the powers from which they had been delivered when they were converted.

(All of these terms can be followed up in the relevant articles in *DPL*.)

FINAL PROJECT – GLOSSARY OF TERMS

2. It was common ground between Paul and Peter that Jews are treated by God as if they had not sinned because of their faith in Jesus. So too are Gentiles. If they then go back to trying to keep the law they will be condemned as sinners (because they cannot keep it perfectly). If keeping the law is required of them, Christ died in vain (2:15–22). This is confirmed by their fundamental Christian experience: the readers had received the gift of the Spirit without keeping the Jewish law (3:1–5).

3. Paul then proves his point by appeal to the OT (3:6–14). Abraham was justified by faith before the law of Moses had been given. Reliance on the law and the inevitable failure to keep it place people under a curse from which Christ has released them by his death. So the law cannot annul the earlier covenant with Abraham; rather it had its own place in God's plan by making people aware of their sin and so leading them to seek justification through Christ (3:15–22). This puts people in a better position than they were under the law; for then they were like slaves but now through Christ they are sons and daughters of God with God's Spirit living in them (3:23—4:7).

GALATIANS 3:24

When a boy ceases to be a child, and begins to be a lad, others release him from his moral tutor and his schoolmaster: he is then no longer under a ruler and is allowed to go his own way. Xenophon, *Constitution of the Lacedaimonians* 3:1 (429 BC; LCL; *HCNT* §766)

4. For Gentiles to accept the law, then, means going back to the tyranny of what Paul calls 'elemental spirits' (4:8–11). He makes an emotional appeal to them to continue to recognize him as God's messenger to them whose only desire is that they mature as Christian believers (4:12–20).

5. Using an allegorical treatment of Scripture Paul argues that the true descendants of Abraham (Christian believers, both Jewish and Gentile) enjoy freedom, but the physical descendants (the Jews) are in slavery (4:21—5:1). He regards acceptance of the law as a form of slavery, since the law comes as a 'package', all of which must be taken on board: there is no freedom to obey some parts and ignore others (5:2–12). Christian freedom is not, of course, freedom to do what you like. It is rather deliverance from the power of 'the flesh' so that people are free to do what God requires. It does not lead to sinful licence but rather enables people to love one another and so to fulfil the real requirement of the law (5:13–15).

6. There are thus two ways of living. One is to live by the 'flesh' and that results in sinful behaviour. People who live under the law are not able to control the flesh because the law does not help them to do so; it can only condemn their failure. The other way is to live by the direction and power of the Spirit of God, which results positively in moral behaviour and enables people to kill their sinful passions. What is fatal is to try to live both ways at the same time; that route leads to an impasse in which you cannot do what you want to do (5:16–26).

7. Finally, Paul urges his readers to support one another in their struggles to live godly lives and to show love in forgiving one another's failures (6:1–6). He reminds them that life according to the flesh and

the Spirit lead to spiritual death and life respectively (6:7–10). Then he takes the pen in his own hand and issues a last appeal to them in which he attacks the inconsistency and dubious motives of his opponents and insists that in the end it

does not matter whether you are circumcised or uncircumcised but whether you place your confidence in the cross of Christ. For Paul only the cross and the Christ who died on it ultimately matter (6:11–18).

'NEW PERSPECTIVE' READINGS OF PAUL

What was Paul reacting to when he wrote negatively about Judaism and the OT law? Influenced by Martin Luther's response to abuses in sixteenth-century Roman Catholicism, Protestants have often claimed that Judaism was a religion of works (rather than faith) with a view to earning or meriting acceptance with God. In *Paul and Palestinian Judaism* (1977), however, E. P. Sanders provided a comprehensive survey of Jewish literature that revealed a very different 'pattern' of Jewish religion which he called *covenantal nomism*. He distinguished 'getting in' to the covenant family of God as a free gift from God and 'staying in' the covenant by thankful obedience to the law; apart from a few exceptional texts, he did not find the idea of individual *merit* to be a central concern. Sanders was not the first to claim that Christians have misunderstood the essence of first-century Jewish religion, but his powerful argument has led many scholars into something of a revolution in their understanding of Paul.

Influenced by Sanders' view of Judaism but disagreeing with his reading of Paul, James Dunn coined the phrase 'the New Perspective' to summarize his own view that the issue Paul was addressing in Galatians was not how an individual could come to be forgiven, but what was required of Gentiles (non-Jews) in order to enter the people of God. All of the first Christians were Jews, and they did not immediately stop treasuring their heritage when they came to faith in Jesus. The greatest issue in first-century Christianity was whether Gentiles had to adopt Jewish religious practices in order to be Christians (cf. Acts 15). Dunn argued that the 'works of the law' which Paul opposed referred to specific practices (such as

circumcision and observing food laws and holy days) that Jews were insisting were necessary for Gentile converts to observe to be part of God's family.

Since Dunn, many variations or 'new perspectives' on Paul have appeared, with N. T. (Tom) Wright's views perhaps being the most well-known. Scholars disagree among themselves on a number of interpretative issues, such as the exact meaning of 'righteousness' and 'justification' or whether the Greek phrase *pistis Christou* (cf. Gal. 2:16; Phil. 3:9) refers to 'faith in Christ' or the 'faithfulness of Christ'. What new perspective (NP) writers share in common is that Sanders' view of Judaism is largely right, representing a correction of an 'old perspective' shaped profoundly by the historical and theological context of the Protestant Reformation.

NP writers do not deny that Paul taught justification by faith or that he would have opposed notions of meriting God's acceptance; they simply don't think the latter was Paul's target. They also would normally assert that Paul did not set 'believing' and 'doing' opposite each other. Paul claimed that faith demonstrates itself in love, as James would agree (Gal. 5:6; cf. Jas. 2:14–26). Instead, the apostle was distinguishing faith *in Christ* from observance of Jewish practices that served to erect and to maintain boundaries between Jews and Gentiles.

Likewise NP writers would not see Paul setting 'law' and 'grace' opposite each other, as though there were no grace in the giving and observing of the law, or no requirement of obedience to the Spirit in the notion of grace. When Paul criticized the law, it was not because

WAS THE LETTER EFFECTIVE?

~~Certainly in the long run the position defended by Paul gained the day.~~ But it was a long and hard struggle, and the problem of 'judaizing' can be seen to lie behind other letters, notably Romans and Philippians. It would seem that the church in Judea and Jerusalem was under constant pressure from non-Christian Jews, especially with the increasing growth of Jewish nationalism in the period up to the war with Rome. It probably

of any antipathy to the importance of obedience to God (cf. 1 Cor. 7:19). His negative comments are in reaction to the insistence that Gentiles had to observe Jewish particulars in order to be included. ✓

Paul's problem was not with the pattern of religion called for in the OT as though it was intrinsically faulty (after all, God had given the Torah to his people, and the psalms are full of praise for that gift), but with Jewish *rejection of Jesus the Messiah*. In Paul's eyes, when Jews refused to follow Jesus as their promised Deliverer and Lord, they were rejecting God's supreme gift and were choosing to rely instead upon the law/Torah; in effect, they were *now* (on the other side of Christ's death and resurrection) seeking a righteousness of their own instead of the new way that God had revealed in his Son.

Where some scholars in the past have understood Paul to have rejected much of his Jewish heritage as a religion of 'works', NP readings typically see more continuity between Saul the Jewish Pharisee and Paul the apostle, with the main difference being his perception of Jesus. Some would prefer to describe the essential change in Paul as a 'calling' to follow the Lord Jesus rather than as a 'conversion' to a fundamentally different pattern of religion.

The NP can help Christians to understand and to appreciate their roots in the Old Testament. NP readings shed new light on texts and offer a way of integrating faith and practice. The more Jewish Paul's faith is understood to be, the less distance there is between his teachings and the strongly ethical message preached by Jesus.

Not everyone has been persuaded that Sanders' thesis about Judaism is correct, however, or that Paul was not addressing a theology of merit. Some texts (especially Rom. 4:2–4 and Eph. 2:8–9) appear to support the 'old perspective'. NP writers have been criticized for not saying enough about fallen humanity's condition and inability to offer the obedience for which God calls. The role of the Spirit in the Christian's life and the basis for final justification at the last judgement are among the other issues needing to be thought through as the debate rolls on.

Michael B. Thompson

Further reading:
J. D. G. Dunn *The New Perspective on Paul*. Grand Rapids/Cambridge: Eerdmans, 2007.

E. P. Sanders *Paul and Palestinian Judaism*. London: SCM/Philadelphia: Fortress, 1977. See also his *Paul, the Law, and the Jewish People*. London: SCM/Minneapolis: Fortress, 1983.

M. B. Thompson *The New Perspective on Paul*. Cambridge: Grove Books, second edition 2010. A simple, clear introduction.

S. Westerholm *Perspectives Old and New on Paul. The 'Lutheran' Paul and His Critics*. Grand Rapids/Cambridge: Eerdmans, 2004. Critical of the NP.

N. T. Wright *Justification: God's Plan and Paul's Vision*. London: SPCK/Downers Grove: IVP, 2009.

'The Paul Page' website <http://www.thepaulpage.com>. The best resource, with many links and downloadable articles.
See also *Exploring the New Testament*, vol. 1, p. 30.

Digging deeper

Paul's teaching in Galatians has been summed up under the two main themes, 'the cross and the Spirit'. Assemble the references in the letter to the cross and death of Christ and to the Spirit, and note the key points that Paul makes about them. In the light of your survey is the proposed characterization of the letter accurate and adequate? Does it fail to cover any significant themes in the letter?

What do you think?

Was Paul right to be so uncompromising in this letter? Might not a little flexibility have been more effective?

became more inward-looking and lost its sense of mission to the Gentiles. Meanwhile, the centre of gravity in the Christian movement shifted to the churches outside Judea and by the end of the century, as was natural, the Christians in the capital city of Rome were becoming increasingly influential. Was Paul right? The verdict of history is clearly on his side, but it cannot have been so obvious at the time. What Paul stood for, and what the conflict helped to bring out clearly into the open, is that it is only and entirely through God's action in Christ that people are justified. Justification is by grace and by grace alone (see p. 55).

But wait a minute. The converse of this statement is that justification is by works, by things that people do, specifically by 'works of the law'. But was that what the Jews believed? A long tradition of interpretation has assumed that in the eyes of Paul the Jews of his time held that justification was by keeping the requirements of the law, and that this was why the Gentiles were expected to keep the law. Then, it is claimed, justification was a matter of gaining a good reputation with God that would counterbalance the sins that had been committed. This view of things has been strongly contested over the last thirty years or so by scholars reminding us that the Jews were God's accepted people through his gracious election of them to be his people, and that they fulfilled the law because they were God's people rather than in order to become God's people. First came the covenant, and then came the law. So keeping the law was what Jews did in order to stay in God's favour rather than to acquire it. (Some hold that Paul did not entirely understand this and offered a misrepresentation of Judaism that has persisted to this day.)

This reinterpretation of Judaism does not really alter the picture all that much. Granted that God had made his covenant with the Jewish people, they still had to keep the law in order to be his people. And many Jewish groups insisted that the Jews by and large had fallen away from God and needed to undergo a spiritual reformation in order to get back into his favour, usually by joining their particular group and following its interpretation of God's requirements. The community at Qumran (see vol. 1, p. 42) could speak a language very like Paul's in which they extolled the grace of God and his pardon for sinners. Even so, what stands out in Paul's writings is his remarkable emphasis on grace that transformed a persecutor of the church into a missionary (1 Cor. 15:8–11).

So it may be the case that Paul's attack was particularly focused on specific groups of Jews (such as the Pharisees). But above all

THE GRACE OF GOD

The key term in Paul's understanding of how God puts sinners right with himself is 'grace'. The word, which he took over from the Old Testament (Gen. 6:8; Exod. 33:12–13; Prov. 3:34), expresses the undeserved favour that God shows to people, specifically to sinners, in forgiving their sins and incorporating them in his family of sons and daughters. Their standing with God rests entirely on his attitude to them and not on anything that they have done to deserve it. It is true that they have demonstrated faith towards God, but faith is not a 'work' in the sense that it is something that they do that places God under an obligation to them in the way that a parent might be constrained not to punish a child who has done some good action to compensate for a misdemeanour. Grace is the fundamental basis for Christian existence (1:3, 6; 2:21; 5:4; 6:18).

WHERE WAS GALATIA?

Paul wrote this letter 'to the churches of Galatia': but to what area of country was he referring, and whom was he addressing when he called his readers 'you foolish Galatians' (3:1)?

The term 'Galatia' was used in Paul's time for two areas. Originally it was the name for the area round Ancyra (mod. Ankara) in the north of Turkey settled by Gallic tribes (c. 250 BC). These were peoples who had begun some time previously to move out of their homeland in central Europe, some westwards to Gaul (modern France) and the rest eastwards. Prevented from entry into Italy and Greece, they finally crossed over into Turkey and settled there, speaking their own form of Celtic language until at least AD 400.

Like many others, their kingdom eventually passed into the hands of the Romans (25 BC) and became part of a larger administrative area (Latin *provincia*) which the Romans named 'Galatia'; the new province was much larger and included the regions of Pisidia and Lydia together with parts of the regions of Phrygia and Pontus (see map, p. 56).

This situation with the same names sometimes being used for local regions and also for Roman provinces is the cause of our problem.

he was opposed to the view that Gentiles must keep the law in order to be justified. His argument was intended to show that the way of the law and the way of Christ are opposed to one another. To be sure, there was no reason why believing Jews should not continue to live by Jewish customs (laid down in the law) if they wanted to, but religiously these were entirely a matter of indifference (Gal. 6:15), and they must never become actions on which people rested their confidence that they would be justified.

The issue then broadens out to cover whatever human qualifications or achievements people may regard as the basis of their good standing with God, whether racial superiority, or moral behaviour, or belonging to the right church, or whatever. The principle enunciated by Paul in Galatians is of wider applicability to all that people put their trust in rather than in Christ.

TO WHOM WAS THE LETTER SENT?

The most important questions to be discussed in introducing this letter are manifestly those concerned with understanding its contents, but we must also attempt to clear up the question of its geographical destination, which is also tied up with the question of its date.

Was Paul's letter addressed to the inhabitants of the old kingdom or the new province? Since the kingdom was in the

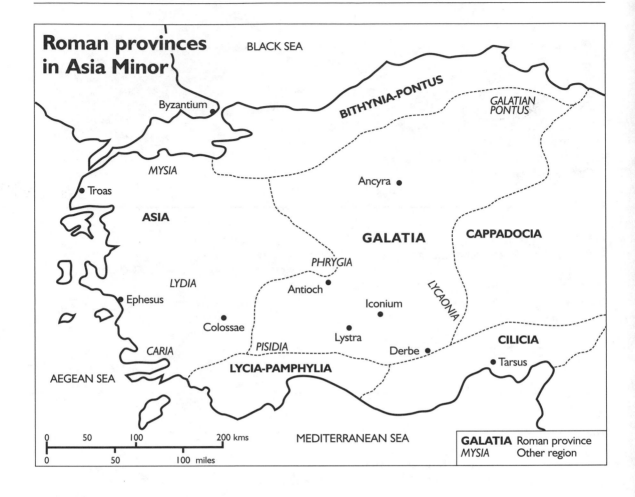

Roman provinces in Asia Minor

BLACK SEA

BITHYNIA-PONTUS

GALATIAN PONTUS

Byzantium

MYSIA

Troas

ASIA

Ancyra

GALATIA

CAPPADOCIA

PHRYGIA

LYDIA

Antioch

LYCAONIA

Ephesus

Iconium

Colossae

Lystra

CILICIA

CARIA

PISIDIA

Derbe

Tarsus

AEGEAN SEA

LYCIA-PAMPHYLIA

0	50	100	200 kms
0	50		100 miles

MEDITERRANEAN SEA

GALATIA Roman province
MYSIA Other region

northern area, the hypothesis that Galatians was sent to it is often called the *north Galatian theory*. By contrast, the alternative hypothesis, that the letter was sent to some location in the province, is called the *south Galatian theory*. This is because we know that on his first missionary campaign (Acts 13—14) Paul visited the towns of Antioch, Iconium, Lystra and Derbe, and then revisited them on his second campaign en route to Troas and so across the Hellespont to Macedonia (Acts 16:1–5) and again on his third campaign (Acts 18:23). It is natural to assume that the congregations in these towns in the south of the province of Galatia were the addressees of the letter.

However, a number of considerations could favour a different solution.

● It is argued that the address 'Galatians' used by Paul (3:1) would properly apply only to the native Gallic people and would be inappropriate for the very mixed population of Lycaonians, Phrygians and others who lived in the rest of the province. If this argument holds, then it would rule out the south Galatian theory and demand that Paul was addressing the north Galatians.
● But did Paul in fact visit the Gallic area in the north? According to Acts 16:6 and 18:23 Paul travelled through 'the region

of Phrygia and Galatia' and 'the region of Galatia and Phrygia' on his way further west. It is argued that this route would have taken him through the region where the Gallic people lived, and it can be assumed that, being Paul the missionary with a burning passion for evangelism, he would have missioned in the area and planted churches.

If these points hold, then we are forced into the north Galatian theory. However, neither of them can be upheld.

● Inscriptional evidence demonstrates that the term 'Galatians' could be used of people living outside the narrowly Gallic region.

F. F. Bruce (1982), p. 16n, refers to an inscription (datable to AD 222) in which a man from Apollonia in Phrygia Galatia thanks Zeus for bringing him back safely 'to my home in the land of the Galatians'. The interpretation of the various fragmentary pieces of evidence is extremely difficult, but the balance of the argument appears to favour the statement above (Hemer 1989, pp. 277–307).

● The two references to Paul's travels most probably refer to the part of Phrygia within Galatia (Acts 16:6) and to the areas previously evangelized in the south (Acts 18:23) rather than to the Gallic kingdom. In any case the Gallic kingdom was rather remote and inaccessible and off the route that Paul was following westwards.

Other arguments help to support the southern hypothesis.

● One small but significant point is that Paul raised a collection of money to alleviate the poverty of the Christians in Jerusalem from the congregations that he had founded, including the churches of Galatia (1 Cor. 16:1). Now in Acts 20:4 we have a list of people who accompanied him on the journey to Jerusalem with the money; in all probability these were representatives from the congregations that gave the money. Even if they were not, however, it is significant that the list includes people from Macedonia, southern Galatia and Asia, but nobody from north Galatia.

● There is also the matter of when the letter was written; it will be argued below that it could have been written before Paul's journey in Acts 16:6 and thus before he could have visited north Galatia, but since this is a controversial point, too much weight should not be placed on it.

WHEN WAS THE LETTER WRITTEN?

We are fortunate in that the letter to the Galatians contains a certain amount of information about the preceding events, which helps us to 'fix' it in relation to Paul's career. Paul found it necessary in the letter to relate the relevant events in his life as a Christian missionary. He therefore describes how he was a persecutor of Christians before his conversion experience in which he received his calling to be a missionary to the Gentiles (1:13–14, 15–17). Three years after his conversion he went up to Jerusalem where he met Peter (or Cephas, as he calls him), and then he went into 'the regions of Syria and Cilicia' (1:18–24). Then after fourteen years he went up to Jerusalem again, this time to discuss the validation by the Christian leaders there of his mission to the Gentiles (which was called in question because it did not require the circumcision of Gentile converts to Christianity). An agreement was reached (2:1–10), which was taken by Paul to allow Jewish and Gentile Christians to eat together in congregational meals. This practice was followed at Antioch until 'certain people came from James' and practised separation at meals; this nearly caused a severe rupture between Paul and Peter and Barnabas who yielded to the pressure imposed by the visitors. At that point the narrative stops and gives way to Paul's arguments on the matter. These arguments then flow imperceptibly into his address to the readers (2:11–14).

Now Paul's narrative can be compared with the account in Acts to see if the latter covers the same ground and, if so, whether this helps us to plot the position of the letter against Luke's fuller story. Paul's conversion and his first visit to Jerusalem are recounted in Acts 9; there are some minor discrepancies between the two accounts, which basically reflect the fact that each account is fragmentary and has a different purpose.

What do you think?

Compare Paul's account of his conversion in Gal. 1:13–17 with the account in Acts 9. Do the differences matter?

Acts further reports that after Paul's first missionary campaign there was a meeting in Jerusalem at which the legitimacy of the mission to the Gentiles was discussed and it was agreed that they did not need to submit to circumcision but should conform to some Jewish customs that would ease fellowship (Acts 15). However, Acts also reports an earlier visit by Paul from Antioch to Jerusalem on which he brought some financial assistance for the Christians there during a period of famine (Acts 11:30 with 12:25).

It is tempting to identify the two meetings in Galatians 2:1–10 and Acts 15. But there

What do you think?

Go through the two accounts of the meetings (Acts 15; Gal. 2:1–10) and make a note of the common features in them. Who took part? What was decided?

Go through the two accounts again and see if there are any significant differences between them. What kind of meetings were they? Are any important features missing from either account?

are some residual problems that cause some disquiet.

From the way Paul tells the story in Galatians, in which he is emphasizing his independence from Jerusalem, it seems probable that he is giving a complete account of his relationships. Yet he has apparently not mentioned the visit in Acts 11:30.

There are essentially two ways of dealing with these discrepancies (See vol. 1, pp. 305–6).

One meeting: Gal. 2 = Acts 15
These two narratives are variant accounts of the same meeting.

● The differences between the accounts are not sufficiently serious to call in question the fact that they describe the same meeting. The differences can be put down to such possible factors as:

Luke's inaccurate historical knowledge of what happened.

Paul's shaping of the story to favour his own position.

The possibility that Luke has run together the account of this meeting and an account of a later agreement, including the 'apostolic decree' of Acts 15:19–21, 29, that was made when Paul was not present.

- As for the visit in Acts 11:30 it can be argued:

  Paul just did not mention it because he saw no need to do so.

  Or it is misplaced in Luke's record and really happened at some other time.

  Or Luke invented it and it never took place.

Two meetings: Gal. 2 = Acts 11:30

The second approach is to argue that the meeting described in Gal. 2:1–10 actually took place on the occasion of the visit mentioned in Acts 11:30, and that this was followed by the dispute at Antioch described in Gal. 2:11–14; as a result of the dispute it was necessary to go over the ground again, and so a second meeting was held in Jerusalem, as described in Acts 15.

In favour of this interpretation it can be argued that:

- provision for the poor figures both in Acts 11:27–30 and in Gal. 2:10;
- both meetings are associated with prophecy or revelation (Acts 11:27; Gal. 2:2);
- the meeting in Gal. 2 was a private one, whereas that in Acts 15 was a larger assembly.

The difficulties with this view are that:

- Luke has not indicated that the Acts 11 visit included such a meeting. But in view of the evangelism of Gentiles that was already going on in Antioch, it is inconceivable that the topic was not being discussed in Jerusalem;
- essentially the same subject was discussed twice before a final agreement was reached. This is hardly a difficulty, as anybody who has tried to steer a difficult proposition through a tricky committee can testify.

THE TWO ALTERNATIVE SCENARIOS

	Galatians	Acts
Scenario 1 – One meeting		
Paul's conversion	1:13–16a	9:1–22
Visit to Arabia	1:17	
FIRST VISIT TO JERUSALEM	1:18–24	9:26–30
SECOND VISIT (FAMINE RELIEF)		11:29–30; 12:25
THIRD VISIT (CHURCH COUNCIL)	2:1–10	15:1–35
Composition of Galatians		
Scenario 2 – Two meetings		
Paul's conversion	1:13–16a	9:1–22
Visit to Arabia	1:17	
FIRST VISIT TO JERUSALEM	1:18–24	9:26–30
SECOND VISIT (FAMINE RELIEF and LEADERS' MEETING)	2:1–10	11:29–30; 12:25
Composition of Galatians		
THIRD VISIT (CHURCH COUNCIL)		15:1–35

Scholars are divided between these two types of solution. Some variants of the 'One meeting' solution reflect badly on Luke's competence as a reliable historian. It also faces the difficulty that the *volte face* of James and Cephas and Barnabas is perhaps less likely after the formal decision in Acts 15 than the less formal private agreement in Gal. 2. These and other considerations incline me to favour the 'Two meetings' solution.

CONSEQUENCES FOR THE DATE OF THE LETTER

After this lengthy discussion we can see that on the 'One meeting' solution, the date of Galatians will be not long after the decision reached in Acts 15. On the 'Two meetings' solution, the date will be after the decision reached in Acts 11 and after Paul's missionary campaign in south Galatia but before the meeting in Acts 15 (since it is not mentioned in Galatians although, had Paul been able to appeal to it, it would have settled the argument). Moreover, it will be the earliest extant letter of Paul (since 1 Thessalonians was not written until after the second missionary campaign was under way). It is on the basis of this weighing of the evidence that Galatians is treated here as the first of Paul's letters (c. AD 48–49), but the case is a finely balanced one.

FOR TODAY'S GALATIANS

What relevance can a letter that is concerned with matters like circumcision and Jewish festivals have for readers today? Are there issues that are still alive today?

- In what ways, if any, can what appears to be a first-century issue about the Jewish law have counterparts in the contemporary church and society? Is 'justification by works' still an issue today?

Focus on theology

The theology of the letter is centred on the cross and the Spirit. Paul's gospel that brings people justification and new life is based entirely upon the gracious action of God in the crucifixion and resurrection of Jesus and becomes effective purely through their response to the good news in faith. Redemption is offered to all people, including Gentiles, and does not require the characteristically Jewish performance of the 'works' required by the law. In the people of God racial and other differences become irrelevant. Paul sees himself as the recipient of a divine revelation that led to his reinterpretation of the OT story of Abraham as the spiritual ancestor of believing Gentiles in that he had faith in God and was justified on account of it long before the law was given to the Jews. The law was not intended to provide a means of justification but rather to make people aware of their sinfulness. The effect of the coming of God's Son and his life and death under the law was to deliver people from the curse that rested upon them for not keeping the law. In their new life they share in the crucifixion of Jesus and also his resurrection life. The Spirit of God enables them to overcome their sinful desires and moral weakness when faced by temptation and to love their neighbours, thus fulfilling what the law really requires of them.

- 'The only thing that counts is faith working through love' (5:6), 'Love God and do what you like' (Augustine, fifth century AD); 'All you need is love' (The Beatles). Many people think that loving is all that we need to do: but what do different people mean by 'love'? Why does Paul put faith in the first place?
- 'There is no longer Jew or Greek, there is no longer slave or free, there is no longer male or female; for all of you are one in

Christ Jesus' (3:28). But clearly people still were Jews and Greeks . . . ; so in what sense did these distinctions no longer exist, and in what ways might the principle be extended and applied to the problems caused by distinctions in modern society, not least between rich and poor?

ESSAY TOPICS

INTRODUCTORY

● Explore the way in which Paul uses the Old Testament to develop his argument in Galatians. (For general discussions of how Paul uses the Old Testament see, for example, M. Silva in *DPL*, pp. 630–42; A. T. Hanson *The Living Utterances of God: The New Testament Exegesis of the Old*, London: Darton, Longman and Todd, 1983, pp. 44–62.)

INTERMEDIATE

● Show how Paul uses different types of approach and argument in attempting to persuade his readers of his case in Galatians.

FURTHER READING

*denotes books assuming knowledge of Greek; most can be used by all students.

INTRODUCTORY

C. K. Barrett *Freedom and Obligation: A Study of the Epistle to the Galatians*. London: SPCK/ Philadelphia: Westminster, 1985 (good exposition of the teaching of the letter).

J. D. G. Dunn *The Theology of Paul's Letter to the Galatians*. New Testament Theology. Cambridge/New York: Cambridge University Press, 1993 (more detailed summary of the theological message).

Commentaries

G. W. Hansen *Galatians*. IVPNTC. Downers Grove: IVP, 1994 (a combination of explanation of what Paul was saying to his readers and of what the relevance of the letter for modern readers might be).

J. Ziesler *Galatians*. EC. London: Epworth/ Valley Forge: Trinity Press International, 1992 (like his *Romans*, exposes the problems clearly).

INTERMEDIATE

J. M. G. Barclay 'Mirror-Reading a Polemical Letter. Galatians as a Test Case' *JSNT* 31 (1987), pp. 73–93 (an important methodological discussion of the pitfalls in attempting to reconstruct the situation behind a letter from ambiguous clues in the letter).

J. M. G. Barclay *Obeying the Truth: A Study of Paul's Ethics in Galatians*. Edinburgh: T. & T. Clark, 1988/Minneapolis: Fortress, 1991 (fresh study with emphasis on the ethical teaching of the letter).

J. D. G. Dunn *The Theology of Paul the Apostle*. Grand Rapids/Cambridge: Eerdmans, 1998 (the most comprehensive recent treatment).

P. F. Esler *Galatians*. New Testament Readings. London/New York: Routledge, 1998 (pioneering study from a social-scientific angle).

R. B. Hays *The Faith of Jesus Christ: The Narrative Substructure of Galatians 3:1–4:11*. Grand Rapids: Eerdmans, 2002 (ground-breaking thesis that Gal. 2:16 and elsewhere refers to the faith shown *by* Jesus).

C. J. Hemer *The Book of Acts in the Setting of Hellenistic History*. Edited by C. H. Gempf. Tübingen: Mohr, 1989 (technical study of the background to Acts).

B. W. Longenecker *The Triumph of Abraham's God: The Transformation of Identity in Galatians*. Edinburgh: T. & T. Clark/Nashville: Abingdon, 1998 (what might it mean for somebody to accept the message of the letter?).

J. L. Martyn *Theological issues in the Letters of Paul*. Nashville: Abingdon/Edinburgh: T. & T. Clark, 1997 (essays by a major commentator on Galatians).

E. P. Sanders *Paul and Palestinian Judaism*. Philadelphia: Fortress/London: SCM Press, 1977 (the classic work that founded the 'new perspective').

E. P. Sanders *Paul, the Law and the Jewish People*. Philadelphia: Fortress Press, 1983 (the implications of Sanders' view of Judaism for understanding Paul).

Commentaries

*H. D. Betz *Galatians*. Herm. Philadelphia: Fortress, 1979 (very technical, but important for its pioneering rhetorical analysis).

*F. F. Bruce *The Epistle of Paul to the Galatians*. NIGTC. Exeter: Paternoster/ Grand Rapids: Eerdmans, 1982 (standard treatment of the Greek text by a major Pauline scholar).

J. D. G. Dunn *The Epistle to the Galatians*. BNTC. London: A. and C. Black/Peabody: Hendrickson, 1993 (good exposition of the 'new perspective' on Paul).

T. George *Galatians*, NAC. Nashville: Broadman & Holman, 1994 (theological commentary).

*R. N. Longenecker *Galatians*. WBC. Dallas: Word, 1990 (fuller than Bruce on Greek text; pays more attention to rhetorical structure).

*J. L. Martyn *Galatians*. AB. New York: Doubleday, 1997 (detailed, with new insights)

B. Witherington III *Grace in Galatia: A Commentary on St Paul's Letter to the Galatians*. Edinburgh: T. & T. Clark/ Grand Rapids: Eerdmans, 1998 (very full on the English text).

Chapter 5

THE LETTERS TO THE THESSALONIANS

In this chapter we shall explore:

- Paul and Silas's mission to Thessalonica;
- what Paul said to new Christians in
  1 Thessalonians;
- what Paul said in his follow-up letter,
  2 Thessalonians;
- whether 2 Thessalonians was in fact written by
  Paul.

PAUL AND THESSALONICA

After the completion of his first missionary campaign Paul felt called by God to travel further west. He and Silas had made their way through the province of Galatia to revisit the young congregations there (Acts 16:1–5). Then they travelled through the western part of modern Turkey (the Roman province of Asia) but felt the urge, communicated in a dream by 'a man of Macedonia', to cross the Hellespont into new territory (Acts 16:6–10). For those of us who are European Christians it was a moment of intense significance, since it was the first recorded venture of Christian missionaries into Europe. However, this is probably to view the incident with hindsight and to invest it with an importance that could not have been realized at the time. Moreover, in any case, Christianity had probably already reached Rome through the return of Roman converts from the Pentecost event in Acts 2.

The new missionary campaign fell into two parts, the first being directed to Macedonia itself, in particular to the cities of Philippi and Thessalonica, and the second to the southern region of Achaia, where Paul visited Athens and Corinth.

THESSALONICA

Thessalonica (mod. Thessaloniki) was founded as a 'new town' c. 300 BC by Cassander, one of the generals of Alexander the Great, who named it after his wife and it rapidly became a leading city in the area. After the Roman conquest of the area it became the capital of the province established by the Romans (146 BC); later in 42 BC it became a free city with its own government and rights of citizenship. Its local magistrates were called 'politarchs' (Acts 17:6), as inscriptions have confirmed. The important Roman road, the Via Egnatia, ran through it from west to east. It became a prosperous administrative and commercial centre with a Jewish presence. Paul's visit here follows his pattern of concentrating his attention on the major cities in the eastern Roman empire.

You can find the account of Paul's visit in Acts 17:1–15. Here we are told that Paul was forced to leave in a hurry after an evangelistic mission that lasted for three weeks and to go on to Beroea and then to Athens. However, the impression that we gain from 1 Thess. 2:7–11 and Phil. 4:16 is that a longer period must have been spent there; perhaps the 'three weeks' in Acts was the period of initial evangelism leading to the formation of a small congregation, and then the missionaries stayed on a bit longer.

Acts describes how when Paul went south he left Silas and Timothy in the north and from Athens he sent word that they should come and join him; they eventually caught up with him in Corinth (Acts 17:14–16; 18:1, 5). There had been opposition directed against both the new converts and the missionaries with the result that Paul had been forced to leave the town by the decree of the city magistrates. It is understandable that he was filled with anxiety as to whether the new church was managing to survive the attacks that were being made on it.

This must now be tied in with the story that we can reconstruct from 1 Thessalonians, where we read that because Satan was hindering him from going back to Thessalonica Paul sent Timothy instead from Athens to convey encouragement and bring back news (3:1–10). These two stories are not in perfect harmony with each other, unless we assume (for example) that there was a rather more complicated travelogue than appears on the surface with Timothy coming south to Athens, then being sent back north to Thessalonica, and finally returning to Paul, presumably at Corinth. In short, Acts has condensed the story.

From the way in which the story is told in 1 Thessalonians, it would appear that the return of Timothy to Paul at Corinth led him to write this letter more or less immediately and send it to Thessalonica. Paul was resident in Corinth for a sufficient length of time for this to happen; he mentions his own distress and affliction in the letter, and this would certainly fit in with the fact that he encountered opposition to his mission in Corinth (Acts 18:5–17). We can therefore date the letter fairly precisely to this period. Since we know that Paul was in Corinth during the time of Gallio's governorship (AD 51–52; see p. 43), the letter will have been written round about this date.

2 Thessalonians contains no similar personal information which could help us to fix its occasion. However, it appears to be a response to a possible misunderstanding of what Paul wrote in the first letter, and it is probable that news that came back to him not long afterwards caused him to write a follow-up letter.

THE STRUCTURE OF 1 THESSALONIANS

1:1	OPENING GREETING
1:2—5:24	BODY OF THE LETTER
1:2–10	Thanksgiving
2:1–16	The mission and its effects
2:17–3:13	Paul's continuing concern for the church
4:1–12	Ethical exhortation
4:13–5:11	Instruction about the *parousia*
5:12–24	Instructions about church life
5:25–28	CLOSING GREETINGS

THE CONTENTS OF 1 THESSALONIANS

From what we have seen about the circumstances of its composition we can deduce that the immediate purpose of this letter will be to express Paul's relief that the church had survived any attacks on it and to give them reassurance and encouragement to continue to stand firm in their Christian faith. At the same time, there could well have been news from Timothy about any specific needs faced by the congregation and perhaps also questions that they had for Paul (5:1), and the letter could deal with these matters. We might also expect that Paul, as preachers are wont to do, would make some general, non-specific comments of the kind that would be appropriate for almost any congregation. And in fact this is what he does within the structure imposed by the conventions of letter-writing.

After the briefest of formal greetings (1:1) he begins as if he is going to follow his normal practice of giving a 'prayer report', an account of the things for which he gives thanks to God and for which he intercedes when he prays for his friends. This procedure (omitted in Galatians because he couldn't get down fast enough to the problems in the churches) enabled him to congratulate the readers on their spiritual progress and to indicate the direction in which they should be continuing. Here there is a very positive mood in which Paul makes use of a well-known triplet of faith, love and hope to summarize the Christian qualities shown by the readers. But then Paul breaks off from his thanksgiving to reminisce over the way in which the readers had demonstrated that they had really been called by God to be his people and had responded positively. The preaching to them had been powerfully effective; its effects had

been such that it was clearly not just a matter of human persuasion but of a divine spiritual inducement to believe. So much so, that news had spread round the whole area, and the other Christian believers had heard about the remarkable conversion of these Gentiles to a genuine faith in God (1:2–10).

THE GOSPEL ACCORDING TO PAUL

For the people of those regions report about us what kind of welcome we had among you, and how you turned to God from idols, to serve a living and true God, and to wait for his Son from heaven, whom he raised from the dead – Jesus, who rescues us from the wrath that is coming. (1 Thess. 1:9–10)

Some scholars have been impressed by the language and content of this brief statement of what it meant for the readers to have become Christians, and have drawn the conclusion that what we have here in fact reflects what Paul would have said to them in his preaching of the gospel. Look up Acts 14:15–17 and 17:22–31 for Luke's summaries of how Paul spoke to predominantly Gentile audiences who worshipped a variety of gods and note the similarities to this description. Paul directed his hearers to the one true God worshipped by the Jews but now revealed in a new way through his Son, Jesus. The first part of his message is similar to what Jews said in commending their faith to Gentiles; the second part is distinctively Christian.

One of the ways in which the church was being attacked was through a smear campaign against the integrity of Paul (and his companions): he was accused of using flattery and distorting the truth simply in order to get converts, and he was motivated by greed. These were stock accusations against the travelling philosophers of the time, but Paul took them sufficiently seriously to call the readers to testify that there was no foundation for them. It was not normally Paul's way to engage in self-defence against Christian rivals but he certainly did so against slanders from outside the church (2:1–12).

What do you think?

'You became imitators of us and of the Lord' (1:6). How do you react to this and to Paul's exhortations elsewhere to 'imitate us' (2 Thess. 3:7, 9; cf. 1 Cor. 11:1)? Are there good reasons why he would have needed to write like this? After all, he couldn't say 'Read the Gospels' or 'Look at the example of Mother Teresa'.

Then he reverts to the readers themselves and the way in which their initial reception of the Christian message as truly coming from God had taken place against a background of opposition. Jesus himself had been opposed and crucified, and this was part of an ongoing opposition from some of the Jews to God's message, which now took the form of trying to prevent Christian missionaries from bringing the gospel to Gentiles (2:13–16). The effect of the mission was to divide the Jewish community. At the bottom of the opposition by some Jews there lay both rejection of Jesus as being the Messiah and fierce opposition to the fact that Gentile converts were not being required to be circumcised and keep the law of Moses. Possibly too there was envy of the Christian success in winning Gentile converts compared with the limited success of the synagogues.

At this point Paul describes his feelings as he thought of his friends facing this opposition, and how he longed to be with them and encourage them but could not do so. So he

Digging deeper

Study 1 Thess. 1:1—2:12. What signs do you find here of Paul's motivation, methods and goals in his work as a missionary? How does he relate to members of the congregation that he has founded? Are there lessons to learn from this for Christian ministry today? (Think out your own response to these questions before turning to a commentary for assistance.)

sent Timothy instead to take his place. And Timothy's return with good news had immensely warmed his heart. Once again Paul is moved to thanksgiving to God for their steadfastness, and he expresses his prayer that he might yet have the opportunity to see them, and that they would in any case continue to grow in their Christian commitment (2:17—3:13).

So far, then, Paul has dealt with the fact of his absence. Now he turns to what he would say to them if he were present with them and most of what follows is teaching. There are a number of themes.

The first is that he encourages them to continue their Christian growth as they have begun (4:1–8). He singles out particularly the need for them to develop in what he calls holiness, and references to this are frequent throughout the letter. This was particularly appropriate for Gentiles who were regarded by Jews as 'unclean' because they did not eat 'kosher' food and because their sexual laxity was considered defiling. Paul was not bothered about the former, but he does insist on the need for sexual morality. The key verse is 4:4, which is variously interpreted. Most probably it means that men are to control their sexual impulses (NRSV: 'your own body') and refrain from immorality and particularly adultery. Paul also commends them for their Christian love for one another and both prays that it will increase (3:12) and urges them to love one another more and more (4:9–12).

SOME PUZZLING CONCEPTS USED BY PAUL

In writing to the Thessalonians Paul uses four terms for the final coming of Jesus:

- 'coming' (Gk. *parousia*, 1 Thess. 4:15). This word means 'presence' or 'arrival' and was sometimes used to describe the visit of a ruler to a city, with all the festive atmosphere which surrounds such a visit. Theologians often use the Greek word as 'shorthand' to refer to the hope of Christ's final coming.
- 'descent from heaven' (1 Thess. 4:16). Linked with the 'clouds' of verse 17, this description echoes the language of Jesus in Mark 13:26; 14:62. The language of 'descending' need not be taken literally, any more than we take literally references to 'going up in the world' or 'coming down from university'.
- 'the day of the Lord' (1 Thess. 5:2). This Old Testament term for the expected day of God's judgement and deliverance (Amos 5:18) is reapplied to the time of Christ's coming for that purpose.
- 'revelation' (Gk. *apokalupsis*, 2 Thess. 1:7; *epiphaneia*, 2 Thess. 2:8). Christ's coming will reveal what is now hidden and will demonstrate the glory of Christ in contrast with the 'incognito' element in his first coming.

These images underline Paul's conviction that Christ's final coming will bring to its promised climax the purpose of God which began with Jesus of Nazareth.

Throughout the letter the horizon of their life is formed by the fact that the Lord Jesus will come from heaven with all his saints and take those believers who are still alive to be with him. It would be fair to say that this hope dominates the outlook of these two letters more than anywhere else in the New Testament with the exception of Revelation.

This teaching had caused problems for some members of the congregation because they thought that those of their number who had already died would be cut out from this event and would have no future.

1 THESSALONIANS 4:13

A tomb inscription from Thessalonica:

Because of her special disposition and good sense her devoted husband Eutropus created this tomb for her and also for himself, in order that later he would have a place to rest together with his dear wife, when he looks upon the end of life that has been spun out for him by the indissoluble threads of the Fates. (A. Boeckh, *Corpus Inscriptionum Graecarum* [Berlin, 1828–77], 1973; *HCNT* §819).

Paul's response to this serious problem was to develop teaching about the way in which those who had died as believers were asleep and would be aroused or resurrected by the Lord to be with him when he came for his people who were still alive on the earth (4:13–18). He bases this teaching on two things. The first is the fact that Jesus himself died and was resurrected, from which Paul concluded that those who believed in him would also be resurrected; to Paul it was inconceivable that those who believed in Christ would be treated any differently by God from the way in which he had resurrected Jesus. The second point to which Paul appealed was a 'word of the Lord', a phrase which might refer to something that Jesus himself had said in his teaching to his disciples or else to a communication by the risen Lord to a Christian prophet (perhaps Paul himself) who then communicated it to the church. The 'word of the Lord' is given in vv. 16f.

PAUL AND THE TEACHING OF JESUS

Paul makes rather less overt reference to the teaching of Jesus than might perhaps have been expected. Even here, where he refers specifically to 'the word of the Lord', some scholars think that he is referring to some kind of direct revelation from heaven. Elsewhere, however, Paul does cite Jesus (1 Cor. 7:10; 9:14; 1 Tim. 5:18b) and the close correspondence between what is said here and the teaching of Jesus (cf. Matt. 24:30–31) suggests that he is doing the same here. Paul's ethical teaching particularly shows signs of influence from the teaching of Jesus. For a careful study which indicates the strong degree of continuity between Paul and Jesus see D. Wenham *Paul: Follower of Jesus or Founder of Christianity?* Grand Rapids: Eerdmans, 1995.

It is puzzling that the readers needed to be reminded of the resurrection in this way, and it is possible that they had not been fully or clearly taught about it earlier or that they had failed to grasp the full significance of what may have been to them a novel teaching.

There was also a fear among the readers that they themselves might be taken by surprise by the coming of the Lord and not be spiritually ready for it. Paul's response was that his coming would certainly be unexpected by the unbelieving world but believers who were spiritually vigilant and living a sober Christian life would be ready for the event and would gladly welcome it when it happened (5:1–11).

What do you think?

'This thought of the future is anything but superfluous mythology . . . Faith in Jesus without the expectation of his *Parousia* is a cheque that is never cashed, a promise that is not made in earnest. A faith in Christ without the expectation of a *Parousia* is like a flight of stairs that leads nowhere but ends in the void' (E. Brunner *The Christian Doctrine of the Church, Faith and the Consummation: Dogmatics*, Vol. 3. London: Lutterworth/Philadelphia: Westminster, 1962, p. 396).

'The mythical eschatology is untenable for the simple reason that the *parousia* of Christ never took place as the New Testament expected. History did not come to an end, and, as every schoolboy knows, it will continue to run its course' (R. Bultmann 'New Testament and Mythology' in H.-W. Bartsch (ed.), *Kerygma and Myth* Vol. 1. London: SPCK, 1953, p. 5).

How do you react to these two statements? How literally or symbolically do you think Paul's language about the future coming of Christ should be interpreted? Can you give *reasons* for your answer, rather than simply expressing assertions or feelings?

The final part of the letter contains the more general kind of instruction that would suit Christians anywhere (it is very similar in content to Rom. 12), but it probably contains some items of particular relevance to the readers. The letter closes with yet another prayer for the readers to be ready for the Lord's coming (1 Thess. 5:23–24).

Focus on theology

The letter is a practical one, intended to encourage its readers to stand firm in their new way of life under persecution. It majors on the doctrine of God as the faithful guardian of his people. Prayers to him are grounded on the assurance that he will protect them. Worries about the future and especially about what happens to believers who have died are answered by repeated reference to the future coming to earth of the Lord Jesus, bringing with him those who have already died but are raised from the dead. The readers are encouraged by reminders of the powerful activity of the Holy Spirit who brought about their conversion and continues to work in their lives to make them like their heavenly Father. But this process of becoming holy (or sanctification) depends at the same time on their active obedience to the purpose of God for their lives. God seeks to make them a holy people, sharing his righteous character, filled with love and alert to withstand temptation. Although little is said about the death and resurrection of Jesus, it is clear that this is the basis of their salvation and their future hope.

THE CONTENTS OF 2 THESSALONIANS

If we take the letter as it stands, it would appear that it takes up the things that Paul had said in the first letter and goes further. The readers are commended because they were now more stable and had progressed in their Christian faith, love and steadfastness (1:3–4). At the same time the violence of the attacks on them appears to have increased; certainly the tone of the comments on the opposition to them is even stronger (1:5–9).

But the most remarkable feature of the letter is the way in which Paul relates how

the congregation was in a state of considerable worry and anxiety because they had been led to believe that the day of the Lord had arrived. This 'day' is evidently a term for that final period of time during which the coming of the Lord himself would take place and not for a literal twenty-four hour period (otherwise the Lord could have come before the letter had been written and sent!). There was thus a flurry of excitement in the congregation, which was not perhaps surprising in view of the way in which this future horizon of the Christian life had been so emphasized in 1 Thessalonians.

There was also another tendency mentioned in the first letter, which had referred to people who were apparently not working for their living and trusting that they would be supported for their daily necessities by other, better-off people (4:11–12). Such 'spongeing' could not but give the church a bad name in the community at large.

In face of these alarming developments a further letter was necessary.

THE STRUCTURE OF 2 THESSALONIANS

1:1–2	OPENING GREETING
1:3—3:16	BODY OF THE LETTER
1:3–12	Prayer report incorporating teaching on persecution
2:1–17	Instruction about the parousia
3:1–16	Instructions about prayer and idleness
3:17–18	CLOSING GREETINGS

In the first part of the letter Paul begins by thanking God for the spiritual progress of his readers and emphasizes their growing steadfastness over against the attacks upon them (1:3). He tells them that he is praying for God to strengthen their resolve so that their conduct will glorify the Lord and they in turn will be glorified in him (1:11–12). The thanksgiving and the prayer are separated by a passage in which the thanksgiving turns into a comment on the situation (1:4–10). The readers were continuing to be attacked or persecuted. This could be seen as an opportunity for them to demonstrate their worthiness for entry to the kingdom of God, since it could be assumed that God in his justice would reward them when Christ is revealed from heaven and is the object of worship by his people. Equally in his justice God will act in judgement against those who do not recognize his rule and do not accept the gospel. Clearly, then, the persecution is raging strongly, and it is sufficiently ferocious for Paul to prophesy the severest judgement upon those responsible for it.

Digging deeper

Work out Paul's theology of persecution and suffering from these two letters.

- What picture of the suffering and persecution of the Thessalonian Christians emerges in these letters?
- What advice do the missionary team offer to the Christians in the face of this suffering?
- What theological themes (such as beliefs about God, his work, his action in history, his people's suffering) do the missionaries focus on in helping the Christians?

In the second part of the letter Paul takes up the suggestion that the Day of the Lord has already dawned (2:1–12). He attempts to refute it by reminding the readers of what he had already taught them, namely that certain other events must take place first, the appearance of a 'man of lawlessness', the removal of restraints on his activity, and the spread of satanic delusions among unbelievers which would in effect shut them in to judgement. This raises even more strongly the difficulties that we have already encountered for modern readers in 1 Thessalonians, with its strong accent on the future coming of Jesus. Three questions arise here:

- What was the origin of this scenario?
- Can we identify to what Paul was referring?
- And what do we make of it two millennia later?

These questions are not easy to answer.

- The *origin of the language* used lies in the apocalyptic tradition with its veiled prophecies of future events and people, and it can probably be traced back to the book of Daniel and to the desecration of the temple by Antiochus Epiphanes (Dan. 11:31; 1 Macc. 1, especially vv. 54–59). This became the accepted imagery for an event of appalling wickedness and impiety (Mark 13:14). The belief in a final, fearsome outbreak of evil on an unparalleled scale before the End was common. The restraining factor probably has its origins in the activity of God or angelic forces holding back evil. It has been thought that a fresh wave of fear of such events was triggered off by the threat of the Roman Emperor Caligula to place an image of himself in the Jewish temple in AD 40–41; the attempt failed, but one never knew when some other Roman ruler might make a fresh try and do something comparable.
- What *Paul was referring to* is not clear. One interpretation is that he meant it literally; did he think that before the end came there would be a literal desecration of the

2 THESSALONIANS 2:4

The insolence with which the emperor Gaius defied fortune surpassed all bounds: he wished to be considered a god and to be hailed as such, he cut off the flower of the nobility of his country, and his impiety extended even to Judea. In fact, he sent Petronius with an army to Jerusalem to install in the sanctuary statues of himself; in the event of the Jews refusing to admit them, his orders were to put the recalcitrants to death and to reduce the whole nation to slavery . . . The Jews replied . . . that if he wished to set up these statues, he must first sacrifice the entire Jewish nation; and that they presented themselves, their wives and their children, ready for the slaughter. (Josephus, *Jewish Wars* 2.184-85, 197 [LCL; *HCNT* §826])

temple in this manner? And if so, what was holding it back from happening? Did he simply think there were hidden, supernatural forces doing so? Or did Paul mean it metaphorically? For example, it has been suggested that he was thinking of some alarming manifestation of apostasy in the church (admittedly not a very likely suggestion). Or did Paul see the church as the force that was preventing the outbreak of this final fling by evil? Or again was Paul simply repeating the prophecies (including the teaching of Jesus) that were current without knowing how they would be fulfilled? We are at the disadvantage that Paul's original readers had received oral instruction from him (2:5) of which we are ignorant.

- And *what do we make of the fact* that nothing that can reasonably be identified as corresponding to this description has happened? The nearest that we have is the desecration and destruction of the Jewish temple in AD 70, but that is not a close fit. Do we conclude that Paul was wrong and

that this is unfulfilled prophecy? Some interpreters would retrieve the situation by saying that there has been an unforeseen long interval of 'restraint' and that the prophecy is still to be fulfilled, even though this would seem to require the rebuilding of a temple in Jerusalem.

So we face problems to which there are no agreed answers. They may cause some embarrassment for people who find that they can go along quite happily with what Paul normally teaches about Christ and salvation and the church but then are disconcerted to find him shifting into this apparently very different mode of discourse that seems to make little sense in the modern world.

Certainly by the end of the chapter Paul has shifted back to his normal discourse, as he expresses his belief that the readers will hold fast to what he has taught them and will not be moved by wild speculations (2:13–17).

In the final part of the letter he takes up the issue of the people who were turning to idleness instead of earning their keep (3:6–13). It has sometimes been suggested that these were people who thought that, if the end of the world was imminent, there was no point in going on working and it would be best to sit down and wait for it to happen, but on the whole this is improbable (the problem was already active in 1 Thess. 4:11f.; 5:14). Paul's response is that people who were lazy should not be given free handouts but expected to work for their living. Winter (1994, pp. 41–60) suggests that the background to the issue was the practice of poorer people seeking the 'patronage' of wealthier people, and that the particular occasion here was the incidence of famine in Greece in AD 51. Such people would give the church a bad name. It is assumed that

APOCALYPTIC AND THE MODERN WORLD

Early Christians in general undoubtedly had a much more pressing belief that the end of the world was imminent than do modern people a couple of millennia later. Under the impact of the first coming of Christ we can well understand how they thought that his second coming could not be far distant. Has the long period since Christ first came altered the character of Christian hope, so that we can no longer believe that his second coming is imminent or let this hope control our outlook for the future?

People today tend to assume that the universe will go on indefinitely, just as it has already existed for billions of years; but a Christian belief in the creation of the universe surely entails that God can also bring history to an end and renew the universe. Already the author of 2 Peter had to remind his readers not to assume that the end would necessarily be immediate (2 Pet. 3:8–10), but nevertheless he still maintained that because of this future hope Christians had to live in an appropriate way and be ready for the Lord's coming (2 Pet. 3:11–13). Does the fact that (like many other Christians) we may die before the end of the world make any significant difference to the way that we ought to live in the light of the judgement and eternal destiny?

The Bible gives vivid descriptions of future events, parts of which at least cannot surely be meant literally (see Chapter 21 on Revelation, pp. 323–46). At the very least they indicate that in many ways the future prospect is very bleak until God intervenes to bring evil to an end; but a generation in whose memory the Holocaust, the Rwanda massacres, the conflicts in the Balkans and the Middle East, September 11th and much besides are still very fresh, should perhaps rather acknowledge the sheer realism of the Bible in recognizing the extent and enormity of evil in the world today. Is there a way in which Christians can believe firmly that the God of love and justice will triumph in the end while recognizing that the path to that end is not fixed? Compare how a chess grand master can be certain of defeating a weak opponent without knowing precisely how the game will proceed to its inevitable end.

the church has some authority over its members and their way of life. (There may be some parallel with the provision for the poor described in Acts 2:44f.; 4:32–37. On patronage see pp. 12–13.)

PROBLEMS IN 2 THESSALONIANS

Although the discussion so far has proceeded on the assumption that 2 Thessalonians is what it appears to be, namely, a follow-up letter to 1 Thessalonians, it has to be recognized that this assumption is open to question. There are some difficulties with the letter, quite apart from that of understanding 2 Thessalonians 2.

- Much of the structure and even the actual wording of 2 Thessalonians is remarkably close to that of 1 Thessalonians, and it could be argued that whoever wrote 2 Thessalonians did so with 1 Thessalonians in front of them and used it as a pattern to follow. But why would anybody, least of all Paul, do that?
- Despite these similarities in wording, there are differences of outlook between the two letters. The most important of these is that in 1 Thessalonians the day of the Lord (i.e. the consummation of human history) is imminent and could come unexpectedly, but in 2 Thessalonians it is more remote and certain events will happen first which

Focus on theology

In a developing situation with real dangers arising from heightened persecution and the apocalyptic hopes of some believers, Paul has to stress the justice of God who will judge persecutors (something that Christians must leave to him to do) and also to insist that this will not happen before the situation gets even worse with the growth of godlessness. The stress on the faithfulness of God and the way in which the conversion of the readers came about indicates that God is not going to abandon them. A further ground for assurance lies in the observable signs of growth in Christian character brought about by the Spirit. The hope of the coming of the Lord Jesus when believers will share in his glory is central as an incentive to continuing faith, obedience and love.

could be interpreted as signs that it was approaching.

- There are other differences in matters of detail, both in the literary style and also in the theology. The former includes the greater use in 1 Thess. of parallel expressions (see e.g. 1 Thess. 2:9, 12; 3:2) and of groups containing three items (see e.g. 1 Thess. 1:5; 2:3, 10). The latter includes a greater stress on the nearness of the *parousia* in 1 Thess. (1:10; 4:17; contrast 2 Thess. 2:3) and a more majestic presentation of Christ as judge in 2 Thess. (1:7–10) and a more frequent use of his title of 'Lord'. These features are thought to be incompatible with common authorship.
- There is quite a lot of inter-personal material in 1 Thessalonians which reflects the warm relationship between Paul and the readers (e.g. 1 Thess. 2:17, 20; 3:6), but there is very little of this in 2 Thessalonians.

If these points are sound, a plausible explanation of them is that 2 Thessalonians is not by Paul but by a later author, who used 1 Thessalonians as a template and precedent for a letter in which he warned later Christians that the end was not as near as they expected (possibly in the aftermath of the destruction of the temple and the growing tendency of Roman emperors to claim divinity and to expect worship from their subjects). (See, for example, Menken 1994; Richard 1995.)

Before committing ourselves to this conclusion we need to ask whether the evidence points to such a drastic reinterpretation.

- If 2 Thessalonians was written by Paul shortly after 1 Thessalonians and to the same people, it would not be surprising if there were close parallels in style and wording, particularly as some of the same ground is being covered.
- The differences between the two letters can be convincingly explained if the second letter is deliberately intended to correct misapprehensions about the nearness of the coming of Christ that partly arose from a reading of the first letter.
- The minor differences in outlook and theology can be shown to be capable of resolution. If Jesus is given a more exalted position than in 1 Thessalonians, this is partly because the theme of the letter led to a greater emphasis on his position and role.
- There is a lack of personal exchange in the second letter, but this is because one of the main themes in the first letter was the relationship between the missionaries and the congregation, and this was not an issue in the second letter, which for its part does address the readers quite warmly (2 Thess. 1:3f.; 2:13; 3:4).

OTHER VIEWS OF THE LETTERS

Other attempts have been made to deal with some of the difficulties, real or imagined, that scholars have found in the letters.

- One hypothesis is that the letters were written by Paul in reverse order, and that they have been ordered as 'first' and 'second' by later scribes purely on grounds of relative length (Wanamaker 1990). This theory doesn't help to solve the difficulties listed above, and it is open to the strong objection that 1 Thess. 2:17—3:10 must surely belong to the prior letter.
- Another suggestion is that the two letters were sent to two different groups of people, with 2 Thessalonians going to a different congregation or being sent to the leaders of the congregation in Thessalonica (E. Schweizer; E. E. Ellis). Again, it is not clear how these theories help to solve the problems, and they are speculations without any solid evidence in their favour.
- Some scholars have argued that the letters do not fit the 'pattern' that we expect in Pauline letters (specifically the fact that Paul makes a fresh start with thanksgiving in 1 Thess. 2:13 after having an earlier thanksgiving in 1 Thess. 1:2) and therefore they have divided up the material and reassembled it to create as many as four letters that satisfy their ideas of what letters should look like (so W. Schmithals; Richard 1995). Such theories assume a degree of rigidity and conformity in Paul that is quite unrealistic. (See further on these issues Marshall 1983, pp. 25–8.)

The cases for and against Pauline authorship are thus finely balanced, but in my view the conventional understanding has more in its favour.

FOR TODAY'S THESSALONIANS

- Paul taught that certain types of sexual behaviour were incompatible with Christian holiness (1 Thess. 4:3–8). Is

holiness a helpful concept for understanding Christian morality today, and what attitudes and practices of the world in which we live might a modern-day Paul find to be incompatible with it?
- In what circumstances is the 'work ethic' of 2 Thess. 3:10–12 appropriate or inappropriate? (Note that the specific problem of people not able to work or to find employment is not the issue in this passage.)
- The man walking down the street carrying a billboard announcing 'The end of the world is nigh' has tended to cast ridicule upon the hope of the coming of Christ which so dominates 1 and 2 Thessalonians. Should and can this hope be rehabilitated in the modern church, and would the church be healthier for it?

ESSAY TOPICS

INTRODUCTORY
- Assess the strengths and weaknesses of the arguments for and against Paul being the author of 2 Thessalonians.

INTERMEDIATE
- Compare the teaching about what happens to believers after death in 1 Thess. 4; 1 Cor. 15; 2 Cor. 5 and Phil. 1 to see if they present a consistent understanding.

FURTHER READING

*denotes books assuming knowledge of Greek; most can be used by all students.

INTRODUCTORY
K. P. Donfried (and I. H. Marshall) *The Theology of the Shorter Pauline Letters*. Cambridge/New York: Cambridge University Press, 1993, pp. 1–113 (summarizes the theology of the letters).

I. H. Marshall 'Pauline Theology in the Thessalonian Correspondence' in M. D. Hooker and S. G. Wilson *Paul and Paulinism. Essays in honour of C. K. Barrett*. London: SPCK, 1982, pp. 173–83 (brief introduction, comparing the teaching of the two letters).

L. Morris *Word Biblical Themes. 1, 2 Thessalonians*. Waco: Word, 1989 (simple introduction).

Commentaries

I. H. Marshall *1 and 2 Thessalonians*. NCB. London: Marshall, Morgan & Scott/Grand Rapids: Eerdmans, 1983 (fuller exposition of the above treatment).

M. J. J. Menken *2 Thessalonians*. London/ New York: Routledge, 1994 (exposition of 2 Thessalonians as a pseudonymous letter).

L. Morris *The Epistles of Paul to the Thessalonians*. TNTC. Leicester: IVP/ Grand Rapids: Eerdmans, 1987 (short introductory-level commentary).

L. Morris *The First and Second Epistles to the Thessalonians*. NIC. Grand Rapids: Eerdmans/London: Marshall, Morgan and Scott, 1991 (fuller treatment).

R. L. Thomas *1 Thessalonians; 2 Thessalonians*. EBC Vol. 12. Grand Rapids: Zondervan, 2006 (introductory-level exposition from a dispensationalist standpoint).

INTERMEDIATE

J. M. G. Barclay 'Conflict in Thessalonica', *CBQ* 55 (1993), pp. 512–30 (helpful analysis of situation behind the letters).

J. M. Bassler (ed.) *Pauline Theology* Vol. 1. Minneapolis: Fortress, 1991 (essays on different aspects of Paul's theology in his early letters).

R. F. Collins *Studies on the First Letter to the Thessalonians*. Leuven: Leuven University Press, 1984 (collected essays by a specialist).

*R. F. Collins (ed.) *The Thessalonian Correspondence*. Leuven: Leuven University Press, 1990 (scholarly essays on all aspects of the letters).

R. Jewett *The Thessalonian Correspondence: Pauline Rhetoric and Millenarian Piety*. Philadelphia: Fortress, 1986 (especially concerned with the structure and situation of the letters).

A. J. Malherbe *Paul and the Thessalonians: The Philosophic Tradition of Pastoral Care*. Philadelphia: Fortress, 1987 (examines Paul's teaching against the background of Hellenistic thinking).

B. W. Winter *Seek the Welfare of the City: Christians as Benefactors and Citizens*. Grand Rapids: Eerdmans/Carlisle: Paternoster, 1994 (the social background of urban life in Paul's time).

Commentaries

E. Best *A Commentary on the First and Second Epistles to the Thessalonians*. BNTC. London: A. and C. Black, 1972/Peabody: Hendrickson, 1988 (the standard work, accepting authenticity of 2 Thessalonians).

*F. F. Bruce *1 & 2 Thessalonians*. WBC. Waco: Word, 1982 (excellent treatment based on Greek text).

G. D. Fee *The First and Second Letters to the Thessalonians*. NIC. Grand Rapids: Eerdmans, 2009 (detailed and reliable).

G. L. Green *The Letters to the Thessalonians*. PNTC. Grand Rapids: Eerdmans/Leicester: IVP, 2002 (good middle-length exegesis).

A. J. Malherbe *The Letters to the Thessalonians*. AB. New York: Doubleday, 2000 (by an expert in the Greco-Roman background of the NT letters; powerful defence of authenticity of 2 Thessalonians).

E. J. Richard *First and Second Thessalonians*. Collegeville: Liturgical Press, 1995 (takes 2 Thessalonians as pseudonymous and adopts the view that 1 Thessalonians is a combination of two separate letters).

*C. A. Wanamaker *The Epistles to the Thessalonians*. NIGTC. Grand Rapids: Eerdmans/Exeter: Paternoster, 1990 (argues that 2 Thessalonians was written before 1 Thessalonians).

Chapter 6

THE 'FIRST' LETTER TO THE CORINTHIANS

In this chapter we shall look at:

- Corinth and the founding of the Christian congregation;
- Paul's earlier letter to the church (before 1 Corinthians);
- problems in the church that prompted 1 Corinthians;
- Paul's response to the problems in 1 Corinthians.

Although Romans is the longest of Paul's letters, 1 Corinthians is not far behind it, and when we take into account 2 Corinthians, it is apparent that Paul wrote more words to the congregation in Corinth than to any other. Moreover, Paul wrote other letters to them that have not been preserved (unless portions of them do survive as insertions into 1 and 2 Cor., as we shall have to discuss later). There was another letter before 1 Cor. (see 1 Cor. 5:9–10) and there was a letter before 2 Cor. (see 2 Cor. 2:4–9), which is generally thought to have been subsequent to 1 Cor. The frequency and the length of the correspondence (which also included at least one written communication in the opposite direction; 1 Cor. 7:1) indicates that the congregation at Corinth and its affairs occupied a very considerable share of Paul's attention during his mission in the Aegean area, although there is nothing in the story in Acts to betray this.

PAUL'S MISSION

Paul's mission took place during his second missionary campaign and is described in Acts 18. Significant features in Luke's story include the accusation of Paul before the Roman governor Gallio. As noted earlier (see p. 43), we can date Gallio's term of office with virtual certainty to somewhere around summer 51 to summer 52, and therefore we have a fixed chronology for his visit.

It is also important that Paul spent something over eighteen months in Corinth, a period long enough to establish a Christian congregation rather than just to win a few converts. He worked with colleagues including Timothy and Priscilla and Aquila. The converts were a mixture of Jews and Gentiles, the latter being contacted primarily through their relationship with the synagogue.

When Paul left Corinth, he went to Ephesus, then back to his home territory, and again

CORINTH

There is a risk of assuming that at this time Athens was the most important town in the Roman province of Achaia. Not only is it the capital city of modern Greece, but it also occupied the most prominent place in the great age of 'Classical' Greece when it was the centre of a culture that was unequalled in the Greco-Roman world. Nevertheless, by the time of Paul it had lost its former political importance, although it was still a cultural centre, and the town of Corinth was in fact the capital city of the province and the seat of the governor.

Corinth itself was an ancient Greek city. It occupied a strategic position on the narrow neck of land (the 'Isthmus') that separated the peninsula known as the Peloponnesus from the main body of Greece. This meant that all transport north and south had to pass through the city. It also meant that there was a short route for traders going east and west that saved them the long (and sometimes stormy) voyage right round the Peloponnesus. There was a slipway across which small boats could be hauled from one side of the Isthmus to the other, and Corinth had ports at Cenchreae on the east (Acts 18:18; Rom. 16:1) and Lechaeum on the west; later Nero attempted to drive a canal across.

The Greek city was destroyed by the Romans in 146 BC, and the Roman city (established in 44 BC) close to the site of the ancient town was a new foundation, and it has been extensively excavated in modern times. Ancient shops have been unearthed and in particular the meat market and the *bema* or tribunal from which the governor would preside over public gatherings and trials; however, it seems that in Paul's time the governor took his seat in the Julian basilica at the east end of the public square. The city was a thriving trade centre. As a result, it also attracted a Jewish population, and a lintel stone has survived bearing the inscription '[Syn]agogue of the Hebr[ews]' The old city had a notorious reputation for immorality, and it is probable that this carried over to the 'new' city.

returned to Ephesus where he spent over two years. Meanwhile he was followed at Corinth by Apollos, who had met up with Priscilla and Aquila in Ephesus and acquired from them a better understanding of the Christian faith, i.e. of the Pauline version of it (Acts 18:24—19:1).

According to Acts 20:1–6 Paul himself then travelled from Ephesus to Macedonia and then to Corinth; then, instead of going directly to Syria, as he had apparently intended, he returned to Macedonia, and then back to Asia and so to Syria (Acts 20:13–16; 21:1–17).

But Paul had a much more complicated set of relationships with the church after its foundation than Acts suggests with its account of the founding visit and its very brief mention of a second one. The story has to be pieced together from hints in the letters, and the evidence is sufficiently scanty and fragmentary to give rise to various different reconstructions; solving the problem is not helped by the fact that many scholars think that 2 Corinthians (and even 1 Corinthians) is a compilation from several fragments of Pauline letters which can then be rearranged chronologically in different ways. We shall set out one possible reconstruction, while noting at each point the main alternatives.

THE 'PREVIOUS' LETTER

From 1 Cor. 5:9–11 we learn that there had been some serious cases of unacceptable behaviour in the congregation, involving possible cases of sexual immorality, greed, robbery and idolatry. (Although Paul mentions all these possibilities and others, some of them may well be 'for instances' rather than actual occurrences). ~~Paul therefore wrote to the congregation the first letter of which we have any knowledge~~. In it he warned the members not to associate with immoral people. The prohibition may have been of any kind of personal contact, but since the congregation held communal meals it is more probable that exclusion from these as a form of discipline designed to lead people to repentance is what is meant. However, the instruction was misunderstood to prohibit any kind of contact with anybody guilty of such faults. This was not only impossible in practice but missed the point that what Paul was writing about was the discipline of members of the congregation. ~~Therefore, Paul had to issue~~ a ~~correction the next time he wrote to them~~.

GETTING BEHIND THE SECOND (FIRST) LETTER

From what Paul said in 1 Cor. 5:9–11 about the misunderstanding of the earlier letter, it is clear that he felt it was necessary to clear up the matter by writing again. What we call '1 Corinthians' is thus really the second letter of which we have evidence. It is a lengthy letter that covers a wide range of

RETRIEVING A LOST LETTER?

Has this 'previous letter', or any part of it, survived? The immediately obvious answer would be that it has not, unless somehow it has been preserved in some kind of disguise. It has been suspected that part of it may be found in 2 Cor. 6:14—7:1.

- The starting point for the suspicion lies in the fact that this passage seems to fit badly into its context; if it were omitted (or so it is argued), the reader would pass straight from 2 Cor. 6:13 to 7:2 with no sense of loss. The passage looks like a digression from what is being said about reconciliation between the congregation and Paul after some breakdown of relationships.
- The contents of the paragraph would be appropriate in the lost letter in that they encourage believers not to form close relationships with sinful people and to keep themselves pure.

These two arguments look quite plausible at first sight, but they are not compelling.

- We lack firm evidence that a compiler edited Pauline material by stringing together fragments in this way. In this particular case, it has been argued that the compiler would have been extremely clumsy since he appears to have broken up a connected train of thought for no apparent reason. To be sure, this argument is open to the objection that the alternative is that Paul himself was writing in a very disjointed and incoherent way. However, at the appropriate point I shall argue that the passage does fit sufficiently aptly into its present context (see pp. 100, 102, 103) and therefore is not an interpolation.
- Although we cannot know all that Paul said in the lost letter, we do know that he was concerned with fellowship with Christian brothers and sisters who sinned, whereas this alleged fragment is concerned with contacts with unbelievers. Again, however, a counter-argument can be mounted, namely that Paul's letter was misunderstood by some of the readers: maybe Paul could have backed up an appeal not to have fellowship with sinful believers with the general comment on not having close contacts with sinners in general that we have in the postulated fragment of the letter.

The arguments are finely balanced, the balance perhaps tipping more against the identification of the lost letter with 2 Cor. 6:14—7:1.

matters, and thus a complicated background lies behind it, which we must now endeavour to reconstruct.

Paul gained his knowledge of the developing situation in Corinth in at least three ways:

● Near the beginning of the letter he writes about reports that he had received from 'Chloe's people' (1:11). These would be members of this woman's household, whether relatives or slaves.
● At the end of the letter he mentions the visit paid by Stephanas, Fortunatus and Achaicus (16:17); since Stephanas at least is not to be identified as one of 'Chloe's people' (1:16; 16:15), this must be a separate (or overlapping) set of visitors.
● In 1 Cor. 7:1 he mentions a letter brought to him by one or other of these groups in which a series of questions were posed by the congregation.

MIRROR READING

A fascinating attempt was made by one scholar (Hurd 1965) to reconstruct from 1 Corinthians what questions and opinions must have been expressed by the Corinthians in their letter and (even more speculatively) what must have been said by Paul (orally or in a previous letter) to give rise to these questions. Other authors have attempted the same exercise at a more popular and less scholarly level (e.g. Frör 1995).

What were these issues, and how did Paul respond to them? Bruce Winter has argued cogently that they arose after Paul had left Corinth as a result of the increasing conformity of some of the members of the congregation to the non-Christian culture round about them and to various social changes, including the advent of famine and the developing cult of worshipping the emperor (Winter 2001).

CONTINUING IMMORALITY

Various remarks in the letter indicate that the kind of immorality castigated in the earlier letter was still prevalent. Some people saw nothing incongruous about taking part in feasts in pagan temples (8:10), where there would be not only idolatry but also immoral behaviour. Even congregational meals were disfigured by gluttony and drunkenness (11:21, 34). There was a particularly reprehensible case of incest and there were instances of litigation between believers (5:1; 6:1–6). Some of those engaging in sexual immorality argued that their behaviour was perfectly acceptable (6:12f.). None of this was surprising, given the fact that some of the congregation were converts from a non-Jewish background and would take time to learn what was appropriate conduct for believers (6:9–11).

It may be surprising that alongside this tendency to loose behaviour there was also some asceticism. This showed itself in some people refraining from sexual intercourse within marriage and others having doubts about getting married (7:1, 36–38). Yet alongside this attitude Paul also foresaw the danger of people not having sufficient self-control to remain celibate and presumably yielding to sexual temptation (7:5, 9).

PARTY SQUABBLES IN THE CONGREGATION

The major theme, with which the letter opens, is that somehow the members of the congregation were splitting up into factions (1:10–12). After Paul's initial visit to Corinth, his place had been taken by Apollos who may well have had a different kind of personality and approach, although Paul appears to rule out any possibility of significant differences of opinion. References to Cephas (Peter) indicate that he had partisans in the congregation, and it is possible that he had actually visited the church, although this is not directly stated anywhere.

This led to a situation in which some members of the congregation were voicing their support for Paul or Apollos or Cephas. Paul adds to this list of party cries the slogan 'I am of Christ' (1:12).

The interpretation of this situation is not easy. Some scholars have denied altogether that there were any distinguishable parties, but that is hard to credit. What can be said with confidence is that there is no indication that the named people were trying to gather support for themselves; the way in which Paul speaks positively of his colleagues rules that out decisively. Whether there was a 'Christ party' is uncertain. The cry 'I am of Christ' is hardly Paul's own riposte, and it is more likely that some people repudiated this idolizing of human leaders (though that hardly constitutes them as a fourth 'party'). This leaves us with the three other groups of Corinthians, and with the question whether there were any significant differences between them apart from this 'hero-worshipping' of different leaders. There were areas of belief and practice where there were differences between Paul and at least some of the Corinthians, and also there appear to have been differences within the congregation over against which Paul takes his own position. Yet it is simplistic to suppose that the different viewpoints reflected in 1 Corinthians can be identified with the Apollos and the Peter parties respectively. It is noteworthy that what Paul tackles in 1 Corinthians 1—4 are not different viewpoints but rather the sort of underlying attitude that led to this rivalry and arrogance. This may have been based on the way in which secular teachers of philosophy (known as

'sophists') competed with one another and expected loyalty and support from their pupils (Winter 2001, pp. 31–43).

THE SOPHISTS

Something of the way in which the sophists played to the gallery and had a high regard for themselves emerges from contemporary comments:

> A sophist is put out in an extempore speech by a serious-looking audience who don't cheer and clap. (Philostratus [c. AD 200]. *Lives of the Sophists* 2.26.3)

It was said of the sophist Polemon (c. AD 100) that 'he used to talk to cities as a superior, to kings as not inferior, and to gods as an equal' (*Lives of the Sophists* 1.25.4).

THE RICH AND THE POOR

It is easy for preachers to hold up the teaching in the New Testament as an ideal for Christians to live by today and then to slide over into commendation of individuals and congregations as ideal models for people to imitate. But alongside the undoubted saintliness of some there was the continuing reality of pre-Christian attitudes and behaviour. Few pastors today would be willing to take on the congregation in Corinth once they had discovered the depth and the range of its problems.

One such problem was that of integration between different social and economic groups. It is perhaps remarkable that the congregations included such a wide range of people; 1 Cor. 1:26 testifies to the mixture. Since it was customary for a household to follow the religion of its head, it is, however, not so surprising that a congregation would include both members of well-off families and also their slaves. There were also lots of people who stood in a patron–client relationship, often where poorer or less privileged people were shown favours by patrons who expected appropriate acknowledgement of their generosity. Thus there could be a circle of 'clients' around wealthy people and the holders of positions in the community. Alongside such there could be freedmen, former slaves whose economic rating would not have been high.

These differences surfaced in the church. From the description of the qualities found desirable in congregational leaders in 1 Timothy 3 and Titus 1 it is evident that normally householders and the more senior men were appointed to these posts, although there were some exceptions (like Timothy himself, 1 Tim. 4:12). Society was much more stratified than is ours today. At Corinth the problem arose at the congregational meals, where there were people eating and drinking to excess and others who were hungry. The meal was not the contemporary 'potluck supper' where the resources are pooled, but rather people brought and consumed their own food. The rich brought copious amounts while the poor had little or none, and the social divisions were embarrassingly plain (11:20–22).

'STRONG' AND 'WEAK' BELIEVERS

Paul refers to two types of people, one of which he categorizes as 'weak' in relation to the question of foods (8:9, 11; 9:22); he doesn't actually name the other group as 'strong', but cf. Rom. 15:1; 1 Cor. 4:10 for this terminology. Two related issues were involved.

First, there was the existence of pagan temples at which meals were held; remains of such temples with dining rooms attached have been found. The meals would have been held, nominally at least, in a religious setting, and if meat was served, it would have been slaughtered and symbolically offered in sacrifice to the deity, as a result of which it was judged unclean and defiled by Jews.

Second, at least some of the meat on sale in butchers' shops would have been treated in the same way; again, archaeology has shown the existence of a shrine in close proximity to the meat market in Corinth. We can imagine the ancient equivalent to a royal warrant sign in the shop window: 'Finest Aberdeen Angus beef as sacrificed to Aphrodite'.

In this situation what did you do as a Christian? Did you say that, since the idols are just human sculptures and the gods represented by them do not exist, therefore offering the animal to them can make no difference to the meat and there is nothing wrong with buying and eating it? Did you argue similarly that going to meals in temples was a social necessity and in any

AN INVITATION TO A PARTY

Chaeremon requests your company at dinner at the table of the Lord Serapis in the temple of Serapis tomorrow, the 15th, at 9 o'clock. (*Oxyrhynchus Papyri* 1.110; second century AD).

This invitation card from Egypt represents exactly the situation pictured in 1 Cor. 8:10: a banquet in the temple of an idol. Excavations in Corinth have revealed the temple of Asclepius; the buildings included a set of three dining rooms with couches round the walls and tables in the centre (Murphy-O'Connor 1983, pp. 161–7).

case the gods didn't exist? Some people in Corinth took that line. Others argued that the consecration to idols really did something to the meat and they could not eat it with a clear conscience (just as they could not offer incense to the Emperor as if he were a god).

The people taking the latter point of view were very probably of Jewish background, since we know that this was the Jewish attitude. The people taking the former view were probably Gentiles. It is tempting to identify them as followers of Peter and Apollos respectively, but that tendency should be resisted; Apollos was also a Jew from Alexandria, and Jews from outside Judea could be just as strict as the Judeans.

An important factor in the argument was that the former group claimed to be acting as they did on the basis of 'knowledge'; they knew that the idols were unreal (8:1–6). And they probably vaunted their superior knowledge over their 'weaker' brothers and sisters.

SPIRITUAL SUPERIORITY AND INFERIORITY

This last comment ties the problem of foods in with another issue that was very significant. Throughout this letter (1:5–7; 12—14) we find that the Corinthian congregation was very concerned with what are broadly called 'spiritual gifts' (Gk. *charismata* or *pneumatika*) and the people who possessed these gifts thought of themselves as 'spiritual' people and on a higher level than other believers who did not have these gifts or possessed only inferior varieties of them. There were perfectly genuine manifestations in the congregation of various gifts, including speaking in tongues and interpreting them, uttering prophecies and other forms of Christian instruction,

performing healing miracles, and so on. Paul was able to commend the congregation for its possession of these spiritual gifts (1:7). At the same time, he was very critical of certain aspects of them. In particular, enormous importance was attached to wisdom, knowledge and eloquence. These may have been a combination of natural qualities and spiritual gifts, but either way they were seen as desirable gifts, and there was rivalry between the possessors of them and pride and confidence in having them.

The background to this problem is debated. We need not doubt that there were charismatic manifestations at Corinth, and that, human nature being what it is, rivalry and pride could develop. Again, the Greek tradition, stretching back to Classical Athens, laid enormous stress on wisdom and eloquence; a 'university education' at this time was primarily training in rhetoric, the art of persuasive speech, and philosophy, the pursuit of wisdom. So there was an environment in which these qualities and accomplishments were especially valued (see especially Winter 2001).

At a later date there developed a movement known to scholars as Gnosticism (Gk. *gnōsis*, 'knowledge'), which involved esoteric knowledge about God and the universe, often expressed in weird mythology. It has been argued that the beginnings of this movement can be traced back as early as the time of Paul in Corinth, so that it could have influenced some of the Corinthian Christians. However, it is better to see here nothing more than the stress on the importance of knowledge which was one of the roots that led in course of time to the development of the particular kind of knowledge that surfaced in the Gnostic sects. It is highly unlikely that fully-fledged

Gnosticism had already developed at this time, since there is no trace of the characteristic teachings and mythology found in Gnosticism.

QUESTIONS ABOUT THE RESURRECTION

In 1 Corinthians 15 Paul raises the question: How can some of you say that there is no resurrection of the dead? (15:12). Since the resurrection of Jesus was part of the foundational Christian preaching, this question is surprising. Or maybe not. From 1 Thessalonians 4 we saw that there were people in Thessalonica who thought that those who died beforehand were somehow excluded from participation in the events surrounding the return of Jesus, and that they had to be instructed that, just as Jesus was raised from the dead, so also would those believers who had 'fallen asleep'. Both Thessalonica and Corinth were in Greece, and popular Greek thought had no concept of the resurrection of the dead; there was generally acknowledged to be an after-life in Hades for the souls of the dead, but nothing more.

THIS LIFE IS ALL THAT THERE IS

'Once a person's blood is spilt, there is no resurrection' (Aeschylus, *Eumenides*, 647f; leading Greek playwright, 5th cent. BC).

'I was not, I was, I am not, I care not' (common tomb inscription from Paul's time).

It is, therefore, intelligible that there could be Greek believers who did not accept the doctrine of the resurrection of the dead and argued against it.

Some scholars think that what they did accept was some kind of 'spiritual resurrection' that had already taken place in the lives of believers (as some people later thought, according to 2 Tim. 2:18). Thiselton 2000, p. 357 (see his index s.v. 'eschatology') has used the phrase 'over-realized eschatology' to describe the mindset of the Corinthians as one of belief that they were already living in the future Kingdom of God. This is not certain, but it would not affect the fundamental point that for them there was no future resurrection of the body. They may also have denied the resurrection of Christ, but it is perhaps more likely that Paul uses this as an accepted starting point from which to argue for the resurrection of dead believers.

written anages)

What do you think?

Before reading further, select any one of the issues that were causing problems in the congregation at Corinth and consider how you would have responded to it if you had been in Paul's situation. Then compare your response with how Paul actually did so as you read on in the letter.

SURVEYING I CORINTHIANS

Paul's response to the news from Corinth was twofold.

His first action was to write this lengthy letter to the Corinthian congregation. It was written from Ephesus (16:8) shortly before Pentecost and possibly before Easter (5:7–8), and it can be dated c. AD 53–4.

Second, in the letter he announces that he has sent (or is sending) Timothy who will be able to talk with them out of his close knowledge of what Paul himself would say to them (4:17; 16:10).

THE STRUCTURE OF I CORINTHIANS

1:1–3	OPENING GREETING
1:4—16:14	BODY OF THE LETTER
1:4–9	Prayer report
1:10—4:21	The party spirit in the congregation
5:1—6:20	Sexual immorality and litigation
7:1–40	Problems regarding marriage
8:1—11:1	Problems regarding food
11:2–16	Women in the church meeting
11:17–34	The Lord's Supper
12:1—14:40	Spiritual gifts in the church meeting
15:1–58	The resurrection
16:1–14	The collection and other matters
16:15–24	CLOSING MESSAGES AND GREETINGS

It should be noted that the variety of topics covered in this letter and some minor problems have led some scholars to postulate that it is really a combination of fragments from two or more original letters. These hypotheses have commanded so little approval from scholars in general that there is no need to summarize or refute them here.

Paul begins the letter by expressing his thanksgiving to God for the spiritual gifts with which the Corinthian congregation was endowed. The situation is not so serious (contrast Galatians) that he cannot find something good to say about them before beginning the process of correction (1:1–9).

PARTY SPIRIT

Then he moves straight into the main theme of the letter, the party spirit and the associated spiritual attitudes (1:10—4:21). Later in the letter he will deal with the problem of how spiritual gifts are to be exercised in the congregational meetings. Already at this point he picks up one aspect of it, namely the emphasis among some of the congregation on wisdom and eloquence, which, as we saw, could be a reflection both of a Greek philosophical mentality and also of an over-concern for showy spiritual gifts. His response to this attitude is to take the readers back to the death of Jesus on the cross, which is powerful to save precisely in its weakness and folly by human standards. The attack at this point seems to be more on the human wisdom that is contrary to the cross than on the spiritual gift of wisdom. Human wisdom cannot save people, but what seems foolish to them is God's wise plan that brings salvation to believers. This can be seen from the observable fact that the majority of the congregation are not wise or powerful people. Their life comes from Christ and not from themselves (1:10–31).

Further, Paul's own message was not couched in wisdom and eloquence. Its powerful effects were due to the Spirit working through it. This is not to deny that there is a wisdom that comes from God, but it is revealed to spiritual people who possess the Spirit, and Paul will maintain that people who quarrel and are envious are not truly spiritual (2:1–16). (He is probably not denying that they have the Spirit, but saying that they have not let the Spirit control their lives fully.)

Against this background Paul can then state that in fact Apollos and himself are merely servants of God who claim and deserve no credit from people and must themselves seek the credit that comes from God. (Cephas/Peter is ignored at this point, probably because he was not an actual missionary to Corinth; unless perhaps the statement about 'no other foundation' [1 Cor. 3:11] is a cryptic correction of false deductions drawn from what Jesus said in Matt. 16:18.) He issues a stern warning to people who are building badly on the foundation of the church and threatening its development by rousing this party spirit. They should realize that the missionaries are not parcelled out to different groups of supporters, but all belong to everybody. Missionaries are simply God's stewards, responsible to him and not beholden to any human supporters (3:1—4:7).

So strongly does Paul feel about this issue that he becomes somewhat scathing about the way in which the Corinthians think of themselves as having received the fullness of salvation while the missionaries suffer abuse and discomfort. Yet in using such strong language he insists that he is trying to win them by love. He warns people who are trusting in their worldly wisdom and position that he will deal sternly with them when he himself visits the congregation again; he is God's servant in the work of his kingdom, and he will match the power of the kingdom against them (4:8–20).

IMMORALITY AND LITIGATION

The reason why Paul feels so strongly is seen in the next section of the letter in which it emerges that these members of the congregation are acting in ways that are contrary to the way of life that arises out of the gospel of Christ crucified (5:1–13). Paul is astounded that there is tolerance in the congregation of a case of incest where one member is living with his father's wife (she was not, however, his mother); worse than that, he claims that they were arrogant about it. This extraordinary claim would seem to imply that these people thought that any kind of conduct was compatible with being a Christian. How was that possible?

Paul demands that the person in question should be severely disciplined. The penalty

certainly involves some kind of exclusion from church fellowship, but the strong wording may imply more: handing over to Satan is meant seriously as a penalty that will hopefully bring the person back to his senses in repentance, or otherwise the implication is that he will come under judgement at the last day. The action is also necessary lest the evil influence spread and affect the congregation as a whole. The congregation is reminded that it celebrates a new passover in the death of Jesus and therefore, just as the Jews did at passover, they must sweep out the 'leaven' of evil. At this point Paul reminds them that this is what he meant when he wrote his previous letter.

---

1 CORINTHIANS 5:1–13

And the Levites shall curse all the men of the lot of Satan, saying: 'Be cursed because of all your guilty wickedness! May he deliver you up for torture at the hands of the vengeful avengers! May he visit you with destruction by the hand of all the wreakers of revenge!' . . . And after the blessing and the cursing, all those entering the covenant shall say, 'Amen, Amen!' (Qumran Manual of Discipline [1QS 2:4–6, 10; *HCNT* §635])

The catalogue of sins is not yet complete. There is also the problem of members of the congregation taking their fellow members to law before the worldly powers instead of settling disputes among themselves. (This is not a prohibition of Christians going to law with non-Christians, which may sometimes be unavoidable.) But worse than this is the attitude displayed which responds angrily to other people taking advantage of them; it would be better to allow that than to wash their dirty linen in public (6:1–8).

All of this leads up to the categorical statement that sin keeps people out of God's kingdom; the list is comprehensive, including the more blatant crimes and the too-easily-tolerated sins like adultery and greed (6:9–11). The list incidentally includes homosexual practices (cf. Rom. 1:24–27; 1 Tim. 1:10).

Finally, Paul reverts to sexual immorality in a section where recent translations assume that he is quoting the kind of things said by the Corinthians and replying to them (6:12–20). From this procedure we may perhaps gain some idea of what members of the congregation had written in their letter to Paul. It looks as though some people thought that what they did with their bodies was their own affair and did not affect their salvation. But Paul insists that their bodies belong to the Lord and that immorality is a sin against a body in which God dwells through his Spirit. If the readers thought that salvation was concerned with the soul and not the body, Paul decisively corrects them.

SEXUAL AND MARITAL ISSUES

At this point in his letter Paul comments, 'Now concerning the matters about which you wrote' (7:1). This phrase informs us that the Corinthians had indeed written to Paul and enquired about his opinion on certain matters; their queries may have arisen out of his earlier oral or written teaching, and this means that the agenda of this letter to the Corinthians is dictated not just by the issues that Paul felt he must raise but also by questions that were raised by the church. The first of these concerns relationships in marriage. The initial problem appears to have been a practice of abstention from sexual relationships within marriage. It is likely that 1 Cor. 7:1b is a citation of a Corinthian point of view; note how here and

elsewhere the NRSV marks such statements as quotations (cf. 1 Cor. 6:12, 13; 8:1, 4, 8; Greek manuscripts had no such devices). It is not clear exactly how these ascetic attitudes may have arisen. One possibility is what has been called an 'over-realized eschatology', according to which some of the Corinthian Christians believed that they were already living in the new age and this led them either to a moral indifference about what they did with their bodies or to an extreme asceticism (see Thiselton 1977–8).

Against this view Paul insists on the propriety of marriage and relationships within it, so that people will not be tempted to immorality (whether as single or married people). What is noteworthy here in the context of Paul's time is that he insists on the equal rights of husband and wife over against each other. Paul admits that his preference would be for singleness and celibacy, such as he himself practised. (We do not know for certain whether he was single or widowed.) But he recognizes that God gifts people differently (7:1–7).

Whether or not his opinion had been asked on other related matters, he proceeds to take them up. He commends remaining single to the 'unmarried' (i.e. probably widowers) and widows, but not absolutely. He urges married couples not to separate, just as Christ commanded. He takes up the question of what to do where one partner becomes a Christian but not the other, and again urges the believer not to break up the marriage, but to acquiesce if the non-Christian partner (who does not feel bound by Christian practice) wishes to separate. From v. 14 it looks as though some believers felt that they were defiled by a non-believing partner, but Paul insists that this is not so. Verse 16 is best taken to mean that if the partnership continues, the believer may be able to convert the unbeliever (7:8–16).

In all this the important thing is to live the life to which God has called them, whatever that may be. In the last analysis it is immaterial whether you are circumcised or not, even whether you are slave or free. Yet he urges slaves to take their freedom if the opportunity comes; so things are not unchangeable, and Paul does not say that God may not call people with a new calling (7:17–24).

Finally, Paul reaches the singles (7:25–40). His advice is that in view of what he calls impending distress people should remain as they are, whether single or married. The main stress is on the single not taking on responsibilities that will cause them pain or hinder them from doing the Lord's work. This is difficult advice in various ways. If the crisis that Paul had in mind was the return of the Lord Jesus and the end of the present world-order, then we have to admit that he was mistaken. However, there is also good evidence that at this time there

were hardships of a more mundane sort, famine and its consequences, and this may be all that is meant (so Winter 2001, pp. 216–225).

FOOD OFFERED TO IDOLS

1 Corinthians 8 introduces us to a fresh topic, which looks as though it may have been another item on the Corinthians' list of points for Paul to elucidate. Paul gets down to basics immediately and directs his remarks to those Christians who claimed the right to act in certain ways because of their (superior) knowledge. Paul will agree to some extent with that knowledge, and also question it in others, but his main concern will be to insist that love must be a prior consideration, the kind of love that can involve self-denial and follows ultimately the example of Jesus.

What is true in the knowledge of these Christians is that there is indeed only one God and one Lord – a staggering statement in itself for a monotheist like Paul to make in a polytheistic culture – and the idols and gods of the Roman world have no reality (8:1–6). Therefore, offering meat to an idol makes no difference to the food and we are free to eat what God has created for us. The problem is that weaker believers, who may think that idols are real, do regard sacrificing to them as sinful and if they are tempted to do so, then they are in fact sinning, since they are deliberately going against what they believe to be commanded by God. For 'strong' Christians to set an example of eating in a temple could be a way of leading them to do what they know to be wrong, with disastrous spiritual results for them. Christian love must come in here and take priority, even if it prevents the 'strong' from doing what is innocuous to them personally (8:7–13).

What do you think?

Paul's advice about marriage is not easy to follow. Why are both getting married and separation from one's wife not recommended (7:27)? Is it really the case that being married diverts a person from the affairs of the Lord (7:32–35)? Was the Roman Catholic Church right after all to insist on a celibate clergy? Without bringing in the evidence of Eph. 5 (which some scholars think was not written by Paul anyhow) can you defend Paul from being basically anti-marriage? Or has Paul something important to say to a society that seems to be obsessed with physical sex?

Paul then illustrates this matter of limiting one's own freedom by reference to his own practice in a different area, but one that was relevant to the situation in the congregation (9:1–27). Although both the OT law and Jesus commanded that those who receive spiritual benefits (such as teaching and pastoral care) should provide for the material needs of the Lord's workers who have little or no income of their own, Paul refused to accept this entitlement and worked with his hands to maintain himself. He saw acceptance as a possible obstacle to the gospel; his experience at Thessalonica was that people could criticize missionaries for living off their converts and being a burden to them. (He was not wholly consistent in the matter, since it is also necessary not to offend people by refusing their loving gifts and care.) It became a matter of principle with Paul to preach the gospel without expecting any material return. He puts the point even more generally by referring to the way in which he had to shape his conduct to the people he was with, living by the law when with Jews and living 'outside' it when with Gentiles. (He doesn't say here what he did in mixed company, but what he probably means is that he accepted table fellowship with Gentiles when they were present in a congregation.) Love demands self-control and self-denial.

After this illustration Paul gets back to the topic, but he now seems to take a stronger line. He is particularly concerned with the way in which idolatry may corrupt people. Even the Israelites on the way to Canaan fell into idolatry with the typical, accompanying immorality of the ancient world, and experienced God's judgement on them. Similar things can still happen (10:1–13).

It follows that the Corinthians, weak or strong, should avoid participation in idolatry. It is not that the gods are real, but there are demonic powers at work in idolatry and pagan religion, and to participate in idolatry is incompatible with devotion to God and can lead to divine judgement. Note that Paul seems to believe quite firmly that God may act in judgement here and now on his rebellious people and not simply at the last judgement (10:14–22).

He sums up with practical advice. It is one thing to eat food bought in the market without enquiring whether this particular animal had been offered in sacrifice (not all were), but if a weaker Christian tells you that it has been offered, then do not set an example that may cause him/her to sin. It is another thing to go to a meal in a temple, and Paul has already indicated that this is unacceptable (10:23—11:1).

What do you think?

'I have become all things to all people, that I might by all means save some' (9:22). How flexible can one be in communicating the Christian message to people of different kinds and cultures? Is there a limit beyond which flexibility becomes unprincipled opportunism? And what if the way of life of those one is seeking to influence is undesirable or even sinful?

Digging deeper

Discuss the adequacy of 1 Corinthians 10:31—11:1 as a basic set of principles for determining Christian ethics. Compare the way in which Paul also argues about a matter involving food in Gal. 2:11–21: are there other principles at work here?

CONGREGATIONAL MEETINGS

With 1 Corinthians 11 we are back in the area of congregational meetings, where Paul begins by taking up two matters that were evidently of concern to him rather than being raised by the Corinthians themselves.

The first concerned the demeanour of men and women when they were engaged in prayer or prophecy in the meeting (11:2–16). The point of the discussion emerges at the end, where Paul holds that the prevailing custom in the churches must also be followed in Corinth, namely that there is a difference between the sexes whereby what is fitting for one is not fitting for the other; thus men wear their hair short and women wear theirs long – or at least they tend to do so. Paul was disturbed that this sort of difference was not being observed and the particular difference that he thought important was that women should wear a veil when taking part in prayer or prophecy, whereas a man should not. This was not a symbol of any inferiority on the side of the women; Paul insists very strongly that man and woman are interdependent and both owe their origin to God; this powerful statement of essential equality before God should not be missed. What Paul is concerned with, then, is a sexual or gender difference that ought to be preserved. The passage, then, is not primarily about the subordination of wives to their husbands, still less of women to men. And the practical requirement is probably related to the sexuality of the woman which could be a distraction to the men at a time when flaunting one's sexuality is inappropriate. The veil was a head-covering, which was the mark of the respectable woman.

This leaves a problem in the first part of the section. Part of the problem is the double reference in the term 'head', which can refer to a person's physical head or to one person in relation to another. There is also the problem of what is conveyed by the term 'head': does it refer to the exercise of superior authority or to being the source of sustenance and direction, or what? Paul envisages a chain of God-Christ-man-wife, which may reflect the Genesis story in which the woman was created out of the man. He is writing against a background in which a wife's behaviour could bring honour or dishonour to her husband, but the reverse possibility is not taken into account; consequently the discussion looks one-sided. In any case, the passage assumes that women may pray or prophesy in church, provided that the proprieties are observed. (See also pp. 91–2.)

In the second part of the chapter (11:17–34) Paul takes up the question of the meal that was a central feature of the congregational meetings. The conduct of this meal was such as to focus the divisions that there were within the congregation and which were making it plain that some people were truly following the Lord while others were not 'genuine' in their faith. Although the details are debated, there is little doubt that some people were consuming large quantities of food and drink (presumably of superior quality) while others had little or none. Thus a rich/poor class distinction was being perpetuated. The meeting was probably held in a rich person's house, which would provide sufficient room for everybody, and the poor people would feel humiliated in that context. People were not realizing that this was a special meal at which the death of Jesus was remembered with all the implications that that had for their life as Christians. Paul's practical solution was that people should eat their meal in their own homes if they felt particularly hungry and should show consideration to one another in the common meal. To fail to do so was to fail to recognize the body of Christ, a phrase which may allude to both the bread representing the crucified body of Christ and to the church which is also spoken of as the body of Christ – a theological point that Paul had already made in 10:16–17, where the sharing of the one loaf constitutes the participants as the one body of Christ. This might seem to be mere theological symbolism but Paul takes it very seriously. He believed that divine judgement could fall upon people who failed to discern this significance in the meal, a judgement expressed in physical illness and even death.

What do you think?

How would you respond to somebody today who feels that their illness or some other unpleasant experience is the Lord's way of disciplining them for sinful conduct? (cf. I Cor. 11:27–32)

SPIRITUAL GIFTS

From these matters Paul turns to the issue of spiritual gifts, which was causing problems in the church (12—14). Although he rejoiced that the church was spiritually gifted, nevertheless this gifting brought difficulties with it. First, he recognizes that there can be counterfeit examples where people could be influenced by demonic powers rather than the Spirit of God (12:1–3).

Second, he develops his main argument, which is that God distributes varied gifts to his people, but as his gifts they are all manifestations of his Spirit; therefore the people who exercise them are not to be regarded as superior or inferior to one another but are all to be honoured equally. Nor should people all desire to have the same gift(s) as if there was something superior to speaking in tongues compared with, say, teaching. While Paul recognizes that some gifts may be greater than others, this does not make the possessors 'greater' than others (12:4–31).

Third, Paul encourages people to seek to have the gifts, but he points out that there is something more important, and that is to have love (13:1–13). Without love the gifts do nothing for the possessor. This leads him into an almost poetic eulogy of love.

Fourth, Paul commends the gift of prophecy over against that of speaking in tongues, which had evidently become the most favoured gift at Corinth. Paul saw value in tongues as a part of one's personal prayer to God but not as part of a congregational meeting unless it was interpreted, and he saw prophecy as superior to it because it was readily understandable. Prophecy could speak to outsiders who came into the meeting, but they would be baffled by speaking in tongues (14:1–25).

Fifth, Paul commends the need for some orderliness in what were evidently unscripted meetings where people took part in a random kind of way. He placed limits on the freedom that was getting out of hand (14:26–33a).

Sixth, he ordered that women should be silent in the churches (14:33b–40). This puzzling statement has been taken in three ways. First, it may refer to a special case of women interrupting the meeting in some

EXPLORING THE NEW TESTAMENT

way (such as in evaluating prophecy, or asking questions of their husbands). Second, it may be interpreted as a complete ban on their taking part (but this would contradict the freedom assumed in 1 Cor. 11). Or, third, Paul did not actually write this. There are some grounds for suspecting that 1 Corinthians 14:34–35 is a much later interpolation into the letter and therefore not part of what Paul wrote. (For these and other options see a commentary on the letter; a particularly full and recent example is Thiselton 2000, pp. 1150–61.)

> ## Digging deeper
>
> What guidelines for church meetings today emerge from Paul's discussion of the Corinthian congregation's meetings? Think of a church you know (or visit one if you don't regularly go to church): what differences would Paul's principles make to the way that meetings are conducted?

THE RESURRECTION

There is an abrupt change of subject in 1 Corinthians 15 as Paul takes up the view of some of his readers that there was to be no resurrection. He responds to this statement first of all by appealing to a brief summary of the gospel as it was understood by the early church generally. It centred on the death and the resurrection of Christ. Paul briefly reaffirms the evidence that Christ appeared to a large and varied number of people including himself and the fact that this gospel was what the Corinthians had accepted (15:1–11). He then argues from this accepted fact to the resurrection of believers in general, holding that if there was no possibility of resurrection in general, then it followed that Christ had not been raised,

which went against the facts and also deprived Christian faith of its content (15:12–19). He reaffirmed that the resurrection of Jesus in fact entailed the resurrection of all believers, using the same kind of argument as in Romans 5:12–21 (1 Cor. 15:20–28). He commented on the existence of practices in the church which presupposed the resurrection: people being baptized in order to be sure of being reunited with their dead relatives and friends (the NRSV translation 'on their behalf' is misleading), and others facing death for the sake of the Christian mission (15:29–34). Finally, he faced up to the major objection that the resurrection of dead people was inconceivable and answered it by developing the idea of a transformation into spiritual bodies appropriate for the life of the world to come over against any suggestion that people were resurrected into physical, perishable bodies (15:35–58).

> ## I CORINTHIANS 15:29
>
> As long as you are alive, be happy, eat drink, live high, embrace others. For this was the End. (Inscription from Aphrodisia [undated; *HCNT* §709])

> ## Digging deeper
>
> 'But someone will ask, "How are the dead raised? With what kind of body do they come?"' What are the key elements in Paul's response to this question (vv. 36–58)? To what extent would this response comfort Christians faced with bereavement or with the prospect of their own death?

IN CONCLUSION

The last chapter (16:1–24) is concerned with various more mundane matters, including

Focus on theology

This letter essentially gives a theological basis for Christian behaviour. Its readers recognized the important role of the Spirit in gifting the congregation, but this was an insufficient understanding of the situation and was leading to disunity and arrogance among them. Faced by these problems, Paul expounded a theology of crucifixion (*theologia crucis* as opposed to a *theologia gloriae*) in which the shame and suffering endured by Christ were not only to take away their sins but also to set the pattern by which his followers are to live. There is a complete reversal of human values in a religion based on the cross, displayed particularly in the self-sacrificing lives of missionaries. Instead of seeking their own position and status, believers are to do everything with a view to glorifying God and not setting a bad example that can lead other believers into spiritual disaster and divine condemnation. Where the congregation was divided by material wealth and poverty as well as by pride in the possession of the more spectacular gifts of the Spirit Paul again placed the death of Christ, as proclaimed in the Lord's Supper, at the centre; he stressed the need for unity and interdependence in the body of Christ and the supreme position of love as a gift of the Spirit to be sought and received by all believers. Where there was uncertainty over the future resurrection of believers, he emphasized the reality of the resurrection of Jesus as the guarantee and pattern of the resurrection of his people, and the importance of this hope as a stimulus to working for the Lord. There is an ongoing need for growth and enrichment ('edification') in the lives of believers as they look forward to the day when they will meet the Lord. The Spirit plays a crucial role in the life of the congregation and the individual believers, but its manifestations can be misused to promote arrogance and lack of respect for others.

the collection of money from the readers to render poor relief to the Christians in Jerusalem and travel plans of himself and other missionaries. The ending of the letter is notable for the utterance of a curse on any who do not love the Lord. This is followed by the prayer 'Our Lord, come', which represents an Aramaic phrase, *Marana tha*, and expresses the hope of the Lord's future coming.

FOR TODAY'S CORINTHIANS

Much of 1 Corinthians seems to deal with issues that no longer trouble us and to involve concepts and ideas that Christians today find difficult. Here are a few examples: how, if at all, might Paul's discussion of them have any relevance or challenge to people today?

- Human wisdom and knowledge are foolish, and human position doesn't matter (1:20, 25, 27–28).
- Church discipline can include as a last resort 'handing over a sinner to Satan' (5:5), and the deaths of members of the congregation can be seen as a judgement for 'eating and drinking unworthily' (11:29–30).
- Paul believes that idolatry and worship of other gods is inspired by real demonic forces (10:20–21).
- Speaking in tongues and prophesying were so prevalent in church meetings that they had to be curbed (14:27–32).

ESSAY TOPICS

INTRODUCTORY
- Make a reconstruction of Paul's understanding of the Holy Spirit and spiritual gifts on the basis of 1 Corinthians.

• What kind of leader does Paul come over as in this letter? Is he a model for church leaders today?

INTERMEDIATE

• Make a study of what Corinth itself was like in the first century and the effects of this environment on the planting of a Christian congregation.

FURTHER READING

*denotes books assuming knowledge of Greek; most can be used by all students.

INTRODUCTORY

J. D. G. Dunn *1 Corinthians*. Sheffield: Sheffield Academic Press, 1995 (extended introduction to the letter).

H. Frör *You Wretched Corinthians*. London: SCM Press, 1995 (imaginative re-creation of the scene at Corinth including letters from the congregation to Paul).

V. P. Furnish *The Theology of the First Letter to the Corinthians*. New Testament Theology. Cambridge/New York: Cambridge University Press, 1999 (straightforward exposition of the theology).

R. P. Martin *Word Biblical Themes: 1, 2 Corinthians*. Dallas: Word, 1988 (simple introduction to the theology).

J. Murphy-O'Connor *St Paul's Corinth: Texts and Archaeology*. Wilmington: Glazier, 1983 (the essential background reader).

Commentaries

C. Blomberg *1 Corinthians*. NIVAC. Grand Rapids: Zondervan, 1994 (sustained discussion of contemporary application of Paul's teaching).

C. K. Barrett *The First Epistle to the Corinthians*. BNTC. London: A. & C. Black/New York: Harper & Row, 1968 (classic work).

F. F. Bruce *1 and 2 Corinthians*. NCB. London: Oliphants/Grand Rapids: Eerdmans, 1971 (good, introductory level work).

R. B. Hays *1 Corinthians*. Interp. Louisville: John Knox, 1997 (excellent middle-length exposition with material for teachers and preachers).

INTERMEDIATE

D. M. Hay (ed.) *Pauline Theology, II: 1 and 2 Corinthians*. Minneapolis: Fortress, 1993 (essays by leading scholars).

*J. C. Hurd Jr *The Origin of 1 Corinthians*. New York: Seabury/London: SPCK, 1965 (classic treatment of the dialogue between the Corinthians and Paul).

*M. M. Mitchell *Paul and the Rhetoric of Reconciliation. An Exegetical Investigation of the Language and Composition of 1 Corinthians*. Tübingen: Mohr Siebeck, 1992; repr. Louisville: Westminster/John Knox, 1993 (technical discussion of the argumentation in the letter).

G. Theissen *The Social Setting of Pauline Christianity*. Edinburgh: T. & T. Clark/Philadelphia: Fortress, 1982 (pioneering work on the social distinctions in the Corinthian congregation).

A. C. Thiselton 'Realized Eschatology at Corinth', *NTS* 24 (1977–8), pp. 510–26.

B. S. Winter *After Paul Left Corinth: The Influence of Secular Ethics and Social Change*. Grand Rapids/Cambridge: Eerdmans, 2001 (excellent use of background to illumine the letter).

Commentaries

G. D. Fee *The First Epistle to the Corinthians*. NIC. Grand Rapids: Eerdmans, 1987 (major work on the English text).

*A. C. Thiselton *1 Corinthians*. NIGTC. Carlisle: Paternoster/Grand Rapids: Eerdmans, 2000 (extremely detailed). See also his article in *NDBT*, pp. 297–306.

B. Witherington III *Conflict and Community in Corinth. A Socio-Rhetorical Commentary on 1 and 2 Corinthians*. Grand Rapids: Eerdmans/Carlisle: Paternoster, 1995 (good, middle-length treatment).

Chapter 7

THE 'SECOND' LETTER TO THE CORINTHIANS

In this chapter we shall look at:

- what happened after Paul wrote 1 Corinthians;
- whether the 'tearful letter' Paul refers to in 2 Corinthians has survived;
- Paul's reconciliation with the congregation in 2 Cor. 1—7;
- Paul's appeal for generous aid for the poor in 2 Cor. 8—9;
- Paul's response to the fresh problems reflected in 2 Cor. 10—13;
- the setting of 2 Cor. 10—13 in relation to Paul's other letters to Corinth.

The document that we know as 'Second Corinthians' contains a fair amount of personal information about Paul, his colleagues and the congregation in Corinth that it is hard to fit into a coherent story. The problem is made all the more difficult because there is some well-founded doubt as to whether what we have before us is one letter or a compilation of material from two or more letters. Those who like literary detective work that involves the possible reassembly of a jigsaw puzzle so that the pieces form incomplete parts of as many as six fresh puzzles will revel in the problem; others may not be so enthusiastic! The tasks

of reconstructing the situation and fitting the letter(s) into it are obviously closely intertwined.

AN OVERVIEW OF THE PROBLEMS

If we read through 2 Corinthians, it is immediately obvious that the first part, up to the end of chapter 7, contains a two-part travelogue by Paul (1:8—2:13; 7:5–16) in which he describes a recently completed journey from 'Asia' (probably this means 'Ephesus') through Troas and across the Hellespont to Macedonia where he met up with Titus, who brought him news from Corinth, and cheered him up. These sections of the letter contain a lot of information about the troublesome relationship of Paul with the church and the ensuing reconciliation. In the middle of the travelogue, but closely related to it, is something more like teaching or a sermon which is largely concerned with Paul's task as a missionary (2:14—7:4).

Then, in chapters 8 and 9 the subject changes, and we have a discussion of a collection that Paul was raising for 'the saints'; this can safely be assumed to be the same activity as the collection for the

95

church in Jerusalem that we read about in
1 Corinthians 16:1–4.

Finally, in chapters 10—13 the subject
changes again and we have a fresh appeal to
the congregation which appears to have
something to do with opponents or critics of
Paul against whom Paul feels the necessity to
defend himself; these opponents were
evidently visitors who were active at the time
in the congregation and consequently they
constituted some kind of threat to Paul's
work with them.

It has long puzzled readers that chapters
1—7 appear to be concerned with the
achievement of some kind of reconciliation
between Paul and the congregation whereas
in chapters 10—13 his tone is rather different
and he is obviously not pleased with some
aspects of their life. This change of tone and
the reappearance of troubles have caused
scholars to wonder whether the two parts
belong to separate letters, but there is no
unanimity on whether chapters 10—13 belong
to an earlier or later letter than chapters
1—7. As for chapters 8 and 9, which tend to
go over the same ground twice, there is
speculation whether one or both of these
chapters constitute parts of separate letters.

It is therefore necessary for us to look at
each of these sections separately to see what
information we can glean about their origins
and the situations that they reflect.

THE EVENTS LEADING UP TO
2 CORINTHIANS 1—7

If we consider chapters 1—7 by themselves,
we find that it reflects a situation in which
Paul had suffered some severe affliction in
Asia that had made him despair of life

(1:8–11) and he also had trouble with the
congregation at Corinth. He speaks of
people in the congregation, including one in
particular, who had caused him pain (2:5).
He says that he did not want to pay another
painful visit to Corinth (2:1), from which we
deduce that he had already paid one painful
visit. This experience appears to have made
him change his mind about plans to travel
via Corinth to Macedonia and then return
via Corinth to his starting point (1:15–23).
In fact, Paul's plans appear to have been
changed more than once. According to 1
Corinthians 16:5–7 he had intended to go to
Macedonia and then visit Corinth, possibly
for a few months over the winter. If this
reference is to the same period of time, what
he is saying now seems to be that he did visit
Corinth (on the way to Macedonia?), but
that the visit was so unpleasant that he
decided that it would not be opportune to
revisit them immediately, and he went back
to Asia by a more direct route.

Instead of revisiting the congregation,
therefore, for the time being it appears that
he wrote yet another letter, in which he tried
to persuade the congregation to change its
attitude to him. In view of the description in
2 Corinthians 2:4 this letter is often referred
to as the 'tearful letter'; it must have been
fairly blunt in what it said (2:3–4, 9; 7:8–12).
Paul also sent Titus to Corinth (7:6–7,
13–16), and he may well have been the
bearer of the letter.

Meanwhile Paul himself had left Ephesus
and moved northwards to Troas, where he
engaged in mission. But he was too worried
about the congregation in Corinth to stay
there, and so he crossed over to Macedonia
in hope of meeting Titus sooner (2:12–13).
And there he did in fact meet Titus who
brought good news that the congregation

had responded to his appeal (7:5–16). Full of joy he responded with another letter, which was apparently to be taken by Titus in advance of Paul's own arrival for his third visit. This letter contained at least some or all of 2 Corinthians 1—7.

The detailed events at this time are not described in Acts. They will fall within the period of Paul's extended missionary work centred on Ephesus (Acts 19); his 'third visit' to Corinth is that mentioned briefly in Acts 20:2–3. The date will be c. AD 52–5.

IDENTIFYING THE TEARFUL LETTER

We would be able to understand the situation better if the 'tearful letter' had survived. Unfortunately there is no unanimity on this matter at the present time. Three different theories exist:

- the letter has not survived in any form;
- the letter is to be identified with 1 Corinthians;
- the letter is to be identified with 2 Cor. 10—13.

The first of these theories must be the answer if neither of the other two can be shown to be plausible.

1. If *the tearful letter has not survived*, we are dependent solely on the evidence in 2 Corinthians for a reconstruction of the situation.

There was evidently one specific individual who had caused grief to Paul. Paul also speaks of somebody else as 'the one who was wronged' (7:12), and it is a moot point whether this is a reference to somebody else in the congregation or to Paul himself. One view is that the person had insulted or otherwise opposed Paul in such as way as to cause Paul pain. The other view is that he had offended or hurt some other member of the congregation and resisted Paul's intervention in the matter. The clear implication seems to be that some of the congregation had sided with him and come out against Paul. We cannot tell what the cause of the contention was, but there is no indication of differences of opinion on theological matters, and it may have been connected with a continuation of the party spirit that led to the writing of 1 Cor. The situation came to a head while Paul was in Corinth (the painful visit), and it certainly became so difficult that Paul felt that he could not return to Corinth so long as the things remained the same.

2. The second possibility is *the identification of the tearful letter with 1 Corinthians*. In 1 Corinthians 5 we certainly have an offender in the congregation in the man who committed incest; possibly a well-off member of the congregation with social position and influence, he could not easily be brought to book for his misdeed. The problem arose before the writing of 1 Corinthians and the man refused to abandon his sinful liaison or submit to discipline despite Paul's pressure upon him. There was a stalemate, with the congregation unable or unwilling to act, and Paul had to leave the church in a state of rebellion against his authority as an apostle. He therefore wrote a letter to them instead of returning personally to deal with the situation, and this letter was 1 Corinthians. In it he deals with the general problem of party spirit in the congregation, and also with the particular problem of disciplining the offender. The letter reflects the powerful emotions that accompanied the writing of it. It was successful in its aims, and was followed shortly after by the writing of 2 Corinthians.

Clearly this theory would give greater precision to our understanding of the situation but without altering our general understanding of it. The difficulties that arise, however, are serious:

- Does 1 Corinthians as a whole look like a letter written out of tears and sadness? There is no doubt that it is a very straight and blunt letter, and that some of the things about which Paul writes must have caused him considerable grief, but it is questionable whether this applies to it as a whole.
- The offence in 2 Corinthians seems to have been more of a personal attack on Paul, whereas in 1 Corinthians we have a case of serious sin against another member of the congregation.
- The reaction described in 2 Corinthians 7:11 does not seem appropriate after a reading of 1 Corinthians.

3. The third theory *identifies the letter with 2 Corinthians 10—13*, which on this view was written prior to 2 Corinthians 1—7 and then attached to it with the loss of its introduction and possibly other material. (This theory would have to assume that the letter had survived as a fragment; then, since it was known to have been sent to Corinth, it was appended to another letter and thus survived.)

If this theory is correct, then we have to assume that some time after the writing of 1 Corinthians the congregation was infiltrated by a number of other missionaries, described by Paul as 'apostles', who must have been giving teaching somewhat different from Paul's own and who were fiercely critical of him as an inferior apostle. They gained a following in the congregation, presumably among those who had formerly been involved in the parties opposed to Paul. Not only so; their teaching did nothing to curb the immorality that was prevalent among some of the congregation (12:21). While the congregation tolerated them, Paul felt that he could achieve nothing and was rejected. He therefore decided not to revisit the congregation, but sent this tough letter instead.

This understanding of the place of 2 Corinthians 10—13 can be defended by various arguments.

- The tone of the letter supports this theory. Paul was accused of commending himself in 2 Corinthians 3:1 and 5:12, and this is exactly what he does in this letter.
- Four sets of passages make good sense if read in reverse order. In each case Paul can be seen as looking back on what had been said previously:

10:6	2:9
11:11; 12:15	2:4
13:2	1:23
13:10	2:3

- In both letters the issue was a rejection of Paul's authority over the church. Watson (1984) argues that the problem in 2 Corinthians 10—13 is Paul's failure to carry out discipline against the offender, and this led to the accusation that he was not a real apostle. He also argues that Paul was accused of misappropriating money (cf. 12:16–18). He thinks that the offences that called forth the tearful letter according to 2 Corinthians 2 and 7 fit this description.

But there are serious objections to this view.

- 10:9–10 could well be a reference to the tearful letter (since it appears to have been stern as well as tearful).
- There is no mention of the individual who had been causing the trouble in the

congregation. Watson's theory fails to explain how the many offenders in chapters 10—13 have been reduced to one offender in chapters 1—7. Also, there is no reference to the visiting apostles in chapters 1—7.

● When Paul wrote the tearful letter, he did so because he had decided not to revisit the congregation for the time being (2:1–4), but in 10—13 he is on the verge of paying his third visit.

● This theory necessitates postulating yet another visit by Titus to the congregation prior to the tearful letter (12:18), for which there is no confirmatory evidence.

● The set of passages that indicate common themes in the two letters would make equally good sense on the traditional order.

Despite Watson's powerful advocacy, the case is not a compelling one. It may be safest to conclude that the tearful letter has not survived.

THE STRUCTURE OF 2 CORINTHIANS 1—9

1:1–2	OPENING GREETING
1:3—9:15	BODY OF THE LETTER
1:3–11	Thanksgiving for Paul's deliverance
1:12—2:13	The rift with the congregation and Paul's 'tearful letter'
2:14—7:4	The existence of a missionary – weakness and strength
7:5–16	The joy of reconciliation
8:1–24	Arrangements for the collection for Jerusalem
9:1–15	Encouragement to generous giving

This outline is incomplete, pending a discussion of whether 2 Cor. 10—13 forms the remaining part of the letter or not. It also includes various passages that in the view of various scholars may not have been part of the original letter; these are discussed below.

SURVEY OF 2 CORINTHIANS 1—7

THANKSGIVING (BERAKAH)

An unusual feature of 2 Corinthians is that it does not begin with the customary 'prayer report' in which Paul expresses his commendation and concern for the spiritual progress of the addressees. Instead there is a *berakah* (Heb. for 'blessing'; cf. 'blessed' in 2 Cor. 1:3) in which he praises God for what he has done in his own life. It is at once apparent that the major thing on his mind at this time is that he has undergone some affliction that threatened his life and it was only thanks to divine intervention that he was rescued (1:8–11). One possibility is simply that he was the victim of a life-threatening accident or severe illness. The other more likely possibility is that he was the object of attack and was in danger of his life, whether because he was physically attacked or because he was in danger of execution. The situation probably arose from his missionary work and could have been any of the life-threatening sorts of experience mentioned in 2 Corinthians 11:23–9. The important point is that the result was to make Paul all the more conscious of the fragility of his existence and to cause him to meditate all the more profoundly on the paradoxes of his life as a missionary. It is also significant that he feels that he shares these experiences with his readers and that he has a very positive relationship with them (1:3–7).

2 CORINTHIANS 1:12

The wise Periander was asked what freedom is, and he responded: A good conscience. (Periander [660–560 BC], as recorded in *Gnomologium Vaticanum* 450; *HCNT* §717)

THE RIFT WITH THE CONGREGATION

But there had been problems, which centred on whether Paul behaved with worldly wisdom or with godly sincerity, and some in the congregation must have taken the former view. There had been a rift. It had led Paul to decide not to visit the congregation on his way to Macedonia (and then on his way back from Macedonia) but to visit them only on the way back. This had led to accusations of vacillation and insincerity. Evidently he had feared that a visit at that point would have been painful as a result of the attitude of some members of the congregation – painful for the congregation and stressful for Paul himself as he spoke out plainly to them (1:12—2:4).

What had caused this situation? Clearly there was one person who had done some wrong and thereby caused pain to Paul and other people. Subsequently, presumably as a result of Paul's appeal, this person had been disciplined in some way by the majority of the congregation, who by taking this action had indicated their loyalty to Paul. (It seems quite feasible to me that the problem was failure to carry out discipline initially against the incestuous man [1 Cor. 5], who had support from some of the congregation; thus to the original sin was added the further fault of refusal to submit to discipline by the man and failure to maintain standards by the congregation.) The effect of the application of discipline had been to cause the offender to repent and seek forgiveness. Paul was now willing for forgiveness to be extended to him and the matter to be brought to an end (2:5–11).

At this point Paul begins to go over the immediately preceding events in his life during the period when he was on his way to Macedonia and uncertain whether the congregation would have done what was required of them. He had sent Titus to Corinth instead of coming himself, and Titus presumably carried the letter to which he refers, but he had to wait anxiously for news of whether Titus's intervention would have the desired effect. So he describes how he left Asia and travelled to Troas to engage in evangelism, but he could not settle to his work, and crossed over to Macedonia in hopes of meeting up with Titus sooner (2:12f.).

This account continues at 7:5, but in the meantime there is a lengthy section, which seems to wander away from the point at issue into deep theological meditation that is also a discussion with the readers (2:14—7:4).

AN INTERPOLATION IN THE LETTER?

It is not surprising that some scholars have regarded 2:14—7:4 as an interpolation into an otherwise coherent and connected narrative. The hypothesis is complicated by the fact that the next-to-last section, 6:14—7:1, is often thought to be a separate interpolation as well. The basic arguments for interpolation are that the style is very different and the narrative would fit together very well if this section was omitted; it appears to interrupt a travelogue that leaves Paul just arriving in Macedonia without telling us what happened when he got there: why does he break off at this point?

However, it has been rightly observed that the end of the digression meshes well with the resumption of Paul's story in 7:4–5. Further, from 7:5 it becomes clear that Paul's time in Macedonia was one of affliction as well as of being with faithful Christians in Thessalonica and Philippi. Therefore it could be quite natural for Paul to think about the deeper nature of his experiences and to apply this to the situation between himself and his readers in Corinth.

THE NATURE OF APOSTLESHIP

The content of this section is particularly dense, and it almost defies summary within the limited space in an introductory book. Essentially Paul begins by thinking of the apostles in three ways:

- they are Christ's captives entirely at his disposal (like the captured opponents of a Roman general forced to march in his celebratory procession);
- they are like an aroma that is breathed both by the lost and by the saved;
- they are motivated to honest dealing as servants of Christ, although there are some who behave differently and with dubious motives (2:14–17).

As Paul says all this, it becomes plain that in effect he is defending himself as an apostle to the Corinthians against the accusations that may have been made against him. In one sense he does not need to do so, because the congregation itself is a testimony to the effectiveness of his ministry, or rather to the effectiveness of what God is doing through him (3:1–3).

This effectiveness is related to the fact that the apostles are God's servants in the new covenant. With the introduction of this thought Paul launches into a comparison between Moses as the servant of God under the old covenant and the servants of the new covenant. His point is that, if the former ministry was accompanied by glory, there is a greater glory associated with the new covenant. He also picks up on the story of Moses hiding his face with a veil ((Exod. 34:29–35) to comment on the veil that can still be on the minds of people reading the law, a veil which is taken away when people turn to the Lord (Jesus). This detail would suggest that Paul has in mind

the teaching of Judaizers who misunderstood the law and tried to apply it to Gentile believers (3:4–18).

The main line of development is that the servants of God engaged in this work do not lose hope in what they are doing. They do not have to resort to insincere methods to achieve their ends. They know that some people will be blind to the gospel, but others will respond when they proclaim Christ. Indeed, their lack of success and human weakness are signs that the power comes from God and not from themselves. It seems that Paul's thought here is decisively affected by the afflictions that he had been suffering, culminating in the near-death experience already mentioned at the beginning of the letter. Moreover, Paul seems to draw a distinction between the readers who

What do you think?

Study 2 Cor. 4:5–6. How does the language used here reflect Paul's own conversion experience (see Acts 9:1–20)? Do you regard it as a complete picture of what is involved in the proclaiming and receiving of the Christian gospel, or would you want to add other elements?

'I believe that the church in our generation needs to rediscover the apostolic Gospel; and for this it needs the Epistle to the Romans. It also needs to rediscover the relation between this Gospel and its order, discipline, worship and ethics; and for this it needs the First Epistle to the Corinthians. If it makes these discoveries, it may well find itself broken; and this may turn out to be the meaning of the Second Epistle to the Corinthians.' (C. K. Barrett, *The First Epistle to the Corinthians*, v–vi)

experience life through his ministry and the ministers themselves who are suffering and dying to bring the gospel to them. Yet the distinction is not sustained, since the readers too suffer, and both readers and preachers will share the same future glory (4:1–18).

All this leads Paul on to a consideration of what death involves. (It is crucial to recognize that throughout this section we are hearing from a man who has recently looked into the mouth of death.) He insists that even if our bodies die and perish, nevertheless God has prepared a heavenly dwelling for us and given us an anticipation of it in the Holy Spirit. Ultimately, therefore, the Christian believer does not want to hold on to life in the body because of this future hope, and aims to please the Lord before whose judgement all must stand (5:1–10).

This explains Paul's zeal to persuade other people to believe, and should convince his readers of his sincerity. Incidentally it provides an answer to his critics who could not understand a person who was prepared to be humanly weak in order that the divine power could work through him. (This remark shows that Paul still has his critics in his sights.) It is not human estimates that matter, for believers live in a new creation, stemming from the reconciling act of God (5:11–21).

All this leads finally into an appeal to the readers, or perhaps to those among them who need reassurance about Paul or to be converted to accepting him, to accept the message that he brings. Ultimately it is a matter of their reconciliation with God. And again Paul insists that the gospel is in fact commended by his experiences and way of

life with its catalogue of weakness and suffering by human standards and its empowerment by God. It is an appeal to those of the readers who still need reassurance to restore relationships with Paul (6:1–13).

With Paul – and not with unbelievers! For to fail to be on Paul's side is not to be neutral but to side with those who are against the gospel (6:14—7:1). There is an echo here of the meals in pagan temples which was an important issue in 1 Corinthians, which suggests that the opposition to Paul included people who were flirting with paganism instead of making a clean break with what Paul saw as inherently dangerous. (There was a vast difference between eating at home meat that had once been offered in sacrifice to an idol in the market and sharing in the actual pagan worship and associated immorality and debauchery in a temple!)

RESUMING THE STORY

So Paul comes to the end of the 'digression' with a further statement of his clear conscience in his relationships with the readers. In fact the knowledge of the reconciliation with them was an enormous relief to him in the midst of his other afflictions (7:2–4).

Thus appropriately he resumes the story of how Titus met him and brought the news of the reconciliation and the renewed loyalty of the congregation to Paul. He expresses his joy at the repentance that had taken place, and comments on the joy that it also brought to Titus who had gone to Corinth with considerable trepidation (7:5–16).

Digging deeper

Write 'the Corinthian story' as it was seen and experienced by Titus. (Use a concordance to check all the places where Titus appears in 2 Cor. and develop your story from those references and what you have read in this chapter.)

YET ANOTHER INTERPOLATION?

In the above exposition I have tried to show how the problematic passage 6:14—7:1 fits perfectly well into the development of Paul's discourse. Nevertheless, the abruptness of the apparent change of subject and the sharpness of the tone in a letter which so far has dealt with a reconciliation already achieved have raised the question whether this section belongs here. Two different theories have been put forward.

One is the view that this section is a fragment from another letter (see above, pp. 78–9, on Paul's 'previous letter' in the discussion of 1 Corinthians).

The other is that the section is not from Paul at all, since what it says does not square with his thought and resemblances have been seen to the Jewish thought expressed in the Qumran documents. The case is by no means compelling. The call to holiness expressed here and the need for separation from unbelievers is in line with Paul's teaching elsewhere (especially in 1 Thessalonians). Nevertheless, a significant number of scholars do find differences from Paul's normal manner of expression, and some suggest that the section was taken by Paul from some other writer and incorporated in his letter (see, for example, Martin 1986, pp. 190–5).

2 CORINTHIANS 8 AND 9

At this point the subject changes from Paul's own afflictions and the problems in the congregation to what he calls this 'ministry to the saints'. From the previous mention in 1 Corinthians 16:1–4 we know that this was a financial collection from the congregations in Paul's mission field for the assistance of Christians in Jerusalem. The link with the earlier part of the letter is that part of Titus's mission to Corinth was to encourage the congregation to do their share in this collection. Paul here cites the sacrificial example of the congregations in Macedonia and urges the Corinthians to emulate it. He reinforces the exhortation with an appeal to the example of Jesus himself. And he encourages the congregation to bring to a successful conclusion what they had already started to do. We learn that Titus was to return to Corinth to complete the collection, accompanied by representatives from other congregations. There is specific reference to two such people, who are curiously not named, but of course if they came with Titus their identity would have been immediately obvious.

Paul continues to write about the fundraising in chapter 9, where it becomes clear that, just as he had encouraged the Corinthians by the example of the Macedonians in chapter 8, so he had also been encouraging the Macedonians by the example of the Corinthians and did not want to have to eat his words! He then makes further general points by way of exhortation to generosity – that God will provide them with sufficient resources to share with others and that blessings will come to themselves through this action.

Digging deeper

You are to give a talk in which you hope to inspire people to give generously towards a project which your group is sponsoring in a country of the Global South: would it be possible to use themes from 2 Corinthians 8—9 to teach, inspire and motivate people about giving?

MORE FRAGMENTARY LETTERS?

In view of the change of topic at this point and the repetition between chapters 8 and 9, some scholars question whether one or both chapters are fragments of separate letters.

- There is really no substantial argument for accepting the theory of some scholars who separate 2 Cor. 8 from 2 Cor. 1—7. The fact that neither section refers to the other is an inadequate reason for separation: letters can have more than one independent topic! In fact, as noted, the two parts of the letter are nicely tied together by the role of Titus.
- More weight attaches to the suggestion that in chapter 9 the topic of the collection appears to be announced as a fresh topic and that the treatment covers much the same ground as in chapter 8. Thrall (1994) thinks that the evidence tilts in favour of separating off chapter 9 as part of another letter, but finds it difficult to explain why the second, separate letter was necessary; Betz (1985) gets round the problem by holding that chapter 9 was sent to a different destination in Achaia.

I am tempted to say that the case for separation raises as many difficulties as it solves. This may be one of those cases where a break in dictation (see pp. 23–4) could lead to some awkwardness and repetition when a fresh start was made.

THE PROBLEM OF 2 CORINTHIANS 10—13

There is an obvious difference in tone when we come to 2 Cor. 10. The confident note of reconciliation in the earlier part of the letter is missing, and there are noises of active opposition. What was happening?

Some visitors engaged on mission had come to the congregation (11:12). They were Jews (11:22), and some of them claimed to be apostles (11:5, 13; 12:11). Paul accused them of preaching 'another Jesus, a different spirit, a different gospel' (11:4; cf. Gal 1:6!). They denied that he was a real apostle or servant of Christ; he couldn't speak well, and he had no 'signs' to prove his apostleship (10:10; 12:12). He was insincere and acted by human standards instead of by God's (10:2–3).

Who were they? Here opinions differ.

- They were *Gnostic Christians* with a Greek background who laid stress on knowledge. If so, they might possibly be associated with the alleged 'Gnostics' of 1 Corinthians. But there is no clear evidence for a Gnostic outlook in 2 Corinthians, and the opposition stemmed mainly from visitors to the congregation. We can safely set aside this view. The remaining options can be taken more seriously.
- The first is that they were *Palestinian Jewish Christians* sent out from Jerusalem to win over the congregation for the legalist party said to be associated with Peter or James. There are two separable points here. There certainly were other Christian missionaries at work, and there were some

who were Judaizers (as we see clearly from Galatians and Philippians). But it is not clear that there was a Petrine party imposing a legalist agenda on the Gentiles. Above all, there is no indication in this part of the letter that Paul is combatting the same kind of Judaizing beliefs as in his other letters. The attack is much more on Paul's own integrity and credentials.

- The second option is that they were *Hellenistic Jewish Christians* who copied the itinerant charismatic preachers of the pagan world and thought of themselves as wonder-workers like (their image of) Jesus. Paul was a failure in their eyes because he lacked their rhetorical and miracle-working skills. Another possibility is that they were Judaizers who associated with the Apollos-party of 1 Corinthians in commending Moses.

- As Barrett has pointed out, evidence in favour of both of these views can be found in the letter (Barrett 1973, pp. 28–30). He therefore combines the two theories by arguing that the opponents were *Jewish Christian rivals of Paul*. They laid great stress on their Jewishness but the Corinthians measured them by their Hellenistic standards of eloquence and possession of the Spirit, and so Paul had to attack both their own claims and the claims made by the Corinthians on their behalf.

- Thrall has replied that miracle-working was also associated with the Jewish Christian missionaries like Peter himself, and therefore Barrett's theory may be unnecessary. She herself argues that what we have is *missionaries from the Petrine mission* who claimed Corinth as part of their field, and who laid stress on their own spiritual competence, reflected in working miracles, possibly seeing visions, and competence in rhetoric (Thrall 2000,

pp. 926–45). A solution along these lines may well be possible, although it must be stressed that there is no evidence whatever that such missionaries were operating under the aegis of Peter himself in their pose as rivals to Paul.

Paul's attack on them accused them of preaching a different gospel. It is not easy to put flesh on these bare bones. Thrall has suggested a form of teaching related to that in the Gospel of Matthew where there is stress on righteousness and obedience to the commands of the earthly and now glorified Jesus (with some stress on observing the law of Moses), and where there may have been some special stress on the gift of the Spirit. This is admittedly speculative.

THE STRUCTURE OF 2 CORINTHIANS 10—13

10:1–18	Paul appeals for obedience and loyalty
11:1—12:13	Paul's 'Fool's Speech'
12:14—13:10	Further appeal and warning
13:11–13	Closing greetings

How does Paul respond to this situation?

First, he insists on the purity of his motives and on his authority as an apostle of Christ. This seems to be an attack on the rivals who were undermining his authority in the congregation that he had founded, and who based their attack in part on what Paul regarded as human qualities and self-commendation (10:1–18).

Second, he saw the effect of the rival mission as being to draw people away from a true devotion to Christ (11:1–15). He attacks both the content of what they said and the rhetoric with which they advanced it. They attacked his apparent lack of rhetoric and his failure to exercise authority and throw his weight about in the church. They seem to have criticised his unwillingness to claim financial support from the congregation (cf. 1 Cor. 9).

2 CORINTHIANS 12:1–10

I feel no shame in recording my own experience, a thing I know from its having happened to me a thousand times . . . I have approached my work empty and suddenly become full, the ideas falling in a shower from above and being sown invisibly, so that under the influence of the divine possession I have been filled with corybantic frenzy and been unconscious of anything, place, persons present, myself, words spoken, lines written. For I obtained language, ideas, an enjoyment of light, keenest vision, pellucid distinctness of objects, such as might be received through the eyes as the result of clearest showing. (Philo [15 BC – AD 50] *On the Migration of Abraham*, 34–35 [LCL; *HCNT* §750])

Third, he is prepared to descend to the level of argument on a human level in order to claim ironically that even by their standards he is a true apostle, in that he is genuinely a Jew, and has worked and undergone hardships as much as or more than anyone else. But having established this common ground, he proceeds to show that the exercise is folly by going on to describe the humiliations that he was prepared to bear for the sake of the gospel; these are the true signs of an apostle in contrast to their showy claims. So, for example, they claimed visions, and he could claim a vision also, but he quickly plays down its significance by referring again to his suffering (11:16—12:13).

What do you think?

'Whenever I am weak, then I am strong' (12:10): paradoxical or meaningless, or what?

Fourth, he insists that he will act in authority when he visits the congregation (and not just in his letters) because of the ongoing immorality that persists among them, and they will discover that Christ does speak powerfully through him (12:14—13:10).

By the end of the letter the super-apostles have disappeared from view, and Paul is concerned only with the Corinthians themselves. May we presume that the super-apostles were temporary visitors? Certainly Paul does not address them directly and in effect say 'Get off my patch!' His real concern is with the people in the congregation and in particular with those of them who are still living blatantly sinful lives or have been seduced by the super-apostles from loyalty to him. After all the strong words that have been written, it is remarkable how the letter ends with a warm greeting and with the first occurrence of the full 'apostolic benediction' (13:11–13).

What do you think?

Could the Paul who wrote 2 Corinthians function as a role model for a church leader today or is he 'an egocentric authoritarian' (cf. Thrall 2000, pp. 955–65)?

THE OCCASION OF 2 CORINTHIANS 10—13

We have already considered the possibility that 2 Cor. 10—13 is to be identified with the 'tearful letter' mentioned in 2 Cor. 2:4. There are two other possibilities:

1. 2 Cor. 10—13 is the second part of the same letter as 2 Cor. 1—9 It can be argued that the situation underlying both parts is essentially the same; there is criticism of Paul in the congregation for his 'worldly' manner of behaviour, which Paul regards as coming from people who judge by outward appearances. Compare the following pairs of passages:

2 Cor. 1:17	10:2
2:9	10:5—6
3:1	10:12
5:12	10:12
6:4–5	12:10

But the difference in tone is a big problem. How could Paul write so confidently about his readers in 2 Cor. 3:1 and 5:12 (cf. 5:20; 6:13; 7:2), if he knew that there was still serious opposition in the congregation? Why is there no allusion in 2 Cor. 1—9 to the serious troubles in 2 Cor. 10—13? In reply it has been suggested that perhaps fresh news came before Paul finished the letter (which may have been composed over a lengthy period). A famous speculation by H. Lietzmann is that he had a 'sleepless night' and was suffering from something like a hangover while he wrote 2 Cor. 10—13 (see further Martin 1986, p. 1 of Introduction)! This last suggestion can hardly be taken seriously; the problem with 2 Cor. 10—13 is not simply a change of mood by Paul but a different situation at Corinth.

2. 2 Cor. 10—13 is part of a subsequent letter written after 2 Cor. 1—9 On this view

Titus came back to Paul after delivering 2 Cor. 1—9 with news of a further outbreak of trouble caused by fresh visitors to the congregation. 2 Cor. 12:18 may suggest that

Focus on theology

No other letter exposes the frailty and weakness of human life so profoundly as this one. By virtue of their humanity believers are like fragile earthenware pots, easily knocked about and broken, open to injury and disease and gradually disintegrating until they perish. If they survive, it is due to the gracious preservation of God, and ultimately to his resurrecting power. Hidden within the pots is spiritual treasure, a divine power that brings renewal and unseen glory. So, although God's people may feel that they brush with death every day, they can have an unshakeable confidence in the God who raises the dead. Even though they face judgement, they can retain this confidence. God's missionaries, who bring this good news and call people to be reconciled to God, are constrained by the love of God. They have a heavy responsibility to proclaim a message that brings salvation and life to believers and the sentence of death to those who will not turn away from sin. This message is not just about conversion; it needs to be continually applied to a congregation that has fallen out with God in the person of Paul. The need to provide for the poor is undergirded by a theology of giving that calls believers to a love like that of Jesus Christ who exchanged his riches for poverty so that the poor might become rich. Riches are for sharing. Criticism of Paul by opponents whom he accuses of boastful confidence in their own achievements is met by a theology of apostleship in which Paul can exult in his weakness and sufferings in the sense that these are occasions when he is aware of the grace and power of God.

the visit announced in 2 Cor. 8:17–24 had already taken place (although one of the accompanying brothers seems to have disappeared from view).

This theory necessitates that the end of 2 Cor. 1—9 and the beginning of 2 Cor. 10—13 have been lost.

These two theories are two different ways of saying that 2 Cor. 10—13 was written some time after 2 Cor. 1—9 and that when Paul wrote the earlier (part of the) letter he had little if any knowledge about the change in the situation that he addresses in this later (part of the) letter. A decision one way or the other does not greatly affect our understanding of the letter(s).

FOR TODAY'S CORINTHIANS

In our discussion of 1 Corinthians we listed some of the things that modern readers might find very strange. But it would have been equally possible to make a list of things that more obviously have abiding relevance and urgency (like the 'praise' of love in 1 Cor. 13). What might figure in such a list from 2 Corinthians?

- The concern and love of a misunderstood pastor. Compare the pictures of Paul that emerge from 2 Cor. 1—9 and 10—13, the combination of weakness and authority, and the over-riding concern for his converts despite their lack of appreciation of what he was doing.
- The outward fragility and inward stability of Christian existence. The missionary is a particularly focused example of how a life for Christ is characterized by suffering of all kinds, in the midst of which there is a conviction of divine calling and empowering and an unquenchable

hope for what God will do in the future.

> Writing 2 Corinthians must have come near to breaking Paul, and . . . a church that is prepared to read it with him, and understand it, may find itself broken too. Yet an earthenware vessel that contains such treasure need not fear breaking; it is the apostolic vocation to carry about the killing of Jesus, and those who accept it are apt to find the funeral transformed into a triumph, as they learn to trust not in themselves but in him who raises the dead. (Barrett, 1973, pp. viii–ix).

- The nature of reconciliation, divine and human. Here we see the way in which the gulf between sinful humanity and God cannot be bridged without the problem of sin being solved at the deepest level by God himself bearing the cost of reconciliation.
- A theology of generosity. Perhaps all that can be said about the motivation for human generosity to those in need is said in 2 Cor. 8—9; there is a remarkable concentration of various kinds of motive here.

ESSAY TOPICS

INTRODUCTORY

- Examine Paul's view of death and what follows it in this letter.
- Write an exegetical study of 2 Cor. 4:1–6 *or* 4:16—5:5 *or* 5:16–21, carefully exploring the main thrust of the passage and the meaning of key words and phrases.

INTERMEDIATE

- Is 2 Cor. 10—13 best considered as part of the same letter as 2 Cor. 1—7 or as preceding or following it as part of a separate letter?

● What insights into the creative possibilities of suffering does Paul develop in 2 Corinthians? How helpful might these insights be for a person today experiencing either persecution for their faith or life-threatening illness?

FURTHER READING

*denotes books assuming knowledge of Greek; most can be used by all students.

INTRODUCTORY

L. Kreitzer *2 Corinthians*. Sheffield: Sheffield Academic Press, 1996 (extended introduction to the letter).

R. P. Martin *Word Biblical Themes: 1, 2 Corinthians*. Dallas: Word, 1988 (simple introduction to the theology).

J. Murphy-O'Connor *The Theology of the Second Letter to the Corinthians*. Cambridge/New York: Cambridge University Press, 1991 (exposition of the theological message).

Commentaries

C. K. Barrett *The Second Epistle to the Corinthians*. BNTC. London: A. & C. Black/New York: Harper & Row, 1973 (on a par with his 'First Corinthians').

F. F. Bruce *1 and 2 Corinthians*. NCB. London: Oliphants/Grand Rapids: Eerdmans, 1971 (good, basic introduction).

C. G. Kruse *The Second Epistle of Paul to the Corinthians*. TNTC. Leicester: IVP/Grand Rapids: Eerdmans, 1987 (entrance level).

M. B. Thompson *Transforming Grace: A Study of 2 Corinthians*. Oxford: Bible Reading Fellowship, 1998 (fine devotional study).

INTERMEDIATE

A. E. Harvey *Renewal through Suffering*. Edinburgh: T. & T. Clark, 1996 (stresses the importance of Paul's 'affliction in Asia' [2 Cor. 1:8] for understanding the development of his thinking).

D. M. Hay (ed.) *Pauline Theology, II: 1 and 2 Corinthians*. Minneapolis: Fortress, 1993 (essays by leading scholars).

F. B. Watson '2 Cor. x–xiii and Paul's Painful Letter to the Corinthians' *JTS* ns 35 (1984), pp. 324–46 (defence of the identification of the painful letter as 2 Cor. 10—13).

F. Young and D. F. Ford *Meaning and Truth in 2 Corinthians*. London: SPCK, 1987/Grand Rapids: Eerdmans, 1988 (an interesting combination of a biblical scholar and a theologian expounding the letter).

Commentaries

P. Barnett *The Second Epistle to the Corinthians*. NIC. Grand Rapids: Eerdmans, 1997 (full-length standard work with some application).

H. D. Betz *2 Corinthians 8 and 9*. Philadelphia: Fortress, 1985.

V. P. Furnish *2 Corinthians*. AB. New York: Doubleday, 1984 (full-length standard work).

*R. P. Martin *2 Corinthians*. WBC. Waco: Word, 1986 (major work on Greek text).

*M. E. Thrall *The Second Epistle to the Corinthians*. ICC. Edinburgh: T. & T. Clark, 2 vols, 1994 and 2000 (the definitive treatment of the Greek text).

B. Witherington III *Conflict and Community in Corinth. A Socio-Rhetorical Commentary on 1 and 2 Corinthians*. Grand Rapids: Eerdmans/Carlisle: Paternoster, 1995 (good middle-length treatment).

Chapter 8

THE LETTER TO THE ROMANS

In this chapter we shall consider:

- the situation that led to the writing of Romans and its purpose(s);
- the manner of Paul's argument;
- the working out of Paul's discourse in detail;
- the place and date of writing;
- the relation of Romans 16 to the rest of the letter.

In the evening I went very unwillingly to a society in Aldersgate Street, where one was reading Luther's preface to the Epistle to the Romans. About a quarter before nine, while he was describing the change which God works in the heart through faith in Christ, I felt my heart strangely warmed. I felt I did trust in Christ, Christ alone, for salvation; and an assurance was given me, that He had taken away my sins, even mine, and saved me from the law of sin and death. (John Wesley *Journal* for May 24th, 1738)

Probably no book in the New Testament has been so influential in the history of the Christian church as the Letter to the Romans. Autobiographical accounts tell us how it was decisive in the initial conversion of, or the renewal of living faith in, such significant figures as Augustine, Martin Luther, John Wesley, and Karl Barth, and through them in the lives of many more.

THE PURPOSE OF THE LETTER

Romans is the longest of Paul's letters and the most systematic, in the sense that a careful argument is developed, even if it is so complex that it is difficult to give a clear analysis of it. Yet it has proved remarkably difficult to offer a compelling account of the reasons for writing it and the goals of the writer.

We can begin by noting four relevant facts in Paul's own situation.

- Paul was hoping to pay a visit to Rome to a church that he himself had not founded and for which, therefore, he had no responsibility and within which he had no particular authority. It will be remembered from his correspondence with Corinth that he was quite touchy about other missionaries working in the congregations that he had founded and equally he avoided working in other missionaries' territories (2 Cor. 10:12–16). However, he wished to visit them only 'in passing' (Rom. 15:24), and the letter is meant to pave the way for the visit.

ROME AND ITS CHURCH

Situated halfway down the Italian peninsula the city of Rome, traditionally founded in 753 BC, had become the centre of a vast empire that encompassed the whole of the area round the Mediterranean Sea. Rome itself was a city of c. one million inhabitants. It was an administrative, military and commercial metropolis, which acted like a magnet to people from all over the empire. It is not surprising that that there was a sizeable population (estimated at 40,000) of Jewish immigrants. Nor is it surprising that Christianity should have reached Rome at an early date, thanks to the movement to and fro of Jews; according to Acts 2:10 there were Roman Jews in Jerusalem at the first Christian Pentecost, and such people will have taken their faith back to Rome with them.

The Emperor Claudius issued an edict banning the Jews from Rome in AD 49. Suetonius, a Roman historian, says that this was because the Jews were continually rioting *impulsore Chresto* ('with Chrestus as the instigator'; Suetonius *Claudius* 25), which many take to be a slightly garbled attempt to describe outbreaks associated with 'Christus' ('Chrestus' and 'Christus' would be almost identical in pronunciation). Whether this be a correct interpretation of the cause of the troubles or not, the ban affected the Christian Jews in Rome, and we read that Aquila and Priscilla were forced to move to Corinth (Acts 18:1–2). With the death of the Emperor in AD 54 the edict lapsed, and the Jews trailed back to their homes.

The Christian church in such a setting was doubtless composed of Jews and non-Jews, just as was the case in other major cities. In a city of this size it would be likely that there were several groups of Christians meeting in different places; Romans 16 contains greetings to a number of people and the church that met in their homes. There were some rich people with the ancient equivalent of detached houses, but most of the congregation probably lived in tenements (Latin *insulae*), high-rise blocks of cheap apartments.

- With his considerable circle of contacts around the Christian world and in view of the fair amount of travel that took place between Rome and other parts of the empire, it would be strange if Paul was not aware of what was going on among the Christians in Rome. Some parts of the letter contain quite specific advice that reflects concrete situations in congregational life. On the assumption that Rom. 16 is genuinely part of the letter (see below, pp. 132–4) Paul did know quite a number of people in the Roman church sufficiently well to send them greetings.

- There is no doubt that this letter is the most lengthy and careful exposition of some major themes in Paul's theology; chapters 1—8 are a sustained theological argument; chapters 9—11 are an equally sustained treatment of a crucial topic; only 2 Corinthians 2:14—7:4 is comparable. We need to ask why Paul wrote at such length and with such care, and why he took up the particular topics that we find here.

- From the letter itself we learn that Paul saw himself as being at the end of one phase of his mission work in the eastern part of the Mediterranean world; he had 'fully proclaimed the good news of Christ' 'from Jerusalem and as far round as Illyricum' (Rom. 15:19), and there was now 'no further place for him in these regions' (Rom. 15:22). Therefore he was on the brink of setting out for Spain as a new, virgin territory for mission, and would visit Rome on the way. It would not be surprising if at such a stage in his life Paul paused to sum up what he had done so far and to set down his message and certain implications of it in a thoughtful manner. This may have been less of a conscious motive and more of an underlying concern in the writing of the letter.

Against this background we can now mention various proposals that have been offered regarding the purpose of the letter. Bear these in mind as you read through the letter and consider which of them (there may be more than one!) make best sense of it.

- Some scholars think that the letter is basically related to Paul's own situation as a missionary, and that the letter is really concerned with *the criticisms of his theology that had been made in the church at Jerusalem which took a different view regarding the salvation of the Gentiles from him* (J. Jervell, in Donfried 1991). Certainly it would be difficult for Paul to write on the issues that he discusses in Romans without the discussions and problems of his immediate past affecting what he was writing.
- We shall consider below the possibility that there may have been more than one edition of Romans with copies being sent to different churches. Building on this possibility, some have proposed that Romans is really a circular letter intended for several churches and that, coming as it does at the end of his mission to the Eastern Mediterranean, the letter was intended to be a kind of 'last will and testament' in which he summed up *his mature understanding of the gospel* for the benefit of the congregations that he had founded (G. Bornkamm; T. W. Manson, in Donfried 1991). The letter is thus a kind of manifesto of Pauline theology.
- A theory which takes into account the church at Rome is going to be much more plausible than these theories which ignore it. The *prima facie* impression given by the letter is that it is written to prepare the way for Paul's intended visit to Rome, and therefore it acts as *a kind of self-introduction by a Christian missionary* who is well aware

that the understanding of the gospel that he has is not universally held by all Christians (Cranfield 1979, pp. 814–23). On this view the letter is very much concerned with Paul's own understanding of the gospel, but he writes about it because of its relevance to his forthcoming visit. The content of the letter is shaped by what Cranfield (1979, p. 818) calls the inner logic of the gospel. From the letter it is clear that Paul hoped for the support of the church at Rome in his mission in the west, and it is understandable that he would want to reassure people about the nature of his message. Jewett (2007) especially has highlighted this function of the letter and thinks that Phoebe in particular was a key figure in winning support for Paul's future mission.

- Various scholars have argued that the specific way in which Paul presents the teaching in the letter is *related to actual circumstances in the church at Rome*. Minear (1971) insisted that the key to the letter lies in the practical application towards its end in which we can see reflected a situation of some disharmony between different groups in the church over the question of ritual observances with regard to food and festivals. These questions ultimately went back to Jew/Gentile problems, and the main part of the letter can then be understood as a theological discussion of the place of Jews and Gentiles in God's plan of salvation, against which the practical, daily problems in the church could be faced and a harmonious solution be found. A further, specific element was the need to encourage the church to internal unity in face of the attacks from outside to which it was subject from time to time. However, not all agree that what is described in Rom. 14—15 is specific to Rome and is motivated by knowledge of the situation there.

Dunn (1988, pp. liv–lviii) has stated that Romans has more than one purpose, and he fits the pieces of the jigsaw together slightly differently to suggest three elements in the total picture.

- **A missionary purpose** To gain support from the church for his mission to Spain.
- **An apologetic purpose** To develop a defence of his understanding of the gospel which he felt to be under attack (cf. 16:17–20), and thus to gain support from the church at Rome for himself against his opponents.
- **A pastoral purpose** To deal with the problem of divisions, real or potential within the church.

Digging deeper

Read through Romans and consider which of the various theories listed above regarding its purpose make best sense.

THE NATURE OF THE ARGUMENT IN THE LETTER

The next stage in our consideration of the letter must be to identify what is going on as Paul develops his argument or exposition in the letter. There is some disagreement as to the precise understanding of what he is trying to do.

- According to Cranfield (1979, pp. 814–23), Paul is setting out the gospel as he understands it, with particular reference to its fundamental nature in relation to Judaism and the Jew/Gentile question.
- A related view is that of Chae (1997, p. 300), who sums up his position: 'Paul's self-awareness of being apostle to the

Gentiles has significantly influenced the shape, the content and the structure of his inclusive soteriological argument in Romans. As apostle to the Gentiles, he boldly presents the theological argument in favour of the Gentiles in his attempt to affirm the legitimacy of Gentile salvation by establishing the equality of Jew and Gentile in Christ.'

- A somewhat different understanding is that of Wright (1991, pp. 194–5, 231–57), for whom the purpose of Romans is to demonstrate that the gospel shows that God is righteous in his dealings in and through Christ.

Again it may be the case that no one of these theories is adequate by itself. Certainly Paul has plenty to say about himself and his own personal involvement in the Christian mission, but the letter is not primarily about himself. It is much more likely that the subject of the letter is the gospel as such. In this there may well be an element of theodicy, in showing that God is righteous (Rom. 3:26), but this seems to me to be more of a side issue arising out of the main subject. Nevertheless, Wright's perspective is valuable in highlighting an element that has perhaps not received adequate attention in evaluating the total picture.

A further preliminary comment is that in the letter we have a remarkable variety of modes and moods.

- **Lots of Scripture** There is much fuller use of the Old Testament in this letter than elsewhere in Paul. If we confine our attention to actual quotations, one estimate gives some 53 quotations compared with only 41 in all the other letters in the Pauline corpus; they are scattered throughout the letter but especially in chapters 3—4 and 9—11.

- **Dialogue** There are also passages where Paul raises questions that people might ask in view of what he has said, so that the exposition borders on a dialogue. The questions are not necessarily the objections of a real opponent, but often serve to carry the discussion forward. (This kind of style is associated with an ancient form of rhetoric called 'diatribe'.)
- **Personal emotion** We also find passages where Paul expresses his feelings in a very intense and personal way (Rom. 9:1–3; 10:1).

Material of this kind ensures that the letter is throughout couched in a lively style that retains interest despite its dense content.

AN OVERVIEW OF THE LETTER

It is impossible to do justice to the letter in a brief summary. What is offered here is simply some guidance as you read through the letter as a whole.

THE STRUCTURE OF ROMANS

1:1–7	OPENING GREETING
1:8—15:33	BODY OF THE LETTER
1:8–17	Thanksgiving, leading into theme
1:18—3:20	The universal sinfulness and guilt of humanity
3:21—5:21	Justification by faith
6:1—8:39	The place of the law; new life in the Spirit
9:1—11:36	The problem of Jewish unbelief; God's future purpose for Gentiles and Jews
12:1—15:13	Practical aspects of Christian living
15:14–33	Paul's future plans
16:1–27	CLOSING GREETINGS

THE OPENING (AND THE CLOSING) (Rom. 1:1–15; 15:14—16:27)

The letter begins with a lengthy greeting in which Paul introduces himself as an apostle/missionary to spread the gospel about Jesus Christ who is God's Son, promised in the Scriptures, and specifically to bring Gentiles to faith (1:1–7).

In the ensuing 'prayer-report', which swiftly glides into personal comment, Paul expresses his confidence in the readers and intimates his desire to share the gospel with them in Rome, and to be encouraged by them (1:8–15). There is a combination here of building up the congregation and of evangelism.

At the end of the letter (Rom. 15:14–33) Paul again expresses his confidence in the readers, but nevertheless states that he felt it necessary to write to them in view of his role as the apostle to the Gentiles, and it would seem that he is justifying that role and the way in which he carries it out. In an autobiographical passage he explains how God has blessed his work to such an extent that he feels that he has completed his work in the Eastern Mediterranean, a task which had prevented him from travelling further west to Rome despite his desire to do so. This explains how he is now on the brink of coming to them. However, first he must visit Jerusalem and he asks for prayers in view of the uncertain reception that he awaited there. The letter concludes with a lengthy set of greetings of people by name, probably those with an active part in the life of the church (Rom. 16). There is a warning against troublemakers, which makes the assumption that the majority of the church have received teaching which is in harmony with that of Paul. And there is a lengthy doxology which sums up some of the main motifs in the letter.

This quick look at the ending of the letter confirms our understanding of the opening and helpfully expands upon it.

THE TEXT IS ANNOUNCED! (Rom. 1:16–17)

But back now to Romans 1! Paul's statement of his plans leads smoothly into a brief statement of the gospel that can be regarded as the 'text', which is expounded in the rest of the letter. Paul wants to proclaim the gospel because it brings salvation to all who have faith, whether they are Jews or Gentiles. This is because in it the righteousness of God becomes evident, for believers, just as Scripture says. This is by no means a summary of all that Paul will say in the letter, but it affirms things that lie at the heart of his understanding:

- The gospel offers salvation. (This implies that people need to be saved!)
- Salvation is offered to and needed by all people, whether Jews or Gentiles.
- Salvation is received by the exercise of faith – again, whether you are a Jew or a Gentile.
- The gospel offers salvation in that it reveals 'the righteousness of God', and again the need for faith is emphasized in such a way as to suggest that there must have been some other view that Paul is combatting.
- The key motif of righteousness by faith is defended as being what the Jewish Scriptures teach. Paul's teaching is firmly based in the teaching accepted by Jews as traditional and authoritative, and is not his own novel idea.

UNIVERSAL SIN AND GUILT (Rom. 1:18—3:20)

Paul's first stage in developing this theme is to justify the need for people to be saved by showing that all stand under the judgement and wrath of God because of their

RIGHTEOUSNESS IN PAUL'S THEOLOGY

The words translated as 'righteous', 'righteousness', 'justify' and 'justification' all represent words from the same Greek root (*dikaio-*). We tend to think of 'righteous' as meaning that a person has a certain type of character, which issues in their doing what is right and pleasing to God. This is broadly true for Paul, but in line with the rest of the Bible he tends to think of righteous people as being those who stand in a right relationship with God, even though they may have sinned against him. God no longer reckons their sins against them – on Paul's view, because of the fact that Christ has borne their sins and died on their behalf; those who believe are thus 'justified' by God's gracious action, and are now committed for the future to living righteously. 'Righteousness' thus is to be understood as a new status conferred on people by God, but a status that is intended to issue in a new, righteous way of life. 'Justification by faith' was a key issue for Paul, because he rejected the Jewish belief that circumcision and other observances of the Jewish law were the requirements for entering into or remaining in God's favour.

sinfulness. He begins with a depiction that clearly applies primarily to the world of non-Jews; the root problem is a failure to recognize the existence and character of God despite the fact of his revelation in nature. He paints a dark picture of human ignorance and folly leading to idolatry and also to sins of a kind regarded as particularly abhorrent by Jews. Paul interprets the miserable and wicked state of humanity as being the result of their failure to acknowledge God and then as being intensified by the judgement of God upon them. Just as Pharaoh hardened his heart against the Israelites in the Old Testament story and was then further hardened by God, so God gives up sinners to an even more debased mind, as a judgement upon them that is also meant to make them realize their sin and need (Rom. 1:18–32).

With all of this, Jewish readers would not have any problems; that was basically how they viewed the Gentiles. But then in chapter 2 Paul moves to address those who share his estimate of the Gentiles to try to show them that they too are sinners, committing essentially the same kind of sins. The Jews thought that they were in a better position because they had been given the law of Moses and they fulfilled its requirements, notably that of circumcision. But Paul emphasizes that it is not possession of the law but the doing of it that matters (Rom. 2:13), and also that circumcision in itself is valueless if it is not accompanied by obedience to the rest of the law (Rom. 2:25). He evidently believes that much of the moral teaching of the law, as opposed to those observances specifically required of the Jews, was also recognized and to some extent practised by non-Jews, so that those who did not have the law of Moses but followed their moral intuition were in a better state than those who had the law but disregarded it. At the same time, this is not to denigrate the law or circumcision or to call in question the justice or faithfulness of God if he judges Jews who fail to keep the law (Rom. 3:1–8).

The conclusion to be drawn, then, is that both Jews and Gentiles are under the power of sin, and again Scripture is drawn in to paint a picture of universal sin (Rom. 3:9–20). Although the primary point is that both groups of people are sinners and the Jews cannot avoid condemnation, it is implicit that the condemnation involves all individuals in both groups, and not just some individuals in both groups. Paul does not mean that all have committed the same sins, but that all have somehow or other failed to pass the test; in the end it does not matter whether you have failed by a great or a small amount if you have not measured up to the standard required.

It follows that the law of Moses did not have the function of saving people in the sense of putting them in the right with God, since it merely told them God's requirements; it did not enable them to keep them (Rom. 3:20).

ROMANS 3:23

[Eve speaks:] And then I quickly persuaded him, and he ate, and his eyes were opened, and he recognized his nakedness, and said to me, 'O wicked woman, what have you done to us? You have made me an alien to the glory of God.' (*Apocalypse of Moses* 21 [first century BC; HCNT §556])

THE MAIN PROPOSITION (Rom. 3:21–31)

But now things are different! What the law in fact does is to point forward to the coming of Christ and the possibility of people getting right with God through faith rather than by trying to keep the law. Instead of them trying to put themselves right with God, God does what is necessary to put them right with himself in that they are set free from their sins and their resultant liability to judgement and wrath through the death of Jesus, which Paul understands as functioning like a sacrifice offered to God. It follows that in granting justification to sinners God is acting righteously and fairly; he does not ignore the sin but provides the sacrifice that cancels it out (Rom. 3:21–26).

Three things follow. First, those who are put right with God in this way cannot boast of it as their own achievement in keeping the law. Second, if justification is not dependent on keeping the law but is by faith, clearly it is open to all humankind and not just to Jews. But, third, all this is not contrary to the law, but rather it upholds the law, since the law itself, as understood by Paul, had the function of pointing people to Christ and not of being in itself a means of justification (Rom. 3:27–31).

The main proposition in the letter has thus been briefly stated. In what follows Paul is concerned to develop its implications more fully and to tackle objections that might be raised against it, particularly by Jews and Jewish Christian readers who may have been influenced by the Judaizing movement in the church to argue for some place for the law in the lives of all Christians.

Digging deeper

With the aid of a commentary study the various pictures in Rom. 3:24–26 of what the death of Jesus achieves; consider where each picture comes from and what it means.

ABRAHAM AS AN EXAMPLE OF FAITH (Rom. 4:1–25)

An immediate possible objection is to cite the case of Abraham, who functioned as a model for Jews in that he might well have been thought to be justified by his good works (cf. Jas. 2:21–26, where it is argued that Abraham demonstrated both faith and works). Paul's response makes several points. In 4:3 he cites the key text, Gen. 15:6, which affirms that it was Abraham's faith that led to him being credited with righteousness. He stresses that since righteousness is said to be God's gift, Abraham cannot have worked to deserve it. He backs up Genesis with a quotation from Ps. 32:1f, which makes the same point (Rom. 4:7–8). Then he is able to use the case of Abraham who was not circumcised until after God had pronounced him righteous to make the point that justification is independent of circumcision, so that Abraham can be seen as the spiritual father of all who believe, whether circumcised or not (Rom. 4:9–12). Moreover, Abraham lived before the law was given, and to make righteousness dependent on the law would invalidate the promise given to Abraham – and to his descendants who follow his path of faith (Rom. 4:13–15). Paul celebrates the fact that Abraham is the 'the father of all of us' and comments on his extraordinary faith which believed in God against all the odds (Rom. 4:16–25). Because he was convinced that God would do what he promised, his faith was reckoned to him as righteousness. By analogy those who believe in the God who raised Jesus from the dead will also be justified, because Jesus is the one through whom our sins are dealt with in his death and resurrection.

THE RESULTS OF JUSTIFICATION (Rom. 5:1–11)

The last word in chapter 4 is 'justification', and Paul uses it to form a catchword link to the next stage in his exposition. The main point that he makes in this section is the certainty of future acceptance with God for those who are justified by faith. Already they enjoy peace with God. Whereas the Jews might place their trust in the law and boast or exult in it as their means of getting right with God, believers exult and are confident in the fact that they will share in the glory of God. At the same time Paul recognizes that the confidence of believers could be shattered by the fact that they have to undergo sufferings in this life. It is not clear whether he is thinking of the sufferings common to all people or of the persecution that might be inflicted upon Christian believers; either way, he asserts that one effect of suffering can be to develop a strong character and so to strengthen hope in vindication by God – a hope that is not empty or imaginary or the fruit of self-effort but is confirmed by the experience of being loved by God that comes as an inner assurance to the believer through the activity of the Spirit of God (Rom. 5:1–5).

The ground for future hope is spelled out more fully. If Christ died for people who were ungodly and had no claims on God's mercy, how much more will God finally save those who have been justified and against whom no condemnation can be raised.

Put otherwise, if Christ died to reconcile God's *enemies* to him, how much more will God finally save and deliver those who are now his *friends* (Rom. 5:6–11)?

CHRIST CONTRASTED WITH ADAM (Rom. 5:12–21)

In the second part of the chapter the magnitude of what Christ has done is developed by means of an extended analogy and contrast with Adam. Adam committed a sin that brought death and judgement upon all humankind because they all sinned like he did; Paul argues from the fact of human death back to human sin. Just how Paul sees the connection between Adam and the rest of humanity is not entirely clear. He does seem to be saying that Adam's sin brought an inescapable fate upon everybody else (Rom. 5:18). But his main intent is to say that in the same way the righteous act (he means the sacrificial death) of one man, Jesus Christ, results in life for everybody else; in view of what Paul says in the immediate context and consistently throughout his writings about salvation

What do you think?

'Paul's great images of salvation – justification, redemption, sacrifice, reconciliation – tell us much more about the experience and effects of salvation through Christ than they tell us about *how* through his death and resurrection Christ achieves salvation': discuss whether you agree or disagree with this. Can you suggest modern images or words that help to convey more clearly to people today what Paul was saying?

What do you think?

Make a comparison in two columns between Adam and Christ, listing the similarities and the differences in what they did and the effects that resulted.

'The historicity of Adam is vital: the biblical view of evil and of salvation (which is also a historical event) hangs upon it.' (H. Blocher, *NDBT*, p. 374): do the theological points that Paul makes in Romans 5 hang upon the view that Adam was a real, historical individual?

and justification being by faith, it is clear that he means here that Christ's righteous act brings justification universally to all who believe. And since the power of God shown in Christ is far greater than the power of sin and death, it follows that far greater blessings are bestowed on believers, who will reign and enjoy the life that God bestows. Moreover, this takes place through the grace of God: it is offered as a free gift.

NO LONGER UNDER SIN AND UNDER THE LAW (Rom. 6:1–23)

From exposition of the nature of justification and new life, Paul proceeds to consider a possible objection or set of objections to it. If justification is entirely a matter of God's favour (grace), people might be tempted to think that it does not matter if they go on sinning, since God will go on being gracious and forgiving. Paul's teaching could thus be thought to open up the possibility of moral indifference and to take away the incentive to sinless behaviour. A new line of defence is mounted against this implied objection. It rests on the fact that early Christian believers underwent the ceremony of baptism. To the outward ritual there corresponded an inward, spiritual reality (just as Paul held that there was a circumcision of the heart alongside physical circumcision, Rom. 2:29). Baptism effectively symbolized the washing away of sins. To Paul it symbolized something more, and he assumed that his readers had the same understanding as himself. It symbolized a sharing in the death, burial and resurrection of Jesus, so that the believer in effect dies and rises in a manner analogous to that of Jesus (Rom. 6:5).

This can be understood in various ways. One way is that believers 'die' in Christ who acts as their substitute in dying for their sins.

Another way is that, as Christ rose from the dead and was exalted to be with God, so too believers will be resurrected to eternal, spiritual life (cf. 1 Cor. 15). But here Paul emphasizes that the death of believers is their death as sinful people, and that they are resurrected to a new life in which they are the joyful servants of God; in dying they become deaf to the appeal of sin and in rising they become open and obedient to the call of God.

But, comes the immediate objection from people like myself, it's not like that in reality. I still hear the voice of temptation to sin and I still yield to it, and I don't always gladly obey the voice of God. Paul's response to this objection appears to be that what he is saying about the status of believers can become a reality as they believe; they have the capacity to be dead to sin and alive to God if only they will believe (like Abraham) in the power of God. Therefore, Paul's doctrinal statement culminates in a passionate appeal to the readers not to yield to sin as their master but rather to yield themselves to God in the confidence that sin will not be their master – 'since you are not under the law but under grace' (Rom. 6:14).

With this closing phrase Paul prepares the way for a fresh aspect of the topic (Rom. 6:15–23). The point of the phrase is that Christians are not under a law that can tell them what to do but cannot help them to do it, but in the realm of grace where God himself enables believers to live the new life. But that phrase could again be misunderstood to suggest that if people are no longer under the law, they are no longer under constraint to live morally in obedience to God. Therefore Paul has to go over the point again. He does so by suggesting that in fact believers face a choice between obedience and disobedience to God, between righteousness and sin, between death and life (Rom. 6:16). So escape from slavery to sin is not escape into a kind of freedom where people do what they like (that would still be bondage to sin!) but into obedience to God. Therefore, believers, having been set free from sin, must not yield to sin but to God. They are set on the path to what Paul calls sanctification (Rom. 6:22), here understood as moral life of a kind that is pleasing to God and the appropriate, required characteristic of his people. And at the end of the path lies the hope of future, eternal life with God – not that it is earned by their obedience, for it remains God's free gift to believers.

THE LAW IS GOOD – BUT IMPOTENT (Rom. 7:1–25)

For Paul's Jewish readers (or for Gentiles who had been converted to Judaism) the question of the law was of paramount importance. The Jews lived life under the law. Paul affirms that Christian believers are not under the dominion of the law but of God's grace. They are no longer under the law. Just as a law is binding on a person only during their lifetime and not after they have died, so the law of Moses is no longer binding on people who have died with Christ and now are living for God. This is seen as a great release, because Paul believed that one thing that the law did was to bring the latent sinfulness in people's hearts to expression. The fact that something is forbidden can often make us want it all the more. In that sense the law made people prisoners in sin (Rom. 7:1–6).

This did not mean that there was anything bad about the law itself. Rather it served to bring the sinfulness that was there all the time out into the open. The law of Moses

appeared to promise life: it said 'do these things and you will live', but in fact nobody is able to keep it. The actual effect of the law was to bring death, because people sinned, rather than life (Rom. 7:7–13).

Why did this happen? It was because of what Paul calls the 'flesh', meaning that as physical beings we are weak and yield to temptations. We know that we ought to do the things that were summed up for Jews in

Digging deeper

There is considerable controversy about what kind of person Paul has in mind when he speaks about the 'I' who is 'sold into slavery under sin' and cannot do what he knows to be right (Rom. 7:14–25).

- Is Paul referring to his own experience or to the experience of humanity in general? (Some commentators note that in Phil. 3:6 he claimed to be blameless before his Christian conversion and conclude that he is not writing about his own experience here.)
- Is the description that of an unconverted person who lacks the power of Christ and the Spirit to deal with temptation?
- Or is it a description of a Christian (note the present tenses!), and if so, does it refer to the 'normal' state of Christians living in a continual tension in their struggle with their sin, or does it refer to the 'abnormal' state when they try to live the Christian life in their own strength without relying on the power of Christ?

Make your own study of the passage; the commentaries give summaries of the arguments for and against the various options (see, for example, Ziesler 1989, pp. 189–95; Moo 1996, pp. 441–51).

the law, but we have not the willpower to do them. Sin has taken over control of our lives and our failure to obey the law makes this obvious to us. A person may delight in the law (as the writer of Ps. 119:97 said), but still be incapable of keeping it. It is a wretched state to be in, tied to sin and consequently under sentence of death. Where can a solution be found? Paul would have said that there was no solution in Judaism, but there was a solution in Christ (Rom. 7:14–25).

ROMANS 7:15–19

[Medea speaks:] 'Desire persuades me one way, reason another. I see the better and approve of it, but I follow the worse.' (Ovid [43 BC – AD 17], *Metamorphoses* 7.20–21; LCL])

NEW LIFE BY THE SPIRIT (Rom. 8:1–39)

In Romans 8 Paul moves into a positive exposition of what this solution involves. There is a new way of life for people who believe in Christ and have been spiritually joined to him. God has set people free from the inexorable bondage to sin and hence to death. Paul repeats the fact that the death of Christ is the condemnation and judgement of sin; therefore believers no longer stand under judgement. But this is not a licence to go on sinning. On the contrary, it is deliverance from the power of sin in order to fulfil what the law requires. And this fulfilment is possible through the power of the Spirit of God. Previously Paul has commanded people to yield themselves to God as though they have been resurrected to new life. Now we learn that this new life becomes real for them because the Spirit of God teaches them what God requires and enables them to do it. Paul makes the point by a rather repetitive comparison between

life that is dominated by the flesh and life that is directed by the Spirit, the one leading to death and the other to life (Rom. 8:1–11).

ROMANS 8:12

So we have two kinds of men, one that of those who live by the divine inbreathing, the other of those who live by blood and the pressure of the flesh. This last is a molded clod of earth, the other is the faithful impress of the divine image. (Philo [15 BC – AD 50), *Who is the Heir of Divine Things?* 57 [LCL; *HCNT* §594])

Just as in chapter 6 Paul exhorted Christians who had risen to new life with Christ not to yield to sin, so now he exhorts Christians who are led by the Spirit to put their sinful natures to death. And he motivates them with the promise of eternal life to come. He then explains how this future life belongs to them; the Spirit whom they have received is the agent whereby they become children of God and are conscious of the fact through calling God 'Abba' (the Aramaic word for 'father'); but if they are children, then they are also heirs along with Christ to the inheritance that God has for them. The metaphor is a bit of a stretch, because God does not in fact die and leave his wealth to other people, but rather all that God has is shared with his Son and his children. But there is a condition tagged on at the end, which Paul then develops at greater length – 'if in fact we suffer with him' (Rom. 8:12–17).

As we have already seen, suffering is part of the human lot, and it may be intensified for believers through persecution and through the hardships of serving Christ. The remainder of the chapter is broadly concerned with this fact (Rom. 8:18–39). Paul stresses that the suffering may appear intolerable, but in fact it cannot bear comparison with the glorious future that awaits believers, and that awaits the creation itself when it is renewed by God. (This is one of the few places where a New Testament writer takes up the question of the future of the universe and looks forward to a renewal of it in a manner that lies outside ordinary human conceptions of what is possible.) He further notes how we are too weak and ignorant even to tell God what we want in prayer, but the Spirit aids us in this also. And he emphasizes that, no matter what the sufferings and setbacks, God can bring about good because his ultimate purpose for his people is to make them into his family and to share his glory with them. And this purpose will be fulfilled precisely because it is God's purpose and nothing can ultimately thwart his intention. His love for his people is so great that he will not let anything separate them from it.

With this thought Paul has reached the climax of this part of the letter. Again it is clear that the letter is concerned to present a picture of God that will reassure his readers. It is a declaration of the rich blessings now and in the future for Christian believers and thus constitutes a powerful incentive to believe in the gospel.

Digging deeper

Set out Paul's key beliefs about the character of God as they are reflected in Romans 8.

THE PROBLEM OF JEWISH UNBELIEF IN THE GOSPEL (Rom. 9—11)

And yet there are people who do not believe the gospel! One of the most powerful

objections to the Christian faith was simply the fact that so many Jews had not accepted it and remained content with the Jewish religion based on the law (Rom. 9—11). How could Christianity be true in light of the fact that so many Jewish people had rejected it? Was there an explanation of their attitude? And what would happen to them in the end? And how did this rejection square with God's election of Israel as his people? Surely what he had purposed he must bring to fulfilment? These are the questions that arise in the central section of the letter. Although these are theological questions, however, we cannot fail to be struck by the fact that what drives Paul in this section is deep sorrow that his fellow-countrypeople do not share his belief in Christ (Rom. 9:2–3).

Paul begins by noting that the Israelites (as he calls them) had received so many benefits and privileges from God that one would have expected them to accept the Messiah who came from among them (Rom. 9:4–5). Then he insists that their failure to do so is not the fault of God through a failure to communicate to them. Throughout Israelite history in the Old Testament it had been a feature that there were some who might be called 'true' Israelites and others who were not. From one point of view this could be seen as a process of divine selection in which he chose out the descendants of Abraham through Isaac (and not through Ishmael) to be his people (Gen. 16—17), and then the descendants of Jacob (and not of Esau; Gen. 25:19–34). It could be said that God decided to show mercy on some and not on others, and even that he hardened the hearts of some so that they did not believe (Rom. 9:6–18).

The consequence that might be drawn from this is that God is unjust to condemn those

123

who were not selected, since it was not their fault that they were not selected. But Paul insists that God is free to show mercy or to withhold mercy as he chooses, just as a potter can decide what different sorts of pots to make from the same batch of clay (Rom. 9:19–21).

Digging deeper

'But we are not simply clay pots, but persons made in the image of God and able to converse with him in prayer!' Is Rom. 9:20 Paul's last word in this letter on God's control of the universe and our status in his sight? Consider (for example) the picture of Abraham in Rom. 4; the love and grace of God even for rebellious sinners in Rom. 5; the status of Christian believers as the beloved children of God (Rom. 8); the dialogue of Elijah with God (Rom. 11:2–4).

In fact, Paul goes on, God has called not only Jews but also Gentiles through the gospel (Rom. 9:22–33). Only a limited number (a 'remnant') of Jews are being saved, and God has called Gentiles as well. Paradoxically, Jews have failed to attain righteousness, i.e. acceptance with God, because, although they strove for it, they did so by the works of the law, which is the wrong way; whereas the Gentiles, who had not striven for it, because they were ignorant of the law, have achieved it by faith. (Paul is speaking here in broad terms: there were other Jews who did believe, like himself, and other Gentiles who did not believe).

By the end of the chapter, therefore, Paul has moved from his initial statement that God has not failed to fulfil his promises, since these promises never included the showing of mercy to everybody, even to all members of the Jewish people, to the assertion that the failure of many Jews to be put right with God stemmed from their own mistaken understanding of how to achieve justification.

This point is repeated in the context of deep personal concern for the Jewish people in Romans 10, where Paul again emphasizes that salvation is available through Christ for all who believe. He develops the contrast between the two ways of doing what the law requires and believing by juxtaposing Scriptures (Lev. 18:5; Deut. 30:11–14), which in his view epitomize them (Rom. 10:5–11). The latter text is regarded as referring to the need for belief in the heart and confession with the mouth that Jesus is the Lord whom God raised from the dead. Then Joel 2:32 is brought in to show that the route of faith is open to 'everybody' (Rom. 10:13). This leads into a comment on the need for messengers to be sent by God to tell people about Jesus Christ (again buttressed by Scripture, Isa. 52:7; Rom. 10:15). So, returning to the original point, Paul can claim that the Jews (broadly speaking) have heard about Jesus, and yet have not believed; they have been disobedient to God (Rom. 10:16–21).

Again Paul returns to the question of whether God has acted unjustly or is open to accusation. Does all this mean that he has rejected his own people, the Jews, and turned to the Gentiles instead? This cannot be so, because even at that time there were some Jews, including Paul himself, who had responded to the Christian gospel. Throughout history, in fact, there had been a core of faithful Jews at times when the mass of the people had turned to idolatry and deserted God. There are Jews who are saved, but it is by grace and not by works (Rom. 11:1–6).

124

How, then, is the limited success of the gospel among the Jews to be explained? Paul reverts to the kind of point made at the beginning of Romans 9, when he spoke of people being 'hardened' by God (Rom. 11:7–12). The Jews by and large have been 'fixed' by God in their unbelief. But in this situation the gospel has gone to Gentiles who have believed and received salvation. Paul sees this situation as one that would make the unbelieving Jews envious of the believing Gentiles. One motive, therefore, and certainly not the only one, for Paul's mission to the Gentiles is to increase this sense of envy and so lead the Jews to seek salvation in the same way as the Gentiles. At this point Paul explicitly says that he is addressing the Gentiles. This implies that up till now he has been primarily addressing Jewish Christians and 'defending' the ways of God to them. But now he tells the Gentiles how wonderful will be the effects if the Jews turn to Christ (Rom. 11:13). Paul cannot forget that he is a Jew and that the Jews had been originally chosen by God. He can therefore remind the Gentiles that they have been brought into the olive tree, which symbolizes the people of God, and they should be appropriately humble and thankful (Rom. 11:17–24). He also reminds them that, although some branches (unbelieving Jews) had been broken off because of unbelief, yet God can graft Jews back into the olive.

God's secret plan has been revealed to Paul. Elsewhere he can refer to God's plan to include Gentiles in his people as a revealed secret. Here, however, there is another aspect of God's secret plan: the 'hardening' of the Jews is temporary, until the full number of the Gentiles is saved, and then there will be a fresh turning of the Jews to receive the gospel; they are not finally excluded, so that there is no possibility of repentance on their part. In the end, the mercy of God is extended to all, to Jews and Gentiles alike, and may be received by all who believe. Thus in the end the ways of God are vindicated (Rom. 11:25–36).

This section of the letter raises some extremely difficult issues. There are critical questions about how Paul uses Scripture, about the relation of hardening to showing mercy, and much besides. It is perhaps this section that is most concerned with 'theodicy', explaining how God is acting justly and compassionately despite appearances to the contrary.

What do you think?

Paul says that Gentile Christians are like wild olives grafted into the original (Jewish) tree. Why does he think it important for Christians to be aware of their Jewish roots? How might this awareness be developed more for Christians today?

'ALL ISRAEL'

The reference of the phrase 'all Israel' in Rom. 11:26 is not certain. One possibility is that Paul is thinking of the 'new Israel', composed of Jews and Gentiles. More probably he is thinking of the Jews, in view of his usage earlier in the letter (see especially v. 25). Some scholars want to restrict the reference to the 'true' Israel (cf. the distinction in 9:6), but that would be tautologous. The alternative is that Paul is thinking in broad terms of the Jews at that particular future point, but without necessarily including every single individual Jew. (Similarly, in the Mishnah [Sanhedrin 10] it can be stated that 'all Israelites have a share in the world to come', but this is immediately followed by clauses that exclude notorious sinners.)

Digging deeper

In the light of (a) Rom. 9—11, and (b) the unfortunate history of Jewish–Christian relations, do you think that it is right for Christians to evangelize Jews? If your answer is Yes, in what circumstances and in what ways might this appropriately be done?

PRACTICAL IMPLICATIONS OF THE NEW LIFE (Rom. 12—13)

Despite these difficulties, one key note of Romans 9—11 is undoubtedly 'mercy', and this term forms the catchword connection to the third main part of the letter (Rom. 12—15), which proceeds to draw the practical conclusions for Christian living in the church from the doctrinal teaching that has preceded. Two chapters deal with this in fairly broad terms.

- Paul begins with an appeal to the readers for dedication of their lives to God, a statement in different terms of the calls to commitment that recurred in Romans 6 (Rom. 12:1f.).
- Next (Rom. 12:3–8) he urges humility, mutual concern and appropriate diligence in the exercise of spiritual gifts of ministry in the congregation (a distillation of the essential teaching in 1 Cor. 12—14).
- A third section (Rom. 12:9–13) stresses the importance of love (cf. 1 Cor. 13).
- This leads to consideration of the Christian attitude to those who persecute believers and personal opponents in general (Rom. 12:14–21).
- In this context of persecution Paul then proceeds to stress the need for believers to be generally submissive to the rulers of the state (Rom. 13:1–7). This instruction may have been especially necessary because

Christians could well have been tempted to take up a hostile attitude to rulers who on occasion persecuted them. It is therefore stressed that these rulers are in fact God's servants to maintain good order in society, and are therefore entitled to respect and obedience.

Digging deeper

In Romans 13:1–7 how does Paul understand the role of the state authorities as serving the purpose of God?

How would you deal with the difficulties involved in teaching from this passage in a country where people are suffering under an oppressive régime?

- Finally, following on from this is a summing up of Christian duty in terms of love for one another (Rom. 13:8–14); such love is regarded as the way to keep the law fully, for observance of the other commandments (Paul cites only the second part of the Ten Commandments) stems naturally from love. If motivation for doing so is required, Paul emphasizes that the day of salvation, i.e. the final day of judgement associated with the coming of Jesus, is not far off and (as in 1 Thess. 5) believers should be living in such a way as to be ready for it, not engaged in activities of which they would be ashamed.

JEWS AND GENTILES LIVING TOGETHER IN THE SAME CONGREGATION (Rom. 14:1—15:13)

Such teaching could have been given in any of Paul's churches, although the instruction about response to the state may have been particularly apt in the centre of Roman administration. The next section of the letter picks up an issue that arose where there were Jewish and Gentile believers together in the same congregation and difficulties were arising because of their different customs and practices with regard to what to eat and drink and what religious festivals to observe. These are essentially the same issues that are reflected in Galatians and 1 Corinthians 8—10. Once again Paul goes over this ground. The teaching given here is much the same, but it is freshly minted and some points stand out the more clearly.

So the main problem here is probably the consumption of meat that had been offered in sacrifice to a pagan god; some people in the church were happy to eat it but others felt that they had to abstain from it. Paul wants to insist that in both cases the people were endeavouring to please God, and he argues that in a case of this kind it is the motive that counts, with the result that different types of conduct may be equally acceptable to God (Rom. 14:1–9). Clearly Paul would not have said this about conduct that was clearly criminal or sinful. It follows that people should not condemn one another over these matters; they are answerable to God alone (Rom. 14:10–12). (The difficulty of course is when somebody believes that what other people regard as neutral is actually sinful.) Also, people should not persuade other people to go against their consciences and thus fall into self-condemnation and sin. There may, therefore, be occasions when it is necessary to abstain from some action because other people think that it is wrong. Ultimately, what matters is not the enjoyment that we get from food but the spiritual blessings associated with the kingdom of God (Rom. 14:13–23).

Paul himself tended to side with the people who recognized that foods and festivals were matters where believers could act with freedom, but he was quite clear that this freedom could need to be limited in the interests of the welfare of other believers. And that is the overriding concern rather than our own satisfaction, just as Christ denied himself (Rom. 15:1–6).

The last part of the discussion makes it clear that (broadly speaking, at least) the advocates of freedom, the so-called 'strong' believers, were Gentiles, and the 'weak' were the Jewish believers, although Paul himself sides with the former group. Since God had called them both to share together in worshipping him, they should do everything possible to welcome one another instead of causing divisions (Rom. 15:7–13).

PAUL'S MISSION – TO ROME AND BEYOND (Rom. 15:14–33)

Finally, Paul reverts to the way in which he has felt it appropriate to write instruction of this kind to the Christians in Rome, since he believes that he may have something to add to what they already know. This instruction is associated with his role as an apostle to the Gentiles. He glides into a statement about the way in which he has carried out this role in the Eastern Mediterranean and is now at last free to turn westwards and visit Rome on his way to Spain. Or almost free; first of all, there is the task of taking the collection raised among the Gentile churches to Jerusalem, and Paul voices his fears that there could be trouble from the non-Christian Jews and even a dubious welcome from the believers. Yet he is full of confidence and anticipation concerning his ensuing visit to Rome.

CLOSING GREETINGS (Rom. 16:1–27)

The body of the letter is complete. The closing section is a mixture of various personal elements. There is a commendation of Phoebe who is to visit Rome, and who presumably took the letter (Rom. 16:1–2). Then there are personal greetings to a host of people, but Paul does not simply name names; he comments on the work that many of them have done in the Christian mission or on other personal matters (Rom. 16:3–16). He warns the readers against people who promote ideas that do not accord with what the readers have learned previously (Rom. 16:17–20). He sends greetings from various people who are with him at the time of writing, including Tertius who acted as his amanuensis (Rom. 16:21–23). At the very end there is a complicated doxology, which refers to the God who has revealed the gospel for the Gentiles (Rom. 16:25–27).

SCRIBES DO STRANGE THINGS

Some curious things that happened in the copying of Romans by later scribes need brief mention.

The first is that some later manuscripts omit the words 'in Rome' in Rom. 1:7 and 15. This is probably linked to the practice of reading in church as part of a lectionary; since the letter was recognized to be appropriate for all Christians everywhere the specific

Focus on theology

Romans is concerned with the place of the Gentiles and Jews in relation to one another in the people of God, with Paul demonstrating to Jewish believers that all people, Jews as well as Gentiles, are sinners in the sight of God and face his wrath; but God has made it possible for all to be regarded as righteous in his sight, i.e. as having a place in his people, through what he himself has done in Jesus Christ his Son. By shedding his blood he is like an atoning sacrifice which cancels out sins, so that God's acceptance of sinners (including Gentiles) as his people is not achieved by ignoring their sin but by an act of deliverance. Since God has so acted, human beings have nothing else to do that would qualify them to be forgiven, such as observing the requirements of the Mosaic law that had been given to the Jews. They are simply to 'believe', i.e. to accept that God has acted in mercy to put them right with himself and to place their confidence in him and not in themselves. The pattern is provided by Abraham who trusted in God and was regarded as righteous before he was circumcised, so that he can be regarded as the father of all who trust in God, both Jews and Gentiles. The present process of justification, whereby people's sin is no longer counted against them, carries the guarantee of future deliverance from the wrath of God at the final judgement. The way in which God has acted creates a kind of inverse parallelism between Adam and Christ. Adam is the source of human sinfulness through whom the infection passes to everybody and they are all destined for death; now in the same way through his righteous deed of dying for sins the one person Jesus Christ brings life for everybody who believes in him. Thus there is one and the same way for all people, whether Jews or Gentiles, to have life.

But does free forgiveness not open up the way for sin to continue in the lives of believers since the sanction of punishment has been taken away? Jews were especially worried that Gentiles would not live righteous lives because they were not brought under the law of Moses as the way to please God.

reference to Rome was deleted in public reading. (Strangely, this did not happen with any other Pauline letters. The problem in Eph. 1:1 [see pp. 172–3] is of a different kind.)

The second oddity is that the doxology, which is printed at the end of the letter, where it is found in the most reliable manuscripts, floats about in the manuscripts (see the footnote in NRSV). In some it occurs at the end of chapter 14 and in some others it occurs both at the end of chapter 14 and at the end of chapter 16! Since the double occurrence is inconceivable in the original letter, it would seem that some scribes were puzzled by it appearing in some manuscripts

at the end of chapter 14 and in others at the end of chapter 16; not knowing which was the correct place, they put it in both places just to be on the safe side.

But why should it come at the end of chapter 14? The most probable explanation is linked to the activities of the second-century Christian, Marcion, who had some radical views about the New Testament. He objected to anything that sounded pro-Jewish, and therefore he limited his collection of Scriptures to the Gospel of Luke and the letters of Paul; even this was not 'pure' enough to suit him, and he cut out the passages that he did not approve of,

Paul therefore brings out the way in which justification involves the death of believers in the sense that they are removed from the sphere in which sin reigns through the law and have entered into the sphere where they share in the resurrection life of Christ and are no longer tied to the fatal combination of sin and death. They have thus been set free to live a new life. On the one hand, they have been set free from life under the law, which was an experience of knowing what they ought to do but being without the power to do it; this is clearly a life apart from the power of Christ, a pre-Christian experience, but one that can be also experienced by believers. On the other hand, it is a life in which the Spirit of God, who brought Christ back from death to life, empowers and enlivens them, enables them to live righteous lives and to know God as their father, and to endure the struggle to live for God in their decaying, mortal bodies, until they enter fully into the glorious state of God's people. They have the assurance that God will overcome every force that is opposed to them.

Does all this imply that God has not kept his ancient promises to the Jews (as descendants of Abraham) to be his people? Paul must both reassure the Jewish believers and ward off the danger of the Gentiles thinking that they have taken their place. He insists that whatever God does is governed by mercy and that he is free to do as he wills. God is free to harden Israel with the result that the mass of the people do not respond to the gospel. This happens because Israel has not sought God in faith but by trying to establish their own righteousness before him. But God does not give up the people for ever, and Paul has an insight into God's ultimate purpose that includes the Gentiles coming into his people now and then the Jews responding to the gospel, so that both groups come into his people. Indeed this is already happening in the church where believers from both groups must welcome one another into the one people of God. Practical measures to bring this about are based on love for all those for whom Christ died.

including Romans 15 and 16. It is therefore conceivable that the doxology became attached to the briefer Marcionite version to make a fitting conclusion to an otherwise incomplete letter.

There is also another, related, possibility. When sections of text are found in more than one place like this, the suspicion may arise that they are not an original part of the text at all, but represent a later interpolation which the scribes were not sure where to insert. The majority of scholars argue that the doxology is different in style and content from Paul's normal writing, and is a later addition to Romans by somebody else who tried to produce a fitting climax for this letter. Certainly it is an appropriate ending to the letter, and in my view the stylistic arguments against it being a Pauline composition are not compelling; it is unlikely to be a late addition to the letter, and is more probably by Paul himself or by somebody very close in time to him.

AGAIN – THE PURPOSE OF THE LETTER

We return to the question of why Paul wrote this letter and reconsider the suggestions listed earlier:

- The view that Paul wrote mainly with his relations with Jerusalem in mind. It is difficult to see why he should write on these issues specifically to the church in Rome, especially as there is no indication in the letter that it was debate with Christians in Jerusalem that was motivating him. The problems in Romans 14—15 are Roman problems rather than Jerusalem problems.
- The theory that Romans was a kind of 'circular letter' intended for several

destinations is not at all compelling. More importantly, the contents of the main part of the letter are clearly intended for Rome (Rom. 1:15; 15:22–29). This is not to say, however, that the contents could not be read with profit by other churches.

- Whatever fuller understanding of the purpose of the letter that we come to hold, Cranfield's commonsense understanding that Paul sets out his gospel for the Roman Christians in view of his hoped-for visit is an indispensable and essential element in it.
- Whatever the actual details of this situation, it seems very probable that Paul would write the letter in the light of his knowledge of the church picked up from his various contacts.
- My own view is that Dunn's threefold summary of the purpose as missionary, apologetic and pastoral has commended itself in my reading of the letter.

THE COMPOSITION OF ROMANS

Romans is perhaps the easiest of Paul's letters to situate in its appropriate place in his career. From the letter itself we have already seen that he had reached the point where he felt that he could turn his attention from the Eastern Mediterranean and look towards the west. Up to this point he had not visited Rome but had 'often been hindered from coming to you' (Rom. 15:22). These hindrances will have included his sense of duty to the work on which he was presently engaged, but they may also have included the difficult situation for Jews in Rome at the time when Aquila and Priscilla were forced to leave the city. But now his intention was to take the collection that he had raised for the poor Christians in Jerusalem and then come to Rome. In 1 and 2 Corinthians Paul was still raising this money, and therefore Romans will come later than these two letters (1 Cor. 16:3–4; 2 Cor. 8—9).

In Acts 19:21 we read how Paul resolved to leave Ephesus and go through Macedonia and Achaia (i.e. Corinth) and then go on to Jerusalem. He said, 'After I have gone there, I must also see Rome.' In Acts 20:1–3 he carried out the first part of this plan, going through Macedonia to Achaia where he stayed for three months. He then changed his plans slightly and instead of going direct to Syria he took a detour by visiting Macedonia once again. According to Luke, the reason for the detour was because of Jewish plots against him. Now Romans 16:1, 23 includes greetings from various Christians who belonged to

AN ALTERNATIVE INTERPRETATION

The dominant interpretation of the theology expressed in Romans, Galatians and elsewhere in Paul's letters has identified justification by faith as a major motif in it, although its centrality and importance have sometimes been played down. The background is forensic (i.e. legal); it sees the human plight as universal sinfulness that renders human beings liable to the wrath of God, i.e. his righteous reaction to evil expressed in their disobedience to his commands that will issue in judgement at the last day. But God in his mercy has borne the judgement in the death of his Son and accepted him as the righteous representative and substitute for humanity by raising him from the dead; all those who put their faith in Jesus Christ participate in his death and resurrection and share the pardon and new life that he has made available for them. As those who have died with him, they are no longer slaves to sin and death but are now free to fulfil the obligations of God's children in holy and righteous living and to enjoy their new status.

This motif, which is expressed particularly in Romans 1—8, has been submitted to an extremely detailed and technical critique by D. A. Campbell who finds all kinds of weaknesses and inner contradictions in it, and who argues especially that it stands in sharp tension with Paul's doctrine of participation in Christ which lays no prior conditions, such as faith, upon human beings, and does not require that a gracious God should propitiate himself before he can offer pardon to sinners.

To make this thesis work, Campbell has to argue that the passages in Romans that appear to teach the traditional doctrine of justification must be reinterpreted, and he achieves this result by proposing that some of the material consists of citations from a 'Teacher' with whom Paul does not agree (cf. the technique in 1 Corinthians 6:12–13; 7:1) together with Paul's refutation of him; the readers would have picked up the non-verbal signals that indicate what was going on. Paul is thus 'a kinder and gentler' apostle than we thought.

The jury has only just assembled on Campbell's case, and in fact has scarcely begun to hear the various scholarly voices for and against his proposal. It is significant that some of the foremost Pauline scholars, who are by no means averse to presenting their own fresh interpretations of Pauline theology, indicate their uncertainty about its conclusions while recognizing the author's brilliant and provocative scholarship. Such a major misreading of Romans as Campbell attributes to virtually all his predecessors is hardly likely, and the need to resort to another voice to account for major parts of the letter such as 1:18–32 when there are no compelling signals is a counsel of despair. Defenders of justification by faith in the traditional sense have generally insisted that the motif is part of a group of images that each contain part of the truth but need to be taken together to get the full picture. And the dogmatic theology (stemming from J. B. Torrance) which gave the nudge to Campbell to explore the possibility of a Pauline gospel that is free from conditions is open to criticism.

Corinth or its immediate neighbourhood: Phoebe from Cenchreae; a man called Gaius who was host to the church and is probably the same person as one of the earliest members of the church in Corinth (1 Cor. 1:14), although it was a very common name; and 'Erastus the city treasurer'.

An inscription from Corinth states:

Erastus pro aedilit[at]e s(ua) p(ecunia) stravit

'Erastus for his aedileship laid (this pavement) at his own expense.'

Although complete certainty is not possible, it could well be that Paul's friend is the same person.

We thus have an interlocking case: the personal travel plans of Paul place Romans clearly at this time when he was intending to take the collection for the poor from Macedonia and Achaia to Jerusalem; and the personal greetings in Romans 16 point unmistakably to Corinth (the reference to Phoebe is sufficient on its own to prove the point, and the other two references fit in nicely as confirmation). The almost irresistible conclusion is that Romans was written during that three-month stay in Corinth and can be dated to c. AD 55.

THE PROBLEMS OF ROMANS 16

Why '*almost* irresistible'? Why not 'only possible'? We have two further problems to deal with before we can close the matter.

Romans 16, the chapter which ties the letter to Corinth, is an unusual chapter for a number of reasons.

- It contains an extraordinarily long set of greetings to people in whatever church is

being addressed: no fewer than 26 people are named. Paul had never been to Rome. How did he know so many people, especially when we remember that no other Pauline letter greets so many people by name?

- Aquila and Priscilla (Rom. 16:3) had left Rome at the time of Paul's first visit to Corinth and then moved to Ephesus where they still were when we last heard of them, whether from Acts (Acts 18:26) or from Paul himself (1 Cor. 16:19, written by Paul from Ephesus). Later still they are in Ephesus (2 Tim. 4:19). So were they back in Rome again at this time?

- In Romans 16:5 Paul greets 'Epaenetus . . . the first convert in Asia': what is he doing in Rome?

- None of the people greeted here are mentioned in Paul's later letters from Rome.

- The strong warning against people who cause trouble in Romans 16:17–20 is surprising, since no such group has been mentioned in the body of the letter.

- Although no early manuscripts of Romans actually omit chapter 16, the earliest manuscript we possess (Papyrus 46) places the doxology (Rom. 16:25–27) in between chapter 15 and 16 instead of at the end of chapter 16.

This evidence has been taken to show that Romans 16 was not addressed to Rome but to Ephesus, a church that Paul knew well, and where several of these named people might be more aptly placed. Two types of theory have been developed.

TWO VERSIONS OF ONE LETTER

| Version for Rome | Rom. 1—15 |
| Version for Ephesus | Rom. 1—16. |

On this theory, of course, Corinth remains the place of composition of the entire letter.

TWO SEPARATE LETTERS

Letter to Rome   Rom. 1—15
Letter to Ephesus   Rom. 16.

On this theory, while the short letter to Ephesus was clearly written in Corinth, the letter to Rome could have been written at any appropriate point in Paul's travels from Ephesus to and from Macedonia and Achaia.

A LETTER THAT IS 63% GREETINGS

Aurelius Dius to Aurelius Horion, my very dear father, warmest greetings. I say my prayers for you every day before the gods of this place. Don't worry, father, about my studies. I am working hard and I'm taking relaxation; I'll be all right. I send my greetings to my mother Tamiea and my sister Tnepherous and my sister Philous; I greet also my brother Patermouthis and my sister Thermouthis; I greet too my brother Heracle . . . and my brother Kollouchis; I greet my father Melanus and my mother Timpesouris and her son. Gaia salutes you all; my father Horion and Thermouthis salute you all. I pray for your health, father. [Addressed] Deliver to Aurelius Horion from his son Dius.
(A. S. Hunt and C. C. Edgar, *Select Papyri*. London: Heinemann, 1932 No. 137, as cited by J. I. H. McDonald, 'Was Romans XVI a Separate Letter?' *NTS* 16 (1969–70) pp. 369–72)

The obvious objection to this second theory is that a letter consisting entirely of greetings is inconceivable. However, this objection is over-ruled by the discovery of other ancient letters doing virtually that!

Nevertheless, this ingenious theory is probably to be rejected. Consider some points on the other side:

- We have already commented on the amount of travel to and from Rome undertaken by people in a position to do so. In the case of Jews such as Aquila and Priscilla, many found their way back to Rome once Claudius had died and his edict lapsed.
- Archaeological evidence shows that some of the names of people mentioned here are more likely to have been resident in Rome rather than in Asia (just as one is more likely to come across the Duke of Argyll's servants in Scotland rather than in Wales).
- The warning tone in Romans 16 fits in with earlier exhortations in the letter suggesting some tension in the church at Rome, and a concluding warning is not without precedent in other letters (1 Cor. 16:22; 2 Cor. 13:11; Gal. 6:12–13; Phil. 3:17–19).
- The letter to the Romans is incomplete if it concludes at 15:33 and we have to assume that the closing greetings have been lost.
- If chapter 16 was not originally part of Romans, why was it tagged on at the end of it and why was the original closing section removed to make way for it?
- Since Romans 16 was less 'edifying' than the main part of the letter, it is likely that some congregations omitted it from their lectionaries, and it would be appropriate

Digging deeper

From Romans 16 what can be learnt about the following:

- the meeting places of the Roman church (see vv. 5, 14, 15);
- how Paul viewed the ministry of women;
- what qualities Paul admired in his fellow-Christians;
- the racial mix represented by the various names (you will need access to a commentary and be able to cope with some Latin and Greek for this one).

to read the doxology at the conclusion of the section of Romans that was read in church (cf. its position in Papyrus 46).

These points seem fairly conclusive to me that Romans 16 was part of one whole letter meant for Rome.

FOR TODAY'S ROMANS

Paul, as a child of his age, addressed his contemporaries. It is, however, far more important that, as Prophet and Apostle of the Kingdom of God, he veritably speaks to all men of every age . . . If we rightly understand ourselves, our problems are the problems of Paul; and if we be enlightened by the brightness of his answers, those answers must be ours. (K. Barth *The Epistle to the Romans*. London/New York: Oxford University Press, 1933, 1963 p. 1.)

So begins one of the most significant theological studies of Romans in the twentieth century. What problems and solutions in Romans might be enlightening for us today in the twenty-first century? Here are a few suggestions, all of them intended as discussion-starters:

- The essential equality of all human beings, both as sinners who all alike have offended against God and as the potential objects of his saving action in Christ (Rom. 3:20–24). Despite all the differences between people, Paul would insist that all share the same sinful nature and that all can be changed into new people by the power of the gospel.
- An incisive treatment of the inability of people to avoid yielding to sinful impulses apart from the new life imparted by the Spirit of Christ (Rom. 7:14—8:11). Where

Marxism and some other political philosophies disbelieve in human fallenness and look to political solutions to deal with society's problems, Paul would insist that we take our captivity to sin seriously, but also recognize that God's Spirit can transform human nature.
- A vision of the re-uniting of humanity into one people through faith in the Messiah (Rom. 11:32; 15:7–13). Paul lamented the deep divisions that existed in the ancient world between the Jews and the Gentiles, and saw how these could be overcome by a common recognition of Jesus as God's Saviour for all humankind. Can the same solution work for today's conflicts?
- A vision of a renewed cosmos with important implications for our attitude to ecology. This is admittedly not a central concern of Paul compared with the problems of humanity, but nevertheless there is the recognition that the universe shares in the corruption and decay of humanity and that it too looks forward to transformation by the power of God (Rom. 8:19–25).

ESSAY TOPICS

INTRODUCTORY
- Is the purpose of Romans to be understood more in the light of Paul's own situation or more in the light of the situation of the Christians in Rome?

- What are the principles for Christian behaviour that underlie Paul's teaching in Romans 12—13?

INTERMEDIATE
- How far can Romans be regarded as a statement of the central aspects of Paul's gospel? What, if any, important issues are not touched on in it?

- If you were a Jewish Christian who believed that observance of the law was necessary for Gentile Christians, would you find Paul's argument in Romans persuasive? What objections might you raise, and how do you think that Paul might respond to them?

FURTHER READING

*denotes books assuming knowledge of Greek; most can be used by all students.

INTRODUCTORY

K. Haacker *The Theology of Paul's Letter to the Romans* Cambridge: Cambridge University Press, 2003 (first-rate introduction from a fresh angle).

P. S. Minear *The Obedience of Faith: The Purposes of Paul in the Epistle to the Romans*. London: SCM Press, 1971 (reads Romans against its Roman background).

R. Morgan *Romans*. Sheffield: Sheffield Academic Press, 1995 (basic introduction with some attention to the influence of Romans).

Commentaries

C. K. Barrett *The Epistle to the Romans*. BNTC. London: A. & C. Black/New York: Harper, 1957 (classic, middle-length commentary).

F. F. Bruce *The Letter of Paul to the Romans*. TNTC. Leicester: IVP/Grand Rapids: Eerdmans, 1985 (good, entrance-level).

C. E. B. Cranfield *Romans: A Shorter Commentary*. Edinburgh: T. & T. Clark, 1985 (abbreviation and simplification of his major work, for which see below).

G. R. Osborne *Romans* IVPNTC. Downers Grove: IVP, 2004 (excellent middle-length exegesis).

J. R. W. Stott *The message of Romans: God's Good News for the World*. BST. Leicester: IVP/Downers Grove: IVP, 1994 (exposition and modern application by a master).

N. T. Wright *The Letter to the Romans*. NIB. Nashville: Abingdon Press, 2002, Vol. X, 393–770 (exciting and provocative).

J. Ziesler *Paul's Letter to the Romans*. London: SCM Press/Valley Forge: Trinity Press International, 1989 (excellent short commentary for students, raising all the major questions).

INTERMEDIATE

D. A. Campbell *The Deliverance of God: An Apocalyptic Rereading of Justification in Paul*. Grand Rapids: Eerdmans, 2009 (immensely detailed attempt to refute traditional views of Paul's soteriology; it is advisable to begin with the next entry).

D. A. Campbell *The Quest for Paul's Gospel: A Suggested Strategy*. London: T. & T. Clark International, 2005 (less technical curtain-raiser for his major work, consisting of separate essays welded together in just under 300 pp.).

D. S.-J. Chae *Paul as Apostle to the Gentiles*. Carlisle: Paternoster, 1997 (an understanding of Romans in the light of Paul's apostleship).

K. P. Donfried (ed.) *The Romans Debate*. Edinburgh: T. & T. Clark, 1991 (essays on the purpose of Romans from scholars of varied persuasions).

D. M. Hay and E. E. Johnson (eds) *Pauline Theology. Volume III: Romans*. Minneapolis: Fortress, 1995 (essays by modern scholars).

M. D. Nanos *The Mystery of Romans: The Jewish Context of Paul's Letter*. Minneapolis: Fortress, 1996 (argues that Paul is writing to a situation in which Christian Jews were still part of the Jewish community and offers an interpretation of the letter that is radically different from the consensus).

M. Reasoner *Romans in Full Circle: A History of Interpretation* Louisville: Westminster John Knox, 2005 (superb introduction to 12 theological themes in Romans and what interpreters have made of them).

A. J. M. Wedderburn *The Reasons for Romans*. Edinburgh: T. & T. Clark, 1991 (fresh survey of the problem of the purpose of Romans).

*N. T. Wright *The Climax of the Covenant: Christ and the Law in Pauline Theology*. Edinburgh: T. & T. Clark, 1991/Minneapolis: Fortress, 1992 (essays on Pauline theology with particular reference to Romans).

Commentaries
*C. E. B. Cranfield *The Epistle to the Romans*. ICC. Edinburgh: T. & T. Clark, Vol. I, 1975; Vol. II, 1979 (traditional exegesis of the Greek text).

*J. D. G. Dunn *Romans*. WBC. Waco: Word, 1988; 2 vols. (detailed work from the 'new perspective' on Paul and Judaism).

R. Jewett *Romans* Herm. Minneapolis: Fortress, 2007 (over 1,200 pp. of exhaustive discussion with many fresh suggestions for interpretation).

D. J. Moo *The Epistle to the Romans*. NIC. Grand Rapids: Eerdmans, 1996 (detailed work on the English text).

T. R. Schreiner *Romans* BECNT. Grand Rapids: Baker Academic, 1998 (similar to Moo in outlook and detail).

Chapter 9

THE LETTER TO THE PHILIPPIANS

In this chapter we shall investigate:

- the founding of the church at Philippi;
- Paul's situation in prison and his contacts with the congregation;
- the problems faced by the church;
- different ways of analysing the structure of Paul's letter;
- the possibility that the letter is composed of parts of several letters;
- the contents of Paul's letter and their lasting significance.

The letters that we have looked at so far all belong to the period of Paul's life as a travelling missionary. With Philippians we move on to a second group of letters in the Pauline collection. They come from a period when Paul was confined within a prison, although it is not certain that they all come from the same imprisonment. In the case of Philippians Paul was not only in prison but was also facing the possibility of imminent death (1:13, 17, 20–26).

PAUL AND THE CONGREGATION AT PHILIPPI

After Paul had had his vision summoning him to Macedonia (Acts 16:9f.), he and Silas

THE DESTINATION OF THE LETTER

Philippi was an ancient town in the northern part of modern Greece that was called Macedonia in ancient times. Built c. 360 BC, it was called after Philip of Macedon, the father of Alexander the Great. After a famous battle in 42 BC in which Antony and Octavian (the later Roman Emperor Augustus) defeated the troops of Brutus and Cassius (the murderers of Julius Caesar) the victors made the town into a Roman 'colony'. This term refers to a place where veteran Roman soldiers could settle on demobilization and enjoy the privileges of self-government and freedom from taxation. This move injected new life into the town, and had the effect of turning a Greek town into one with a more strongly Roman character. After the defeat of Antony and Cleopatra in 31 BC further veterans were settled there. Luke aptly describes it in Acts 16.12 as 'a leading city . . . and a Roman colony'. Nevertheless, the bulk of the population was probably Greek (Oakes 2001). There do not appear to have been many Jews in the town at the time of Paul's visit, since apparently there was not a synagogue, but only a few Jewish women who gathered for prayer (Acts 16:13).

came here from Asia. They met up with a number of Jewish women, including a businesswoman named Lydia, and their message met with an encouraging reception. Lydia was baptized and opened her house to them.

The rest of the story of how Paul and Silas exorcized a slave girl who told fortunes and found themselves thrown into prison as a result of the ensuing commotion can be read in Acts 16:16–40. The person who wrote the parts of Acts related in the first person was evidently present for some part of the time (Acts 16:12–17; cf. 20:6).

When he was set free, Paul travelled south from Philippi through Achaia (the southern part of modern Greece) to Athens and Corinth, where he spent at least 18 months. He then crossed over to Ephesus, paid a flying visit to Caesarea and Antioch, and returned to Ephesus where he spent more than two years in evangelism. Then he journeyed north again to Macedonia, and it can be safely assumed that he visited Philippi again (Acts 20:1f.). He then went on south to Corinth.

Paul intended to return from Corinth direct to Jerusalem, but his plans were changed at the last minute, and he decided to return to Macedonia. In Acts 20:6 we read how he sailed from Philippi to Troas on the first stage of his journey to Jerusalem for what turned out to be his final visit.

When Paul refers to 'the churches in Macedonia' and their generosity despite their difficult situation in 2 Cor. 8—9, he was doubtless thinking of the church in Philippi.

All of this probably happened some years before the writing of the letter and it casts very little light on the circumstances that led to its composition. It does at least show that Paul had visited Philippi at least three times

and therefore probably developed a close relationship with the church; it also indicates that the congregation were generous to other Christian believers, despite their own poverty (2 Cor. 8:2). Here, then, it is necessary to take into account both Paul's own position and the situation of the church as they are reflected in the letter itself. Paul wrote his letter because of what had been happening to him, especially as it affected the church at Philippi, and also because of what he had heard about the needs of the church.

PAUL'S SITUATION

As the letter makes clear, Paul was a prisoner at the time of writing and there was some kind of threat to his life. We know that he spent time under house arrest in Rome (Acts 28:16) and Eusebius records his death there (*Hist. eccl.* 2:25; see p. 186). A Roman citizen such as Paul was (Acts 22:25–28) had the right of appeal to Caesar and could not be legally executed away from Rome. If the death he feared when he wrote Philippians was death by execution (rather than by illness), then he must have been imprisoned at this time in Rome and nowhere else.

Two factual pieces of evidence drawn from the letter fit this conclusion. The 'praetorium' or 'praetorian guard' (Gk. *praetōrion*) in 1:13 will be the members of the praetorian regiment who were stationed in Rome, and in 4:22 'those in the emperor's service' (lit. 'Caesar's household') will be members of the imperial civil service.

In this case the letter will belong to the period at the end of Paul's life when he was imprisoned in Rome (Acts 28) and will have been written several years after the

ALTERNATIVE VIEWS OF THE ORIGIN OF THE LETTER

But this reconstruction has been questioned. Various messages and messengers passed between Philippi and Paul, and it has been argued that the difficulties in communication and the length of the journey make Rome seem unlikely. The reference in the letter to the gifts Paul received from Philippi when he first worked in Macedonia and the suggestion that only now 'after so long' – several years later – the church had helped him again (4:10, 15) seems inappropriate, if not impolite. Could the letter be redated? There are two possibilities.

We know that Paul was frequently imprisoned (2 Cor. 11:23). The only other imprisonment of Paul for any length of time recorded in Acts is in Caesarea, and this could possibly be the place from which he wrote. The word 'praetorium' can then have its other well-attested meaning of a governor's HQ in an *imperial* province (such as existed in Caesarea), and 'Caesar's household' refers to travelling diplomats. The letter is brought nearer in time to the mission to Philippi (c. AD 57–59).

However, we do not know that Paul expected to be set free in Caesarea and able to visit Philippi again. A compelling case for preferring Caesarea to Rome has not yet been offered.

One strongly supported and apparently very plausible location is Ephesus in view of the length of time Paul spent there and the vigorous opposition that he experienced. The case for Ephesus as then being the place of imprisonment from which Philippians was written has been powerfully defended, not least because of the relative proximity of the two towns. If the letter was written from here, it would of course be much nearer in time to the founding of the church (c. AD 53–55) and would thus fall in the period of Paul's missionary travels rather than of his later imprisonment.

But there is what may be a fatal objection. According to Bruce (1989, p. 11) there is no known example from this period of the use of the term 'praetorium' for the government headquarters of a *senatorial* province such as Asia was at this time (for the distinction between imperial and senatorial provinces see pp. 8–9). If this linguistic point is correct, the Ephesian hypothesis is not viable.

foundation of the church. Its date will be somewhere in the early 60s when Paul was in Rome.

From the letter we learn that the members of the church at Philippi had an especially close relationship to him and regarded themselves as his partners in the work of the gospel. They had entered into an arrangement to provide him with financial help in the early days of the church, and had sent money to him in Thessalonica (4:15–16). When they heard of his imprisonment, they had sent another monetary gift to him by the hand of Epaphroditus, who was one of their own Christian group. It was no doubt intended that he would stay for some time and help Paul. But Epaphroditus fell ill, whether on his way to Paul or after he arrived. The illness was sufficiently severe and lengthy for there to be great concern over him at Philippi. This implies that news about him travelled back to Philippi.

Epaphroditus was anxious over the effect that the news of his illness would have on the church. Paul, therefore, decided that it was best for Epaphroditus to return home instead of staying on to assist him, and the

TRAVEL FROM PHILIPPI TO ROME

Communications in the ancient world were certainly not as good as they are today, even when our planes are delayed, the trains break down, snow blocks the road, or the e-mail is out of action. The temptation is to think that travel was virtually impossible or took an enormous length of time. Certainly far fewer people travelled, and it took much longer to get anywhere.

However, the situation should not be exaggerated over much. Huge armies of foot and mounted soldiers traversed enormous distances. The missionary work of Paul would have been impossible without the existence of sailing ships that cruised around the coasts of the Mediterranean and across the open sea during most but not all of the year (cf. Acts 27:9–12). Roman roads provided routes for the military and for ordinary travellers. Journey times were counted in days rather than hours, but since nobody knew anything else people simply took them as necessary. Again, there were plenty of risks to be taken (2 Cor. 11:25–27; Acts 27—28), but people did take them. (See 'Travel in the Roman World' *DPL*, pp. 945f.)

One oft-quoted inscription found at Hierapolis in Asia Minor on the tomb of a merchant records that he travelled to Rome no less than seventy-two times. He needed no passport anywhere in the Empire. Provided he did not bring merchandise with him, he would have to pay no customs duty, though he was liable to pay a small tax for using the road. It is clear from the pages of the Acts that Christians made the maximum use of the Roman road system, and that it formed an unconscious directive to their evangelism. What a merchant could do for financial advantage, a Christian could do in the cause of the gospel. (M. Green *Evangelism in the Early Church*. London: Hodder and Stoughton/Grand Rapids: Eerdmans, 1970 p. 16, citing *CIG* 3920.)

letter was written to accompany him back home (2:25–30).

From the letter we also learn that Timothy was soon to visit Philippi, and it was Paul's hope that he would be able to return with news of the church. All this, however, was only a preliminary to a possible visit by Paul himself. He intended to delay sending Timothy until he had a better idea of his own future, and he was confident that that future would include the possibility of his own return to Philippi (2:19–24).

These travel plans adequately explain the direct occasion of the letter. But what would Paul want to say in a letter at this time? Naturally he wanted to give news about himself and his own situation to his friends. They would be wondering about his imprisonment and its effects and perhaps would naturally assume that his detention would hinder his work as a Christian missionary. Paul wanted to assure them that this was not the case, that the reasons for his imprisonment had become known to the people round about and had thus provided an opportunity for witness, and that other Christians in the area had taken fresh courage from his example to proclaim Christ.

They would also have been worried as to how his imprisonment would end. Imprisonment in the ancient world was used mostly as a means of keeping people in custody until their trial and not as a form of sentence (except for situations like debt). Paul evidently anticipated the possibility of execution, and had come to terms with it. But he knew that his friends were praying for him, and he expressed his confidence that the answer to their prayers would be his deliverance and consequently the opportunity for him to give them further help. All this had to be explained to the readers.

Peterlin (1995) hypothesizes that the congregation was divided in its attitude to Paul's imprisonment, some being bewildered by it and thinking that this was a sign of Paul's failure, since God had not rescued him from it.

THE SITUATION AND NEEDS OF THE CHURCH

The main reason for the letter, however, was Paul's need to give some pastoral advice to them immediately without waiting until his hoped-for future visit. There were three specific concerns.

ATTACKS ON THE CHURCH

The church was experiencing pressure of some kind, so that Paul can speak of it being called to 'suffer' for Christ (1:29–30). Christians might face hostility from other people at any time in the ancient world. Organized persecution of the church by the government was not a factor at this time, but Christians might well find themselves suffering discrimination, verbal abuse and other harassment from their neighbours.

Digging deeper

Read through the letter noticing evidence of the presence of this hostile pressure on Christians and consider how Paul responds to it. How does he try to help them to face it? Is there evidence to support the proposal by Oakes (2001) that this pressure would have ultimately been economic rather than necessarily physically violent?

Paul's frequent appeals in the letter to them to be joyful may reflect a situation in which they were feeling unduly depressed.

TENSIONS WITHIN THE CHURCH

There was quarrelling in the church; two women are specifically named in this connection (4:2), but it had spread more widely. Euodia and Syntyche occupied leading roles as workers in the church, and probably some of the members had lined up in support of them. If church groups met in their respective homes, this would have helped to foment divisions and rivalries. A considerable amount of attention is given to the need for unity and harmony in the church in the letter; trace the development of this theme in the letter.

What was causing the tensions? The problems may have been due simply to ordinary human causes, to petty jealousies and rivalries. Again, if the church was the object of attack from outside, then there may have been tension over how to respond, with some people taking a hard line and others an easier line. We simply do not know for certain the underlying causes.

A RIVAL VERSION OF THE GOSPEL

In 3:2 Paul warns his readers to beware of a group whom he describes variously as 'the dogs . . . the evil workers . . . those who mutilate the flesh'. He draws a contrast between them and Christians who are 'the circumcision', i.e. 'the true circumcision'. He suggests that the people whom he is opposing put their confidence in the physical, namely on the marks of Jewish piety and zeal. Later on he puts himself forward as an example to follow, and he warns against people who are enemies of the cross, 'who make appetite their god' and 'take pride in what should bring shame' (3:19 REB).

Who were these people? Three things are said about them.

- 'Dogs' was an insulting term used by Jews for Gentiles. It is generally thought that Paul is throwing it back at Jews who were attacking his gospel with its insistence that Gentiles did not need to be circumcised or keep the Jewish law.
- Elsewhere Paul uses the term 'workers' to signify his missionary colleagues. 'The evil workers' refers to missionaries of whom Paul disapproved. They were probably not native members of the church at Philippi but were part of a group of travelling missionaries who followed in Paul's footsteps. But it is not clear whether the group had actually visited Philippi. There is no indication that any of the members of the church had succumbed to their teaching. They appear to be a potential danger, but nevertheless one that needed to be strongly guarded against.
- 'Those who mutilate the flesh' is a bitter pun in Greek on 'circumcisers'. These were people who practised circumcision as a Jewish rite, or else Paul would not contrast it with the Christian circumcision in the next verse. In all probability they urged circumcision upon Gentile Christians.

This description is virtually certain to be that of so-called Judaizing Christians, people who claimed to be Christians in that they accepted Jesus as the Messiah but who held strongly that to be 'proper' Christians and members of the people of God all Christians had to be circumcised and observe the Jewish law. They dogged Paul's footsteps and tried to persuade his converts that what Paul had told them was insufficient. They put their trust in the physical – in the

outward signs of religiosity, including circumcision – and they went about urging this message on the Gentile Christians. They were similar in outlook to the opponents whom Paul attacks in Galatians, whom he accused of preaching a different gospel and of making the cross useless.

Was this group the same as those who are accused of being enemies of the cross in 3:17–19? It would be strange if Paul were to introduce a fresh group of opponents at this point without any clear signals that he was doing so. Paul used equally strong language in Gal. 1:8f. against Judaizers.

A difficulty with this view is that these people were 'making appetite (Gk. koilia, lit. the stomach, womb) their god'. However, the Greek word koilia can refer to any of several physical organs and not simply to the stomach. It can be used euphemistically for the sexual organ, so that Paul may be saying that they regard their circumcision as an idol. But it is certainly possible that Paul is referring to people who were living immoral lives, indulging in bodily pleasures and sins, and perhaps vaunting their freedom to do so (cf. Rom. 16:17–18; 1 Cor. 5:11; 6:9–10).

In the middle of the chapter (3:12–16) Paul refers to a group who thought of themselves as 'mature', and it may be that this refers to people who thought that one had to go on beyond the message of the cross to acceptance of Judaism in order to be a full, 'mature' Christian. They may have thought that maturity and sin were not incompatible.

THE STRUCTURE OF THE LETTER

So far, in trying to work out the situation of the letter, we have been engaged in what is sometimes called 'mirror-reading' – trying to gain a picture of the community addressed from the image of it that is presented in the letter. We have assumed that the letter is meant to deal with the needs arising from the situation of the author in relation to the readers and of the readers in relation to him. We therefore are working in the expectation that the content of the letter is shaped by these needs. But it may also be shaped by the requirements of a particular pattern of writing.

PHILIPPIANS AS A LETTER

Philippians clearly falls into the familiar pattern of a Pauline letter, with the Christian development of the salutation (1:1–2) and closing greetings (4:21–23). However, this analysis does not take us very far when we try to analyse the intervening 'body' more closely. We can detect the presence of various types of material which were common in ancient letters – such as the opening expression of good wishes or prayer report (1:3–11), statements about the writer's own situation (1:12–26), discussion of a forthcoming visit to the recipients (2:19–30), and exhortation or instruction (e.g. 4:2–9). But recognition of the formal 'shape' of the letter does not help us greatly to understand what is going on in it, any more than recognition of, say, the broad shape of a musical composition like a symphony or sonata takes us far in understanding just what the composer has achieved within the constraints of a particular structure.

PHILIPPIANS AS AN EXAMPLE OF RHETORIC

Recent scholars have examined various books of the New Testament and analysed them against what is known of the theory and practices of ancient rhetoric. This approach presupposes that the formal shape of Philippians is that of a written speech, in which the writer behaves like an ancient orator who is attempting to persuade his audience of some proposition.

Ancient speeches were classified into three different types, namely:

- **Judicial** concerned with accusation and defence.
- **Deliberative** concerned with persuasion and dissuasion.
- **Epideictic** concerned with praise and blame.

Broadly speaking, the first of these was used in court proceedings, the second in political meetings, and the third in ceremonial gatherings. Philippians has been interpreted as 'deliberative', its aim being to show what kind of life is worthy of the gospel.

Two quite different attempts to structure the letter in this way have been offered by D. F. Watson and L. G. Bloomquist respectively (D. F. Watson 'A Rhetorical Analysis of Philippians and its Implications for the Unity Question' *Novum Testamentum* 30 (1988) pp. 57–88; L. G. Bloomquist *The Function of Suffering in Philippians*. Sheffield: Sheffield Academic Press, 1993). It should be noted that ancient writers use a variety of Latin terms for the different parts of a speech. Deliberative speeches were obviously not all structured the same way, and there is room for disagreement among modern scholars as they try to reconstruct the structure of a speech and the functions of the different elements.

Watson's analysis:
INTRODUCTION (*Exordium*) (1:3–26)
Aimed at securing the goodwill of the audience and preparing for the main subject.

THEME (*Narratio*) (1:27–30)
A statement of the concerns for which the Introduction has prepared the way. It contains the theme which will be elaborated and defended in the rest of the speech, in this case that the Philippians are to live a life that is worthy of the gospel and to stand firm and united against any opponents.

ARGUMENT (*Probatio*) (2:1—3:21)
The heart of the speech, offering arguments and examples to support the case. It can be subdivided into three main parts with a 'digression':

FIRST DEVELOPMENT (2:1–11)
After the proposition has been restated, the argument is reinforced by an example, that of Christ himself.

SECOND DEVELOPMENT (2:12–18)
Paul appeals to his own authority and example.

DIGRESSION (*Digressio*) (2:19–30)
Aids the argument by exemplifying the kind of life that is desired in the readers. It is not recounting material about Timothy and Epaphroditus simply out of general interest but basically in order to show how the readers should live.

THIRD DEVELOPMENT (3:1–21)
Contains argument by example (that of Paul himself) but also attacks directly a different way of life which is contrary to the gospel.

FINAL APPEAL (*Peroratio*) (4:1–21)
The climax of the speech in a 'peroration' which is intended to sum up the argument and press it home. It has two parts:

RECAPITULATION (*Repetitio*) (4:1–9)
Repetition of basic points in a fresh way.

APPEAL (*Adfectus*) (4:10–20)
An emotional appeal to the readers to secure agreement with the writer.

Bloomquist's analysis:
Exordium (1:3–11).
Reaffirmation of good relations with the readers and introduction of theme of suffering.

Narratio (1:12–14)
Brief account of the situation.

Partitio (1:15–18a)
Brief statement of the case to be developed.

Argumentatio (1:18a—4:7)
The main development of the case.

Confirmatio (1:18b–26)
Paul himself as an example of suffering to be followed by the readers.

Exhortatio (1:27—2:18)
A persuasive development of the *Confirmatio*.

Exempla (2:19–30)
Timothy and Epaphroditus as examples of suffering.

Reprehensio (3:1–16)
Attack on a group of opponents who live 'in the flesh' instead of following the way of Christ.

Exhortatio (3:17—4:7)
Use of Paul himself as an example of the Christian way.

Peroratio (4:8–20)
Various themes, including thanks to the congregation for its support of Paul.

Each analysis supports a unified theme right through the letter. However, they are probably too neat and ignore the fact that letters may have several diverse themes. For example, it is hard to believe that the material about Timothy and Epaphroditus is used primarily as an example for the readers. Although 1:27–30 is the key to the main theme in Paul's teaching to the Philippians, not everything in the letter is necessarily tied to that one theme. And the fact that the ~~two analyses are so different from each other makes one wonder if the approach is an appropriate one~~.

Analysis by content

~~I fall back on the view that an analysis of the contents gives us the best way into the structure of the letter.~~

THE STRUCTURE OF PHILIPPIANS

1:1–2	OPENING GREETING
1:3—4:20	BODY OF THE LETTER
1:3–11	Opening prayer-report
1:12–26	Paul's own situation and prospects
1:27—2:18	Appeal for unity and humility in the church
2:19–30	Future visits to Philippi by Paul and his colleagues
3:1—4:1	Warning against Judaizers
4:2–9	Practical instructions for life in the church
4:10–20	Thanks for a gift to Paul
4:21–23	CLOSING GREETINGS

This analysis attempts to do justice to the letter as a letter with the prayer-report as part of the letter structure. The basic divisions in the letter are fairly clear and correspond to those of Watson. The difference is that I am not claiming that they form a tight rhetorical structure.

THE DEVELOPMENT OF THE MESSAGE

Paul begins the letter with a prayer-report which reflects the two main themes that are on his mind: first, the work of the gospel in which he and the readers share, and which may seem to be hindered by his imprisonment; and second, the spiritual growth of the readers in love (1:3–11).

He develops the first of these topics, explaining the problems in his own situation and showing how these are not really problems. In fact, the gospel is being proclaimed. And he himself is confident that he will continue to oversee his mission rather than be snatched away from it, however much he might desire to depart and be more close to Christ (1:12–26).

What do you think?

Is Paul's attitude to death, in which he prefers it to life, an unhealthy, jaundiced view of life? Or can it be understood as a healthy corrective to the view that this life is all that there is and all that matters?

From this thought of his continuing care for the churches he moves to the particular instruction that he wishes to give the readers. They are to live a life worthy of the gospel, and specifically to live together in unity, being prepared for any suffering that might result, and withstanding any opposition (1:27–30).

There must be inner unity in the church based upon humility – a point reinforced by the example of Christ whose humiliation was

---

PHILIPPIANS 2:12–13

All is foreseen, but freedom of choice is given; and the world is judged by grace, yet all is according to the excess of works. (*Pirqe Aboth* 3:16 [2nd–3rd cent. AD; *HCNT* § 796])

vindicated by God (2:1–13) – and this must be accompanied by a good witness to the world around them (2:14–18).

Digging deeper

Assemble the teaching in this letter on unity in the church and discuss in what ways it could be helpful to the cause of Christian unity today both within individual congregations and between congregations and denominations.

The focus of this section lies in the summary of the 'career' of Jesus in 2:6–11. Since the theme of the context is humility and service and the passage about Jesus culminates in his exaltation, it has been argued that the example does not altogether fit the lesson to be drawn from it; furthermore, the use of rhythmical prose and unusual language has led to the proposal that this is a pre-formed piece, originally a celebration of the humiliation and exaltation of Christ, which is here put to secondary use so that vv. 6–8 function as an example. On this view the passage is a pre-Pauline 'hymn' which Paul has incorporated in the letter. Alternatively, it can be argued that the passage does fit into its context and was composed specifically for it; its theme is not only the humble service demonstrated by Christ but also his lordship over believers. He is a 'lordly example' (a phrase used by L. Hurtado).

After this basic instruction, Paul returns to the links between himself and the church, and refers specifically to what may be called the outward occasion of the letter, the impending visit of Timothy (and hopefully also of himself) and the return of Epaphroditus as the bearer of the letter (2:19–30).

Digging deeper

Discuss whether what Paul says about Jesus Christ in the letter could be seen as setting up a comparison and contrast with the Roman Emperors of the time (from Augustus to Nero). See what was said by and about the Emperors in C. K. Barrett *The New Testament Background* London: SPCK/San Francisco: Harper & Row, 1987 Ch. 1. See also Oakes (2001).

What do you think?

Consider how Epaphroditus and Timothy can be seen as exemplary figures to further Paul's appeal for Christian character among his readers (Phil. 2:19–30). Compare them with the example of Jesus (2:6–11) to see if there are any similarities between them.

Then he moves to a fresh topic: the danger of rival missionaries with an appeal to Gentile Christians to be circumcised and keep the Jewish law. Woven into this section is a warning against some kind of claim to maturity which was being made by some of the church members and which possibly lay behind some of the divisions in the church (3:1—4:1).

What do you think?

Why was Paul so tolerant of the rival preachers in 1:15–18 and so intolerant of the rival missionaries in 3:2? Is intolerance sometimes a justifiable Christian virtue?

Next, Paul returns to the question of division in the church and speaks out openly to some of the people who were causing the problems. This merges into some rather general exhortation that is concerned with positive Christian living (4:2–9).

Only after all this does Paul return finally to the initial theme of the work of the gospel and to the help that he had received from the church. It forms a fitting climax to the letter as he expresses his gratitude and prays that God will provide for the needs of the readers who, we suspect, may have impoverished themselves in their concern for other Christians (4:10–20; cf. 2 Cor. 8:1–5).

Focus on theology

Paul is in prison and facing the threat of death; he writes to Christian believers quarrelling with one another. He develops a theology of death in which it becomes the gateway to a better life than can be known on earth because it brings one closer to Christ. Christ himself is depicted as one who had the highest privileges alongside God but voluntarily surrendered the exercise of them to become a servant; as such he has been vindicated by God the Father raising him from the dead and exalting him. He is thus both Lord and example for his people. They (like Paul) are called to participate in his sufferings and look forward to sharing in his resurrection. Christ's example of rejecting self-seeking should be expressed in their lives in service of one another and oneness of purpose. In this way they will be a united people, strengthened to face persecution and be like lights in a dark world. Here is a profound theology of union with Christ that leads to confident hope and sheer jubilation despite suffering.

PHILIPPIANS – ONE LETTER OR SEVERAL FRAGMENTS?

Not everybody agrees that the kind of analysis of the letter as a coherent whole offered above is convincing. There are two problems with it:

- At the beginning of chapter 3 there is an abrupt shift from 'Finally, my brothers and sisters, rejoice in the Lord' in the first part of 3:1 to the strong warning in 3:2 against 'evil workers' and the generally impassioned tone of Phil. 3 as a whole. 'Finally' in 3:1 could suggest that the end of a letter was in sight. The attack on the 'evil workers' who have not been mentioned in the earlier part of the letter suggests that a new and different situation is now in mind.
- In 4:10–20 Paul offers thanks for a gift sent to him by the Philippians through Epaphroditus. Why does Paul delay this matter to the end of the letter? Would it not have been more natural to do so earlier, perhaps in connection with the passage about Epaphroditus's visit?

For these reasons it has been proposed that Philippians contains parts of two, or more probably three, documents which have been combined to form one letter. A typical proposal (out of many) is:

Letter A	Letter B	Letter C
	1:1—3:1	
		3:2–21
	4:4–7	
		4:8–9
4:10–20		
	4:21–23	

Letter A was sent by Paul when he received a gift from the Philippians. Then he wrote a longer letter (Letter B) dealing with the question of unity in the church. Finally, when he heard that a new and dangerous situation had developed in the church, he wrote Letter C to deal specifically with this problem. Later, these letters were combined into one. Letter B was enlarged by the insertion at suitable points of Letter C (with a slight alteration of order at the end) and Letter A. Whatever introductory and concluding matter was originally present in Letters A and C was dropped.

This decomposition of the letter is unnecessary and unconvincing.

- 'Finally' (Gk. *to loipon*) in 3:1 can equally well mean 'furthermore' and is not necessarily a sign of the closing of a letter. The change of topic in chapter 3 is abrupt but not impossible, especially when we bear in mind that letters were not necessarily dictated and written in one continuous session.
- The presence of opponents in the church has already been hinted at earlier in the letter, and there is a remarkable number of common themes, extending to the use of the same (sometimes unusual) vocabulary between chapter 3 and the earlier chapters.
- There is nothing unusual about Paul discussing gifts and money at the end of a letter (cf. 1 Cor. 16); he had in fact already alluded to the topic in passing earlier (1:5; 2:25).
- The letter has a perfectly coherent structure.
- The same distinctive vocabulary and motifs can be shown to be present in all three parts of the letter and they function to tie the letter together as one integrated whole.

FOR TODAY'S PHILIPPIANS

Various items make this letter of special interest.

- Paul's attitude to death. In 2 Corinthians Paul wrestles especially with the fragility of human existence, particularly as a missionary. Here in Philippians he takes a positive view of what lies after death for the Christian believer. Perhaps now feeling his age, he seems to prefer the state of being with Christ rather than continuing to live in this world. Can this be defended as a healthy attitude in a younger person? Or does Paul in fact get the balance right?
- The mission conducted by Paul and its relation to the witness of a local congregation. This letter is significant for the light it sheds on the work of other preachers and for the partnership of a congregation with Paul in evangelism. Elsewhere in Paul's letters it might appear that only specially called travelling apostles and missionaries were involved in evangelism; here it becomes evident that other Christians also were 'speaking the word' (1:14), and Paul was glad about what was happening, even if there were aspects of the evangelism that caused him concern.
- Paul's concept of 'knowing' Christ and sharing in his sufferings and resurrection. 'Knowing' Christ (3:10) is something that Paul rarely refers to directly, yet it was obviously central in his Christian experience. Such a relationship is realized in willingness to share the suffering of Christ (in the service of the gospel). For Paul it was an on-going experience leading onwards to a developing maturity.
- Above all, the formal prose description of the career of Christ Jesus in 2:6–11 with its

profound implications for christology. Paul rarely discusses the role, status and nature of Jesus Christ as the Son of God and Lord as a theme in its own right; here he does do so in a way that brings out the paradox of One who was equal to God and yet renounced the privileges of this position in which he could exercise sovereignty in order to be a servant of God as a human being. Such self-denial is recognized by God as what it truly means to be a lord, using one's position not for one's own sake but in service. (Note especially the phrase 'something to be exploited' [Gk. *harpagmos*].)

ESSAY TOPICS

INTRODUCTORY

● Write an exegetical study of Philippians 2:6–11. Use at least two commentaries and consider carefully alternative interpretations of key phrases (including 'something to be exploited' in verse 6) held by different scholars.

INTRODUCTORY/INTERMEDIATE

● Who are the people attacked or criticized by Paul in Phil. 3? Is he dealing with one or more different groups of opponents? What are the key elements in his response to them?

INTERMEDIATE

● Evaluate the arguments for and against the view that Philippians 2:6–11 is a previously formed 'piece' by Paul (or unknown early Christians).

FURTHER READING

*denotes books assuming knowledge of Greek; most can be used by all students.

INTRODUCTORY

G. F. Hawthorne *Word Biblical Themes: Philippians*. Waco: Word Books, 1987 (introductory level).

(K. P. Donfried and) I. H. Marshall *The Shorter Paulines: Thessalonians, Philippians and Philemon*. Cambridge/New York: Cambridge University Press, 1993 (exposition of the theology).

Commentaries

F. F. Bruce *Philippians*. NIBC. Peabody, Mass.: Hendrickson, 1989 (excellent entrance-level).

D. Flemming, *Philippians*. NBBC. Kansas City: Beacon Hill, 2009 (excellent on application).

I. H. Marshall *The Epistle to the Philippians*. EC. London: Epworth/Valley Forge; Trinity Press International, 1992 (exegesis with discussions of how to expound key themes).

R. P. Martin *Philippians*. NCB. London: Marshall Pickering/Grand Rapids: Eerdmans, 1980 (good middle-length exegesis).

J. A. Motyer *The Message of Philippians: Jesus our Joy*. BST. Leicester: IVP/Downers Grove: IVP, 1984 (exposition for modern readers).

INTERMEDIATE

R. P. Martin and Brian J. Dodd (eds) *Where Christology Began: Essays on Philippians 2*. Louisville: Westminster/John Knox, 1998 (survey of the recent debate on the meaning and significance of Phil. 2:6–11).

P. Oakes *Philippians: From people to letter*. Cambridge/New York: Cambridge University Press, 2001 (fascinating reconstruction of the situation at Philippi as a Roman *colonia*).

*D. Peterlin *Paul's Letter to the Philippians in the Light of Disunity in the Church*. Leiden: Brill, 1995 (sees disunity in the church as the key to understanding the letter).

*N. T. Wright *The Climax of the Covenant: Christ and the Law in Pauline Theology*. Edinburgh: T. & T. Clark, 1991/Minneapolis: Fortress, 1992, pp. 56–98 (revision of 'Harpagmos and the Meaning of Philippians ii.5–11', *JTS* ns 37 1986 pp. 321–52; the major, technical treatment of the crucial term in Phil. 2:6).

Commentaries

M. Bockmuehl *The Epistle to the Philippians*. BNTC. London: A. and C. Black, 1997/Peabody: Hendrickson, 1998 (the most recent full treatment of the English text).

G. D. Fee *Paul's Letter to the Philippians*. NIC. Grand Rapids: Eerdmans, 1995 (detailed discussion of English text).

*G. F. Hawthorne *Philippians*. WBC. Waco: Word Books, 1983 (full treatment of the Greek text).

*P. T. O'Brien *The Epistle to the Philippians. A Commentary on the Greek Text*. NIGTC. Grand Rapids: Eerdmans/Carlisle: Paternoster, 1991 (full treatment of the Greek text).

*M. Silva *Philippians*. Chicago: Moody Press, 1988 (essentially a discussion of the Greek text with less emphasis on theology).

Chapter 10

THE LETTER TO PHILEMON

This is the shortest of the surviving letters of Paul, yet even it is quite long by the standards of the personal correspondence of the time that have survived on papyrus in the sands of Egypt. It is sufficiently short that its omission from the New Testament would not have been surprising, but it was probably preserved simply because it was yet another precious fragment from Paul.

Like all the other letters ascribed to Paul (with the exception of those to Timothy and Titus) it is addressed to a Christian congregation rather than to an individual, but nevertheless it is primarily meant for one of the named individuals greeted at the outset. Philemon is greeted as Paul's fellow-worker and the greeting is extended to 'the church in your house'. This must mean that Philemon, as a householder, was the leader of a small Christian group that comprised his household and some friends. Thus Paul addresses them all about a matter that primarily concerns Philemon himself.

THE PEOPLE IN THE STORY

- Paul – former travelling missionary – now confined in a Roman prison;
- Timothy – Paul's younger fellow-worker;
- Philemon – leader of a Christian church in or near Colossae;
- Apphia – probably the wife of Philemon;
- Archippus – another leading Christian in Colossae (cf. Col. 4:17);
- Onesimus ('useful') – a slave belonging to Philemon;
- Epaphras – another missionary colleague of Paul, also now in prison;
- Mark, Aristarchus, Demas, Luke – other colleagues of Paul.

PAUL, PHILEMON AND ONESIMUS

It gradually becomes apparent, after the courteous beginning to the letter, that the real concern is with a slave of Philemon's called Onesimus, a typical slave-name that expressed the hope that its bearer would be a useful member of the household.

Onesimus as a slave had evidently not been useful to his owner, and somehow he had come in contact with Paul in prison. (We are not sure where Paul was in prison. The usual assumption is that it was in Rome. But some scholars think that Ephesus is more likely, being so much nearer to Colossae, and

Caesarea has also been proposed. See the discussion of this point in the section on Colossians pp. 166–7.)

Though concrete evidence is lacking, the traditional understanding of the situation is that he had run away from his master, probably with some stolen goods or money, and somehow came into contact with Paul. This reconstruction assumes that Onesimus was a 'runaway' in the technical sense of a slave attempting to escape from his slavery, and therefore liable to heavy penalties if he was caught and returned to his master.

● But where is the evidence that he was a runaway?
● And how did he come up against Paul the friend of his master in prison?
● And how could Paul have any authority to 'send him back', as if he were somehow in charge of his fate?

HOUSEHOLDS AND SLAVES

Where modern families have vacuum cleaners, washing machines, dishwashers, and many other labour-saving devices and gadgets, their not-so-remote ancestors would have had servants (if they were able to afford them) to do the house-keeping and help to look after the children; even people of quite modest means could hire some help for times of special need such as just after the birth of a new child. In an earlier period these functions were fulfilled by slaves: persons who belonged to their masters and mistresses and who could be bought or sold at prices reflecting their skills and usefulness. In many cities more than a quarter of the population were slaves.

Where the typical modern family consists of parents and children (the so-called 'nuclear' family) the ancient, comparatively well-to-do equivalent was a household that included in addition other relatives and the slaves. Such domestic slavery existed alongside agricultural and industrial slavery where slaves did the work on farms or in other types of industry and commerce including the civil service. People became slaves through being the children of slaves, or through selling themselves in order to pay their debts, or through being prisoners of war. The ancient world depended economically on them and could not have survived without them.

The conditions of service varied enormously. Owners had enormous power over their slaves if they misbehaved, including the right to physical punishment and even execution. Moreover, if slaves ran away, it was the duty of anybody who found them to return them to their owners. At the same time, many slaves worked in good conditions and shared in the fortunes of the families to which they belonged and, in strong contrast to the typical picture of modern slavery as a lot from which there was no escape, it was quite common for ancient slaves to be set free (the process known as 'manumission'), whether on payment of a ransom (either by friends and relatives or out of their own tiny income) or simply at the owner's will. Sometimes manumission was accomplished by a 'fictitious' purchase of the slave for a sum of money by a god:

The Pythian Apollo bought from Sosibius of Amphissa for freedom a female slave, whose name is Nicaea, by race a Roman, at a price of three silver minas and a half-mina. Former seller according to the law was Eumnastus of Amphissa. He has received the price. The deed of sale Nicaea has entrusted to Apollo for freedom. (Inscription from early second century BC at Delphi, in C. K. Barrett *The New Testament Background: Selected Documents*. London: SPCK/San Francisco: Harper & Row, 1987 §54)

The stock picture of slaves is of people who were lazy and dishonest, but this was by no means true of them all, any more than it is true that all Aberdonians are mean and tight-fisted with their money. (See further articles in *DPL*, pp. 1098–1102; *DNTB*, pp. 1124–7.)

These problems make the traditional solution less likely. A better solution may be that Onesimus had fallen out with his master and made his way to Paul as a known friend of Philemon who might give him sanctuary and negotiate on his behalf. In such a situation the slave was not technically a 'runaway', for he intended to return to service. Could it then be that Onesimus was being, as he thought, treated badly by his master, or had he committed some misdemeanour or crime for which he expected to be punished, and did he therefore go to Paul for help? This suggestion entails the fact that Onesimus was not necessarily faced by extreme penalties from his master, and certainly not by the penalty for being a runaway. Nevertheless, he was still in an unpleasant situation.

> I appoint you by this instruction as my representative to journey to the most illustrious Alexandria and search for my slave called . . . aged about 35 years, with whom you too are acquainted, . . . and when you find him you are to deliver him up, having the same powers as I should myself, if present, to . . . imprison him, chastise him and to make an accusation before the proper authorities against those who harboured him, and demand satisfaction. (*Oxyrhynchus Papyri* 14.1643)

Whatever the exact route by which he reached Paul, there now occurred a decisive change in the situation. When Paul comments that he has become Onesimus' 'father', he is using a metaphor found elsewhere in his letters for being the person through whom somebody is brought to Christian faith. In plain terms, Onesimus was converted through the agency of Paul (cf. Timothy in 1 Cor. 4:17; the members of the congregation at Corinth in 1 Cor. 4:14–15). With the conversion there went a change in character, such that Paul could see in this young man a potential for working with him in the Christian mission that continued despite Paul's own imprisonment.

So this letter is written. It is first and foremost Paul's duty to effect the reconciliation between Onesimus and Philemon: to intercede on behalf of Onesimus so that he will be received back and forgiven. That would be essential whether or not Onesimus had become a Christian. Even if he had not been converted, he could still have sought out Paul as the ancient equivalent of an 'Arbitration and Conciliation Advisory Service' and asked for his help on a purely secular level.

What do you think?

Is it always appropriate for Christians to forgive the wrongs they suffer from other people? For example, should a battered wife go on forgiving her husband?

But there was this additional complication that now Onesimus was going back home as a Christian believer. Was that going to make things easier or more difficult? It could have the latter effect. For now Onesimus was a Christian, and all Christians are brothers and sisters to one another.

If this was the first time that Philemon had had to face this situation in reality (as opposed to whatever theoretical teaching he may have received about Christian brotherhood and sisterhood), it could well have been extremely difficult for him to receive back Onesimus not simply as a slave but now as a brother so far as their common faith was concerned.

But it went even further than that. For Paul tells him that now Onesimus is to be to him a beloved brother not just on the spiritual level of their belonging together in the church but also on the ordinary level of their relationship within the household. It's as if Paul is saying: 'he's not to be your brother just on Sunday in church, but on Monday morning as well in the home and the workshop'. It is an enormous demand to make.

Note, however, that there were some people in the ancient world, including the Jewish group known as Essenes (see vol. 1, p. 42), who believed that all human beings were brothers and sisters to one another.

PHILEMON 16

Not a single slave is to be found among them, but all are free, exchanging services with each other, and they denounce the owners of slaves, not merely for their injustice in outraging the law of equality, but also for their impiety in annulling the statute of Nature, who mother-like has born and reared all men alike, and created them genuine brothers, not in mere name, but in very reality, though this kinship has been put to confusion by the triumph of malignant covetousness, which has wrought estrangement instead of affinity and enmity instead of friendship. (From a description of the Essenes in Philo [15 BC – AD 50], *Every Good Man is Free* 79 [LCL; *HCNT* § 846])

Or it could be that the conversion was going to make things easier for Philemon, in that he would find it easier to forgive and accept somebody whose life truly had changed from being useless to really living up to his name as useful.

Digging deeper:
WHAT STRATEGIES OF PERSUASION DOES PAUL USE IN THIS LETTER?

Read through Philemon and assess Paul's strategies of persuasion, using the list of questions below.

- What might be significant about the way in which Paul addresses the letter not just to Philemon but to the congregation as a whole? Is this a legitimate form of pressurization on him?
- How does Paul use his 'prayer report' in which he tells Philemon about his Christian qualities for which he gives thanks to God? Is Philemon the kind of person who is likely to respond positively to Paul's request? Or is Paul guilty of 'buttering him up'?
- What picture does Paul paint of the 'new' Onesimus and his own relationship to him?
- Having intimated that a request is coming in v. 8 when does Paul actually make it?
- Is Paul really offering to pay off any debts that Onesimus has incurred, or is this a way of asking Philemon to write them off (vv. 18–20)?
- What does Paul hope that Philemon will do that will be 'even more than I say' (v. 21)?
- Is v. 22 a veiled threat (I'm coming to see if you've done what I'm asking of you!)?
- Is Paul commanding Philemon (cf. vv. 8, 14, 21) or is he genuinely persuading him?

So that is the major theme of the letter. There is one further complicating factor, which is that, having recognized the potential of Onesimus, Paul hoped that it might be possible for him to spend some time with him as a missionary colleague. In a study of Paul's colleagues a German scholar, W.-H. Ollrog, has developed the plausible theory that Paul expected the congregations he founded to help him in his missionary work not only by their prayers and by their gifts but also by providing personnel on a short or longer term basis to assist him in his work. Paul's hope was that Onesimus might be able to do this as the delegate of the congregation led by Philemon.

The interesting thing now is to see how Paul goes about the matter of persuading Philemon to act in this way.

THE STRUCTURE OF THE LETTER

1–3   OPENING GREETING

4–22   BODY OF THE LETTER (REQUEST)
    4–7   Prayer report
    8–14   Paul's request regarding Onesimus, the new Christian
    15–22 Fuller development of request
        15–16 The new relationship between Onesimus and Philemon
        17–20 The resulting reconciliation with Onesimus
        21–22 Recapitulation and a further request

23–25 CLOSING GREETINGS

A case might be developed that Paul is an authoritarian figure who is wielding the iron fist in a velvet glove. There are scholars who think that he was a self-centred manipulative figure who used all kinds of dubious means to pressurize his converts into doing what he wanted. But it can also be argued that the motivation is entirely genuine. What must not be overlooked is that, whatever some modern people think about tracing power struggles behind every relationship, the ancient world recognized that there were structures of authority, and this was true of the early church where apostles did have a certain authority; the important question was how authority was exercised, and it was important that those in authority learned to follow the example of the 'servant-king' (to use Graham Kendrick's apt phrase).

What do you think?

What kind of authority, if any, should be exercised in the church today? If so, who should have it, and how should it be exercised?

THE OUTCOME

Did the appeal work? Was Philemon persuaded? The odds are heavily in favour of a positive answer. The fact that the letter has been preserved indicates that Philemon responded favourably to it. There was at least reconciliation between Philemon and Onesimus.

But the matter cannot be left there. Paul was confident that Philemon would do even more than he asked (v. 21). What exactly was that 'more'? It is surely difficult to read Philemon in any other sense than that Paul says in effect: 'Onesimus has become a Christian. I would have loved to keep him with me as one of my colleagues, but I wouldn't force the point . . . I am sure that you will do what I ask – and more.' If that is not a request for Onesimus to join Paul's circle, I do not know what more would need to be said.

Moreover, we have the fact that Ignatius wrote in his letter to the church at Ephesus (c. AD 110):

> In God's name I have received your whole multitude in the person of Onesimus whose love passes utterance and who is moreover your bishop. (Ignatius, *Ephesians* 1:3; cf. 6:2)

THE LIBERATION OF SLAVES

The general setting free of slaves was certainly not something advocated by early Christian teachers. Such a revolution would have been totally impracticable in the ancient world and would have led to the downfall of Christianity. But isolated cases could occur (since, as we have noted, manumission was not that uncommon). The important issue is whether the teaching given in this letter, according to which your slave should be your brother or sister both as a fellow-Christian and as a fellow-human being, leads to a situation which is really incompatible with the institution of slavery. It took time for this insight to be appreciated, but is it not the case that if we follow through the implications of this letter we shall move beyond the early Christian acceptance of the *status quo* to the revolutionary stance of William Wilberforce?

It is a not unreasonable suspicion that he is referring to the same person.

But if this reading of Philemon is accepted, then it would surely follow that Onesimus was probably released from slavery. There

Focus on theology

Within the normal Christian format of a Pauline letter, Philemon reflects the defining role of faith and love in deepening the spiritual experience of believers and their sharing with one another that increases their joy. Such qualities can flourish despite adverse circumstances, and they also lead into fresh experiences such as the love relationship between slave-owners and slaves that eventually led to the recognition of the incompatibility of slavery with the gospel. If believers live a life that is determined by a relationship to Christ and so lived 'in him', this has profound effects on interpersonal relationships.

would be no point in Philemon retaining him as a slave if he was letting him go to serve Paul – although it must be confessed that it would be perfectly possible to do so especially if the period of help was regarded as limited.

I therefore side with those who think that Paul was hinting at the manumission of Onesimus in order that he might become a colleague of Paul.

FOR A TWENTY-FIRST-CENTURY PHILEMON

Much of the contemporary relevance of this letter has already emerged above. Here are a further couple of points.

● Consider the letter as an example of how Christian conduct can be understood as the appropriate consequence of acceptance of the gospel.
● Admittedly Paul wrote at length about Philemon's relationship to Onesimus because of his own personal interest in having the latter as his colleague. Allowing for that special element in this case, to what extent should church pastors and elders intervene in what might be regarded as the personal and domestic life of members of the congregation?

ESSAY TOPICS

INTRODUCTORY

● What guidelines for Christian living and social ethics might be drawn from a study of this letter?

INTERMEDIATE

● What are the theological grounds for rejecting slavery? Are there other situations analogous to slavery in the world today that Christians ought to be seeking to change?

FURTHER READING

INTRODUCTORY

F. F. Bruce 'St Paul in Rome: 2. The Epistle to Philemon' *BJRL* 48 1965 pp. 81–97 (excellent, introductory survey).

(K. P. Donfried and) I. H. Marshall *The Theology of the Shorter Pauline Letters*. Cambridge/New York: Cambridge University Press, 1993 pp. 175–91 (brief account of the theology).

W. J. Richardson 'Principle and Context in the Ethics of the Epistle to Philemon' *Int* 22 1968 pp. 301–16 (general study).

INTERMEDIATE

J. M. G. Barclay 'Paul, Philemon and the Dilemma of Christian Slave-Ownership' *NTS* 37 1991 pp. 161–86 (exposes the difficulties and problems in interpreting the letter).

J. D. M. Derrett 'The Functions of the Epistle to Philemon' *ZNW* 79 1988 pp. 63–91 (a lawyer looks at the letter in the light of its background).

M. J. Harris *Slave of Christ: A New Testament Metaphor for total devotion to Christ*. Leicester: Apollos, 1999/Downers Grove: IVP, 2001 (within a broader theological concern contains much useful background on ancient slavery).

N. R. Petersen *Rediscovering Paul: Philemon and the Sociology of Paul's Narrative World*. Philadelphia, Fortress: 1985 (important discussion of the letter from a social-scientific angle).

S. C. Winter 'Paul's letter to Philemon' *NTS* 33 1987 pp. 1–15 (argues for a non-traditional understanding of the setting).

Commentaries

Most commentators treat Colossians and Philemon in the same volumes. Therefore for commentaries on Philemon see the bibliography on Colossians. In addition there are two volumes devoted to Philemon alone:

M. Barth and H. Blanke *The Letter to Philemon*. ECC. Grand Rapids: Eerdmans, 2000 (a mere 579 pp. on a one-page letter!).

J. A. Fitzmyer *The Letter to Philemon*. AB. New York: Doubleday, 2000 (much more compact, but still lengthy).

THE LETTER TO THE COLOSSIANS

In this chapter we shall explore:

● why Paul wrote a letter to a church that he had never visited;

● how he responded to the 'philosophy' that was threatening the congregation;

● whether Paul was in fact the author of the letter.

THE PLANTING OF THE CONGREGATION

Most of Paul's mission work was conducted in the major cities and centres of communication of the Roman world and consequently his letters are addressed to such places. Colossians is the exception. Paul himself had not visited the town, as Col. 2:1 clearly implies. He mentions a local believer called Epaphras as the evangelist who was responsible for the planting of the church (1:7; 4:12–13). What had happened was that as a result of Paul's own missionary work in the provincial capital city of Ephesus 'all the residents of Asia heard the word of the Lord' (Acts 19:10) through the work of Paul's associates in the mission. Epaphras visited Paul and brought news of the congregation, in response to which Paul wrote this letter; Paul describes him as a fellow prisoner (like Aristarchus) in Phlm. 23, although he oddly does not so describe him in Colossians. Whether this means that he voluntarily stayed with Paul to help him in his prison or that he himself had been arrested is not clear; in any case it was not he who took the letter to Colossae but rather Tychicus (4:7).

WHERE WAS COLOSSAE?

The town of Colossae was one of a group of three in an inland area of the Roman province of Asia in the valley of the River Lycus about 100 miles from Ephesus. The other towns were Laodicea (Col. 2:1; 4:13; Rev. 3:14–22) and Hierapolis (Col. 4:13), which also had Christian congregations in them. They were small towns on a Roman road and they were devastated by an earthquake c. AD 60–64. There were Jewish settlements in the region.

WHY WAS THE LETTER WRITTEN?

As with other New Testament letters, we have to resort to what we call mirror-reading in order to try to reconstruct the circumstances that lay behind the writing of the letter.

summary

- Paul had an opportunity to communicate with his friends in this area through a visit that was planned by his colleagues Tychicus and Onesimus. The latter belonged to Colossae (or the neighbourhood) from where he had found his way to Paul, become a Christian and was now about to return. This return journey could well be the same one on which he returned to his master Philemon bearing the letter that dealt with his own situation. Tychicus was a missionary colleague of Paul (also mentioned as a messenger in Eph. 6:21). Admittedly Tychicus is not mentioned in Philemon, but there was no need to do so; the reason why he is mentioned here is to authorize him as a representative to speak on Paul's behalf in addition to being the bearer of the letter – this is a letter of commendation, such as was familiar in the ancient world (cf. 2 Cor. 3:1). Paul, then, would naturally use this occasion to give personal news about his own situation in the light of which his friends could pray for him with fuller understanding (4:2–4).
- At the same time, as a good pastor with a concern for congregations for which he was indirectly responsible, he would offer them some general Christian teaching which would help them to develop in their spiritual life both as individuals and as a church. A good deal of what is said in this letter could have been written to any similar congregation and indeed continues to be relevant to other congregations centuries afterwards.
- However, the letter is also sharply focused on a particular problem that was apparently peculiar to this area. (It is noteworthy that Ephesians, which in many respects stands very close to Colossians in its content, does not reflect this problem.) It is common to speak of 'the Colossian heresy', as if there was a definable body of strange ideas, which had infected the church. Paul, however, saw it as a threat to the congregation, presumably due to outside or marginal influences, rather than as something that had taken hold of them, and therefore his letter has more of the character of a prophylactic than of a cure for an illness. The general impression that we get from the letter is that Paul was grateful for the spiritual state of the church, and his language is that of commendation and warning to them not to get led astray rather than of condemnation of any members of the church and urgent appeal to give up wrong beliefs and practices. But what exactly was this threat?

THE 'PHILOSOPHY'

Various strange beliefs and practices are listed in the letter:
- 'Philosophy and empty deceit, according to human tradition, according to the elemental spirits of the universe.' (2:8, cf. 20)
- 'The rulers and authorities.' (2:15; cf. 1:16; 2:10)
- 'Self-abasement and worship of angels.' (2:18)
- 'Matters of food and drink or of observing festivals, new moons or sabbaths.' (2:16)
- 'Do not handle, Do not taste, Do not touch.' (2:21)
- 'Dwelling on visions.' (2:18)

We came across the same phraseology, 'the elemental spirits of the universe', in Galatians (Gal. 4:3, 9) and saw that the phrase could refer to the individual components of a series (and hence to elementary teaching), to the elements that compose the material world, to the stars and planets, or to cosmic spirits associated with the planets. Each of these possible meanings has been canvassed by scholars. Was Paul simply referring to elementary religious teaching (rather than perhaps to the 'wisdom' that comes from God and that people are incapable of receiving if they are unspiritual)? Or was he thinking of the way in which the four elements of earth, air, fire and water were associated with powers over human beings? Or was he thinking of the influences exercised by the heavenly bodies? When we hear of the 'host of heaven' in Judaism it is not easy to differentiate between the heavenly bodies and heavenly beings. (At a later date the elements were taken up into Gnostic teaching about the hierarchy of powers between God and the material world, but this material is too late for us to be confident about asserting that it was current in the first century.)

In Colossians 2:8 the parallelism with 'human tradition' suggests that the 'elements of the world' is some kind of teaching. In Colossians 2:20 Christians are said to have died to the elemental spirits and need no longer to be governed by various regulations. There is, therefore, a possibility that the reference here is simply to some kind of teaching characteristic of this world as contrasted with divine teaching.

However, in Galatians 4:8f. there is a parallelism between the elements and 'beings that by nature are no gods', and this could suggest that some kind of spiritual powers that issue commands and hold people in their grip are meant.

Further, the centres of power and influence have been overcome by Christ (1:16; 2:10, 15). It is, therefore, possible that the elements are to be linked up with these hostile powers that control the world.

The researches of various scholars, especially of Arnold (1995), have demonstrated that in the religions of Phrygia there was a belief in one high god surrounded by many intermediaries, and in the existence of evil spirits and powers that had tremendous power over people. It would be very natural for converts to Christianity to continue to believe in these beings. We may compare how Christians today can still believe in ghosts and magic and be scared to walk under ladders on Friday because it is an unlucky day, although in their rational minds they should know that this is all superstitious nonsense.

It has also been discovered that the Phrygian religions were hot on ways of dealing with these hostile powers. There were also more friendly powers and these could be induced to provide protection by various ascetic practices. These practices could include various sorts of initiation rites (which could provide occasions for heavenly visions). And just as modern-day Christians may still 'touch wood' to ward off evil influences, so did both Jews and Christians in the ancient world practise ways of warding off evil

'To Zeus Most High and the good angel, Claudius, Achilles and Galatia, with all their household, made a thank offering for deliverance.' (Second-century AD inscription from the neighbouring region of Caria; Arnold 1995, p. 71.)

'The thirty-sixth [sc. heavenly world ruler] said, "And I am called Rhyx Mianeth. I hold a grudge against the body; I demolish houses; I cause the flesh to rot. If anyone writes on the front entrance of his house as follows, 'Melto Ardad Anaath,' I flee from that place." ' (*Testament of Solomon* 18:40, cited from *OTP* I p. 981.)

161

influences. The Judaism of this area was particularly syncretistic, and the requirements of the Jewish law could have been seen as ways of keeping in favour with the angels who were on the side of God's people and could protect them from the hostile powers.

If we put these various things together we can now appreciate how some Christians could have been attracted to similar practices in order to deal with the threat of the hostile powers. The references in Colossians 2 to following regulations with regard to food and drink and to Jewish festivals (new moons and sabbaths are specifically Jewish) and then to self-abasement and worship of angels point clearly in this direction.

This adoption of Jewish practices is something distinct from the judaizing that we came across earlier in Galatians and elsewhere, where the issue was keeping the Jewish law in order to be justified with God. Yet there is a set of references to circumcision in the earlier part of the chapter (2:11, 13), which indicate that the Gentiles were not to think that they needed to be circumcised, and it may be that the old, judaizing insistence on circumcision was also present (though Arnold 1995, p. 296f. disagrees). It was not, however, the main issue.

THE STRUCTURE OF THE LETTER

As with other Pauline letters, there are a number of places where paragraphs have a transitional function and it is a moot point whether they should be attached more closely to what precedes or to what follows; for example, many scholars would regard 1:13–14 as the conclusion of 1:3–12 rather than the commencement of 1:13–23.

1:1–2	SALUTATION
1:3—4:6	BODY OF THE LETTER

	1:3–12	Prayer report
	1:13–23	Christ – head and reconciler
	1:24—2:5	Paul's mission and authority to teach the congregation
	2:6–23	Attack on the false teaching
	3:1—4:6	Exhortation to Christian living (including 'household table')

4:7–18	CLOSING MESSAGES AND GREETINGS

PAUL'S TEACHING IN THE LETTER

We have seen that there are actually two agendas in this letter, one of dealing with the syncretistic teaching and the danger it constituted to the church, and the other of giving general Christian teaching, especially on Christian behaviour. These two agendas are related to one another, in that attention to the heretical teaching and the way of life that it imposed would inevitably tend to diversion from and neglect of the truly Christian way of life. Paul's positive teaching in the first part of the letter is thus meant both to provide a refutation of the heresy and to lay a doctrinal basis for a mature Christian life. Although he does not deal specifically with the heresy until he reaches 2:8, it will quickly emerge that the earlier part of the letter is skilfully designed to lay a foundation for what will be said there.

The letter begins, then, with a prayer report that states both what Paul thanks God for in the present life of the congregation and what he prays may happen with them in the future (1:3–12). Conventional language is used but there is no reason to regard it as other than sincere. The readers are characterized by faith and love, which are motivated by their hope for what God has in store for them in the future. Like people in the rest of the world the gospel had come to them and was like a plant bearing fruit. For the future Paul's prayer is centred on knowledge and understanding, living a life that is appropriate for the people of God, being filled with the spiritual resources to persevere in such a life, and being thankful to God. These themes will recur later in the letter.

It is not easy to be sure where the prayer report ends and Paul slides over into a doctrinal statement about what God has done in making the readers members of his people. Verse 13 begins a doctrinal statement loosely tagged on to the preceding material by a relative pronoun 'who' (lost in most recent translations), and this tagging on with relative pronouns continues in vv. 14 and 15. By v. 15 we have clearly left the prayer behind, and in my view this has already happened at v. 13. What happens is that we get a statement of what God has done in setting the readers free from the power of darkness (note the power language!) and placing them in the kingdom ruled by his Son, and taking away their sins. Here is the basic statement that the readers are no longer under the power of the hostile world and their sins cannot be held against them by anybody.

Then there comes a remarkable statement that describes the authority of God's Son (1:15–20). There is a certain balance about it with vv. 15–17 roughly parallel to vv. 18–20; the former statement affirms the priority and superiority of Christ as the image of God over all of creation, including the various powers, while the latter statement affirms his superiority over the church as the first to rise from the dead and his role as the reconciler of the universe.

Probably the majority of scholars hold that this is a preformed statement which has been incorporated by Paul at this point, perhaps with some editing to make it fit the context better; some even hold that it is a pre-Christian text about some cosmic power which has been christianized. I see no need for these speculations; the text looks as though it has been created to deal specifically with the situation in Colossae, although it could well be based on earlier formulations and phraseology about Christ.

The important thing about it is that it asserts the priority of Christ before creation (like Wisdom in Jewish literature or the Word in John 1) and on that basis can argue that even the powers were created by him and therefore are inferior to him; then it asserts in the same way his superiority over the church. From there it goes on to a new statement, that all the fullness of God was in Christ and that he has reconciled everything in the universe to himself. Therefore there is no need to placate these powers or seek help from any of them. These points are made as assertions, but they would carry weight for Christian readers because the fundamental points (Christ as creator and Christ as exalted and reconciling the world) were already accepted Christian teaching and also because they were made by Paul, a Christian apostle. The mention of reconciliation is important because it enables Paul to remind the readers that their good standing with God depends on their continuation in the faith and not moving away from it (1:21–24).

Then Paul turns to his authority to teach as a servant of the church the secret revealed by God to him that God's purpose is to make people complete in and through Christ; this is why despite his imprisonment

look at the descript of Jesus in col —

163

1 paragraph discuss 1 then look at Top

COLOSSIANS 1:18

For as in an animal the head is the first and best part and the tail the last and meanest, and in fact not a part which helps to complete the list of members, but a means of swishing off the winged creatures which settle on it, so too he means that the virtuous one, whether single man or people, will be the head of the human race and all the others like the limbs of a body which draw their life from the forces in the head and at the top. (Philo [15 BC – AD 50], *On Rewards and Punishments* 125 [LCL; *HCNT* § 803])

Digging deeper

The phrase 'cosmic redemption' is sometimes used to indicate that the scope of God's new creation is wider than just the church. Does Paul have such a concept? What is implied by his reference to 'cosmic reconciliation' in Col. 1:20?

What do you think?

Paul makes frequent references to rebellious superhuman powers: how can we conceptualize this part of his framework of thought? Does it help us to understand the nature of evil better? Is it simply a peculiarity of 'Western culture' to deny the thought of a cosmic power of evil (or powers), and are other contemporary cultures more insightful on this point? In the light of Colossians can you think of modern examples of people with fears that have not been resolved by their Christian faith? How might Paul try to help people overcome these fears?

and the consequent suffering he bends every energy to sharing this knowledge with his readers so that they may receive the fullness of wisdom that comes from Christ. They have been standing firm in this: let them continue to do so (1:24—2:7).

The implication of all this is that all the knowledge and power that they need is contained in Christ and available to them through their faith in him. All divine power is in him and not in any other spiritual entities. As Gentiles they have been fully initiated into a new life through a baptism (symbolized by their water-baptism) as a result of which they have shared in Christ's death and resurrection. Their sins have been forgiven. Not only so, but the

principalities and powers have been disarmed by Christ and are under sentence of death (2:8–15).

So there is no need to fear them or to do things to placate them or to invoke the help of friendly powers. They have died as far as the powers are concerned (just as believers have died to the law, in Galatians 2:19 and Romans 7:4). They need not submit to human regulations as a form of self-abasement to win the favour of the powers (2:16–23).

In this way Paul has dealt with the threat of a diversion from attention to the aspects of the Christian life that really matter. He now summons the readers to be what they really are, people who have died to the sinful world and now live to God. Therefore, they can be told to 'kill' their sinful passions, which include both the baser sins and also the sins that might be thought less reprehensible, but which nevertheless are strongly condemned in the New Testament, the sins of personal

HOUSEHOLD CODES

Col. 3:18—4:1 is the first example that we have seen of sets of instructions given to people who stand in the mutual relationships that existed in the ancient household, wives and husbands; children and fathers; slaves and masters. Similar teaching is found in Eph. 5:21—6:9 and fragmentary instructions in 1 Tim. 6:1f.; Titus 2:9f.; 1 Pet. 2:18—3:7, sometimes supplemented by teaching to other groups within the community and household. A fixed form of instruction is being followed, known to us from other ancient sources, particularly from documents on household management, e.g.:

> And now that it is clear what are the component parts of the state, we have first of all to discuss household management; for every state is composed of households. Household management falls into departments corresponding to the parts of which the household in turn is composed; and the household in its perfect form consists of slaves and freemen. The investigation of everything should begin with its smallest parts, and the primary and smallest parts of the household are master and slave, husband and wife, father and children; we ought therefore to examine the proper constitution and character of each of these three relationships, I mean that of mastership, that of marriage (there is no exact term denoting the relation uniting wife and husband), and thirdly the progenitive relationship (this too has not been designated by a special name). Let us then accept these three relationships that we have mentioned. There is also a department which some people consider the same as household management and others the most important part of it, and the true position of which we shall have to consider: I mean what is called the art of getting wealth.

> Let us begin by discussing the relation of master and slave, in order to observe the facts that have a bearing on practical utility, and also in the hope that we may be able to obtain something better than the notions at present entertained, with a view to the theoretic knowledge of the subject. For some thinkers hold the function of the master to be a definite science, and moreover think that household management, mastership, and statesmanship and monarchy are the same thing, as we said at the beginning of the treatise; others however maintain that for one man to be another's master is contrary to nature, because it is only convention that makes the one a slave and the other a freeman and there is no difference between them by nature, and therefore it is unjust, for it is based on force.

> Since therefore property is a part of a household and the art of acquiring property a part of household management (for without the necessities even life, as well as the good life, is impossible), and since, just as for the definite arts it would be necessary for the proper tools to be forthcoming if their work is to be accomplished, so also the management of a household must have his tools and of tools some are lifeless and others living (for example, for a helmsman the rudder is a lifeless tool and the lookout man a live tool – for an assistant in the arts belongs to the class of tools), so also an article of property is a tool for the purpose of life, and property generally is a collection of tools, and a slave is a live article of property. (Aristotle, *Politics* 1.2.1–4. Aristotle [384–322 BC] was one of the two greatest Greek philosophers, and wrote in much detail on many aspects of knowledge.)

relationships. Perhaps surprisingly, there is a reminder that they are now new people in a new situation where racial and social distinctions are irrelevant – and, therefore, not to be seen as barriers between people (3:1–11).

The readers have been told to put their minds on 'things above'; these turn out to be the qualities of Christian character in which people love one another, live peaceable lives, submit to the teaching of Christ and only do what they can do in the name of Jesus (3:12—4:6).

Within this section specific instruction is given on behaviour in the family or household (3:18—4:1).

The content of Paul's teaching is not dissimilar to that in secular sources, and it is clear (especially from 1 Peter) that one aim of the teaching was that Christians would show the expected respect and conformity to custom and so commend the gospel; advocates of 'women's lib' in the first century would have created enormous difficulties for evangelism. The general rule is that Christian obedience to Christ includes respect for the social norms.

The letter closes with a remarkably long set of notes about various people who send greetings or are to be greeted (4:7–18). From them we can see something of the variety of people who worked with Paul in his mission, free and slaves, male and female, Jewish and Gentile. There is also the typically Pauline emphasis on the need for prayer both for himself and for the congregations. We also

Digging deeper

Compare Col. 3:18—4:1 with the passage from Aristotle (p. 165). What are the similarities and the differences? Does it surprise you that Paul's instruction is so similar to that of his non-Christian contemporaries? What, if anything, is specifically Christian about the practical teaching that is given in Colossians? Certainly the Christian teaching goes beyond the secular in its motivation of serving the Lord and gaining his approval and in the stress on love and the fact that masters are as much subject to God's judgement as are slaves. But does that make a real difference? Is Paul's teaching really nothing more than ordinary rules for decent living, such as any good ethical teacher of the time might have offered?

learn (what we might well have guessed) that letters to one congregation would be shared with others in the neighbourhood.

What do you think?

How do you think that Paul would word his instructions for Christians in family and employment relationships today?

PAUL'S CIRCUMSTANCES

In Colossians 4:3 Paul mentions that he is in prison and also refers to a certain Aristarchus as his fellow-prisoner (4:10). This narrows down the possible periods in his life at which this letter may have been written. Further, the distinctive vocabulary which he uses about both Christ and the church in this letter (see 1:18) can be seen as a development of his earlier thinking; since he does not use it in the same way elsewhere (except in Ephesians), this would suggest that this letter belongs to a period after his other correspondence with the churches. These two arguments point to one of the times when we know for certain that Paul was imprisoned for a lengthy period of time, namely the imprisonments in Caesarea and in Rome. The traditional view of the letter is that it was sent from Rome. The argument for this view rests on the assumption that the letter belongs to the same period as Philippians, which (as we concluded earlier) was most probably written from Rome.

OTHER POSSIBLE PLACES OF ORIGIN
Nevertheless, the case for another origin bears examination. An analysis of the possibilities must also take into account any clues that can be gleaned from Philemon,

since there is every indication that Colossians and Philemon belong together.

Caesarea has also had its supporters. The argument is that Paul refers to himself in Phlm. 9 as 'now also a prisoner', which suggests that he has newly become a prisoner and thus fits Caesarea rather than Rome, and that Paul expected to be taken overland to Rome via the road through Asia Minor and then onwards across northern Greece to the Adriatic coast by the Via Egnatia, so that a visit to Colossae on the way would be feasible (Phlm. 22). The second of these points does not constitute an argument for the hypothesis but merely explains what would have been possible if it were true; while the first of them reads too strong a nuance into the phrase. The case is weak.

A stronger case can be made for *Ephesus*. We saw, however, that Philippians could not have been written from Ephesus unless it was known Roman practice to call the governor's HQ the 'praetorium', and so far, despite the plentiful references that we have to this term, none have the desired reference. However, Ephesus would be a possibility if Colossians belonged to a different period of imprisonment from that to which Philippians is assigned. Ephesus is much nearer than Rome is to Colossae, so that communications would have been much easier. But otherwise there are no really strong pointers to Ephesus, and this theory would probably require placing Colossians earlier than Romans, which is very unlikely.

We are left with the conclusion that Paul's Roman imprisonment is the most likely option without being able to offer any compelling proof of the point.

DID PAUL WRITE COLOSSIANS?

So far we have simply assumed that Colossians is a genuine letter by Paul. One of the main arguments in favour of this assumption is simply that the reconstruction of the situation and the way in which the writer of the letter responds to it makes sense in the context of Pauline authorship.

However, we have seen earlier, in the case of 2 Thessalonians, that suspicions may arise where a letter attributed to Paul is not written in his characteristic style, reflects a situation that doesn't correspond with that of his lifetime, or says things that go beyond or outside what Paul might reasonably be expected to say. Many scholars feel such difficulties about this letter. What kind of arguments arise in this particular case?

ARGUMENTS AGAINST PAULINE AUTHORSHIP

- The *vocabulary* and *style* are different from those of Paul. There is a large number of unpauline words (see the lists in Lohse 1971 pp. 84–91). The syntactical style is rather full and loose, with lots of genitives, a lack of infinitives, a love of participles, etc. The way in which the argument is conducted is unpauline.
- Some of the *doctrinal teaching* is unpauline. The christology in 1:15–20 is new. Christ is said to be the 'firstborn' and the 'beginning'; he contains the fullness of deity. Believers are said to be already raised with him (3:1; they have newness of life in Rom. 6, but are not explicitly said to be 'raised'). There is no mention of the Holy Spirit. Whereas in earlier letters the church is likened to a body, here the imagery is developed by reference to Christ as its head (1:18).
- The *position of authority* ascribed to Paul and Epaphras is typical of later claims

made for the transmitters of church tradition.

- The long *list of greetings* could have been copied from Philemon in an attempt to persuade readers that the letter was really from Paul.

- A *later occasion* for the letter is feasible. It could have been written to defend Pauline doctrine against Gnostic inroads after his death. The writer used Paul's name to indicate the kind of things that he would have said if he had still been there to say them and to invoke his authority for them.

ARGUMENTS IN FAVOUR OF PAULINE AUTHORSHIP

Such points need to be carefully examined to see whether they are demonstrable and will bear the burden of proof.

- The *vocabulary* is not strange, and some of the unusual words belong to the discussion of the 'heresy'. We may compare four letters of roughly the same length, two of which are certainly by Paul and two that are doubtful. (The Pastoral Epistles are excluded from the reckoning because of the stronger doubts over their authenticity.) It is clear that there is no distinction between the four letters on this point.

	Gal.	Phil.	Col.	Eph.
Total no. of words	526	448	431	529
No. of words not used elsewhere by Paul	98	85	74	94
Percent. of words not used elsewhere by Paul	18.6	18.9	17	17.6

- The *style* is more of a problem. Two major books have been written, arguing respectively for the presence and absence of Pauline features. Some differences can be established, but then we must ask: how far can one and the same author vary his style?

- The *doctrinal* teaching does contain elements not found in the earlier letters of Paul. But did Paul never develop or change his theology, especially to cope with new situations, or pick up material from other Christians? May not the presence of heresy have been a catalyst to make him work it out more fully?

- Paul claims a similar position of *authority* for himself and his colleagues in his earlier letters (e.g. Rom. 16:1f. and, strikingly, Phlm. 17).

- The *list of greetings* is not strange in a letter written at the same time as Philemon.

- The *early church* accepted Colossians as readily as any other letter of Paul.

Thus it is an arguable position that, although the letter does have some differences in style and theology from other letters of Paul, these are not sufficient to call its authenticity into question as a later letter of Paul rising to the demands of a new situation. Some scholars resolve the problem by proposing that the letter was written in Paul's name by a colleague with a good deal of freedom – specifically Timothy, who is named as a co-author; to it Paul then attached his autograph as an indication that he accepted it as his own letter (4:18).

What do you think?

Which set of arguments on the authorship of Colossians do you find more persuasive, and why?

FOR TODAY'S COLOSSIANS

- Consider what the Christian response to post-modernism should be in the light of the way in which the cosmic lordship of Christ in every area of human thought and life is asserted in this letter.

● 'Hold to Christ, and for the rest be totally uncommitted' (H. Butterfield *Christianity and History*. London: Collins, 1957 p. 189): read the letter as a possible justification of this precept for life.

● Note the central place that prayer by Paul for his readers (and by them for him) has in this letter (and in his other letters) and what he prays for. Compare the place and nature of intercession in your congregation.

Focus on theology

Faced by an apparent threat to Christian faith caused by some kind of intellectual teaching which led to subservience to alien powers and found expression in a new kind of legalistic ritualism, Paul develops the implications of his earlier teaching about the person of Christ. He emphasizes his superiority to all other powers in the universe in virtue of his being the Son of God who shared in creation, who is filled with divine power and exercises it throughout the universe, and whose death and resurrection are the only and fully adequate means of defeating the hostile powers and restoring the universe to peace with God. Believers have no cause to fear the rebellious powers and follow their commands. They constitute the church, which is like a body of which Christ is the head, and which is commissioned to proclaim this reconciliation with God that specifically brings together Jews and Gentiles. They are joined to Christ and his power flows through them to enable a new way of peaceable and loving behaviour that anticipates the life to come.

ESSAY TOPICS

INTRODUCTORY

● In what ways is the teaching about Christ in Colossians a development from what Paul says in his earlier letters about him?
● Write an article for a thoughtful magazine (such as *Time* or *Newsweek*) expressing how you think Paul would respond to 'New Age' beliefs in the light of the way in which he argues in Colossians.

INTERMEDIATE

● Explore and assess the other suggestions that have been offered by scholars regarding the nature of the teaching opposed by Paul in Colossians.

● List the different types of language used in Colossians to explain the way in which people are saved (redemption, resurrection, etc.) and their resulting status (saints, believers, etc.) and do a fuller study of one or more of them in the light of the broader usage in the New Testament.

FURTHER READING

*denotes books assuming knowledge of Greek; most can be used by all students.

INTRODUCTORY
C. E. Arnold *Powers of Darkness: Principalities and Powers in Paul's Letters*. Downers Grove: InterVarsity Press, 1992.
(A. T. Lincoln and) A. J. M. Wedderburn *The Theology of the Later Pauline Letters*. Cambridge/New York: Cambridge University Press, 1993 (careful study of the theology).

Commentaries
R. P. Martin *Colossians and Philemon*. NCB. London: Oliphants, 1978/Grand Rapids: Eerdmans, 1981 (entrance-level).

M. M. Thompson *Colossians and Philemon* Grand Rapids: Eerdmans, 2005 (stresses the theology of the letters).

B. J. Walsh and S. C. Keesmaat, *Colossians Remixed: Subverting the Empire*. Downers Grove: IVP/Milton Keynes: Paternoster, 2005 (commentary writing like you've never seen it before. You'll love it, even if you don't agree with all of it).

N. T. Wright *Colossians and Philemon*. TNTC. Leicester: InterVarsity Press/Grand Rapids: Eerdmans, 1986 (short, but stimulating).

INTERMEDIATE

*C. E. Arnold *The Colossian Syncretism: The Interface Between Christianity and Folk Belief at Colossae*. Tübingen: Mohr, 1995 (major technical study of the 'heresy' at Colossae).

M. D. Hooker 'Were There False Teachers in Colossae?' in B. Lindars and S. S. Smalley (eds) *Christ and Spirit in the New Testament: Studies in Honour of Charles Francis Digby Moule*. Cambridge: Cambridge University Press, 1973 pp. 315–31 (argues that there weren't!).

T. J. Sappington *Revelation and Redemption at Colossae*. Sheffield: Sheffield Academic Press, 1991 (specialist monograph on main themes of the letter).

W. Wink *Engaging the Powers: Discernment and Resistance in a World of Domination*. Philadelphia: Fortress, 1992.

N. T. Wright *The Climax of the Covenant: Christ and the Law in Pauline Theology*. Edinburgh: T. & T. Clark, 1991/Minneapolis: Fortress, 1992, pp. 99–119 (reprint of 'Poetry and Theology in Colossians 1:15–20' *NTS* 36 1990 pp. 444–68; detailed study of the major christological passage).

Commentaries

F. F. Bruce *The Epistles to the Colossians, to Philemon, and to the Ephesians*. NIC. Grand Rapids: Eerdmans, 1984 (middle-length by an outstanding commentator on Paul).

*J. D. G. Dunn *The Epistles to the Colossians and to Philemon*. NIGTC. Grand Rapids: Eerdmans/Carlisle: Paternoster, 1996 (probably the best on the Greek text for the beginner).

*E. Lohse *Colossians and Philemon*. Herm. Philadelphia: Fortress Press, 1971 (translation of major, technical German commentary).

*P. T. O'Brien *Colossians, Philemon*. WBC. Waco: Word, 1982 (detailed, middle-length work).

Chapter 12

THE LETTER TO THE EPHESIANS

In this chapter we shall tackle these questions in turn:

- the readers of the letter;
- the twin agendas of the writer;
- the development of the message;
- the unusual features that raise doubts about Pauline authorship and an assessment of them.

The letter to the Ephesians is surrounded by greater uncertainties than any of those that we have considered so far. To whom was it sent? What exactly is it, and what is its situation and purpose? And by whom was it composed?

As a starting point we may observe that the paragraph which deals with the transmission

PAUL AND EPHESUS

Ephesus was an ancient Greek city with a long history and by this time a major city of the Roman empire, the capital of the province of Asia, an important and prosperous commercial and administrative centre. Extensive remains have been excavated, including a theatre with a seating capacity of 24,000 people.

Not surprisingly after a brief preliminary visit at the end of his second missionary campaign (Acts 18:18–21) Paul spent the major part of his third campaign, amounting to at least two years, establishing a congregation in Ephesus (Acts 19) and, after a further trip to Macedonia and Greece, he had further contact with the leaders of the church at a meeting in Miletus on his subsequent return journey to Jerusalem (Acts 20:17–38).

- Read the story of Paul's contacts with Ephesus in Acts 18—20.

Luke has confined himself to the more exciting incidents in the story and is tantalizingly silent on much else that we would like to know. Since Paul faced hostility in the city and since we know that he endured several imprisonments in the course of his travels (2 Cor. 11:23), the odds are very high that at least one of these imprisonments happened during the lengthy time that he was in Ephesus.

Later, according to 1 Timothy, he left Timothy in charge of the continuation of the mission work in Ephesus (1 Tim. 1:3).

of the letter to the recipients by the hand of Tychicus is identical with the wording of the corresponding paragraph in Colossians (cf. Eph. 6:21–22 with Col. 4:7–8.; cf. 2 Tim. 4:12). This would imply that the letter was sent (or was intended to be understood as sent) to some other group(s) of believers on the same trip, and therefore at the same time and presumably in the same region.

TO WHOM WAS THE LETTER SENT?

Sometimes scholars think that the wording or development of ideas in a biblical text doesn't make good sense, and they rearrange or rewrite the material to offer better sense, although there is no objective basis for doing so. We have seen an example of this in the dissection of 2 Corinthians. At other times, problems arise because there are different versions of the text in the various manuscripts that have been handed down, and we need to decide which version (if any) is original, what it signifies, and how the other versions developed. This is our difficulty with Ephesians.

The oldest manuscripts of this letter begin:

> Paul, an apostle of Christ Jesus by the will of God, to the saints who are also faithful in Christ Jesus.

What we expected to read, of course, and what we do find in some translations of the New Testament, is a wording which includes some precise reference to the destination of the letter:

> Paul, an apostle of Christ Jesus by the will of God, to the saints who are at Ephesus and also faithful in Christ Jesus.

The latter wording is based on the majority of the manuscripts, and causes no great

surprise, although you might be puzzled as to why Paul says that the saints are '*also* faithful'. Since it was Paul's practice to keep in contact with the congregations that he founded, the composition of a letter to Ephesus would not be at all surprising, perhaps indeed something to be strongly expected.

Nevertheless, there is the fact that the oldest known form of the letter does not mention Ephesus, and the later wording is rather awkward in the Greek, as if somebody had made a clumsy interpolation to fill a surprising gap. Other factors are also relevant:

- The writer writes to the readers as if he and they were personally unacquainted with each other (1:15; 3:2).
- There are no concrete details about the readers or indications that the letter is written to a specific audience and situation, although every other Pauline letter to named recipients reflects something of a local situation.

These points are sufficient to demonstrate that this is not a letter in the usual sense to one specific congregation that was well known to Paul. Hence three questions arise:

- **What kind of document was this?** It certainly has the general shape of a letter with the usual formal features. Was it then originally sent to a congregation that was unknown to Paul or to a group of churches (to be passed round from one to another; cf. Col. 4:16) or simply to Christians in general wherever they happened to be? In this last case it would be a so-called 'catholic' epistle (cf. the very general addressees in 2 Pet. 1:1 and Jude 1). One often-repeated suggestion is that the letter may have been meant for a number of churches, each of whose names could have been inserted in a gap in 1:1. (We know of no precedents for this technique, but that does not mean that it could not have happened.)

- **Was it sent to any particular destination?** The facts that it was later thought to be for Ephesus and that it has links to Colossians strongly suggest that it may have been meant for congregations in Asia. This is a very early guess. The second-century Christian Marcion identified it with the letter to Laodicea of Col. 4:16, and the modern scholar A. Harnack followed this up with the unlikely suggestion that the name had been excised because Laodicea turned out to be an unfaithful congregation (Rev. 3:16)! But Paul's lost letter to Laodicea would probably not have been so formal and impersonal. Nevertheless, the hypothesis that the letter was meant for Asian congregations in general remains very plausible.
- **How did the name of Ephesus get attached to it?** We cannot be sure. If it was a letter intended for several congregations, a copy may have been sent to Ephesus or otherwise have come into the possession of the church. Or at a later date it was assumed that Paul must have sent a letter to such a major congregation as the one at Ephesus and that this was it. It would certainly have been possible for somebody to relate Eph. 6:21f. to 2 Tim. 4:12 and draw an obvious conclusion.

WHAT IS THE LETTER?

Probably the most common route into the problem of Ephesians is by way of Colossians. The two letters share the same broad shape, with a first part that is essentially doctrinal and a second part that is essentially practical. Their theological vocabulary and ideas are very similar and set them apart from the other Pauline letters, and they share a remarkable amount of wording with each other, although (except in Eph. 6:21f.) the common words and phrases are combined in very different ways. Ephesians knows nothing of the particular heresy that was threatening the church at Colossae. It has often been said that, whereas Colossians is more about Christ, Ephesians is more about the church, and specifically about the unity of Jewish and Gentile believers in Christ. The style of Ephesians is also somewhat different, with a greater tendency, particularly in Eph. 1—3, to the composition of extremely long rambling sentences. For example, the heart of Eph. 1 consists of two long Greek sentences, 1:3–14 and 15–23, although English translations break them down for readability. To some extent these peculiarities of style may be attributed to the fact that here Paul is using the language of prayer rather than of argument, and the prayers tend to drift over into instruction of the readers.

The letter may be characterized in part as a celebration of the salvation that is experienced by the writer and his readers, set in a context of praising God for what he has already done (Eph. 1—2) and praying for what he will do in the future (Eph. 3). As is common in expressions of praise, the writer describes the nature of salvation, so that he is simultaneously teaching the readers, making them more fully aware of the nature of their experience; in doing so he clearly wishes to remind them of certain important aspects of their salvation which have practical implications (Eph. 4—6) and also to enable them to praise God with greater understanding of the wonder of his love for them.

Two specific agendas underlie this presentation.

THE UNITY OF THE CHURCH

The first of them is a concern to emphasize the unity of the church. In Ephesians 1 and 2 there is a curious alternation of the pronouns 'we/us' and 'you'.

What do you think?

Go through a copy of the letter and underline the two sets of pronouns ('we/us' and 'you') in Eph. 1—3: can you see any pattern in their use?

It seems most likely that 'we' refers to the author and his Jewish Christian compatriots and that 'you' refers to the readers, understood as Gentile Christians (see especially 2:11), although he can also use 'we' to refer to 'all of us who are Christians'. He uses this device to describe how the readers as Gentiles have come to share in the spiritual blessings in Christ that originally came to Jewish believers in Christ. He is trying to express the wonderful character of salvation and at the same time to emphasize that through it the Gentiles, who once were excluded from the blessings given to the Jewish people, now fully share in them through Christ.

Now that they are incorporated into one Christian community he urges them to maintain this unity, and in chapter 4 he develops this theme in a way that is separate from the Jew/Gentile issue, by describing how God has given various different gifts to the church in the form of people with different functions, such as evangelism, pastoral care and teaching, so that together they may enable believers to grow in faith,

knowledge and love and not be led astray by false teaching.

A further aspect of this is that the practical teaching that follows is concerned with weaning the Gentile believers away from the kind of dissolute life that was assumed by Jews to be characteristic of them (although 2:3 shows that Paul was not so naive as to assume that the Jews themselves were free from such tendencies).

'POWER' LANGUAGE

A further underlying agenda is indicated by what has been called the 'power' language in the letter.

What do you think?

Go through the whole letter and mark the various words indicative of power, authority and might, noting in each case who has the power. What does the use of these words suggest to you about Paul's concerns in the letter?

The preponderance of such language, comparable with what we have seen in Colossians, indicates that, alongside the problem of sins that needed to be forgiven, the readers also faced the problem of supernatural, evil powers that were thought to influence and even control their destiny. There is no indication that the readers were attempting to deal with this problem in the sort of way that is condemned in Colossians, but they were still affected by it. Therefore in this letter the superior power of Christ is strongly emphasized; what God is doing through the creation of the church is to defeat these beings. What might appear to be simply a conflict initiated by human beings who persecute the church and imprison its members (including Paul, Eph. 6:20) is in fact a battle in which believers are attacked by these supernatural powers, but for which God has provided them with the resources for victory.

What do you think?

Understanding the life of the believer and the church as a spiritual battle against the devil and other cosmic powers (Eph. 6:10–17) is not a natural idiom for many Christians today. How, if at all, can this way of thinking be helpful in the modern world?

THE STRUCTURE OF THE LETTER

1:1–2   OPENING GREETING

1:3—6:20 BODY OF THE LETTER
  1:3–14   Thanksgiving (berakah) for salvation for both 'us' and 'you'
  1:15–23   Prayer report, asking for spiritual enlightenment
  2:1–22   Theological description of the readers' conversion, leading to a reminder that reconciliation is 'horizontal' and 'vertical'
  3:1–21   Further prayer report, incorporating meditation on the 'mystery' that the Gentiles are included in God's plan
  4:1–16   Appeal to live in unity in the church
  4:17—5:20 The new life in contrast to the old
  5:21—6:9 Christian relationships in the household
  6:10–20   Appeal to readers to share in spiritual conflict

6:21–4   CLOSING NEWS AND GREETINGS

A QUICK SURVEY OF THE LETTER

The broad structure of the letter is plain. Since Paul is not writing to a specific congregation he does not begin with a prayer report that catalogues particular aspects of their spiritual progress, but instead he uses a general thanksgiving (equivalent to a Jewish berakah; cf. 2 Cor. 1:3–4; 1 Pet. 1:3–9; Luke 1:68–79) in which he thanks God for his gift of salvation, planned in eternity past and now realized in the lives of himself and his readers (1:1–14).

What do you think?

Read Eph. 1:9–10. Think through, with the aid of one or two commentaries, what Paul means here and what the passage implies for God's purpose for his creation.

From this thanksgiving he moves naturally into a prayer for the spiritual progress of the readers, which is principally concerned with a fuller realization of the spiritual resources that they now have through Christ, and here he stresses the superior power of Christ to every opposing power in the universe (1:15–23).

In 2:1 the main verb 'he made alive' found in some translations (RSV; cf. AV [KJV]) is not present in the Greek; what we actually have in vv. 1–3 is a long description of the state of the readers before their conversion, a situation of death and condemnation; then in vv. 4–5 the writer at last gets to the main verb as he elaborates on what God in his mercy has done to deliver these people from death in sin. There is a stark contrast in the

175

original sentence between the total hopelessness in 2:1–3 and the astounding deliverance in 2:4–7.

The new element in this description of what God has done is the insistence that the reconciliation of both Jews and Gentiles to God through the cross is at the same time the bringing of them together in one people, thus breaking down the former barriers that existed between them (2:11–22).

EPHESIANS 2:14

No foreigner is to enter within the fence and enclosure surrounding the sanctuary. Whoever is caught so doing will himself be the cause of his ensuing death. (Jerusalem temple inscription [first century AD; *Orientis Graecae Inscriptiones Selectae* 598; *HCNT* § 526])

Digging deeper

In 2:1–10 what are the marks of the readers' states before and after their conversion? How has the change happened? Can this description be regarded as typical of conversions to Christianity in general?

It took a long time for Jews and Gentiles to realize that the age-long, deeply seated division between them was now overcome. In chapter 3 Paul therefore spends time referring to the way in which this realization had come about through a new revelation of God's purpose given to the Christian apostles and prophets and especially to himself (3:1–13). A further prayer for the readers that they may know the love and power of God follows appropriately (3:14–21).

Now that God has brought together diverse people in the one church, it is important that they maintain and grow more fully into their unity. This is to be accomplished through the rich variety of gifts with which God has endowed the church. Here we may have an echo of the problems in Corinth where there tended to be rivalry between people with different gifts (and their partisans) instead of working together to build up the body (4:1–16).

The practical instruction in the remainder of the letter (4:17—6:20) is very similar to that in Colossians but it is developed more fully throughout, and particularly in the extended treatment of the way in which husbands should love their wives (5:25–33).

In the course of this exposition of life in the church we can detect various new emphases:

- The concept of a plan of God that is being worked out in history is expressed. God's plan to create a church composed of his sons and daughters and his purpose to reunite his divided universe in Christ goes back to before the creation of the world (1:3–14; 2:11–22; 3:7–13).
- The understanding of Christ as the person in whom all the fullness of God himself is present is shared with Colossians (1:23). This divine power is effective in the lives of believers since Christ can be said to be in them (3:17).
- Christ himself as the agent of all that God does to bring salvation and victory to his people. The phrase 'in Christ' is frequently included to indicate that Christ is the agent through whom God acts (1:3, 10, 20; 3:11; 4:32). At the same time, the Holy Spirit also has a vital role as the agent of salvation (1:13; 2:18, 22; 3:16; 4:3f.).
- The state of the Christian believer as one of resurrection from 'death' to new life

(2:5f.), so that believers can be said to be now 'in the heavenly places' (1:3; 2:6), although this does not remove them from the sphere of the hostile powers (3:10).

- Whereas in earlier writings Paul uses the term 'church' (Gk. *ekklesia*) predominantly to mean a single congregation of believers, here (and also in Col. 1:18, 24) he envisages one universal church composed of all believers everywhere, which constitutes the body of which Christ is the head (1:22; 3:10, 21; 5:23–33).

WHO WROTE THE LETTER?

As in the case of Colossians, we have assumed so far that the letter is what it appears to be, namely a composition by Paul himself. But we have already unearthed some points that raise similar doubts about the origin of the letter. There is the general closeness of the letter to Colossians, itself of questionable authorship, and the fact that Ephesians seems to go even further than Colossians in its development of new theological ideas. There is also the unusual general character of the composition, unlike any other letter of Paul in its somewhat impersonal nature. These points must now be supplemented by others that combine to produce a formidable case.

ARGUMENTS AGAINST PAULINE AUTHORSHIP

- **Language and style** Although a knowledge of Greek is necessary to appreciate the full impact of the argument, the English reader can still recognize that the style is somewhat different. The sentences are extraordinarily long and ponderous. Some of the phraseology, especially the strings of genitives, is unusual (e.g. 'the working of the power of his might', Eph. 1:19).

- **Theological differences** Different words are used for familiar Pauline expressions (Paul always refers to 'Satan', but we have 'devil' in 4:27; 6:11; Paul uses 'justify', but we have 'save' in 2:5, 8). Some words are used with slightly different senses; 'mystery' is used especially of God's purpose for the universe (1:9; 3:3–4, 9; 5:32; 6:19), whereas elsewhere it is used in more varied ways; 'economy' is elsewhere the task of a church leader (as in Eph. 3:2), but here it is God's plan of salvation (1:10; 3:9). Whereas in 1 Cor. 12 the head was just one of the parts of the body, now it is identified as Christ (1:22; 4:15; 5:23; so also in Col. 1:18; 2:19). There is little reference to his death and *parousia*. There is, it is said, a much more positive view of marriage than in 1 Cor. 7.

- **Relation to earlier letters** There are many parallels with striking passages in Paul's earlier letters that suggest that Ephesians is the work of a person who knew them and wove together a new tapestry on the basis of the earlier materials. Compare Eph. 1:3 and 2 Cor. 1:3; Eph. 1:13 and 2 Cor. 1:22; Eph. 3:7 with Rom. 12:3 and 1 Cor. 3:10; Eph. 3:8 and 1 Cor. 15:9f.; Eph. 4:28 with 1 Cor. 4:12; Eph. 4:16 + 5:23 and 1 Cor. 11:3; Eph. 5:2 + 5:25 and Gal. 2:20.

What do you think?

In what ways is the theology of the church in Colossians and Ephesians different from, or a development of, the teaching in Paul's earlier letters? (Consider in particular the foundation of the church [2:20], the use of the terms 'body' and 'head' [1:22f.; 4:15f.], and the teaching about spiritual gifts and ministry [4:1–16].)

- **Atmosphere** The theological atmosphere is said to be typical of *early catholicism*, the post-apostolic type of theology: the church was regarded as an institution dispensing salvation, increasing veneration was paid to the apostles and theology became backward looking. The emphasis on Paul's role as apostle to the Gentiles (Eph. 3:1, 8) and on the foundational position of 'apostles and prophets' in the church (Eph. 2:20; 3:5) could point to this later period.
- **Relation to Colossians** The final point is admittedly somewhat ambiguous. There is a large amount of common phraseology shared by Ephesians and Colossians. This would not be surprising were it not for the varied way in which the same words and phrases are used. But it is difficult to assess its significance. There are four different theories:

1. Somebody used Colossians as a source or model for Ephesians.
2. Both Colossians and Ephesians are based on some earlier document that is no longer extant ('S' in the diagram below).
3. There are places where Colossians looks less developed than Ephesians and places where the reverse is the case. So perhaps there was an earlier version of Colossians, on which somebody based Ephesians, and then later somebody revised Colossians in the light of Ephesians. (It does make you wonder what kind of people the early Christians were and whether they had files on disk long before the rest of us had computers!)
4. The resemblances are due to one author writing both Colossians and Ephesians at the same time.

In diagrammatic form these theories can be represented as follows:

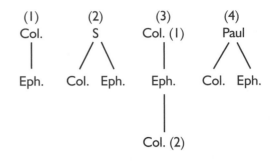

Any of the first three of these interpretations of the evidence is hard to harmonize with Pauline authorship.

Digging deeper

Consider the following parallel passages in Colossians and Ephesians and discuss whether they are explicable as the work of one and the same author using the same basic thoughts and ideas in different ways or demand some other explanation: Eph. 1:4/Col. 1:22; Eph. 1:7/Col. 1:14, 20; Eph. 1:15–16/Col. 1:4, 9; Eph.3:1–5/Col. 1:25–7; Eph. 3:9/Col. 1:26; Eph. 4:2/Col. 3:12; Eph. 4:31–32/Col. 3:8, 12; Eph. 5:19f./Col. 3:16; Eph. 6:21–22/Col. 4:7.

These arguments convince many scholars that Ephesians is the work of a disciple of Paul who has written a sort of catholic epistle closely based on his teaching in his other letters. It was perhaps meant to recall Christians in Asia to Paul's gospel. An older suggestion is that the letter was written to stand as a kind of introduction to a later collection of Paul's writings; but we do not know of any such collection in which Ephesians occupied the first position. The view that somebody summed up Paul's teaching and formulated it in a new way to give us what has been called 'the quintessence of Paulinism' is more probable. Tychicus and Luke have been suggested as authors; the former suggestion is irrefutable, since we have no other composition with which to compare it, while the latter is refuted by the rather different style and theological idiom of Acts.

ARGUMENTS FOR PAULINE AUTHORSHIP

- The vocabulary is Pauline (see on Colossians, p. 168). The unusual style could be partly due to the use of liturgical phraseology (many of us tend to adopt a different style of speech when we are praying). One scholar says that the style is 'more liturgical than controversial'. Traditional ethical material has also been used.
- The theology does go further than Paul's earlier statements. The question is whether Paul himself could not have created the same developments as are here being ascribed to a later writer. Was Paul incapable of using the same kind of material in both Ephesians and Colossians with different kinds of spin for different situations and needs?

Digging deeper

With a concordance trace the use of the term 'mystery' (Gk. *mustērion*) in the Pauline letters; use commentaries on the passages to see whether it has a consistent meaning and reference.

- So-called early catholicism has its roots in Paul himself, and was a natural development as he grew older and saw the need to preserve and consolidate the tradition. But in fact the thought of Ephesians is very unlike the early catholicism of the second-century Christian writers (such as Ignatius). The real problem here is perhaps whether the historical Paul saw himself in the way described here and would have spoken about himself in this way. There is certainly nothing about the situation and general content of the letter to point decisively to a post-Pauline date.

- Early Christians had no doubts about the Pauline authorship of the letter. (But that may prove only that a later writer did a good job of producing a letter that looked Pauline.)

Digging deeper

Arrange a debate on the motion, 'This house believes that Paul did not write Ephesians'. Let two or three people present the case for the motion and others against. The debate will work perfectly well even if participants are not necessarily themselves convinced about the case that they are arguing but work hard to 'stand in the shoes' of people who do hold that view.

WEIGHING THE PROBABILITIES

The problem is one of relative probabilities. Clearly those who think Colossians is not by Paul will argue that the case against Ephesians is even stronger. But even scholars who accept Colossians still have doubts about Ephesians. However, Paul's own versatility is evident from his acknowledged writings and is arguably broad enough to encompass the rich theology of Ephesians. The biggest problems lie in the style and the relation to Colossians.

It is probably the majority view at present that Ephesians is the work of a later writer who has endeavoured to present what he knew of Paul's teaching in a form that would speak more particularly to the needs of his situation. He drew on his detailed knowledge of Paul's letters, including especially Colossians, with which there are extensive parallels in wording, although the thought is often developed differently.

As in the case of Colossians, a solution may be sought in the hypothesis of the ghost

Focus on theology

This extraordinary composition with its long complex sentences is a prayerful celebration of the God whose purpose, conceived before the world was made, of creating a holy people has been brought about through his Son and confirmed by the gift of his Spirit. This new people includes the readers, and the letter aims to make them more aware of the wonder of their redemption and the power of God that continues to be active to transform them. The letter focuses on the way in which their reconciliation to God through the death of Jesus Christ also reconciles them as Jews and Gentiles to one another as one people of God, and it exults in this remarkable work of God which is his 'new purpose' conceived long ago and now revealed through Paul himself. Such a divine calling carries profound consequences for the life and behaviour of God's people. He provides gifts of charismatically empowered agents to build up the unity of the new people. As in Colossians there is a fairly detailed account of the changed behaviour that should be shown by believers when compared with that of the surrounding world. And also, as in Colossians, there is an awareness of the spiritual dangers that they face and against which they must be continually vigilant.

writer. In view of 6:21–22 the speculation mentioned above may be worth pursuing. Did Tychicus, as a close associate of Paul, have some share in, or was he entrusted with, the actual composition of a letter that bears Paul's authority and was composed with his cooperation and approval? In that case the letter would not be pseudonymous in that it is not an unauthorized attempt to deceive the readers regarding the real author. Consequently, the objection that early Christians, with their high regard for truth, would not have attempted to deceive people about the authorship of their letters, does not arise.

Another possibility is that a shorter letter by Paul (the letter to the Laodiceans, mentioned in Col. 4:16) has been extensively revamped by a later writer (Muddiman 2001).

But such hypotheses may be unnecessary. It all depends whether you think that this letter falls outside the parameters of what an exceedingly able and versatile Christian theologian was capable of composing.

FOR TODAY'S EPHESIANS

- Ephesians traces what is wrong in the world to evil powers that have taken control of it but over whom Christ is superior; Christian believers are consequently involved in a spiritual warfare. Is this perspective embarrassing or helpful to modern believers? Is it more credible in the so-called post-modern world than in the world of scientific materialism?
- The unity of the 'one body' of believers drawn from Jews and Gentiles is a major theme in this letter. What forms does the problem of Christian disunity take today, and how might Ephesians direct us

A WRY COMMENT ON THE AUTHORSHIP QUESTION

Many years ago there was in an English school a much beloved bachelor master whom the boys called Puddles. He had, however, decided mannerisms of speech, which showed among other occasions whenever he recited a favourite poem on the prehistoric animal called Eohippus. Once in holiday-time when a large group of his old boys was gathered together at Woodbrooke College to share again in his leadership, they arranged to have a little competition to see which of them could most perfectly imitate him in the recitation of his well-known selection. In order to ensure the impartiality of the judges chosen for the contest they were seated in the audience, while the contestants spoke in turn from the stage, but behind the curtain. Unknown to judges and audience Puddles himself slipped in backstage as one of the contestants and when the merits of each were scored by the judges and the winners announced, it was found that Puddles was himself awarded third place in the competition. (Cadbury 1958–59, pp. 101–2)

towards appropriate action in response to the problem?

● Ephesians commends what has been called a 'love patriarchalism' in the household and family (i.e. the exercise of authority over wife, children and slaves by the [male] head of the household); this was an appropriate Christianization of the patriarchalism of first-century society. What if anything has it to teach Christians today about family life and relationships in a somewhat different social setting?

ESSAY TOPICS

INTRODUCTORY
● Write an exegetical study of Eph. 2:1–10 or Eph. 2:11–22, drawing out the flow of the argument and the meaning of key words and phrases.

● Plan a series of six group Bible studies on Ephesians. For each session write a brief introduction to the theme(s) of the chapter, four or five questions which will enable the group to engage with the issues raised by the chapter and to relate them to their own lives, and a short summary of the chapter for a 'take home' leaflet.

INTERMEDIATE
● Get hold of a copy of the letter of the early second-century Christian leader, Ignatius, to the Ephesians and compare it with the New Testament letter. What conclusions can be drawn from the similarities and differences? (There are several translations of Ignatius, e.g. M. Staniforth [tr.] *Early Christian Writings: the Apostolic Fathers*. Harmondsworth/New York: Penguin, 1968.)

FURTHER READING

*denotes books assuming knowledge of Greek; most can be used by all students.

INTRODUCTORY
E. Best *Ephesians*. Sheffield: JSOT Press, 1993 (good introduction to the issues).

H. J. Cadbury, 'The Dilemma of Ephesians', *New Testament Studies* 5 1958–59 pp. 91–102 (balanced discussion of authorship).

A. T. Lincoln (and A. J. M. Wedderburn) *The Theology of the Later Pauline Letters*. Cambridge/New York: Cambridge University Press, 1993 (excellent study of the theology).

Commentaries
G. B. Caird *Paul's Letters from Prison (Ephesians, Philippians, Colossians, Philemon) in the Revised Standard Version*. Oxford: Oxford

181

University Press, 1976 (brief, but penetrating treatment).

L. Kreitzer *The Epistle to the Ephesians*. EC. London: Epworth Press/Valley Forge: Trinity Press International, 1997 (some unusual exegesis coupled with modern application).

P. Perkins *Ephesians*. ANTC. Nashville: Abingdon, 1997 (lots of basic exegesis in a succinct format).

J. R. W. Stott *God's new society: The message of Ephesians*. BST. Leicester: IVP/Downers Grove: IVP, 1979 (excellent modern application).

M. Turner 'Ephesians' in Carson, D. A. (et al.) *New Bible Commentary. 21st Century Edition*. Leicester: IVP/Downers Grove: IVP, 1994 (very brief but sound exegesis).

INTERMEDIATE

C. E. Arnold *Ephesians: Power and Magic. The concept of power in Ephesians in light of its historical setting*. Cambridge/New York: Cambridge University Press, 1989 (pioneering work on the 'power' language).

T. Moritz *A Profound Mystery: The Use of the Old Testament in Ephesians*. Leiden: Brill, 1996 (exactly what the subtitle says).

Commentaries

*E. Best *Ephesians*. ICC. Edinburgh: T. & T. Clark, 1998 (very detailed exegesis of Greek text).

F. F. Bruce *The Epistles to the Colossians, to Philemon and to the Ephesians*. NIC. Grand Rapids: Eerdmans, 1984 (excellent middle-length work).

H. W. Hoehner *Ephesians: An Exegetical Commentary*. Grand Rapids: Baker Academic, 2002 (immensely detailed study of the Greek text with a strong defence of Pauline authorship).

*A. T. Lincoln *Ephesians*. WBC. Dallas: Word, 1990 (a good alternative to Best).

J. Muddiman *The Epistle to the Ephesians*. BSNT. London/New York: Continuum, 2001 (good middle-length commentary on the English text).

*P. T. O'Brien *The Letter to the Ephesians*. Leicester: Apollos/Grand Rapids: Eerdmans, 1999 (full-length treatment of Greek text with defence of Pauline authorship).

Chapter 13

THE LETTERS TO TIMOTHY AND TITUS

In this chapter we shall consider:

● the difficulties surrounding the origin of these letters;
● their addressees and possible dates of composition;
● the teaching of each of the three letters;
● the identification of their setting in relation to Paul.

LETTERS THAT ARE SOMEHOW DIFFERENT

The three letters addressed to Paul's colleagues in mission, Timothy and Titus, clearly belong together as a group.

● They are the only letters addressed to individuals in positions of church leadership.
● They are broadly concerned with the same topics of how Christian leaders should behave both in their own personal lives and in their supervision of the congregations. The designation as 'pastoral' epistles (i.e. epistles for pastors) is apt.
● They are united by a common literary style and way of thinking which marks them off from the other Pauline letters.

This last point raises very sharply the question of their origin. There is a danger of letting this question dominate the discussion to the exclusion of all others. It must therefore be insisted that the most important thing is to determine the message of the letters in their context. Nevertheless, at the outset it may be helpful to catalogue the various possibilities and their consequences for interpretation. We can distinguish four types of solution that are currently on offer.

● **Pseudonymous composition** The letters were written a considerable time after Paul's death (perhaps 40 years) by somebody who was anxious to recall the church to its Pauline roots; his intention was to pass off the letters as if they came from Paul. In doing so, however, whether deliberately or unconsciously, he presented a rather different picture of Paul's theology than the historical one.

● **Incorporation of Pauline material** The letters were composed by a close disciple of Paul soon after his death, making use of any written materials left by Paul (including a last letter from Rome to Timothy) together with recollections of his teaching. The whole was put together to ensure that Paul could still be heard by a subsequent generation, and the original intention was not to deceive anybody about the origin of the letters.

- **Composition by an amanuensis writing during Paul's lifetime and with his authority** We know that Paul's letters were normally dictated to a scribe (apart from the last few sentences; Rom. 16:22; Gal. 6:11). Probably his normal practice was to dictate more or less word for word, but there could have been occasions when for whatever reason he conveyed the gist of what he wanted to say to the scribe who then wrote it up appropriately.
- **Direct authorship** by Paul who wrote or dictated the letters in his normal manner.

W.A

THE PROBLEM OF NON-PAULINE AUTHORSHIP

Before proceeding further it is necessary to consider the implications of adopting any of these four types of position. There is no problem for those who believe that they can accept either of the last two solutions. In both of these cases the letters are authentic letters of Paul, written either directly by him or on the basis of his instructions and with his authority. However, problems arise with the first two positions.

The first position involves *pseudonymity* (sometimes also called *pseudepigraphy*) in which somebody falsely claims the name of some other author for what they themselves have written; Paul is named as the author in order to deceive readers into thinking that he wrote something that he did not write. The second position, as described above, is different. It involves what I call *allonymity*, that is to say, the writing of a letter by somebody other than the named author, but without the attempt to deceive people: from

the beginning the readers knew what was going on.

Some scholars find it hard to believe that the morally reprehensible practice of deceit could be involved in the composition of books that the Christian church has accepted as Scripture. Consequently, they are loth to accept the first position. One may want to debate whether a 'faith commitment' based on the status of the letters as Scripture can have a place in an objective critical investigation of the origin of the letters. I shall come clean on the matter and say that this consideration does weigh with me and leads me to enquire very carefully whether we are really shut up to this hypothesis or whether, if there is no other option, I need to review the implications of my faith commitment.

Those who do not think that this faith commitment is relevant to the issue tend to argue that the moral standards of the ancient world were not those of today (with its great emphasis on literary propriety), and that an element of deceit was ethically permissible if the ends in view were praiseworthy and could not be otherwise achieved. Pseudepigraphy was a common enough practice, as with the pseudonymous letters attributed to Plato and many (usually heretical) Christian documents from the second century onwards.

The matter is not as simple as that.

- The early Christians were strongly committed to truth both in theory and in practice, and the practice of pseudepigraphy would have been inconsistent with this.
- This attitude is reflected in the clear rejection of inauthentic documents by

early Christians from the second century onwards.

- These inauthentic documents were the product of heretics and opponents of mainline Christianity who sought to pass off their teaching as if it had come from leading first-century Christians.
- Suggestions that Christian opinion was more lax in the first century and hardened only in the second century under the pressure of heresy have no solid evidence in their favour.
- One may well question whether documents falsely purporting to be by Paul could have been produced by AD 100 or so and accepted by other Christians.

The second position avoids these problems. It claims that the letters were written by a colleague of Paul not long after his death to make available to the next generation of Christian leaders the kind of instructions that he gave to Timothy and Titus because these were still relevant and necessary. There was no intention to deceive, and the first readers were aware what was going on. It has to be admitted that with the passage of time the letters came to be thought of as being from Paul himself, but the fact that this happened is not a reason for condemnation of the original author. It could be added that the difference between the second and third positions is one of degree, the difference being whether Paul himself was able to give his imprimatur to what had been written in his name whether before or after his death.

A possible weakness of the second position is that it must remain speculative whether it represents what actually happened.

In the ensuing discussion we shall need to compare the merits of these four positions to

see which is best supported by the evidence (or which is rendered unlikely by the evidence). For further discussion of pseudonymity see pp. 234–8.

TO WHOM WERE THE LETTERS WRITTEN?

Paul was the leader of a Christian mission in the countries that stretched round from Jerusalem in the east to Illyricum (the west of the Balkan peninsula) in the west (Rom. 15:19). He always worked with colleagues, and reference is made in these letters to Titus working in Cyprus and to Timothy in Ephesus.

Using a concordance it is not too difficult to reconstruct something of the missionary work and travels of these two men. Timothy joined Paul on his second missionary campaign (Acts 16:1–3), visited Thessalonica, Philippi and Corinth, and was with Paul when he wrote Romans, 2 Corinthians, Philippians, Colossians, 1 and 2 Thessalonians and Philemon. Titus was Paul's companion at Jerusalem (Gal. 2:3; never mentioned in Acts) and visited Corinth more than once.

According to 1 Tim. 1:3 Timothy was stationed at Ephesus as overseer of the churches. In 2 Tim. 4:9–13 he is summoned to visit Paul in prison, travelling via Troas. According to Titus 1:5; 3:12 Titus had been left in Crete, but is summoned to join Paul in Nicopolis.

If the letters are authentic or are based on authentic material, then 'Timothy' and 'Titus' are these historical characters and the teaching in the letters is meant for them as they cope with the problems of their congregations. If the letters are post-Pauline, then the letters are meant for church leaders of the author's generation.

WHEN WERE THE LETTERS WRITTEN?

Can we use this information about the named recipients to identify the occasion of writing the letters, whether the actual occasion (if Paul himself wrote the letters) or the scenario that is envisaged (if they were written by somebody else)? There are three possibilities.

Late in Paul's career

The traditional view is that the letters belong to *a period after the release of Paul* from his two years of imprisonment in Rome as recorded in Acts (Acts 28:30–31). He must be assumed to have revisited the Aegean area, but was later arrested and imprisoned for a second time at Rome, and then he was executed. 1 Timothy and Titus belong to the period of renewed missionary activity, and 2 Timothy comes from his second imprisonment, shortly before his death. The possibility of this reconstruction is supported by three considerations.

● If Philippians and Philemon come from Paul's 'first' imprisonment in Rome (as we argued earlier), they reflect a strong hope of release and travel in the east (Phil. 2:24; Phlm. 22). Paul's earlier plan to visit Spain (Rom. 15:24, 28) could easily have been given up after the long delay in reaching Rome. Or he may have travelled both west and east.

● Although Acts contains strong hints of impending martyrdom (20:23–25, 29, 38; 21:13), it is hard to see on what charge Paul could have been executed, and there is a good case that he was released.

● 'Tradition' reported by Eusebius affirms this view (cf. 1 Clem. 5:7; Acts of Peter 1–3, 40; Muratorian Canon).

'Tradition has it that after defending himself the Apostle was again sent on the ministry of preaching, and coming a second time to the same city suffered martyrdom under Nero. During this imprisonment he wrote the second Epistle to Timothy, indicating at the same time that his first defence had taken place and that his martyrdom was at hand.' (Eusebius, *Hist. eccl.* 2:25)

The weakness of this scenario is that, although it is possible, it rests on (reasonable) conjecture.

Earlier in Paul's career

Various scholars have speculated that the letters themselves (or portions of them) could have been written *earlier in Paul's career*.

For example, Robinson (1976) dates 1 Timothy at Acts 20:1f. (from the Troad after leaving Ephesus), Titus while Paul was en route for Jerusalem (Acts 20), and 2 Timothy from Paul's imprisonment in Caesarea to Timothy who was then in Philippi. This particular reconstruction runs into difficulties with 2 Timothy, since the personal data in 2 Tim. 1:17 place Paul firmly in Rome.

Some of the difficulties can be alleviated if we allow that the letters as we have them are post-Pauline compositions but contain some genuine fragments of Paul's correspondence. Harrison (1921) isolated three fragments, which he fitted into Paul's last visit to Macedonia and Illyricum and his Roman imprisonment. However, once the fragments have been tentatively identified, they are so brief and so lacking in concrete details that the possibilities of placing them historically open up very widely, and hypotheses are even more open to the charge that they can be neither proved nor disproved.

A fictitious setting

The previous two solutions are those held by scholars who believe that the letters or portions of them are authentic. Scholars who hold that *the letters are not genuine* hold that the writer assumed the kind of scenarios during Paul's life just described and created fictitious personal data accordingly. The personal data may be based on genuine fragments of Paul's correspondence incorporated in the letters but are essentially part of the apparatus of pseudonymity, designed to create an illusion of historical reality.

WHAT ARE THE LETTERS ABOUT?

Before we plunge more deeply into the problem of the origin of the letters we need to see what the letters themselves actually say, primarily for their own sake but also so that we may have a basis for asking what kind of situation and author must be postulated to account for them.

THE STRUCTURE OF THE LETTER TO TITUS

1:1–4   OPENING GREETING

1:5—3:11 BODY OF THE LETTER – INSTRUCTIONS
          TO THE CHURCH LEADER
          1:5–9   Instructions to Timothy – The
                   appointment of elders
          1:10–16 and the danger from opponents
          2:1–15   Teaching for the church – How
                   believers are to relate to one
                   another
          3:1–11   Teaching for the church – How
                   believers are to live in society

3:12–15   PERSONAL INSTRUCTIONS

3:15   CLOSING GREETING

AN OVERVIEW OF TITUS

The Letter to Titus is distinguished by a lengthy greeting which gives Paul's credentials as an apostle in such a way as to become a brief exposition of the nature of the Christian message with which he was entrusted by God and which is implicitly shared with his colleague Titus (1:1–4).

The letter goes straight into its theme without a thanksgiving or prayer report (similarly in 1 Timothy). This is probably because it has the character of a 'mandate' or letter of instruction to a delegate. Titus is Paul's helper rather than his colleague. The instruction in 1:5 is general and particular.

The particular element is taken up immediately in the rest of the chapter. There are weaknesses in the congregations that are evidently due to the lack of proper local leadership. The usual interpretation is that the congregations were comparatively young and had not yet developed a system of leadership that would keep some unruly elements in order. Titus is to ensure the appointment of suitable people to act as elders, who appear to be also known as overseers or bishops. The former term identifies them more in terms of status (the senior members of a community) while the latter term is more expressive of their function of supervision, which includes teaching. The emphasis is on their blameless Christian character and their competence to teach the truth (1:5–9).

The reason for their appointment is because of the activities of other people who have been attracted by some form of Jewish teaching; this appears to have been a

Digging deeper

Make a list of the qualities and qualifications that you would look for if you were appointing a church leader. Then compare it with the lists in Titus 1:5–9 and 1 Tim. 3:1–13. What similarities and differences are there? Does today's church have anything to rediscover in the emphases expressed in these New Testament lists?

speculative, allegorical interpretation of Jewish stories and genealogies from which probably some strange rules of conduct were drawn. The whole thing appears to have been the sort of nonsense that cannot be refuted by the use of reason (like the teaching of some weird modern sects), and it did not lead to moral conduct; rather those who professed it were morally dubious in their lives (1:10–16).

Now comes some more general instruction to be conveyed to the church. Over against this time-wasting drivel (as the author saw it), Titus is encouraged to give wholesome teaching. This is summed up in two sections of the letter. The first of them (Titus 2) is concerned with sober Christian conduct, which is spelled out in fuller detail for different age and gender groups in the church, including slaves. Their position in service to their masters is simply assumed as the norm in society, but even in their lowly position they can add lustre to the Christian faith by the quality of their service (2:1–10). The exhortation to such behaviour is backed up by a short summary of the gospel which develops the theme that the purpose of God's act of redemption was to create a people who would live godly lives and do good (2:11–14).

In the second section the same pattern is repeated. This time the instruction is common to all believers and concerns their relationships with society at large (3:1–2), and again it is backed up by a doctrinal summary which describes how God had saved them from a life of dissipation and evil to one in which they have been renewed by the Holy Spirit so that they may live good lives (3:3–8).

This section concludes with a direction to avoid profitless discussions with the opponents and to take disciplinary measures if necessary against people who refuse to conform (3:9–11). And the letter then finishes in the usual manner with some personal notes (3:12–15).

Focus on theology:
TITUS

Practical instruction about congregational leadership and decorous Christian conduct is backed up by theological statements about the salvation event, which encompasses both the manifestation of the grace of God in Jesus Christ and the revelation of its significance through proclamation of the gospel. There is a universal offer of redemption to all people, delivering them from evil to live godly lives as the people of God while they look forward to his final glorious manifestation in the coming of Jesus Christ.

THE STRUCTURE OF 1 TIMOTHY

1:1–2	OPENING GREETING
1:3—6:21a	BODY OF THE LETTER
1:3—3:16	TEACHERS AND CHURCH LEADERS

	1:3–20	Instruction to avoid false doctrine
	2:1–15	Instruction on prayer

3:1–13   Qualifications for overseers and deacons

3:14–16   The church and the mystery of the faith

4:1—6:21a   THE ATTITUDE OF THE CHURCH LEADER TO THE CHURCH AND THE GROUPS IN IT

4:1–16   Timothy's duties as a teacher in the face of heresy

5:1—6:2a The treatment of various groups in the church

6:2b–21a True and false teachers contrasted

6:21b   CLOSING GREETINGS

AN OVERVIEW OF 1 TIMOTHY

The first letter to Timothy is similar to Titus in taking the form of a mandate giving him a renewal of his orders for supervision of the church in Ephesus. From the first chapter we see that some kind of Jewish-based speculation on the law was again causing problems in the church and diverting people from concentration on godly living. The author is not opposed to the law, but insists that it is being misused (1:3–11).

'LET A WOMAN LEARN IN SILENCE'

Probably no paragraph in the New Testament has caused as much upset in the modern church as 1 Tim. 2:11–15 with its apparent silencing of women in church, which has led to situations where women have had no vocal part whatever in the meetings, except participation in the singing, and have been excluded from any kind of leadership positions. In a world where the equal rights of women with men have come to be generally recognized many people have rejected this paragraph outright as falling below the standards of the gospel which elsewhere have raised the dignity of disadvantaged groups of people, both women and slaves.

It is likely that the gospel did bring a measure of emancipation to women, and evidence elsewhere in the New Testament shows that they had some share in ministry. In the situation depicted here it is plausible that at least some of them had been infected by the heretical teaching that was present in the congregation and, like the men concerned, they had to be restrained. Some of them would have had little or no education. It is also probable that in a world where there was a patriarchal ethos and women did not on the whole take part in public affairs, some of the women were exercising a freedom which did not go down well with their conservative menfolk, and some of them appear to have been vaunting some kind of superiority over men (the much-discussed extremely rare verb 'have authority' [Gk. *authenteō*] appears to refer to an improper kind of authority). The appeal to the case of Adam and Eve may be nothing more than the use of a type of argument which would have some force with people who were using passages from Genesis to support their own (odd) ideas and behaviour. And the reference to bearing children is a reminder that people don't need to be teachers and church leaders to be truly 'saved'; God is just as pleased if they do their ordinary tasks in a godly and faithful manner. If we reach down to the principles underlying this instruction, given in a rather different social and ecclesiastical situation from our own, we may find that the application of it will also be rather different and does not impose the same restraints upon people today. For rather different approaches to the problem see: J. R. Beck and C. L. Blomberg (eds) *Two Views on Women in Ministry*. Grand Rapids: Zondervan, 2001; J. Piper and W. Grudem (eds) *Recovering Biblical Manhood and Womanhood: A Response to Evangelical Feminism*. Wheaton: Crossway, 1991; R. W. Pierce and R. M. Groothuis (eds) *Discovering Biblical Equality: Complementarity without Hierarchy*. Downers Grove: IVP, 2005 (second edn).

I TIMOTHY 1:9

The one who does no wrong is in no need of law. (*Sentence of Antiphanes* [408/405–334/331 BC, cited in Stobaeus, *Anthologium* 3:349; *HCNT* § 828])

What do you think?

Consider the comments made above on 1 Tim. 2:8–15 and discuss them in the light of the observation that 'hermeneutics is a way of getting round passages in Scripture that we find difficult'.

He then gives an account of his appointment as a servant of Christ, into which is incorporated the story of his conversion and a statement of the gospel (1:12–17), and then he reminds Timothy of his own calling to be faithful, despite the opposition that he may encounter (1:18–20).

In 1 Timothy 2 he deals with matters that needed attention in the church. First, he concentrates on the congregational meetings and insists on the need for prayer at them (2:1–7). The ultimate aim of the prayer is for people to be saved, since God wants all people to be saved and Christ as the mediator died for all; the proximate aim of the prayer is for rulers to create peaceable conditions in which Christians may live their lives without fear (and presumably be at liberty to witness to their faith). He gives instructions on what the men must do if their prayer is to be effective and then on what the women must do (2:8–10). In both cases the conduct expected extends outside the meeting room to their life generally.

Then, having mentioned the women in connection with prayer, he adds as a rider that the women should not teach and have authority over the men but should recognize that they can fulfil their Christian duty by fulfilling their responsibilities in bearing and bringing up children (2:11–15).

In 1 Tim. 3:1–3 we have instructions similar to those in Titus 1 regarding the

appointment of suitable people as church leaders; here the organization is a little more complex, in that alongside the overseers we also have deacons and 'the women' (probably female deacons rather than the wives of deacons).

All of this instruction regarding the life of the church is backed up by a doctrinal reminder of the nature of the church as God's household (which must be administered in an orderly manner) and as the bulwark that is meant to support the truth of the gospel. That gospel is then briefly summarized in a memorable but somewhat cryptic saying, the force of which appears to be that the sublime secret revealed in our Christian religion is the revelation of Christ, who is confirmed in numerous ways as God's agent and who is to be preached to the world so that people everywhere may believe in him (3:14–16).

Next we have a section in which first of all the ascetic tendencies of the false teaching are stated and refuted (4:1–5), and then there is a lengthy direct address to Timothy as to how a Christian leader is to behave in such circumstances (4:6–16).

Sensitivity towards different groups of people in the church is commended. In particular, a young male leader must be careful to treat older people and women in appropriate ways (5:1f.). (Again, we remind ourselves that Timothy is living in a different culture from our own with different conventions in relationships.) A remarkably long section deals with the problem of care provided by the congregation for destitute widows; here is a window on the beginnings of social care in the church (5:3–16). There are some general instructions on discipline in the church (5:17–25), and a comment on instruction for slaves (6:1–2a).

Finally, there is another long section in which teaching regarding rich and poor people is interspersed with advice to Timothy as a pastor (6:2b–19).

---

1 TIMOTHY 6:10

The love of money is the mother city of all evils. (Bion the Sophist [3rd cent. BC, cited in Stobaeus, *Anthologium* 3:417; *HCNT* § 838])

This section is interesting for its revelation that congregations included people who were well off and tempted to wrong use of their wealth as well as people who had little or nothing.

THE STRUCTURE OF 2 TIMOTHY

1:1–2	OPENING GREETING
1:3—4:8	BODY OF THE LETTER – TIMOTHY AS A CHURCH LEADER
	1:3–18 The need for Timothy to show courage and to hold fast to the gospel
	2:1–13 Exhortation to be strong and to endure suffering
	2:14–26 The church leader and his opponents
	3:1—4:8 Ungodliness and the consequent need for faithfulness and truth
4:9–18	APPEAL TO VISIT PAUL SOON – CLOSING INSTRUCTIONS
4:19–22	CLOSING GREETINGS, REPETITION OF APPEAL TO COME, AND FINAL BLESSING

AN OVERVIEW OF 2 TIMOTHY

2 Timothy is unlike Titus and 1 Timothy in that it is not a mandate giving orders but is rather a friendly letter of personal encouragement from a Paul who feels that he is approaching the end of his life. It has, therefore, to some extent the character of a 'testament', a last letter from an old man to his family and friends. Consequently, it

---

Focus on theology:
1 TIMOTHY

Against a background of disputes, non-Pauline teaching on the law and some form of asceticism, the letter develops a theology of Christian living (godliness) that rests on the revelation of Christ as the divinely vindicated Saviour of all humankind. God's universal saving purpose through Christ, demonstrated in the conversion of Paul from a sinful way of life, should lead the church to pray for everybody. Congregational leadership must provide sound teaching and exemplify godly living. The doctrine of creation provides an antidote to a pointless asceticism in respect of diet and marriage. A particular danger to godliness is caused by greed and love of money instead of setting one's hope and desire on the future coming of God's kingdom with the manifestation of the Lord Jesus Christ.

contains no instructions on congregational order. It does describe the hard times that the church is experiencing and that will get worse, and in particular it is concerned with Paul's own harsh experiences in an ancient prison with the threat of death hanging over him. Although, therefore, the letter contains many of the same elements as the other two letters and reflects the same general outlook and theology it is rather different in structure and content.

Thus, the letter does begin with a prayer report in which Paul is grateful for Timothy's faith (1:3–7). But, whereas in other letters Paul moves on to report how he intercedes for his readers, here the thanksgiving merges into an exhortation to Timothy regarding what is lacking in his Christian life and witness. Although he has the Spirit of God in him to empower him for his service, he needs to fan that Spirit into flame so that he may have the courage and strength that he needs for a very testing time. To encourage him further Paul describes how he himself was saved and called as a Christian leader and has to endure suffering which he is able to bear thanks to his trust in God. At the same time the call is not just to courage but also to faithfulness. Opposition to the gospel continues and there is a temptation to the Christian leader to succumb to false teaching instead of preserving faithfully the gospel which has been committed to his keeping, like a deposit placed in the hands of a banker (1:8–18).

A major part of the letter, then, is an appeal to Timothy to be strong, to be prepared for a tough, self-denying life, like a soldier on active service (2:1–7). He is to remember the examples both of Jesus (who was vindicated by God after his suffering) and of Paul, who bears his sufferings for the sake of the salvation of God's people. There will be no crown without first bearing a cross (2:8–13).

Then Timothy is warned against descending to useless bickering with opponents; his duty is rather to present the truth faithfully. Yet there must not be a quarrelsome spirit with opponents but rather a gracious manner so that they may yield to persuasion and admit their error (2:14–26).

At the same time, the long-range forecast is not good. There will be continuing moral and spiritual decline even in the church (3:1–9).

Digging deeper

What measures are proposed in the Pastoral Epistles for dealing with teachers and teaching that the author believes to be wrong and mischievous (see, for example, I Tim. 4; 5:19–21; 6:3–5, 20f.; 2 Tim. 2:2, 14–26; 3:1–9, 16; 4:1–5; Titus 1:9–16; 3:9–11)? What place should there be in the church today for freedom and diversity of opinion on Christian doctrine and practice, and what contribution do the Pastoral Epistles make to discussion of this point?

2 TIMOTHY 3:8

And next in order came Jannes and Jambres, Egyptian sacred scribes, men judged to have no superiors in the practice of magic, at the time when the Jews were being driven out of Egypt. (Numenius of Apamea [2nd cent. AD; cited by Eusebius, *Hist. eccl* 9:8; *HCNT* § 840])

So again Paul reminds Timothy of his own example of fortitude in coping with suffering (3:10–14). It is hard here to distinguish between suffering as a result of persecution from outside the church and suffering as a result of harassment from within it by opponents; the reason for this may be that the line between the two was hard to draw. When Paul was attacked by fellow Jews, there were occasions when they successfully summoned the help of the local rent-a-mob (Acts 17:5) or even tried to get the magistrates to take their side (Acts 18:12–17). The later history of religious wars shows how easily the church and secular forces get entangled with one another.

Despite all these pressures Timothy is urged to stick to the teaching of the Scriptures, which, rightly understood, point to salvation through Jesus Christ (3:15–17).

All of this teaching is underlined by a solemn 'charge' in which Paul in effect places Timothy in the presence of God to enforce what he is saying (4:1–5). A sense of pathos is introduced as Paul speaks of his own impending death and hope of divine approval (4:6–8). The letter concludes with a lengthy list of instructions concerning Paul's own welfare and the continuation of his work by his colleagues (4:9–22).

What do you think?

There is an enormous emphasis in the Pastoral Epistles on the place of teaching and learning in the congregation and its meetings. Has the writer gone too far in emphasizing the intellectual side of Christianity over against its experiential and practical sides? Do modern congregations get the balance right?

Focus on theology:
2 TIMOTHY

Instruction to a comparatively young leader is based on his being equipped by the Spirit to bear courageous witness to the gospel, following the pattern of Paul and treasuring and passing on his teaching of the gospel; Timothy must be prepared to bear suffering as one aspect of participating in the death of Christ. He is to be nourished by the Scriptures which are God's own words for the guidance of his people. In all this Paul himself and Timothy have been given a solid basis for endurance to the end through the promises of the faithful God to his servants, which assure them of his sustaining presence and his safeguarding power in accordance with his saving purpose.

WHAT IS THE SITUATION REFLECTED IN THE LETTERS?

Our survey of the letters has hopefully indicated that for all their individual differences they all share much the same situation and outlook, and therefore we can consider them together rather than separately. Various aspects of them require attention:

OPPOSITION AND HERESY

From the point of view of the author the congregations assigned to Timothy and Titus are affected by people who differ sharply from them in their outlook.

- There were speculations based on weird interpretations of passages from the Jewish Scriptures – the 'myths and genealogies' (1 Tim. 1:3–4; Titus 1:14; 3:9).
- They followed ascetic practices, including abstinence from certain foods and from sexual relationships (1 Tim. 4:1–3).

193

- They probably spoke of their theology as 'knowledge' (1 Tim. 6:20); clearly it was a kind of intellectualism that led to lots of debate and argument (cf. 2 Tim. 2:23; Titus 3:9).
- Some of them claimed that 'the resurrection is past already' (2 Tim. 2:18).
- They are accused of moral licence and even depravity (1 Tim. 1:19; 2 Tim. 3:1–9; Titus 1:15–16).

Various explanations of this combination are possible – always assuming that we are dealing with one basic type of people. Some scholars dismiss the accusations of immorality as typical mud-slinging to blacken the reputation of opponents. ('If you can't think of good arguments against them, just call them names.') But moral looseness was and is often a concomitant of weird thinking.

In the second century there was a broad movement that we now call 'Gnosticism' which laid much stress on esoteric knowledge of myths about the creation and nature of the universe, that postulated a strict dualism between spirit and matter or between God and the world, and that could include ascetic practices. It is tempting to see in the 'heresy' here a form or forerunner of this common Christian heresy. However, there is no clear reflection of typically Gnostic beliefs in the letters.

We also know that around the turn of the century there were groups who practised fairly strict asceticism (and invoked Paul as the champion of their beliefs and practices); their views are reflected in the *Acts of Paul* (see box). Some of these ascetic groups included women who abandoned marriage for a religious life. It has been suggested that asceticism of this kind was essentially the

problem reflected in these letters. But there was more to the situation than just asceticism.

> ' "Who is he that is inside with you, the false teacher who deceives the souls of young men and maidens, that they should not marry but remain as they are? ..." And Demas and Hermogenes said to him, "Who this man is, we do not know. But he deprives young men of wives and maidens of husbands, saying: 'Otherwise there is no resurrection for you, except you remain chaste and do not defile the flesh, but keep it pure.' " ' (*Acts of Paul and Thecla*. 11f.; a second-century apocryphal account of Paul's missionary journeys, stressing his ascetic teaching. W. Schneemelcher [ed.] *New Testament Apocrypha*. Cambridge: James Clarke/Louisville: Westminster/John Knox, 1992, vol. II, p. 241)

The Jewish character of the teaching, or rather the sectarian-Jewish character, is significant. The concern with the law, the admittedly Jewish speculations, and the ascetic practices can all point in this direction. We also know that Paul taught that believers were raised to new life with Christ, and it is quite possible that some people misinterpreted his teaching to mean that the resurrection itself had taken place. If we put these two elements together, the Jewish speculations and the misunderstanding of Paul, we have an adequate explanation of what was going on. It bears some resemblance to the kind of things that went on in Corinth and Colossae.

THE DEVELOPMENT OF CHURCH ORDER

The antidote to the false teaching is a combination of sound teaching and the appointment, as leaders, of people who combine upright character and soundness in the faith. The position of Timothy and Titus is that they are helpers of Paul who are increasingly trusted with the kind of supervision that he formerly exercised directly over the congregations that he had founded. They represent a level of superintendence that stems from the Pauline mission.

At the local level the congregations are to appoint leaders. These are referred to as elders, a term referring to the senior members in a community or to those of their number appointed to act as leaders. They were characteristic of Jewish local organization. The term overseers or bishops is also used, apparently for the same people (or possibly for a narrower group within the group of elders), and the term indicates their functions. The deacons in 1 Timothy 3 appear to be a subordinate group who may have assisted the overseers.

This kind of set-up is closest to that in Philippians where we also have overseers and deacons as terms used for church leaders (Phil. 1:1). Later writers outside the New Testament have different combinations of names. Ignatius (who wrote letters to various congregations including Ephesus c. AD 110) espoused a set-up in which a local congregation would have a bishop in charge with elders and deacons in subordinate roles. The situation in the Pastoral Epistles looks to be closer to Philippians than to Ignatius.

Elsewhere in Paul's letters there is very little on the organization of the church and the appointment of leaders. With the passage of time, the growth of the church and the rise of opposing factions, there was the greater need for order and discipline.

CHRISTIAN LIVING AND PASTORAL CARE

It may be significant that the letters are addressed to leaders rather than to congregations. This could reflect a stage

in development when the leaders were becoming more prominent and responsibility for congregational affairs was shifting to them rather than resting on the congregation as a whole.

In this situation there could also be a tendency to look back to earlier days and to venerate both the first leaders and their teaching. Some scholars detect in the letters a tendency to reverence Paul and to present a somewhat idealized picture of him as a pattern or paradigm for later leaders. Could Paul have referred to himself in the kind of way in which he is described here, for example as 'the foremost' of sinners (1 Tim. 1:15)? Was the historical Paul likely to have been so – dare we say – complacent about receiving a heavenly reward (2 Tim. 4:8)? In short, is the picture of him here idealistic and hagiographical rather than authentic self-description?

It is in the light of these considerations that many scholars begin to doubt whether the letters come from Paul's own lifetime and to ask whether they come from a later period. It has been urged that the heresy is like second-century Gnosticism, that the church organization looks rather more developed than we would expect in Paul's time, and that the picture presented of him looks like later veneration.

Each of these points is debatable, and there are certainly good grounds for some hesitation about them. As I have already indicated, the heretical teaching could easily belong to Paul's time or shortly after; the church organization fits into a time when Paul saw the need for measures to deal with growth and heresy (cf. Rom. 16:17–18); and the claim that the letters venerate Paul is open to question (e.g. the 'heavenly reward' is not just for Paul but for 'all who have longed for his appearing'). These factors, then, are not entirely conclusive.

However, there are two other factors that must be taken into account before a verdict is reached.

LANGUAGE AND STYLE
Consider the following points:

- Out of a vocabulary of 901 words in the Pastorals, 335 (incl. 37 names) are not found elsewhere in Paul. This proportion, amounting to 37%, is double what we found in the other letters that we tested (see p. 168). (It has been argued that the vocabulary is more characteristic of a second-century writer, but in fact the words were current in the first century.)
- Many common Pauline words are not used at all. These include: uncircumcision, die, free, to work, to preach the gospel, to give thanks, to boast, heaven, spiritual, to do, wisdom, body, son, to rejoice, soul.
- The style is different from that of Paul's other letters. There are long strings or lists of nouns and adjectives, some use of rare words and a different sort of argumentation. Paul has a varied fund of 'connective tissue' (conjunctions and other

particles), but over a hundred items from it are missing in the Pastorals.

These facts are relatively easy to establish. It is more difficult to assess their significance. Some scholars will argue that we must not underestimate the versatility in style of a competent writer; but this does not explain why in this particular set of letters the writer acted differently from normal. Others plead that a person's style may change with age; but there is no hard evidence that this is so (apart from cases of senility), and common observation suggests that it is simply not true. The difference in literary style is a problem.

THE THEOLOGY AND THE WAY IT IS EXPRESSED
Even more weight attaches to the actual content of what is said. Literary style and method of argumentation are closely linked. The different literary style is accompanied by a different way of thinking.

- There is an absence of the kind of things that Paul tends to say from one letter to another; the writer can make do without a lot of his characteristic theological vocabulary. For example, there is a relative lack of reference to God as father, new life 'in Christ', and the work of the Spirit in the believer.
- There are new ways of expression. There are phrases like 'the saying is trustworthy', which are not used by Paul. The coming of Christ is expressed in terms of epiphany, a technical term used by Paul only in 2 Thessalonians 2:8. Christian living is described in terms of godliness and self-control and similar words which are not used or scarcely used by Paul elsewhere. There is more of the language and ethos of Greek-speaking Judaism than we find elsewhere in Paul; why would Paul have

adopted this rather different idiom in addressing his colleagues Timothy and Titus?

EVALUATING THE EVIDENCE

Let us now try to pull these points together and evaluate the various theories that have been built upon them.

We have seen that the three letters belong together in general style, situation and content. They have a style of composition which does differ from that generally used by Paul, and the theology is certainly expressed in different ways, although there is a good case that it is not inconsistent with Paul's thinking; Paul could have read through these letters and said, 'Fundamentally I'm in agreement with what is said here', but he might well have added: 'although I might have expressed myself differently'. But there are also problems in that a good deal of the material consists of instruction about matters on which Timothy and Titus, as Paul's companions over several years, might well have been expected to be fully informed. (However, to be fair, it is relevant to respond that Ignatius also wrote a letter of counsel to another church leader, Polycarp, in which he gave him some equally dazzling glimpses of the obvious, and that such material may have been included for the congregations to overhear.) Added to this we have seen some reason to wonder whether the self-portrait of Paul in the letters is altogether lifelike.

NOT BY PAUL?

For these reasons many scholars argue that the letters are not by Paul (e.g. Barrett 1963; Collins 2002; Davies 1996; Hanson 1982; Harrison 1921). They come from a much

later period (c. AD 100) when Paul's gospel was being ignored or forgotten and there was a development of strange doctrines and practices in the church that were subversive of it. These doctrines could be seen as somewhat akin to Gnosticism.

In this situation an unknown writer attempted to retrieve the position by writing to church leaders, urging them to withstand the heretical teachers and to return to Pauline teaching. In order to do so effectively he chose to invoke the authority of Paul rather than any of his own, and he therefore wrote so as to give the impression that it was Paul writing. This meant that he had to compose letters to Paul's historical companions, since he could hardly have Paul writing anachronistically to the people of his own day. (He could have composed 'catholic epistles', but he didn't go down that route.) 'Timothy' and 'Titus' thus stand for church leaders in his own time. In so doing he depicted Paul as an example of conversion, calling and suffering that should be paradigmatic for later Christians.

He fell back on traditions of what Paul had taught, and may well have used some of his letters. But he was not himself Paul, and his theological outlook and manner of expression were different, and these differences from Paul are evident. Thus the letters contain accents that are different from those of Paul; some things that were central to Paul are passed over, and there are some fresh nuances.

The writer was successful. What he wrote was orthodox and his attempt to impersonate Paul was not discovered; the letters were accepted by other Christians and became attached to the collection of Paul's letters. And, it can be argued, what the author was doing was not regarded as morally reprehensible; it was a stratagem demanded by an extremely critical situation, and it worked.

WRITTEN OR DICTATED BY PAUL?

At the other end of the scholarly spectrum is a by no means insignificant or uncritical group of scholars who argue that the letters (or at least 2 Timothy) are by Paul (e.g. Fee 1988; Guthrie 1990; Johnson 1996; Mounce 2000). They recognize that there are differences in style and expression from the other letters of Paul, but they claim that these are well within the range of a versatile writer. Some of them arise from the fact that the subject matter is different from that in the other letters, and it has been argued that the unusual words are mostly in passages dealing with such topics.

Other differences are partly to be explained through the facts that Paul is writing to colleagues rather than to congregations and would adopt a different style; I could compare how one of my daughters, when working in Ghana, wrote accounts of her family's life and mission work in quite different idioms depending on whether it was a prayer letter for the home congregation or a letter to her relatives (and again there were intriguing differences between the ways in which she put things to her parents and to her sisters!).

A further factor could be the use of existing traditions, which Paul has incorporated in the letters. This view is particularly developed by Ellis (1999), who identifies a large amount of such material. However, the criteria for identifying tradition need careful examination, it is not clear why Paul would have cited so extensively (against his practice in other letters), and the peculiar style of the

letters is fairly consistent and not confined to particular passages.

There is also the fact that Paul was dealing with a situation of powerful opposition to himself and his colleagues, and therefore his instructions would be rather different from what they would have been in a stable situation. As we have noted, the general situation in the letters is one that could be set within the period of Paul's own lifetime. If Paul was in prison, then he could well have needed the help of a scribe, and given him greater freedom than usual.

A MIDDLE WAY?

Each of these two theories has its weaknesses. The former theory is open to the objections that none of the evidence demands so late a date for the letters. The likelihood of an orthodox writer attempting a pseudonymous composition and getting away with it is low. There is, in any case, no firm evidence that any Christian writers or scribes had any doubts that the letters were Pauline. Some scholars draw attention to the fact that Marcion (c. AD 140) apparently did not have them in his rather select canon of Scripture (Luke's Gospel and the Pauline letters); however, this does not necessarily imply that he was ignorant of them or rejected them as not being Pauline composition, but simply that he disagreed with their teaching.

A third type of theory attempts to avoid the criticisms that can be levelled against the other two (Marshall 1999). It avoids the difficulties caused by the unusual style and thought of the letters compared with those of Paul by suggesting that they are the work of a slightly later writer who was concerned to let Paul speak to the ongoing needs of the church. And it avoids the difficulties caused by the theory of late, pseudonymous origin by proposing that the letters were actually written much closer in time to Paul and that they were composed without any intention to deceive their readers. They represent the kind of instructions that Paul gave to his colleagues, perhaps incorporating elements from his actual correspondence with them, but adapted to deal with a worsening situation in the churches.

Whichever of these views is adopted, the letters convey much the same message. They show a writer dealing with the growth of heresy in the church and they describe the measures to be adopted. The treatment of this problem is put in a setting of personal instruction for the way of life of church leaders and members.

FOR TODAY'S CONGREGATIONAL LEADERS

- There is much emphasis in the Pastoral Epistles on the importance of 'sound doctrine' and on the danger of heresy and false teaching and practice in the church. Is there a danger today of going to the opposite extreme by tolerating a wide variety of beliefs and patterns of behaviour?
- The importance of appointed leaders and teachers: is there any danger in the contemporary emphasis on 'every member ministry'?
- Compare the teaching in 1 Tim. 6 on the proper use of wealth with that in 2 Cor. 8—9 on generosity and the teaching in the Gospels about 'selling all that you have' (Luke 18:22; cf. 14:33). What might a contemporary 'theology of money' look like?
- Much of the teaching about character and behaviour in the letters reflects ideals held

in the ancient world (e.g. the stress on self-control, godliness and submissiveness). What might Christians today learn from the picture of the godly life in these letters? Are there any particular virtues upheld in today's society, that contemporary Christians would do well to emulate?

ESSAY TOPICS

INTRODUCTORY
- Write a study of 'the person and work of Jesus' on the basis of the evidence in the Pastoral Epistles.

INTERMEDIATE
- 'The way in which Paul is made to speak about himself in the Pastoral Epistles looks more like the portrait that a later venerator of him would have than an authentic record of what he himself would have said': discuss whether the picture of Paul is artificial compared with the kind of way that he talks about himself in (for example) Phil. 1 and 2 Cor. 1—7.

FURTHER READING

*denotes books assuming knowledge of Greek; most can be used by all students.

INTRODUCTORY
M. Davies *The Pastoral Epistles*. Sheffield: Sheffield Academic Press, 1996 (introductory matters; favours pseudonymity).

R. T. France *Women in the Church's Ministry*. Carlisle: Paternoster, 1995/Grand Rapids: Eerdmans, 1997 (non-technical discussion of the subject in the New Testament and the problem of its modern application).

F. Young *The Theology of the Pastoral Letters*. Cambridge/New York: Cambridge University Press, 1994 (excellent survey of the theology).

Commentaries

C. K. Barrett *The Pastoral Epistles*. Oxford: Oxford University Press, 1963 (succinct and sharp).

M. Davies *The Pastoral Epistles*. EC. London: Epworth Press/Valley Forge: Trinity Press International, 1996 (some critical comments to challenge traditionalists).

G. D. Fee *1 and 2 Timothy, Titus*. NIBC. Peabody: Hendrickson, 1988 (excellent entrance-level).

D. Guthrie *The Pastoral Epistles*. TNTC. Leicester: IVP/Grand Rapids: Eerdmans, 1990 (the classic introductory treatment).

P. H. Towner *1–2 Timothy and Titus*. IVPNTC. Downers Grove/Leicester: IVP, 1994 (combines exegesis and some application).

INTERMEDIATE

R. A. Campbell *The Elders: Seniority within Earliest Christianity*. Edinburgh: T. & T. Clark, 1994 (detailed, fresh study of the problem of elders and bishops).

E. E. Ellis *The Making of the New Testament Documents*. Leiden: Brill, 1999 (comprehensive treatment of the subject, assigning the Pastoral Epistles to Paul's lifetime).

P. N. Harrison *The Problem of the Pastoral Epistles*. Oxford: Oxford University Press, 1921 (the classic linguistic argument for post-Pauline authorship).

A. J. Köstenberger and T. L. Wilder (eds) *Entrusted with the Gospel: Paul's Theology in the Pastoral Epistles*. Nashville: B&H Academic, 2010 (comprehensive set of essays on aspects of the theology).

I. H. Marshall 'Recent Study of the Pastoral Epistles' *Themelios* 23.1 1997, pp. 3–29 (see also author's contribution to Köstenberger and Wilder's symposium).

J. A. T. Robinson *Redating the New Testament*. London: SCM Press/Philadelphia: Westminster, 1976 (argues for the early

dating of the New Testament books including the Pastoral Epistles).

P. H. Towner *The Goal of our Instruction*. Sheffield: Sheffield Academic Press, 1989 (the major study of the theology and ethics of the letters).

D. C. Verner *The Household of God: The Social World of the Pastoral Epistles*. Chico: Scholars, 1983 (examines the centrality of the motif of the household).

Commentaries

R. F. Collins *I & 2 Timothy and Titus: A Commentary*. NTL. Louisville: Westminster John Knox, 2002 (particularly good on citing non-biblical texts that illumine the background of thought).

A. T. Hanson *The Pastoral Epistles*. NCB. London: Marshall Pickering/Grand Rapids: Eerdmans, 1982 (some stimulating original interpretations that don't always work).

L. T. Johnson *Letters to Paul's Delegates. 1 Timothy, 2 Timothy, Titus*. Valley Forge: TPI, 1996 (stresses the nature of the letters as instructions to Paul's junior colleagues).

W. L. Liefeld *1 and 2 Timothy, Titus*. NIVAC. Grand Rapids: Zondervan, 1999 (particularly concerned with application on the basis of careful exegesis).

*I. H. Marshall (in collaboration with P. H. Towner) *A Critical and Exegetical Commentary on the Pastoral Epistles*. ICC. Edinburgh: T. & T. Clark, 1999 (very detailed treatment of the Greek text).

*W. D. Mounce *The Pastoral Epistles*. WBC. Dallas: Word, 2000 (detailed treatment of the Greek text).

J. Twomey *The Pastoral Epistles Through the Centuries*. Blackwell Bible Commentaries. Malden, MA/Oxford: Wiley-Blackwell, 2009 (fascinating section-by-section account of how the letters have been understood and misunderstood down the centuries).

Chapter 14

PAUL – THE MISSIONARY THEOLOGIAN

In this chapter we shall consider:

● Paul's view of humanity and its need;
● how people could get right with God in Judaism and in Paul's theology;
● the importance of faith;
● the new life of believers in relation to God the Father, Jesus Christ and the Holy Spirit;
● Paul's new understanding of God;
● the community of believers and its corporate life;
● the new shape of Christian behaviour in general and in some particular areas;
● the Christian hope and its relationship to life here and now.

Now that we have surveyed the career of Paul and the various letters attributed to him, it is time to put all the material together and see what general picture of his thought emerges. What follows will inevitably be a rather selective summary of some of the main themes that we find in Paul's letters. In our earlier discussion we stressed the fact that Paul was a missionary, but his letters also show that he was a creative, theological thinker. These two elements are crucial for understanding him. Perhaps a third element should also be included, namely that Paul experienced frequent opposition and as a result spent a considerable amount of time in imprisonments and knew that the threat of death was a very real one.

What do you think?

Is it fair to expect a single, coherent, systematic theology from Paul? On the basis of your knowledge of his letters how far do you think that he did his theologizing on the hoof, so that his thought was continually developing new insights? How far did he have 'core' beliefs that remained constant?

PAUL AS AN APOSTLE

The key term that sums up these roles of Paul is 'apostle', a term that was in use in the ancient world to signify a messenger acting as an agent on behalf of the sender. Paul describes himself as both an apostle and a slave or servant of God or of Jesus Christ. There were other apostles in the Christian movement, in particular the twelve apostles appointed by Jesus himself during his lifetime who continued to be active in the church at Jerusalem in its early days.

'Twelve' is in a sense a 'complete' number, corresponding to the number of the twelve tribes of Israel, and Luke almost seems to limit the number of the apostles to the twelve. Only in Acts 14:4, 14 does he use the term rather casually of Paul and Barnabas. It is not clear why he is so coy in this respect. Paul himself evidently knew of a wider number of apostles and even of people whom he described as 'false' apostles. He could also refer to people who were apostles of the churches (2 Cor. 8:23) rather than of Christ himself. In the fuller sense of the term it referred to people who had seen the risen Jesus Christ and been commissioned by him as missionaries (1 Cor. 9:1–2; Gal. 1:15–16). Such people were also constituted as trustees of the new revelations that God gave at the foundation and early development of the church, and they had authority to set up congregations and to supervise their growth. It was in this way that Paul saw himself. Thus his activities as a

missionary and as a communicator of God's message formed a united whole. It is, therefore, not inappropriate to speak of him as a missionary theologian, meaning that his theology developed in the interests of his work as a missionary and was also shaped by it. His theology provides the foundation for his mission.

HUMANITY AND ITS NEED

The presupposition of the work of a missionary is that he/she has an answer to a problem faced by at least some people. Therefore, underlying Paul's theology there is a set of beliefs or assumptions about humanity and its need.

CREATION

For Paul humankind is God's creation, traced back to Adam (and Eve). Adam, the progenitor of the human race in the story in Genesis, is important for Paul who establishes a contrast between him as the introducer of sin into the world and the Second Man, Jesus, who acts as Saviour (Rom. 5:12–21). The rest of the created universe is involved in the need that leads to the new creation and will share in it (Rom. 8:19–23).

HUMAN NATURE

Of all the New Testament writers Paul has the most developed and complex understanding of human nature and personality. He uses the terms 'body' and 'flesh' frequently to refer to human nature. Less frequent are 'mind', 'heart', 'soul' and 'spirit'. It is difficult to describe his anthropology in a 'neutral' kind of way, since he uses it largely to describe the nature of the Christian believer. Nevertheless, some points are fairly clear:

EVANGELISM AND THEOLOGY

Paul's letters are all addressed to people who were already Christian believers and contain his theology of the Christian life. We have little direct information as to what Paul preached as an evangelist. All that we have are the 'sermons' in Acts (principally in Acts 13, 14 and 17 together with his autobiographical defences of himself before Jewish and Roman audiences in the later chapters), and these are very short summaries of what may be presumed to have been much longer discourses (as Acts 20:7 indirectly testifies!). Nevertheless, since preachers often remind their Christian audiences of the way in which they became Christians, we can reconstruct the basic contents of Paul's evangelism without too much difficulty, even if some points remain complex and difficult. Echoes of Paul's preaching can be picked up from Rom. 10:8–13; 1 Cor. 15:1–11; 1 Thess. 1:9–10.

Flesh

Flesh (*sarx*) is the substance of which humans are made (1 Cor. 15:39; Rom. 2:28). Therefore, it refers to the sphere or character of the existence of Jesus as a man (Rom. 1:3; 8:3). 'Flesh' can signify what we would call 'humanity' (Rom. 3:20; 1 Cor. 1:29). It refers to what is outward and visible as opposed to what is inner and spiritual (1 Cor. 5:5; 2 Cor. 7:1). Hence it can be used to refer to human relationships as opposed to spiritual ones (Rom. 4:1; 9:3). It can be used to designate the sphere of or mode of human existence (Gal. 2:20; Phil. 1:22, 24). By nature it is weak and mortal (2 Cor. 4:11; 7:5). And yet people put their confidence in it instead of in God (Gal. 6:12–13)!

Frequently 'flesh' is used to designate that part or aspect of humans that is liable to sin and can be taken over and empowered by sin. Paul can use 'fleshly' to refer to sinful human nature (1 Cor. 3:1; Rom. 7:14; 2 Cor. 10:4). Flesh can almost appear as a power that controls us. It refers to human life apart from God – life 'according to the flesh' (2 Cor. 1:17; 10:2–3) and thus hostile to God (Rom. 8:7). People may seek 'salvation' on this level (Gal. 3:3; Phil. 3:3).

What do you think?

Misunderstanding of Paul's use of 'flesh' has led many people through the centuries to think that Christianity has a negative attitude towards the human body and sexuality. Do you think this is still the case? How can we help people towards a truer understanding of Christian perspectives on these issues? (The Pauline material is especially to be found in Rom. 7:14—8:13; Gal. 5:13–26; Eph. 2:3, 11–14.)

Body

Curiously there is no word for 'body' in Hebrew. In Paul 'body' (*sōma*) is used in ways that are parallel to 'flesh'. It refers to outward, physical existence (Gal. 6:17; 2 Cor. 10:10). It can refer to the whole person (1 Cor. 6:18–20; Rom. 12:1); it can be used to refer to oneself (Rom. 6:12–13). Human bodies are mortal (Rom. 6:12; 8:11). The body can be subject to hostile powers (Rom. 6:6; 7:24). But whereas 'flesh' is incapable of redemption, the body can be redeemed and transformed (Rom. 6:6; 8:23; 1 Cor. 15:44, 51).

SIN

Sin (*hamartia*) is universal (Rom. 3:23). Paul treats the human race as a unity in sin and somehow relates this to Adam (Rom. 5:12–21). Sin is fundamentally disobedience towards God, but one can sin against a fellow human being (1 Cor. 8:12).

Sin is also related to the 'law' i.e. the revelation of God's will associated with Moses. It was in the world before Moses, but the effect of the law is to bring it out into the open; it is like a hidden power, which can be prodded into life. Hence there was death right from creation (Rom. 5:13–14).

Sin can also be regarded as a kind of power that keeps us under its sway (Rom. 7:7–13). It is fundamentally alien to our true being, yet takes us over completely.

Sin leads to death, regarded as its 'wage' or reward (Rom. 6:23). Death is regarded as the divine judgement on sin; the word 'penalty' is hardly used. Paul prefers to talk of divine 'wrath' (*orgē*; Rom. 1:18; 2:5; 5:9; Eph. 5:6; 1 Thess. 1:10).

What do you think?

Paul's use of 'wrath' to describe God's reaction to sin is perhaps the aspect of New Testament theology that people find most distasteful. The language of 'retribution', which states that people must somehow make up for their sins by paying a recompense or undergoing a penalty, is often questioned by people who are trying to rethink how society should deal with those who break its laws.

The question is as old as the New Testament: 'But if our injustice serves to confirm the justice of God, what should we say? That God is unjust to inflict wrath on us? (I speak in a human way.) By no means! For then how could God judge the world?' (Rom. 3:5–6). The problem is eased by the fact that divine wrath is not presented by Paul as an arbitrary, unbridled fit of temper or anger but rather as the outworking of his judgement upon sin and evil. It is more like the response of a judge acting on behalf of a community to uphold its laws.

Do you think that Paul's concept of God's wrath is an application of human categories to God? Or should our ideas of justice and the functions of judgement in the community be based on what the Bible has to say about God's ways as judge? See C. D. Marshall *Beyond Retribution*. Grand Rapids: Eerdmans, 2001, for a full discussion of justice, human and divine.

GETTING RIGHT WITH GOD

From the plight we move to the solution. Paul, of course, was not alone in offering an answer to human need. His Jewish contemporaries believed that they were the possessors of the answer. However, there is much debate over just how they envisaged it, and not all Jews necessarily understood the situation in the same way. Here are three different modern interpretations of how the Jews understood the matter.

JUSTIFICATION BY WORKS

According to the traditional understanding of the matter, God provided a way for the Jews to get right with God and achieve salvation (the cancelling out of their sins) by the performance of the works required by the law (Gal. 3:12); and equally failure to keep the law resulted in being under God's judgement ('cursed'; Gal. 3:10). But this salvation was only for Jews and for those Gentiles who accepted the requirements of the law, including circumcision, the observance of Jewish festivals and the practice of Jewish food restrictions. Paul replaced salvation by works of the law with salvation by faith, and thus opened up the way for Gentiles to be saved without having to keep the law and become in effect practising Jews.

COVENANTAL NOMISM

This traditional understanding of what Judaism taught has been strongly challenged by recent scholars (principally E. P. Sanders; see pp. 52–3). Judaism, they say, taught that salvation was through belonging to God's people, which rested on God's gracious election of Israel into the covenant. Obedience to the works of the law ('nomism') followed on from this as the means by which one stayed within the covenant and not as the meritorious means of admission.

THE MARKS OF BELONGING

J. D. G. Dunn's refinement of this position is that performance of the works of the law was not so much the means of staying in the covenant as rather the outward sign that one was 'in'; such visible actions as circumcision, Sabbath observance and food laws marked off the Jews from the unsaved Gentiles.

On any of these views of Judaism, entry into the covenant or salvation for Gentiles entailed the adoption of Judaism. And it was assumed that all Jews were automatically 'in', apart from notoriously wicked sinners.

PAUL'S RADICAL ALTERNATIVE

Whichever of these views is correct, the radical teaching of Paul was that salvation depended upon the grace of God displayed specifically in the 'Christ-event' (shorthand for the sending of God's son into the world, his death and resurrection). The significance of this event was expressed in various ways:

- Christ became a 'curse' so as to deliver people from the *judgement* due to those who do not fulfil the law (Gal. 3:13).
- Christ died as a sacrifice of *atonement* (Rom. 3:25) in order to deal with human sin.
- Christ became 'sin' for us that we might become '*righteousness*' (2 Cor. 5:21).
- God acted in *grace* (Rom. 3:24; 4:16; 5:15; 2 Cor. 6:1; Eph. 2:5). This word designates free and unmerited favour (Rom. 4:4) which acts to save sinners, whether Jews or Gentiles.

THE LANGUAGE OF SALVATION

There are five main ways in which the process whereby God deals with sin and sinners is expressed by Paul.

SACRIFICE

The Jewish religion had at its centre an elaborate system of animal sacrifices to God offered at the temple in Jerusalem; these sacrifices had various functions, but most important were those offered for sin and which had the effect of cancelling out the effects of the sins committed by God's people. Paul understood the death of Jesus by analogy with these sacrifices as itself a sacrifice, which replaced the Jewish system and made it obsolete. He can refer to the death of Jesus as a sin offering (Rom. 8:3 NRSV mg.) and he described it as a 'sacrifice of atonement' (Rom. 3:25; or 'place of atonement' [NRSV mg.], corresponding to the lid of the box in the temple on which the high priest annually poured the blood of a sacrifice; Lev. 16:15f.). The death of Jesus is compared to that of the Passover lamb (1 Cor. 5:6–8), and there are references to his 'blood', a term that carries nuances of sacrifice (Rom. 5:9; 1 Cor. 10:16; 11:25; Eph. 1:7; 2:13).

JUSTIFICATION

This is primarily a legal metaphor. The verb 'justify' reflects the Hebrew verb *hitsdîq* (from *tsadaq*, 'to be just, in the right'), which means essentially 'to give a person a righteous status' in the sight of God. Traditional Roman Catholic theology took it to mean 'to make righteous' in the sense that God gave people a righteous nature. But the Greek verb has more the force 'to declare righteous' (like the Hebrew verb) rather than 'to make righteous'. The idea is that the person who has been placed in a bad relationship to God by sin is now put into a good relationship and thus becomes 'righteous' in the sense of 'enjoying God's favour' (Rom. 3:24–30; 1 Cor. 6:11; Gal. 2:16–17; Titus 3:7). Traditional Reformed theology has taken justification to mean 'to confer the righteousness of Christ' on a person, but it is debatable whether it has this positive force or simply means (negatively) 'to forgive'.

Justification has often been regarded (especially by followers of Martin Luther) as the heart of Paul's theology. It can certainly be seen as the framework for understanding much of his theology. But Paul also uses a variety of other pictures to express the nature of God's act.

REDEMPTION

This is ultimately a metaphor from the setting free of captives, especially slaves. Normally this took place by the payment of a ransom (cf. Isa. 43:1–4; 52:3). But the metaphor is especially used in the OT of God delivering captives by his mighty power (Deut. 7:8), and it has been argued that the idea of paying a price is not integral to the metaphor. In fact two lines of thought occur: first, the redemption of captives resulting in their freedom from bondage – i.e. to sin and hence to death (cf. Ps. 130:8; Gal. 3:13; 4:5); second, the purchase by God of his people to belong to him (a change of masters; 1 Cor. 6:20; 7:23). In both cases, however, the action is linked directly to the sacrificial death of Jesus (Rom. 3:24; Eph. 1:7).

RECONCILIATION

This is the language of diplomacy, which was used extensively in Greek thought to refer to establishing peace between warring persons. One side may take the initiative, or a mediator may intervene. The metaphor implies that people are at enmity with God, but he acts in the death of Christ to offer them reconciliation; this is proclaimed to them in the gospel, and they must make their response (2 Cor. 5:18—6:2; Eph. 2:16; Col. 1:20–21). Rom. 5:9–11 shows the close parallelism with justification.

SALVATION

This term is used primarily to refer to the future state of deliverance from judgement and entry into God's favour with its associated benefits (Rom. 5:9–11; 13:11). Nevertheless, it also refers to the present state of people who have been through the experience of justification (Rom. 8:24; Eph. 2:5, 8). Essentially it refers to deliverance from a fatal situation (whether illness or danger).

Digging deeper

Use a concordance to find the main references to these five pictures used by Paul for understanding what Christ did to put us right with God. Outline the key features of each of them. Which of them is most meaningful for people of today? Are there important elements of truth that would be lost if we set aside any one of them?

FAITH

For Paul faith is the fundamental human attitude that receives the divine gift. Faith is the correlate of grace and the antithesis to works (Rom. 1:17; 3:22; Gal. 3:2, 5). More closely defined, it appears to be basically acceptance of a gift, but includes belief in the truth of God's promises (even when they seem incredible, Rom. 4:18). It therefore rests upon 'hearing' – and is preceded by the preaching of the gospel (Rom. 10:14). It also involves commitment, and it finds expression in 'working by love' (Gal. 5:6).

Faith is clearly required of Gentiles. For Paul it is of crucial importance that it stands in antithesis to the works of the law (Rom. 3:27–28; 9:32; Gal. 2:16; Eph. 2:8–9). One does not need to become a Jewish proselyte in order to be saved and be a member of God's people.

What do you think?

'Faith is believing something for which there's no evidence.'

'Faith is believing six impossible things before breakfast.'

What does Paul say about faith (for example, in Rom. 4), which helps to correct misunderstandings of faith such as these?

But Paul goes further than this. He teaches quite plainly that the Jews themselves have gone the wrong way. They are regarded as lost and in need of salvation. They also need to believe in order to be saved. He regards Judaism as having gone astray, and it is difficult to avoid the impression that somehow they have put their trust in the works of the law and seen them as a means of establishing their righteous status in the sight of God; he develops this point at length in Rom. 9—11. Clearly this position would not win Paul friends, for in effect it disqualifies Judaism. Paul appears to teach one way of salvation for all; if Jesus is the God-given Messiah, then Jews who reject him disqualify themselves from his people.

All this raises the question of how Paul saw the law of Moses. He appears to regard it as obsolete as a way of salvation but its ethical requirements express the will of God, which is now to be fulfilled through the Spirit (Rom. 8:4).

THE NEW LIFE OF BELIEVERS

From Paul's teaching about how people are saved we move on to consider the situation of those who are saved. For Paul 'salvation' is generally understood in terms of future deliverance from the wrath of God against sinners. Those who have put their faith in Christ constitute the new people of God who are now on their way to this ultimate salvation. But what is their present status, and how are they to live in the intervening period?

At the risk of being over-schematic, we could say that the situation of Christian believers is determined by their relationship to God, who is understood as Father, Son and Spirit.

GOD AS FATHER

Paul's understanding of God as Father is essentially the same as that of Jesus. One of the 'new things' that Jesus did was to take up this concept, which was effectively marginal in the Old Testament, and to make it central. Whereas in the earlier stages of the Jewish religion God was understood to be the Father of the Jewish people (Exod. 4:22; Deut. 32:6; Jer. 31:9, 20) and to have a specially close relationship to their king (2 Sam. 7:14; Ps. 89:26), there was some limited recognition of him as standing in a similar relationship to godly individuals, and people might pray collectively to him as their Father (Ps. 68:5; 103:13; Jer. 3:4, 19). Jesus took a quantum-leap forward in that he saw himself as closely related individually to God as his Father and taught that this same close relationship was open to all his followers (see vol. 1, pp. 178, 191–3). To accept the message of Jesus about the kingdom of God and to become a follower of Jesus carried with it the privilege of entering into a filial relationship with God. What Jesus taught as something new became the accepted understanding of the early Christians, and was taken for granted by Paul. It is Paul who preserves for us the fact that Christians at prayer even used the intimate Aramaic word 'Abba' to address God (Rom. 8:15; Gal. 4:6). So for Paul 'the God and Father of our Lord Jesus Christ' (2 Cor. 1:3) is also the Father of all believers (2 Cor. 1:2). (This entails that Paul is using 'fatherhood' to designate a spiritual relationship which is true only of believers; the common understanding that God is the father of all human beings is seriously mistaken.)

What do you think?

Is it impossible for people to appreciate the meaning of God as father if they have experienced their human father as oppressive, abusive or absent? Are some feminists right in their protest against the use of male father-language of God? Does the occasional biblical picture of God as like a mother (Isa. 66:13) offer a helpful supplement or alternative to father-language?

'IN CHRIST'

Paul expresses the relationship of believers to Christ in a characteristic way that can easily be overlooked. The phrase 'in Christ' (and equivalents such as 'in him') is used about 165 times in the Pauline letters, primarily to establish this relationship. It occurs in a variety of constructions, such as these:

2 Cor. 5:17	If anyone is in Christ, there is a new creation.
Rom. 16:2	You may welcome her in the Lord
Rom. 14:14	I know and am persuaded in the Lord Jesus that . . .
Rom. 16:13	Greet Rufus [who is] chosen in the Lord.
Rom. 6:23	. . . the free gift of God is eternal life in Christ Jesus our Lord.
Rom. 8:39	The love of God [which is] in Christ Jesus our Lord.
Rom. 12:5	We, who are many, are one body in Christ.
Col. 1:16	In him all things . . . were created.
2 Cor. 1:20	In him every one of God's promises is a 'Yes'.

Difficulties have sometimes arisen in understanding the phrase because people assumed that it must have the same force every time it is used. This is not so. There are four main types of usage.

Ordinary usage It is the appropriate construction with numerous verbs that are naturally and normally followed by 'in' to express the basis of confidence, exultation, rejoicing, etc. ('to trust in' and 'to rejoice in'; see Phil. 1:14; 2:19, 24; 3:1, 3–4; 4:1, 4, 10, 13). The basis and foundation of Christian experience lies in Jesus.

Use with verbs of divine action In an instrumental or causal way it expresses the means by which divine blessings come to people as well as the means through which God works in the world (e.g. in creation). Jesus is seen as the channel through which God carries out his work in the lives of believers (see Phil. 3:14; 4:7, 19; 2:1). The thought of Christ as the channel or means of God's blessings implies that believers must come into a personal relationship with Christ in order to receive them, but it seems to be over-translation if we take the phrase, as some scholars do, to mean 'in virtue of your union with Christ'.

Use with verbs of human action In a more circumstantial way the phrase expresses the parameters affecting behaviour. Christian behaviour is determined by 'the Lord'; see

Phil. 2:29, 'Welcome him in the Lord'. Here 'in the Lord' qualifies the verb 'welcome' rather than the pronoun 'him'. We may paraphrase the command to mean: 'Receive him in a Christian manner'. The fact that the reference is to 'the Lord' rather than to 'Christ' may suggest that it is Jesus as the one who has authority over conduct in the church who is in mind, and that the phrase should be taken to mean something like 'in the manner appropriate to the situation in which Jesus is Lord' (cf. Phil. 4:2).

Adjectival use The phrase 'in Christ' can function adjectivally to describe the state of Christians (see Rom. 8:1; 16:7, 11; 2 Cor. 5:17; 12:2; Phil. 1:1; 3:9; Eph. 1:1; Col. 1:2; 1 Thess. 4:16). In the salutation in Phil. 1:1 (cf. Col. 1:2; Eph. 1:1) Paul writes to 'all the saints [who are] in Christ Jesus'. He is characterizing his readers as saints by virtue of the fact that they are 'in Christ'. Two types of understanding exist.

● The phrase could express *'incorporation in Christ'* or 'union with Christ'. One explanation is that the phrase is shorthand for 'in the body of Christ' (cf. 1 Cor. 12:18; Col. 3:15); this breaks down on the fact that the latter is not a phrase that Paul uses. Appeal has also been made to the idea of corporate personality so that Christ and believers form in effect one person, but this hypothesis has also fallen from favour because it rests on a misunderstanding of Hebrew thought. The phrase might indicate belonging to a group of people who are united to Christ, and so what is true of him is or will be true of them.
● Another possibility is that the phrase refers to a state of being determined or affected by the fact of Christ – a kind

of *circumstantial usage*. Believers are in a situation that is controlled by the fact of Christ crucified and risen. This will affect how they behave by contrast with people whose lives are not determined by the death and resurrection of Jesus.

These two types of understanding can be brought together. The phrase on occasion expresses close union between Christ and the believer. We can see this from the way in which Paul can also speak of Christ being 'in' the believer (Gal. 2:20); similarly, in the Gospel and Epistles of John we have the concept of mutual indwelling, where the language must surely be metaphorical (John 6:56; 14:20; 15:4–7; 17:21–23; 1 John 2:5–6, 24–28; 3:24; 4:13–16). At the same time, if believers are united with the Christ who died and rose again, then their existence and behaviour must be determined by the pattern of Christ. All this can be expressed in the phrase 'participation in Christ', which has recently become popular to indicate a relationship that is closer and deeper than other phrases like 'believing in Christ' or 'being united with Christ'.

Whatever be the usage, it is clear that the effect is to show that the Christian life is utterly dominated by the Christ who humbled himself, died and was exalted, the crucified and risen Christ. It further demonstrates something of the Pauline understanding of Christ. For him it is the crucified and risen Christ who is the basis of Christianity. God's blessings come through him. Christian believers are united to him, and the basis for their faith and the controlling factor in their behaviour lie in him. His cosmic lordship and his spiritual character are thus expressed.

THE WORK OF THE SPIRIT

A third feature of Paul's understanding of the life of the believer is expressed by reference to the Spirit of God. Reference to the Spirit is surprisingly rare in the teaching of Jesus, and in the depiction of the life of the early church in Acts the Spirit figures largely (but not exclusively) as the power which guides and empowers the church in its mission, specifically by filling individuals to do things that would appear to be beyond their natural capacities. Nevertheless, the gift of the Spirit is poured out at Pentecost and subsequently on believers in general and is conceived as a permanent possession rather than merely as a spasmodic empowering for particular occasions. It is to Paul that we have to turn for a more comprehensive and explicit understanding of the Spirit as the agent of God who somehow exercises an influence in people.

We have seen how the lives of people can be dominated and influenced by what Paul calls 'the flesh', so that their selfish and immoral passions get the better of them. But there is another possibility, namely that people are dominated and controlled by the Spirit. It is not easy to explain what sort of influence this is. Consider, however, how a virus or something similar, which causes physical illness and weakness and can have psychological effects such as depression or lassitude, may attack a person. The virus cannot be seen or felt but the effects are real enough. Equally, a person may take some medicine or drug, and again the working is not visible but the effect can be to impart health, to give enthusiasm and vitality. In both cases we are thinking of something that affects the person at the physical level, and over which they have no control once it has been taken (they could decide whether or not to take it), and it becomes a given factor in a situation whether for bad or good effects. We might compare the working of sin or the flesh, on the one hand, and the Spirit of God, on the other, as outside factors that dispose us one way or another, making us too weak to withstand temptation or strong enough to resist it, making us despondent or filling us with the capacity for hope. The influences are, of course, not physical like the viruses or drugs, but are something analogous in the spiritual sphere.

The analogy is crude (and therefore dangerous), but it may help to understand the kind of way in which Paul understands the Spirit. A new factor comes into a person's life enabling them to do things that otherwise they could not do. The Spirit is placed in close relationship to *faith*, so that the Spirit is the divine agent in the Christian life and is complementary to the human response of faith (Gal. 5:5). The Spirit is evidently received by faith (Gal. 3:2–3, 14). But the relationship between the human act of faith, by which people are saved, and the divine bestowal of the Spirit is impossible to elucidate any more clearly. We may think of them as complementary aspects of the same process.

The Spirit is associated with baptism, the rite of Christian initiation (1 Cor. 6:11; 12:3, 13). Corresponding to the physical act of baptism with water, there is a baptism with the Spirit, in which the Spirit becomes active in the person. He is received as a gift bestowed by God (Gal. 3:2, 14; 4:6; 1 Thess. 4:8; 1 Cor. 2:12; Rom. 5:5). He can be said to 'live' in believers (1 Cor. 3:16; Rom. 8:9) and to convey life. His presence is indispensable to the Christian life. A person who does not have the Spirit does not belong to Christ (Rom. 8:9).

The Spirit is associated with the new relationship of believers to God in which they are his adopted children (Rom. 8:14–15; Gal. 4:6). The Spirit gives Christian 'assurance' (Gal. 4:6; Rom. 8:16) and is the 'guarantee' of God's further gifts (2 Cor. 1:22; Eph. 1:13–14). He conveys the love of God to believers and makes them feel loved (Rom. 5:5). The presence of the Spirit is thus the subjective sign that a person is a child of God. When a person acknowledges Christ as Lord or prays to God as 'Abba', this is done by the Spirit and is a sign of the presence of the Spirit.

The presence of the Spirit leads to 'sanctification' and the qualities of Christian character (Rom. 14:17; Gal. 5:22; Eph. 3:16; Col. 1:8; 1 Thess. 1:6; 2 Thess. 2:13). Thus, the requirements of God's will expressed in the law are fulfilled by the Spirit. Only through the Spirit can believers fulfil the law (Rom. 8:4). Nevertheless, sanctification is not an automatic process over which the believer has no control. There is the possibility of continuing tension between the flesh and the Spirit in the believer (Gal. 5:16–26; cf. Rom. 7:14–25 which depicts a situation with which Christians may be all too familiar).

What do you think?

How does Paul cope with the paradox of sanctification – God gives the power of the Spirit to those who yield their lives to him, but how do you get the power to yield your life when you are controlled by self-centredness? Do we not need the Spirit to overcome our self-centredness? (Look especially at Rom. 8:1–13; Gal. 5:16–26; Phil. 2:12–13)

THEOLOGICAL IMPLICATIONS FOR PAUL'S UNDERSTANDING OF GOD

The ways in which Paul writes about the relationships of believers with God the Father, Jesus Christ and the Holy Spirit raise the important question of how he understands these beings.

His view of *God the Father* as the one God who created the universe and is sovereign over its history is fully in line with the teaching of Judaism, which in turn was based on the Jewish Scriptures, our Old Testament.

Likewise, Paul took over the Jewish understanding of God's agents, including the angels and especially the *Spirit of God*. Increasingly the Spirit is seen as the form in which God is active in the world. Although the Spirit is understood as a power that can affect human beings, there are indications that the Spirit is also seen as personal; the Spirit can be grieved (Eph. 4:30) and is said to intercede with the Father in prayer for God's people (Rom. 8:26f.). The implications of this personalizing of the Spirit are not developed by Paul.

But the same cannot be said about *Jesus*. There was a 'slot' in Judaism for Jesus to occupy, namely as the Messiah, who would be God's personal agent ruling over his people. Although the Messiah appears to have been thought of as a human figure, early Christians quickly came to think of him as more than human. Jesus had referred to himself as God's Son, and did so in a way that was suggestive of a personal relationship. He was raised from the dead, and this was understood in the light of Ps. 110 as an enthronement beside God. When Paul experienced his vision of the risen

Jesus at his conversion, he understood Jesus to be 'the Son of God' (Gal. 1:16). It may be that from this time he also understood Jesus to be 'the image of God' (2 Cor. 4:4). By the time that he wrote Philippians he understood Jesus to be a figure who was the image of God and equal with God, but who became a human being and submitted to God like a slave to a master, and then was subsequently exalted to sit beside God and bear the name of 'Lord' which (at least in this context and in various other passages) was clearly not just a title indicative of sovereignty but was God's own title or name shared with his Son (Phil. 2:6–11). The exalted language persists in the later letters with the declaration that all the fullness of God is in Christ (Col. 2:9) and with the use of the title 'God' for him (so in Titus 2:13 and also in Rom. 9:5, but here the rendering is not absolutely certain [cf. NRSV mg.]).

We thus can see a development, whether in the thought of Paul himself or stretching on into later letters composed in his name, whereby Jesus is placed alongside the Father. Thus it is that right from his earliest writings Paul names Jesus alongside God the Father as the source of the salvation bestowed by God and as his partner in creation (1 Cor. 8:6). Again, the Spirit is variously referred to as the Spirit of God (1 Cor. 2:11–14; Rom. 8:9, 14; specifically of the God who raised Christ, Rom. 8:11), and as the Spirit of Christ (Gal. 4:6; Rom. 8:9–10; Phil. 1:19). He is even called 'the Lord' in 2 Cor. 3:17–18. This process climaxes in the naming of the Lord Jesus Christ, God and the Holy Spirit alongside each other in the benediction at the end of 2 Corinthians (13:13). Paul's theology is implicitly trinitarian, but he never stops to work out the consequences of this understanding.

Digging deeper

Explore how Paul understands the nature and relationships of the Father, Son and Spirit in Romans 5—8. How far, if at all, can his thought be said to be 'implicitly trinitarian'?

THE COMMUNITY OF BELIEVERS

If our exposition of Paul's thought stopped at this point, we would be left with the impression that his message was concerned purely with how individuals might get into a right relationship with God and live lives that were pleasing to him. This would be a fatally one-sided and inadequate understanding of Paul, for it quickly becomes apparent that what motivated him was the creation of a people who would be reconciled to God and form his people. All Paul's letters (except the three to leaders) are addressed to groups of Christians, and it is their character as a community which is significant.

The key term '*church*' is used frequently by Paul simply to mean the group of Christians in a locality (e.g. Rom. 16:1, 4, 5, 16; 1 Cor. 1:2). Generally Paul refers to 'the churches' when he means Christians in several places. In a locality there may be one or more churches in households (Rom. 16:5; 1 Cor. 16:19; Col. 4:15; Phlm. 2). Sometimes, however, Paul may be thinking of the totality of Christians (1 Cor. 10:32; 12:28; 15:9), and this is particularly so in the later letters (Eph. 1:22; 3:10, 21; 5:23–32; Col. 1:18, 24).

The word '*saints*' is used in a similar way as a collective term for God's people (e.g. Rom. 1:7; 1 Cor. 1:2; Phil. 1:1; 1 Cor. 14:33).

Both of these terms take up Old Testament language for *the people of God*. It becomes apparent that Paul sees his task as the reconstitution of a people of God who are defined by their acceptance of Jesus as the Messiah and Lord appointed by God. This people stand in continuity with the people of God whose roots stretch back to Abraham; it looks as though Paul traced a line of faithful people back to Abraham, who were to be distinguished from the disobedient Israelites who were condemned by the prophets, and also that in his own time he distinguished between the Jews who accepted Jesus and those who rejected him and thereby cut themselves off from God's people. And, of course, the people of God now included the Gentiles who believed in Jesus and were thus grafted in, like branches being grafted into a living vine. The church can accordingly be understood as 'the Israel of God' (Gal. 6:16) and it is seen as the inheritor of the promises made to Israel in the Old Testament. For Paul salvation, whether for Jew or Gentile, is by faith and involves acceptance of Jesus Christ as Lord (Rom. 10:9–13).

A local congregation can be likened to a *body* in which various parts help one another and all are important (Rom. 12:5; 1 Cor. 10:17; 12:12–27). It is called 'Christ's body' (1 Cor. 12:27). At this stage the thought is purely of the mutual relationship of the parts and nothing is said about the relationship to the world. In later letters this metaphor is developed in terms of the 'head'. The church is now a body of interrelated parts which function together and 'grow' under the leadership of the Head and by means of the power that flows from it (Col. 1:18; 2:19; 3:15; Eph. 1:23; 4:4, 12, 16; 5:23, 30). The metaphor expresses the unity of the church and the inter-relatedness and complementarity of the individuals who compose it.

Like the individual believer (1 Cor. 6:19), the church is compared to a *temple* or building in which God is present (1 Cor. 3:16–17; 2 Cor. 6:16; Eph. 2:21). The spiritualization of the temple idea is here fully carried through.

MINISTRY AND THE FUNCTIONS OF THE CHURCH

There is a sense in which the church is the church when its members meet together. These meetings of local congregations are characterized by 'edification', i.e. by activities that strengthen and build up the lives of the members individually and corporately (1 Cor. 14:3–5, 12, 26; 2 Cor. 10:8; 12:19; Eph. 4:12; 1 Thess. 5:11). But what is to be developed? Paul mentions such qualities as: love (Eph. 4:16); peace; the good of others (Rom. 15:2); knowledge, encouragement and comfort (1 Cor. 14:3–5).

The congregation is the place where the Spirit is active. He produces unity in the church (Eph. 2:18, 22; 4:3–4). Believers share together in the gift of the Spirit (2 Cor. 13:13; Phil. 2:1). He distributes spiritual gifts (1 Cor. 12; 14:2, 12). The Spirit's power is demonstrated in the working of miracles (presumably, in the main, of healing; Gal. 3:5) and also in enabling the various charismata that build the church up. Paul has a theology of spiritual gifts rather than of natural abilities harnessed to divine service. (We can assume that he doesn't disregard natural abilities; it is rather that in the context he is talking purely about what the Spirit does.)

What do you think?

When Christians think about the Spirit of God, they can often be divided into those who are excited about spiritual gifts and those who focus on the Spirit's work in developing Christian character and behaviour. If you found this kind of division in your congregation, how would you try to help the two groups to learn from Paul that both are important?

In 1 Cor. 12 Paul lists various charismatic people – apostles, prophets, teachers, workers of miracles, healers, helpers, administrators, speakers in various tongues, etc. (12:28; cf. 12:8–10; Rom. 12:6–8); there is a simpler list in Eph. 4:11. The various tasks and functions carried on in the congregation are done by those who have the appropriate 'charisma' rather than by people who are 'appointed' by the rest of the congregation to do them. These tasks are what we would call aspects of 'ministry' in today's language. They are manifestly carried out by the members of the congregation, and we gain the impression that they were spread among the congregation as a whole and not confined to a small minority of participants.

At the same time, some people do seem to have been appointed to act as leaders. Apostles were apparently 'appointed' by the risen Lord, and at Corinth there were some locally appointed leaders (1 Cor. 16:15–16 – evidently from among the first converts). It is therefore misleading to separate sharply between charisma and appointment and to contrast an original charismatically endowed congregation (1 Corinthians) with a later institutionalized church where a limited number of people are appointed to specific offices (the Pastoral Epistles); elements of

both are present throughout and the change is one of emphasis, not of kind.

Nevertheless, there was probably a development towards a more organized system of leadership as the church grew and spread. In his earliest references to local leadership Paul refers vaguely to those who labour and are *over the church* (1 Thess. 5:12) or who *teach* (Gal. 6:6). In Phil. 1:1 Paul addresses the *overseers* and *deacons*. A similar pattern is found in the Pastorals where we have overseers or elders (1 Tim. 3:1–7; 5:17; Titus 1:5–9) and deacons (1 Tim. 3:8–13) in the local churches, but all under the oversight of Timothy or Titus (who function like Paul, perhaps with the role of *evangelist*,

OVERSEERS AND SERVANTS

Overseer (NRSV: 'bishop'; Gk. *episkopos*) was a term used of people with financial, teaching and pastoral responsibilities. It looks as though 'elder' and 'overseer' were closely related terms.

Deacon (Gk. *diakonos*) originally means a servant, especially one serving at table, and could be used of any type of worker in the church in their capacity as servants of Christ and of their fellow-Christians; in Philippians and 1 Timothy it has developed a more restricted reference to those with lesser responsibilities than the bishops.

Digging deeper

Read 1 Cor. 12—14. Draw up a list of the differences between what happened in Christian meetings at Corinth in Paul's time and in a contemporary congregation known to you. How can you account for them, and is a 'return to New Testament Christianity' possible or advisable?

2 Tim. 4:5). Their tasks were pastoral and didactic, and Paul himself is presented as an example to follow.

> ### What do you think?
>
> Different church traditions and denominations have different patterns of ministry and leadership, yet all of them tend to argue that their pattern is derived from the New Testament. Do you think that they are indulging in special pleading, or are New Testament patterns varied enough to allow for them all (or perhaps most of them)?

WHAT PRINCIPLES SHAPE CHRISTIAN BEHAVIOUR?

The basis for Christian living is theological. We have seen how some letters have a more or less doctrinal section followed by a more or less practical section (Romans; Ephesians; Colossians), while some can use doctrine to back up practical teaching (Titus). At other times doctrine and practice are closely linked in discussions of individual aspects of behaviour.

FIVE GENERAL PRINCIPLES

● Life *'in Christ'* is life that takes on the shape of the death and resurrection of Jesus. Hence the believer has 'died' to sin and 'lives' to righteousness (Rom. 6; Col. 2—3). This leads to the understanding of ethics that has been summed up in the paradoxical command: 'be what you are'; the imperative is 'given' in the indicative. Believers have a new status as 'saints' and possesses a new ethical power. They can be encouraged to follow the example of Christ in self-giving and humility (Phil. 2:5–11).

● Life 'in the Lord'. Paul's use of this phrase indicates that life is lived in the new situation that is controlled by the presence of Christ as Lord (Rom. 16:2, 8, 11–13; Eph. 6:1; Phil. 2:29; 4:2; Col. 3:18; 1 Thess. 4:1). Hence the believer can be said to be under the law of Christ (1 Cor. 9:21) and must imitate the Lord (1 Cor. 11:1).

● Obedience is required to *the commands of God* as mediated by the apostolic teaching, including that of Paul himself (Rom. 1:5; 6:16; 15:18; 2 Cor. 7:15; 10:5; 2 Thess. 1:8; 3:14; Phlm. 21).

● Believers are also summoned to *'live by the Spirit'* (Gal. 5:16–26; Rom. 8:1–13). The Spirit is understood as the source of moral guidance, teaching believers how they are to live, but also as the source of spiritual power, enabling them to follow this guidance; Paul makes this point by contrasting life in the Spirit with trying to live by the law of Moses which gave no help to people struggling to keep its commandments (Rom. 8:3).

● Believers are to live in the light of their *calling and future hope*. They are to live lives worthy of God who has called them to be his people (1 Thess. 2:12; 4:7; Eph. 4:1; 2 Tim. 1:9) and to 'run the race' to its goal (Phil. 3:14). They are to remember that they will come before God's judgement (Rom. 14:10–12; 2 Cor. 5:10). They should endeavour to be ready for when the Lord comes (Rom. 13:11–14; 1 Thess. 5:1–11).

> ### What do you think?
>
> Study 1 Thess. 5:1–11 with the help of a commentary. According to Paul, what impact should the hope of Christ's coming have on the lives of Christians?

THE NEW WAY OF LIFE

Holiness and sanctification God's call is to *holiness* (1 Thess. 4:7) and *sanctification* (2 Cor. 7:1). These two terms translate words from the same Greek root, and describe the kind of conduct that is appropriate for the people of a righteous and loving God. In plainer terms Paul tells his readers to live a life that is worthy of the Lord and that brings credit to him (1 Cor. 10:31; Eph. 1:12).

Love for one's neighbour This involves putting no stumbling block in the way of others (Rom. 14:13; 1 Cor. 8:13; 10:32) and counting other peoples' interests as highly as one's own (Phil. 2:3–4).

Liberty/freedom is also upheld. The believer is set free from the power of the flesh (Rom. 7:14–25) and also from sin (Rom. 6:18, 22) and is not enslaved to other people, yet must pay regard to them (1 Cor. 7:21–22; 9:19; 2 Cor. 3:17; Gal. 5:1, 13). Thus Paul could side with the 'strong' at Corinth, who were not troubled by scruples about the food that they bought in the market, but he insisted emphatically that they pay regard to the weak and not act in ways that could lead them into sinning by disobeying their consciences (1 Cor. 10:29).

The Jewish law Controversy surrounds the place of the Jewish law in regard to Christian conduct. Paul appears ambivalent. On the one hand, justification is no longer by the works of the law (Rom. 3:28; Gal. 2:16; 3:11) and believers are not 'under the law' (Rom. 6:14f.). On the other hand, the law is perfectly good (Rom. 7:6) and believers are called to fulfil the requirements of the law (Rom. 8:4). Although one is justified by faith alone, this does not mean that being a Christian is simply a matter of believing in Christ and nothing more. It is a faith that works by love (Rom. 13:10; Gal. 5:14). Thus the law is upheld and Paul is able to rebut charges of antinomianism, i.e. that Christian conduct is not concerned with the requirements of the law. Ethical teaching can be drawn from the OT generally (and not just from the actual Torah or law of Moses). It does seem that Paul worked with some kind of distinction between the commandments in the law of Moses which were done away with in Christ (in effect the ritual ones and those which were peculiarly 'Jewish') and those which were of abiding and universal validity, although this distinction is never made explicit. In any case, Paul also makes a contrast between the letter and the spirit (Rom. 2:29; 7:6; cf. 2

Digging deeper

'If you let yourselves be circumcised, Christ will be of no benefit to you. I testify to every man who lets himself be circumcised that he is obliged to obey the entire law.' (Gal. 5:2–3)

'For the whole law is summed up in a single commandment, "You shall love your neighbour as yourself".' (Gal. 5:14)

'If you are led by the Spirit, you are not subject to the law.' (Gal. 5:18)

'Bear one another's burdens, and in this way you will fulfil the law of Christ.' (Gal. 6:2)

Does Paul have a consistent understanding of the law? Did his views develop and change? Or is he simply inconsistent? Explore his teaching about the law (see the relevant articles in *DPL*, especially pp. 529–44, 975–9).

Cor. 3:6–7), which implies that mere outward, literal fulfilment of specific laws is not to be confused with the fuller and deeper obedience that comes from the heart; there is a distinction between keeping the letter of the law in a mechanical kind of way and the love of God which leads to delight in doing his will in ways that go beyond the strict letter.

Perfection? Does Paul expect Christians to be 'perfect' in the sense of 'sinless'? He puts this ideal before them (1 Cor. 1:8) and sees it as their ultimate goal (Phil. 1:10; 1 Thess. 5:23), but he recognizes the possibility of temptation and falling into sin (as a reading of 1 Cor. would quickly establish). Church discipline is needed to deal with blatant sins (1 Cor. 5; 1 Tim. 5:20). But Paul's ultimate belief is that God is at work in the lives of believers to make them holy and blameless (1 Cor. 1:8; Phil. 2:12–13).

SOME SPECIFIC AREAS OF CONCERN

RELATIONS BETWEEN MEN AND WOMEN
Paul goes along with the society of his time, which taught the subordination of the wife to the husband (1 Cor. 11:3; Eph. 5:22–4; Col. 3:18). Yet at crucial points he undermines it, by insisting on oneness in Christ (Gal. 3:28) and by stressing equality in so fundamental a matter as physical sexual relationships (1 Cor. 7:3–4; cf. 11:11–12). He is variously seen as a confirmed patriarchalist or as a person with new insights who is following the principle of *festina lente* ('hasten slowly!'). He follows the teaching of Jesus on divorce and remarriage – but develops it pastorally (1 Cor. 7:10–16) – and he follows the teaching of the OT in an emphatic rejection of homosexual relationships (Rom. 1:26f.; 1 Cor. 6:9; 1 Tim. 1:10).

SLAVERY
Slavery is assumed and taken for granted; Paul issues guidance for the better running of the institution, but at the same time his stress on the kinship of masters and slaves *both in the Lord and in the flesh* (Gal. 3:28; Phlm. 16) in effect undermines the institution. Paul himself does not yet take that step of affirming that slavery is incompatible with this kinship, but that is the logical issue of his basic Christian understanding of humanity.

THE STATE
Earthly obligations are obligations and must be taken seriously (Rom. 13). The question of an unjust state is not raised (although the reigning emperor was Nero!), but it is not difficult to guess what Paul would have said to a state that forbade the proclamation of the gospel.

MONEY AND POSSESSIONS
2 Corinthians 8—9 contains the fullest NT teaching on Christian giving to help the needs of other Christians who are poor. With God's gift of Christ in the background, and the way in which Christ himself became poor, believers are called to sacrificial giving, confident that God will provide them with both what they need for themselves and what is superfluous to their needs to give to others. At the same time Paul is not so idealistic as to fail to take careful practical measures to avoid temptations to avarice and mismanagement of church funds (cf. also 1 Tim. 6).

THE FUTURE FOR THE WORLD AND BELIEVERS

The common view of the Jews was that the world would not last for ever; there would be an intervention of God in history to bring it to an end. The present age would be succeeded by the age to come. There would be a judgement carried out by God upon all humankind with the righteous entering into God's new world and the unrighteous being condemned to punishment or destruction. The dead would be raised up to be judged. Jews believed that they would enjoy God's favour (except for notorious sinners who had not repented), but the Gentiles would be judged.

Paul shared this framework of thinking, but decisively modified it. He believed that God had entrusted the final judgement to Jesus, before whom everybody would have to appear (2 Cor. 5:10; cf. Rom. 14:11–12). He further taught that those who had been justified by faith through the redemption achieved by Jesus could approach that judgement with confidence, knowing that they would not be condemned. Nevertheless, he also taught that people would be judged on the basis of their deeds (Rom. 2:6). How are these two apparently different statements to be reconciled? One possibility is that Paul believed that believers would not be condemned at the last judgement but that they would suffer reward or loss according to the quality of the lives that they had lived (cf. 1 Cor. 3:12–15).

Paul further developed the concept of resurrection. Believers in Christ are already being transformed from within; when they die, their body of flesh perishes, but it will be resurrected and transformed into a spiritual, glorious body, appropriate for life in the new world (1 Cor. 15; 2 Cor. 5:1–10; Phil. 3:21). He has little to say about the nature of this new life. But he believed that the highest good in this life is a personal relationship with Christ (what he calls 'knowing Christ',

Phil. 3:8), and he appears to regard life after death as a fuller opportunity for precisely this (Phil. 1:21–23).

The presence of the Spirit in believers now is the guarantee of their future life; what believers enjoy now is the first instalment of what they will fully enjoy in the future (2 Cor. 1:22; 5:5; Eph. 1:13–14; Rom. 8:23; 15:13). He gives hope (Rom. 15:13); he is the agent in resurrection (Rom. 8:11).

From all this it follows that Paul thought of Christian existence in terms of 'already – not yet'. He believed that the decisive intervention in human history had been made by God in the first coming of Jesus and through him believers *already* experience the power of the new creation. *Yet* they still live in perishable bodies, surrounded by temptations in the 'old world', and they look forward to the completion of what God has already begun with the second coming of Christ, the resurrection of believers to new life and the transformation of the universe. The 'last things' (as these future events are traditionally called) are not a kind of appendix to New Testament theology but rather the full realization of what God has already begun to do through Christ.

What do you think?

What effects did Paul's beliefs about the future ('eschatology') have on his understanding of how Christians should live in the here and now? Useful starting points for discussion can be found in: Rom. 13:8–14; 1 Cor. 15; 2 Cor. 4:13—5:10; 1 Thess. 5:1–11. See also articles on 'apocalypticism' and 'eschatology' in *DPL*, pp. 25–35, 253–69.

THE MISSIONARY OBLIGATION

The character of Paul's thinking means that there is an obligation laid upon believers to share the Christian message with other people, since it is only through faith in Christ that people can escape from their sin and begin to live a new life which is pleasing to God and which will lead in the end to eternal life with him; apart from faith people continue to be dominated by sin and will ultimately receive their 'wage' for serving it in the form of death. So the task of proclaiming the gospel is committed to believers. Some believers are specially called to take part in the evangelistic mission, such as Paul himself (Rom. 1:14; 1 Cor. 9:16). Although little is actually said about it, Paul also assumes that by being believers, living changed lives, and speaking about their faith, Christians generally will bring the light of the gospel to the communities round about them (Eph. 6:15; Phil. 2:15–16; 1 Thess. 1:8).

What do you think?

In the church today it is perhaps unusual for some-body to be both an evangelist and a theologian. Why do you think this is? Does the church lose something as a result?

ESSAY TOPICS

INTRODUCTORY

- 'Paul: apostle of liberty' (the title of a book by R. N. Longenecker): to what extent is this an apt characterization of Paul as a theologian?

INTERMEDIATE

- Is it possible to discern any developments in the understanding of Christ and the

Spirit as we progress from the earlier to the later Pauline letters?

FURTHER READING

*denotes books assuming knowledge of Greek; most can be used by all students.

INTRODUCTORY

J. A. Fitzmyer *Paul and his Theology: A Brief Sketch*. Englewood Cliffs: Prentice Hall, 1989 (entrance-level).

M. J. Gorman *Apostle of the Crucified Lord: A Theological Introduction to Paul and his Letters*. Grand Rapids: Eerdmans, 2004.

M. B. Thompson *The New Perspective on Paul*. Cambridge: Grove Books, second edition 2010 (excellent brief introduction).

D. Wenham *Paul: Follower of Jesus or Founder of Christianity?* Grand Rapids: Eerdmans, 1995 (discusses how Paul's thinking is dependent on Jesus).

V. Wiles *Making Sense of Paul: A Basic Introduction to Pauline Theology*. Peabody: Hendrickson, 2000 (simple introduction to some aspects of his thought).

N. T. Wright *Justification: God's Plan and Paul's Vision*. London: SPCK, 2009.

N. T. Wright *What Saint Paul Really Said: Was Paul of Tarsus the Real Founder of Christianity?* Grand Rapids: Eerdmans/Oxford: Lion, 1997 (introductory guide by a major interpreter).

J. Ziesler *Pauline Christianity*. Oxford/New York: Oxford University Press, 1990 (excellent alternative to Fitzmyer).

INTERMEDIATE

D. A. Campbell *The Quest for Paul's Gospel: A Suggested Strategy*. London: T & T Clark International, 2005 (attempts to understand Paul's doctrine of justification in a non-traditional way).

*W. D. Davies *Paul and Rabbinic Judaism: Some Rabbinic Elements in Pauline Theology*.

London: SPCK, 1955/Philadelphia: Fortress, 1990 (fundamental, rather technical study of Paul's relation to Judaism).

J. D. G. Dunn *The Theology of Paul the Apostle*. Grand Rapids: Eerdmans, 1998 (massive work from the 'new perspective', but clear and readable).

*S. Kim *The Origin of Paul's Gospel*. Grand Rapids: Eerdmans, 1981; Tübingen: Mohr, 1984 (pioneering research on the way in which Paul's conversion led directly to his new understanding of Jesus).

R. N. Longenecker (ed.) *The Road from Damascus: The Impact of Paul's Conversion on His Life, Thought and Ministry*. Grand Rapids: Eerdmans, 1997 (how Paul's theology grew out of his conversion).

I. H. Marshall *New Testament Theology: Many Witnesses, One Gospel*. Downers Grove/ Leicester: IVP, 2004 (fuller treatment of the theology of each of the Pauline letters).

H. Ridderbos *Paul: An Outline of his Theology*. Grand Rapids: Eerdmans, 1974/London: SPCK, 1977 (hardly an 'outline' at 587 pp. Solid pre-'new perspective' exposition).

E. P. Sanders *Paul, the Law and the Jewish People*. Philadelphia: Fortress, 1983 (how Sanders understands Paul from his 'new perspective').

T. R. Schreiner, *Paul, Apostle of God's Glory in Christ: A Pauline Theology*. Leicester: Apollos/ Downers Grove: IVP, 2001 (less technical than Dunn).

M. Turner, *The Holy Spirit and Spiritual Gifts Then and Now*. Carlisle: Paternoster, 1996/Peabody: Hendrickson, 1999 (good chapters on Paul).

B. Witherington III *Paul's Narrative Thought World: The Tapestry of Tragedy and Triumph*. Louisville: Westminster/John Knox, 1994 (readably expounds Paul's theology in terms of the 'stories' that underlie it).

Chapter 15

NEW TESTAMENT LETTERS – INTERPRETATION AND AUTHORSHIP

In this chapter we shall study:

● what is meant by 'understanding' the NT letters;

● how we get a message for our own times from the writers;

● arguments for and against the proposal that it was an acceptable practice in the early church for the writer of a letter to present it as the work of someone else such as the apostle Paul or Peter.

This chapter picks up in more detail three questions that have already been touched on as we worked through the letters of Paul. Now that we have studied these letters individually we are in a better position to reflect generally on these two issues, which will of course come up again in discussion of Hebrews to Revelation. First, we explore the process of understanding these ancient texts and interpreting them for today's world. Secondly, we summarize various critical methods used to interpret texts. Thirdly, we examine the view that some NT letters were not written by the named authors but by someone else who attributed them to the named authors. This is the issue of pseudonymity, from the Greek for 'false name'.

UNDERSTANDING WHAT WE READ IN NEW TESTAMENT LETTERS

How should we read the letters in the New Testament? More precisely, is there some kind of method that we should follow?

When I originally drafted the preceding question I included some extra words: 'Is there some kind of method that we should follow *in order to understand them*?' The use of that word 'understand' represents my instinctive – or should I say 'conditioned' – approach to the matter. By nature or by training I assume that the primary purpose of reading a letter is to *receive* the message that the writer is conveying; but to do so an act of communication must take place in which I come to understand what she or he is saying. However, like all other approaches based on a presupposition, this one deserves at least to be questioned; maybe there are other approaches.

One such approach would be to begin with the fact that the New Testament letters are part of a body of literature, and therefore it is appropriate to consider them as such. The reason why people *read* literature is because they find it enjoyable; there is some kind of aesthetic experience in store for them. Then study of literature would be concerned with the nature of this experience and how the letters function to provide it. Doubtless one could also *study* them from this angle; there are, to be sure, various studies of the Bible generally as literature, asking questions about how the Bible 'works' as literature, how the writers achieve their effects. The letters of Paul and his colleagues could form a set of texts to be read and studied in a course on Greek literature. I have to recognize the legitimacy of the enterprise.

Yet, I suspect that this would be rather like reading the dialogues of Plato as literature rather than as philosophy. No doubt Plato wrote in the way that he did in order that he might be as effective a proponent of his philosophy as possible, and it is a proper exercise to ask questions about how he did

it, and whether he did it well. Equally one can ask corresponding questions about the New Testament writers. But, just as we would miss the point if we did not read Plato's writings as philosophy, so we would fail to appreciate the New Testament letters for what they really are if we did not see them as Christian documents written to help Christian believers in their belief and practice.

Or again, we might compare the way in which people might enjoy and study Christian music simply as music while neglecting the faith that inspired it and is expressed in it; if we did so, we might have enjoyed ourselves, but we would have missed out something that is more important.

So I return to my original instinct that the New Testament letters are Christian documents and that the primary thing to be done with them is to understand them as Christian communications. The word 'understand' may suggest that we are interested simply in the communication of information, but a letter will often have other functions. If it says 'Thank you for your present for my birthday', it is not just conveying the information that the writer is feeling gratitude, but it is the action by which the writer actually thanks me. When somebody writes 'Love from Mary', the statement is a way of actually loving a distant person, just as a kiss or a hug is not just a physical action but something more. We have learned to recognize that written texts do other things besides simply conveying information. So to understand a text includes more than just recognizing what the words mean; consciously or unconsciously we recognize that we are being thanked or are being loved, and so on.

GIVING A NAME TO IT

The technical term for what we are doing here is 'hermeneutics' (I used to think that I was hearing the name of an obscure German scholar – Herman U. Tix). This word, formed like 'mathematics' or 'physics', simply means 'the science of interpretation'; it covers the topic of what we are doing when we try to understand a text and how we should go about it (and not go about it).

Sometimes, however, people use the term (especially in the singular form 'hermeneutic') to refer to the particular way in which they are interpreting a text. One instance is the 'hermeneutic of suspicion', in which you question whether what appears to be going on in the communication is really what is happening: is there a hidden agenda? For example, we considered whether in the letter to Philemon Paul is simply trying to persuade his reader to act in a certain way or is really forcing him to do so (see pp. 154–5).

TWO RELATED ACTIVITIES

Before we can understand the New Testament letters we have to recognize that to do so depends on what we are trying to do. Essentially there are two associated but distinguishable activities in which we may be engaged.

● The first of them is the task of trying to understand what the letter-writer was saying to the original readers. It is surely self-evident that this is what we must do because there would be difficulties if we misunderstood a passage and proceeded to base our modern practice on a misunderstanding. But to misunderstand a passage means to fail to apprehend what Paul was saying, and to ask what he was saying is clearly to ask what he was saying to his first-century audience in Corinth.

Take, for example, a simple matter of identification. In 2 Cor. 8:18 Paul says that he is sending a certain 'brother' with Titus 'who is famous among all the churches for his proclaiming the good news'. He did not need to name the person because the readers would know who was meant, but we do not know: who was he? Here is a typical example of the problem of understanding what was being said to the original readers.

● The second activity is when we overhear what Paul is saying to his original readers and ask what (if anything) we can get from it for ourselves, who are not the originally intended readers but are separated from them by two thousand years and all kinds of differences.

The verse just quoted (2 Cor. 8:18) comes from a section of the letter in which Paul was urging the readers to generosity and making arrangements for a donation from them to help impoverished Christian believers in Jerusalem. Can we work out Paul's theology and practice of generosity from the letter and how (if at all) can we apply the same principles to our own situation? In other words, if Paul was writing to us today about our Christian giving, what would he say to us?

Any reading of the letters has to recognize these two broadly distinguishable activities. They are applicable, of course, to reading any document that was not originally addressed to us and not just to writings that we may regard as 'Scripture'. A modern American might read through what Abraham Lincoln said to his contemporaries and ask whether it still says something to modern Americans, and, if so, what. Some people may read ancient writings simply for interest and enjoyment (as we might read poetry or novels), but even in such cases it would be difficult to avoid some kind of engagement with the text, whether we respond to it positively or negatively. One could read ancient philosophers, like Plato or Aristotle, purely to find out what they said and to enjoy the way in which they said it, but it would be very hard to do so and not to learn something from them that is of value to modern people also.

It may well be that simply recognizing the difference between these two activities is the most important thing to do in response to our initial question. However, matters are not quite so simple! We need to recognize that these two activities are closely inter-related.

Let us list some of the various problems that arise, drawing our illustrations from 1 Corinthians.

● It is basic that we need to know *whether what we are reading is what Paul actually wrote*. We do not have the original manuscripts of any of the writings of Paul (or his amanuensis). The later copies of the lost original of 1 Cor. vary from one another in 13:3 where *either* Paul wrote 'if I hand over my body so that I may boast' but a later scribe making a copy made a mistake here and wrote 'if I hand over my body so that I may be burned', *or* Paul wrote 'if I hand over my body so that I may be burned' and a later copyist made a mistake and wrote 'if I hand over my body so that I may boast'. A mistake either way was very easy since the difference between them in Greek is very tiny (*kauchesomai* or *kauthesomai*). There was no problem for the original readers who obviously had only one form of wording before them, but it is a problem for us who do not know for certain which of the two forms it was (though most interpreters today side with NRSV and TNIV to favour 'boast'; ESV has 'be burned').

● Paul may use *phrases which the first readers understood, but which are now less clear to us*. For example, presumably the original readers knew what Paul meant by women having a head-covering 'because of the angels' in 1 Corinthians 11:10, but modern readers may well be baffled by the phrase. However, some references in the Dead Sea Scrolls indicate that probably the thought is of the angels as God's agents watching over his people to preserve decorum and in their worship. Again, in 1 Corinthians 12:8 Paul refers to various forms of message given in the congregational meeting as 'the utterance of wisdom' and 'the utterance of knowledge'. Doubtless the congregation in whose midst these things happened knew what Paul was talking about, but modern readers may well wonder how these two types of utterance were distinguished from each other.

What do you think?

Here are a few lines by the English cricketer Ian Botham:

> I took seven wickets in the morning session as their last eight wickets fell for 43, to complete the best return by an England bowler since Jim Laker had taken nine for 37 and ten for 53 against Australia at Old Trafford in 1956. (Botham: *My Autobiography*. London: CollinsWillow, 1994, p. 89.)

For someone unfamiliar with the game of cricket, how puzzling is this sentence? How might they find out what the various phrases mean and what the significance of these events is?

In what ways is that process of interpretation similar to, and different from, the process of understanding puzzling statements in New Testament letters?

● Problems arise for us because we live in a different culture from the New Testament writers and their audiences and *we do not appreciate their customs and assumptions*. We shall have difficulties in understanding 1 Corinthians 11 where Paul discusses some kind of head-covering for women, traditionally translated as a 'veil', because most of us do not know exactly what sort of covering is meant and (more importantly) what the wearing of it signified for people at that time. (Compare how wearing a bowler hat used to be the indication that a person was the foreman in some industries; what, if anything, is conveyed by the wearing of a baseball cap by people who are not actually playing baseball?) The reference seems to be to the hair or other head-covering that distinguished a woman from a man.

- Other problems may be *difficulties both for us and for the original readers*. In 1 Cor. 7:21 Paul says to slaves, 'Were you a slave when called? Do not be concerned about it. Even if you can gain your freedom, make use of your present condition now more than ever.' But the last few words could also be understood to mean 'avail yourself of the opportunity' (see the NRSV text and margin for these two possibilities). The difficulty arises because 'your present condition' and 'the opportunity' are both attempts by translators to identify the reference of what Paul wrote, which was simply 'it'. It is not clear whether 'it' refers to the opportunity to gain freedom or to the state of slavery: is the reader to use the opportunity to gain freedom or to decide to remain as a slave? Paul's wording may well have been as ambiguous to early Christian readers as it is to us today (Jerome and Chrysostom differed in their understanding of it).

Or, again, when Paul said 'Any man who prays or prophesies with something on his *head* disgraces his head' (1 Cor. 11:4), his audience, like us, could well have been uncertain whether the head that is disgraced is his literal head or his metaphorical head, Christ (v. 3), or refers to both.

These are fairly straightforward, more or less factual questions. But other questions may be rather different. These arise when These arise when the discussion about what the passage could mean for today may influence our judgment.

- There are some Christian groups today where it is still the practice for the women to wear some kind of head-covering in worship services. People who accept this practice follow what they think is the apparent sense of this passage in 1 Cor. 11, which appears to require women to have a head-covering when engaged in prayer or prophecy, and they think that they are simply doing what God requires of them according to this passage. They are assuming that whatever Scripture says that is not obviously tied to the original situation continues to be valid instruction for Christians today.

- Others may be unhappy with this requirement because it is seen as impracticable or pointless in the modern world. Some of them may be comfortable with recognizing that the passage teaches something that is unacceptable today and rejecting it as evidence of a male-chauvinist attitude on the part of Paul that we can no longer share. Some commentators do attribute to Paul a whole set of unacceptable attitudes on the basis of which they feel that they can dispute his authority as a teacher for the church today.

- Others may also reject a literal application of the passage today, but they may do so by arguing that the original meaning of the passage is different from what the traditionalists think. Paul was not talking about women wearing a veil or other head-covering but rather about their having long hair (as compared with men) and this was a sign of a gender difference (rather than of subordination).

- Still other readers may recognize that Paul was requiring some kind of head-covering, but then argue that, although this may have been appropriate at that time and in that culture, the principles behind Paul's teaching would have a different application in the different situation of today, where a veil or differences in hair length do not have the symbolical significance that they had then. They then face the problem of what to do instead of wearing a head-covering, or perhaps they just do nothing (like people who do not follow the command to disciples to wash one another's feet but do not do something else that would express the symbolism in the contemporary mode).

Here are four different approaches to a problem and they arise from different modern reactions to the text:

● The first, very conservative attitude is prepared to accept whatever Paul wrote quite literally – well, not altogether literally, because generally women in this tradition wear hats rather than veils, wear them throughout the worship service, and are not in fact allowed to prophesy or pray aloud! This approach thinks it is 'neutral', but in fact it may be suffering from an inability to move with the times or (even worse) from an unacknowledged desire to maintain a patriarchal attitude towards women. To do them justice, however, we should recognize that people who adopt these practices are probably honestly trying to follow biblical teaching as closely as possible.

● The second, very radical attitude rejects the authority of Paul and in some cases may have a bias to present a consistent picture of him as a time-bound, patriarchal teacher.

● The third approach is to investigate whether the traditional understanding of what Paul is saying and of what theological principles underlay it is actually mistaken and therefore to see whether it may be possible to re-interpret what Paul says so that his teaching can be adopted today. Here there is the danger of sometimes (not

necessarily in this particular case) accepting less-likely solutions because they fit in better with our contemporary mood.

● The fourth, somewhat different approach recognizes that Paul does advocate practices that do not make sense today, but argues that behind his practices lie valid principles that require to be applied differently in a different cultural situation.

It is not the case that any one of these approaches will always be the right one or that any one of them is always to be rejected. For example, contemporary unease with a specific interpretation of a text may be the cue that alerts the scholar to a more accurate interpretation of it. At other times, the interpretation may be unchallengeable, and one of the other solutions may be appropriate. The lines down which the scholars go may well be influenced, consciously or unconsciously, by their pre-set attitudes, and they need to be aware of this temptation. However, in all cases, the test of the acceptability of a solution ought to be whether it provides the best understanding of the text. We must distinguish between the *motives* that lead people to explore a particular solution and the *reasons* that can be adduced to justify the solution; it is ultimately the reasons that matter and not the motives. The difficulty is that our evaluation of the reasons may still be influenced by our motives and presuppositions. I am conservative in religious temperament, and I have to recognize that my conservatism may sway my judgement unacceptably.

In the end, therefore, the solutions to our problems may well rest on better exegesis of the difficult texts and upon being able to distinguish between the theological principles and their practical applications which are affected by the social and cultural setting in which they are made. Those who consider themselves bound by Scripture as their supreme authority need to be particularly careful to understand Scripture well so as not to follow their own principles under the mistaken belief that they are necessarily what Scripture teaches.

What do you think?

Discuss Romans 14:1–23. It appears to tell believers to refrain from eating meat and drinking wine because of the effect this may have on their 'brothers and sisters'. Find out what was the nature of the problem that Paul was facing. What were the considerations and principles that guided him? Why was he so concerned about it? Is the conduct that he recommended a pattern that we should follow? Do we face the same problem and, if so, should we adopt the same solution? Are there any similar problems that we have? If so, do the principles expressed in his teaching in this chapter give us guidance that we can follow? And what practical forms of conduct might be right and necessary for us? There are some people today who abstain from eating meat (vegetarians and vegans) and some others who abstain from drinking alcohol (abstainers or teetotallers): do they do so from the same motives and for the same reasons as Paul states here, or are they guided by other considerations? How far are people influenced by their church traditions or other personal factors?

SPEECHES IN THE FORM OF LETTERS?

Letters can be understood as what writers would say aloud if they were able to be present with the people to whom they were writing. They are a substitute for the spoken word. It is not surprising, therefore, that the question has arisen as to whether the kind of analysis made of the spoken word can be applied to the letters. In the ancient world the formal speech occupied a place that was more central than it is in society today. Even today, however, a speech in a law court or a public assembly will naturally follow certain rules and tend to have an appropriate structure. This was all the more the case in the ancient world, where rhetoric was the main component of a higher education, and the nature of speeches was analysed in great detail as regards their various types, their logical structure, the types of arguments that should be used, and the different ways of achieving persuasive force. It is therefore possible to give a reliable, detailed account of ancient rhetorical theory.

There were three types of speeches that dealt with proving a case in court (forensic), or encouraging an assembly to follow a particular line of action (deliberative), or celebrating some person or their achievements (epideictic).

There was a recognized structure which involved an introduction, the statement of the point to be argued, an account of the circumstances leading up to the statement, the development of appropriate arguments with refutations of opposing arguments, the emotional appeal, and so on. If the New Testament letters can be analysed in this kind of way, then we would have a better understanding of the function of the different parts of the letter and so be able to appreciate better just what the author is trying to do at each stage.

This approach has been developed most carefully in the case of Galatians, but it has

Digging deeper

In his commentary on *Galatians* (Dallas: Word, 1990, pp. cxiv–cxix), R. N. Longenecker notes examples of different rhetorical tactics used by Paul:

● the appeal to *ethos*, the personal character of the speaker. In Gal. 1—2 Paul argues from his own status as an apostle of Jesus Christ and the recognition of that status by the pillars of the church in Jerusalem.

● the appeal to *pathos*, making an emotional appeal to the audience. In Gal. 4:12–20 Paul reminds his readers of their personal concern for him when he was with them and his corresponding parental concern for them. He expresses astonishment and passion in 1:6–10.

● the appeal to *logic*. Paul uses various types of logical argument to make his case, such as the appeal to example (the case of Abraham as a man of faith, Gal. 3:6–18), or the use of the 'slippery slope' in Gal. 5:2–4.

Examine some other letter (e.g. 2 Timothy) to see if these (and any other) rhetorical tactics are employed by the author.

also been attempted with other letters such as Philippians (see pp. 142–5). It may simply be because the approach is a new one, but the fact is that different scholars analyse the same material in remarkably different ways, and this casts serious doubt as to whether the approach is always viable. It is quite possible that some letters may have a rhetorical structure and that others do not have one. Some scholars have expressed strong reservations about the whole assumption that letters can be analysed as speeches, and I share their

scepticism. What can certainly be recognized is the use of various rhetorical devices or means of making one's point and persuading the readers.

ENTERING INTO THE SITUATION

One of the difficulties in understanding the Gospels is their very general character. They were probably written for fairly broad audiences who can be described in general terms. It would thus be possible for many different people to pick them up and read them with profit. In this respect they would be like many modern books that are sold far and wide; the author has not had to stop to think too precisely about the audience beyond assuming that they will have the general knowledge and intelligence to understand what is being said. But a letter is generally very specific and deals with a particular situation. For example, it may announce travel arrangements that are peculiar to the occasion. Equally, however, something may be said to the original readers that is just as true and relevant for other people who listen in to what is said. Some authors have specifically written letters that were meant to be overheard by other people. Although 2 Corinthians was written to deal with the particular needs of the Christian group in Corinth, Paul intended that it should be read by other Christians through Achaia, although he did not include any material specifically addressed to them (2 Cor. 1:1). The churches at Colossae and Laodicea were specifically told to exchange and read the individual letters sent to them (Col. 4:16). The letters to Timothy and to Titus end with greetings addressed to *you* (plural!), which suggest that they were to be shared with the congregations that the named recipients oversaw. The so-called 'general letters' are apparently intended for fairly wide audiences over broad geographical areas. We can, therefore, make a broad distinction between letters intended more for specific, limited groups and those intended more for a wider distribution. It is the former set which may cause the greater difficulty for readers other than the small groups to which they were originally written.

THE FRUSTRATIONS OF LISTENING IN TO OTHER PEOPLE'S CONVERSATIONS

'Do you not remember that I told you these things when I was still with you? And you know what is now restraining him, so that he may be revealed when his time comes.' (2 Thess. 2:5–6). *But we don't know!*

'You know that it was because of a physical infirmity that I first announced the gospel to you.' (Gal. 4:13) *But we don't know what it was!*

'Otherwise, what will those people do who receive baptism on behalf of the dead?' (1 Cor. 15:29) *But we don't know what 'baptism on behalf of the dead' was!*

A problem with reading the New Testament letters is that like any letters they represent one side of a two-way conversation. Anybody who has listened in to a person speaking into a telephone and was unable to hear the voice of the person at the other end knows how difficult it can be to understand the force of remarks made in response to the other partner in the conversation. To some extent it is possible to work out what must have been said by the other person from what has actually been heard, but the process is fraught with difficulty and the likelihood of alternative reconstructions can be high.

This is obviously the situation with Paul's letters. We generally have no other direct sources of information that will help us to understand the situation into which he was writing. Instead we have to reconstruct the situation from Paul's response and use the reconstruction of the situation to explain why Paul wrote in the way that he did. The process is often called *mirror-reading*. In 1 Corinthians 7 Paul gives some teaching about sexual relationships and marriage which has often been thought to be one-sided and to ignore the positive aspects of marriage: he may appear to be almost grudging in his approval of the married state. At least part of the explanation will lie in the fact that he was doing nothing more than replying to some specific questions from the congregation and that he was doing so in a situation that he described as one of extreme distress; he was not trying to give a balanced picture of Christian marriage. We might compare how an anxious parent might try to dissuade a son or daughter from an unsuitable match by presenting a rather bleak negative picture of the things that can go wrong with a marriage, even though they do hope to see a happy marriage to a more appropriate partner in due course.

The tendency with mirror-reading has been to find specific situations in the recipient congregation to account for every topic that the writer takes up, and very often to detect opponents and interlocutors at every point. This has led to some justifiable reactions. For example, readers have been invited to reconsider whether there really were opponents to Paul's understanding of the gospel at Colossae. (The consensus is that there were, but it was entirely proper to ask the question.) Questions have also been asked about whether the practical teaching given in the letters is necessarily specific to the readers or is simply drawn from a general fund of instructions that could be addressed to any congregation. (Martin Dibelius was well known as a scholar for understanding as much of the New Testament as possible as generalized teaching that was not tied to specific situations. See, for example, the discussion of his interpretation of James, p. 262.)

GETTING THE MESSAGE

How, then, do we approach the letters? Clearly we begin by trying to understand them in their original setting. This means that we need to know whatever is relevant about the readers, their situation and needs, and the writers and the factors that would dispose them to write in the way that they did. The letters arise out of the inter-relationship between writers and readers.

Second, it is helpful to distinguish between the problems of understanding at the micro- and the macro-levels. The former is concerned with understanding the individual words, phrases and sentences. The latter is concerned with understanding the total effect of these small units when they are used to form a composition. One guide comments on the need to read the letters as wholes, as they were meant to be read originally, rather than in short excerpts. This should be dazzlingly obvious, but how rarely it is done in practice. A letter as a whole has something to say, and it needs to be read right through in the order in which it was written, rather than in brief extracts plucked from their contexts (as happens with readings of Scripture in many church settings or personal Bible study). Even the use of commentaries, necessary though they are, can hinder the process in that it slows down the reading of the actual text to a snail's pace.

THE ODD THINGS THAT SCHOLARS DO

When we receive a letter from a friend, we do not usually try to come up with an outline. Why should we do it with Paul's letters? Part of the answer is that these letters are a little longer . . . than the typical personal letter; keeping in mind where the shifts occur helps orient the reader. But there is a more fundamental issue here. Even a friend's casual letter has a certain structure, whether the writer was conscious of it or not. In some cases, to be sure, the argument may be a little incoherent, and one could not come up with an intelligible outline. It is always true, however, that our ability to understand a letter (or any other document) is tied to how accurately we perceive its structure. This process of identification is largely unconscious, but if we receive a longer and more complicated letter, we may start asking ourselves structural kinds of questions ('Is the lawyer talking about something else in this paragraph, or am I missing the connection?'). The more explicit we are about these issues, the more sensitive we become to the information that the context provides. (M. de Silva, in Kaiser and de Silva 1994, p. 131)

How do we go on to appropriate the message for ourselves? Here our predispositions inevitably come into play. For myself I share the view expressed by Karl Barth at the beginning of his commentary on the letter to the Romans:

Paul, as a child of his age, addressed his contemporaries. It is, however, far more important that, as Prophet and Apostle of the Kingdom of God, he veritably speaks to all men of every age. (K. Barth, *The Epistle to the Romans*. London: Oxford University Press 1933, p. 1)

It can be suggested that, when Paul wrote to the Christian congregation in Rome, he said the kind of things that he would have said to any group of Christians but did so in a manner relevant to the particular needs of his readers as he understood them. He was, therefore, saying things that he believed were true for any Christian readers and applicable to them. But, if this is granted, then it would follow that these things will also be true for any other group of readers, and the things said about the world at large will also remain true, assuming that there is a basic similarity or identity between the original readers and the original world addressed by Paul and the later readers and world. Just as we can generalize what Paul says to the Romans to reconstruct what his message to other readers would have been, so we can move from what he would have said to them to what he would say to us. Thus, most obviously, cultural differences will affect the way in which things are said or commands are expressed. Nearly 60 years ago J. B. Phillips paraphrasing Paul's letters for today substituted for the command 'Greet one another with a holy kiss' (1 Cor. 16:20) the words 'A hearty handshake all round', thereby trying to express the principle that lay behind Paul's command with what was the cultural equivalent in English society at that time; today 'give one another a warm hug' might be the cultural equivalent.

Greater problems might arise where the underlying principles appear to be timebound. 'Wives, be subject to your husbands' (Eph. 5:22) may be thought to rest on a principle of male or husbandly authority over wives that is hard to justify in the Western world today.

What do you think?

Somebody once suggested to me that 'hermeneutics' is the art of making the Bible say something different when you don't like what it appears to be saying. Was he right? Can you think of any passages in the New Testament letters that might tempt you to develop this 'art'?

'All have sinned' (Rom. 3:23) might be thought to rest on an understanding of human nature that is no longer shared in a world where human faults may be explained by a mixture of other factors, psychological, social and so on. In such cases interpretation is more difficult. Do we argue that Paul is expressing principles that are valid even if the modern Western world rejects them, or do we claim that they are now outmoded in the light of advances in human knowledge and ethics? These are questions that cannot be avoided. If we find the principles to be of dubious validity, basically there are three possible routes to follow.

- To reject them as invalid.
- To accept them and to insist that it is modern culture that is wrong and not Paul.
- To ask whether we have correctly identified the underlying principles and

---

Digging deeper

'We must first discuss what Paul meant in addressing his first readers and then work out from that what he would say today': how adequate is this as a way of relating the New Testament letters to the lives of Christians today? Try it, for example, on such passages as 1 Cor. 8; Eph. 6:1–9; 1 Tim. 3:1–7. (Help from commentaries will be necessary for this exercise! See the bibliographies on these letters, pp. 94, 181–2 and 199–200.)

whether there may be some deeper principle, which was expressed one way in the culture of the first-century world and will be expressed in a different way in our world. This 'different way' must, of course, be something that arises out of, and is faithful to, Paul's teaching as a whole, and is not simply an accommodation to prevailing fashions.

What do you think?

'I want to be free to say sometimes "Paul was wrong" ': within the context of Christian belief is there such a freedom, and, if so, in what ways, if any, might it be limited?

CRITICAL METHODS IN THE STUDY OF THE NEW TESTAMENT

In order to help to answer some of the questions raised here, New Testament studies as a discipline has developed a range of approaches. Very often these are borrowed from neighbouring disciplines within the university, making theology something of an interdisciplinary subject.

HISTORICAL CRITICISM

Historical criticism, sometimes called the historical critical method, is concerned with establishing historical realities that might affect our understanding of what a text means. It grew out of the development of interest in classical history and archaeology in the eighteenth and nineteenth centuries and as part of a quest for more 'objectivity' in biblical interpretation. So, for example, we might be interested in the social make-up of the population of Corinth, and its reputation for (what we would now call) entrepreneurial

initiative, in trying to find a context for Paul's discussion of group rivalries in 1 Cor. 1—4.

FORM CRITICISM

This approach, more commonly used in study of the Gospels, is concerned with the form that passages take, and what this might tell us about their use prior to inclusion within the written texts as we have them. So it is commonly held that both Phil. 2:6–11 and Col. 1:15–20 consist of pre-Pauline hymns that Paul has incorporated into his letters – purely on the basis of their written form.

SOURCE CRITICISM

Again, this discipline is most concerned with the source documents of the Gospels, but also is used in the study of letters. We have seen that most scholars believe that what we call 2 Corinthians is composed of two or more earlier documents which have been brought together (see pp. 97–100, 103–4, 107–8). There are also several theories about the composition of the book of Revelation, either as originating as a series of visions over a long period of time, or as a text which has been edited once, twice or even three times!

REDACTION CRITICISM

This focuses on the way an author has made use of his or her sources and shapes the material to offer a distinctive perspective, so again has been made use of in relation to the Synoptic Gospels. But there continues to be considerable debate about the relation between Paul's portrayal of himself in his letters and the way Luke edits his sources to depict Paul in Acts, highlighting some of Luke's particular concerns already evident from his Gospel.

TEXTUAL CRITICISM

We have literally thousands of manuscripts and manuscript fragments from the early centuries, and these have some variations in them. Textual criticism is the discipline of deciding which is the most likely original text. For the vast majority, there is little significance in the variations, and these do not affect any key doctrinal issues. But on some occasions the variations contribute to discussion of an important issue. For example, we have already noted (p. 92) that the injunction for women to be silent in 1 Cor. 14:34–35 may be a later interpolation, and this is a continuing subject of debate.

CANONICAL CRITICISM

'Canon' is the Greek word for reed or measuring rod, and the 'canon' of Scripture refers both to the rule of life that Scripture invites us into, but also the 'rule' governing what we include in what we call Scripture. Canonical criticism is concerned with reading one part of the NT in the context of what else the NT (and, ultimately, the whole Bible) says. Thus we need to read what James says about faith, works and the example of Abraham (Jas. 2:14–26) in the light of what Paul says about faith, works and the example of Abraham (Romans 4) and vice versa.

LITERARY CRITICISM

This is the name given to a range of approaches which have become important in the last 40 years and derive from more general approaches to literature. They are concerned with understanding the shape and effect of the text as we have it. Narrative criticism looks at the key features of stories and how they work. Of particular importance to the NT letters, rhetorical criticism is concerned with the shape and effect of texts as arguing a case. For example, in 1 Cor. 15 we can find either three categories of rhetoric according to Greek thinking, or four categories according to Latin thinking, and this gives important insights into the

way Paul is making his case. For another example, see the discussion of rhetoric in Philippians on pages 143–5.

SOCIO-RHETORICAL CRITICISM

An important area of recent development, this approach seeks to combine aspects of literary criticism and historical criticism, in exploring the rhetorical impact of texts for their first audience. Championed particularly by Ben Witherington III, it involves attending both to the rhetorical shape of the text and what we know of the expectations of original readers in their historical context. (It is distinct from so-called 'social-scientific' reading, which is more controversial.)

RECEPTION HISTORY AND READER-RESPONSE CRITICISM

The study of a text's 'reception history' is concerned not so much with the text itself, but how it has been read and interpreted over the centuries. The book of Revelation has been read in an almost bewildering variety of ways, many of which have been highly influential in the church and in culture, and this gives us some clues as to the nature of the text. Closely related to this, reader-response criticism explores the ways in which readers have or might have responded to a text.

IDEOLOGY CRITICISM

Ideology criticism covers a number of approaches in which the ideological perspective or convictions of the critic form a key part of the approach to the text. This ideological position might be in relation to wealth and poverty (liberation readings), issues of gender and sexuality (feminist and gay readings) or global politics (post-colonial readings). These approaches highlight the fact that no reader approaches texts from a 'neutral' point of view, but brings intellectual, philosophical and cultural assumptions which shape the task of interpretation.

These approaches are best understood as addressing issues in different stages of the writing and reading of the NT, exploring either the world 'behind' the text (historical, form, source, redaction), the world 'of' the text (textual, canonical and literary, with socio-rhetorical bridging these two worlds) or the world 'in front of' the text (reception, reader-response and ideology criticism).

None of these methodologies is value-neutral, in that they all make assumptions about the nature of reality and how we can be confident about the truth of assertions made about the texts in question. However, the different methods make assumptions in different ways. For example, historical critical approaches make assumptions about what kind of evidence may be used in reconstructing the nature of (for instance) the first-century world. At the other end of the spectrum, ideology criticisms will usually make ideological assumptions, such as prioritizing the experiences or perspectives of a particular group, though this is often done to bring a counter-perspective to what is seen as the previously dominant interest group in reading these texts.

THE QUESTION OF PSEUDONYMITY

Another question which has arisen in the discussion of some of the Pauline letters, and which will arise again in relation to other letters, is the issue of pseudonymity. Did the people whose names appear at the beginning of NT letters actually write them? Although it is a natural assumption that they did, some scholars during the last 200 years

have questioned the authorship of certain letters. Books deliberately attributed to an author who is not the real author are called 'pseudonymous' (Greek for 'falsely named') or 'pseudepigraphical' ('falsely attributed'). The NT letters most widely regarded as pseudonymous are 2 Peter and the Pastoral Letters (1–2 Timothy and Titus).

Pseudonymity is a different matter from anonymity. Hebrews names no author, nor does 1 John (the title in our Bibles is not part of the actual text of the letter, but an addition based on early church tradition). And 2 and 3 John name a mysterious 'elder' as their author. Of course, the identity of the author of these documents would be known to their *readers*, and may have been on a tag that was attached to the letters but was not part of the letters themselves. One cannot imagine the readers of Hebrews scratching their heads and saying, 'Who on earth of all our wise friends has sent us this elaborate document?' But the author is not named in the document as we have it, and therefore to us it is anonymous. But with no author named, it does not raise the problem, which arises in the case of pseudonymous letters: is *deception* at work in the attribution of the letter to someone other than the real author?

Debates about whether the named author of a letter is the real author normally focus on whether the style of writing and theological perspective of the document and the historical situation that it presupposes are compatible with the named author, such as Paul or Peter. This book discusses those questions in the appropriate chapters. But we explore here a cluster of underlying questions: Is the idea of pseudonymous NT letters acceptable in principle? Or does it involve deception that is incompatible with NT ethics? Was pseudonymity a recognized literary convention in NT times, so that the early church would accept a pseudonymous letter without regarding it as deceptive? (See also pp. 34–6.)

THE TRADITIONAL VIEW

'Paul, an apostle of Christ Jesus by the will of God' (2 Tim. 1:1). Most readers of the Bible have taken letter openings like this at face value as an indication of the real author. In this they have followed general Christian practice since the second century. In the debates about whether a book should be regarded as Scripture, authorship was a crucial question. Eusebius has quite a nuanced discussion of this question in *Hist. eccl* 3.3 (early fourth century).

Because it appears to sanction deception, the notion of pseudonymity has been regarded as morally unacceptable. Early Christians attached great value to truthfulness and openness. Therefore, it has been argued, pseudonymity and canonicity are simply incompatible.

It is too easy to resist the possibility of pseudonymity in the NT on dogmatic grounds, without considering the real difficulties thrown up by NT documents themselves when they seem to be out of character with the author to whom they are attributed. It is these difficulties that originally motivated scholars to suggest that some letters might not have been the work of the claimed author. It is also too easy to say, as many scholars have said, 'Pseudonymity was widely practised in the ancient world, so there is no problem about regarding NT books as pseudonymous; the writers were simply following normal practice. If we decide that a certain book was not written by Paul or Peter, that doesn't necessarily mean it has no value or should be thrown out of the NT.'

Nevertheless, we find that many commentaries and some standard Bible dictionaries state the view that pseudonymity was an accepted practice without giving more than cursory attention to the difficulties which this view poses. We find this approach, for example, in F. W. Beare's comment on 1 Peter: 'The use of the pseudonym need not trouble us in the slightest; the feeling that it is somehow fraudulent is a purely modern prejudice' (*The First Epistle of Peter* [Oxford: Blackwell, third edition 1970], p. 48).

It is true that many books from the Greco-Roman world are pseudonymous, including letters. There are genuine letters of the philosophers Plato and Epicurus, and there are later letters written in a similar style and attributed to them. Among the 94 letters attributed to the first-century philosopher and miracle-worker Apollonius of Tyana there is just a handful of genuine ones. But there are three problems with the view that the church simply took over Greco-Roman usage.

First, we cannot simply assume that Christians would adopt a practice that was acceptable in the surrounding world, particularly if there was an issue of truth and deception. Second, not often enough is it recognized that pseudonymity raises particular questions in relation to *letters*, which may not apply to other types of literature. Different 'rules' and assumptions apply to different types of literature. In our own day, for example, we are familiar with the idea of a novel being written under an assumed name. But if we discover that a book labelled as an autobiography was in fact written by someone quite different without the consent of the book's subject we feel cheated. And we might not take kindly to finding that a letter written in the name of someone we respect was in fact written by someone else without her consent, because we attach particular value to the named author of this personal type of communication.

Third, the matter is complicated by the fact that ancient documents are not always what they appear to be at first sight. The letters of Plato, Epicurus and Apollonius (both the genuine and the pseudonymous ones), though they have the superficial appearance of letters, are quite unlike Paul's. They are not addressed to a specific situation, making quite detailed responses to specific issues. They use the letter form, rather as Plato's dialogues use the dialogue form, as an elegant way to present what is essentially a philosophical treatise (or, in the case of Apollonius, usually a brief word of wisdom). In this case, they are not so clear-cut a precedent for pseudonymous letters in the NT.

ALTERNATIVE SUGGESTIONS

In recent years the supposed 'stigma' of pseudonymity has been challenged from various angles. In particular:

- D. G. Meade argues that the issue of NT pseudepigraphy should be studied in the light of Jewish tradition whereby an original body of material deriving from an authoritative figure (e.g., Moses, Isaiah or Solomon) was developed by the addition of further material attributed to the original figure.

Thus, for example (as even many conservative scholars accept), Isaiah 40—66 was added to the material handed on from Isaiah of Jerusalem even though it was probably created over 150 years later. In such cases 'attribution is primarily a claim to authoritative tradition, not a statement of literary origins' (Meade 1986, pp. 1–2). In a similar way, some letters attributed to Peter and Paul were conscious attempts to affirm the authority of the apostles and the tradition stemming from them, and to apply their teaching afresh. There was no intention to deceive, but rather to honour the tradition and make it present for a new generation (Meade 1986, pp. 42, 177–9).

Meade suggests that pseudepigraphy was accepted by first-century Jewish Christians, but that in the second century attitudes changed. This was because the now mostly Gentile church did not understand the Jewish tradition and was less tolerant of pseudonymity because it needed to discriminate between orthodoxy and heresy and to exercise control over writers of Christian literature (Meade 1986, p. 206).

- P. J. Achtemeier argues for the legitimacy of pseudonymous writing by appealing to the idea of the 'therapeutic lie'. This concept was expressed by Plato when he suggests it is sometimes appropriate for a doctor to deceive a patient or for politicians to 'deceive a city or enemy for the good of the state' (*Republic* 389b–c). Also, the view was expressed by ancient writers (including the second-century Christian Tertullian, *Against Marcion* 4.5) that students who expressed in writing their masters' teaching should attribute their writing to their teachers rather than seek to build their own reputation (Achtemeier, *1 Peter*, Philadelphia: Fortress, 1996, pp. 40–41).
- R. J. Bauckham, recognizing that a widespread practice in the Hellenistic world was not necessarily acceptable to Christians, suggests that the few pseudepigraphical letters known from Judaism (*1 Enoch* 91—105; Letter of Jeremiah, 1 Baruch,

2 Baruch 78—87) provided a model for Christian usage. The last three of these letters all purport to address the situation of Jews during the Babylonian exile of the sixth century BC, but were actually written to address the needs of Jews in a later, parallel situation of distress. The Letter of Jeremiah presents the prophet as foreseeing the situation of the real readers in the later situation. *1 Enoch* 91—105 and *2 Baruch* 78—87 are 'testaments' or farewell messages in which the supposed authors foresee and address the situation of the real readers of a later generation.

Bauckham sees these letters as a model followed by 2 Peter and 2 Timothy, which also contain a significant element of 'testament' (see 2 Tim. 4:1–8; 2 Pet. 1:12–15; Bauckham 1988). In this light, 'the pseudepigraphical device is . . . not a fraudulent means of claiming apostolic authority, but embodies a claim to be a faithful mediator of the apostolic message' (Bauckham 1983, pp. 161–2).

FURTHER REACTIONS

While providing a positive way forward in the search for a legitimate role for pseudepigraphy in the early church, these approaches have not gone unchallenged. It is often pointed out that in the one specific instance where a letter circulating among Christians was discovered by the church to be a second-century pseudepigraph, the letter (*3 Corinthians*) was immediately rejected and its author removed from his office as presbyter (Tertullian, *On Baptism* 17).

Bauckham responds that 3 Corinthians was rejected on grounds of unorthodox teaching rather than pseudonymous authorship (Bauckham 1983, p. 162). But it is arguable that the initial reason for its rejection was the fact that it was falsely attributed to the apostle, even though the author protested that he had done it 'from love of Paul', and that the point about false teaching (women being allowed to administer baptism!) was Tertullian's own later reflection on the document.

Meade's proposal that pseudepigraphy was accepted by first-century Christians but rejected in the second century fails to do justice to the reality of heresy in the first century, and the consequent need from the beginning to be wary of documents which lacked apostolic authority. This concern is evident, for example, in 2 Thess. 2:2; 3:17, and in other places where Paul draws attention to his own signature on letters written by an amanuensis (1 Cor. 16:21; Gal. 6:11).

Nor does his earlier argument, that pseudonymous Christian literature was modelled on the development of traditions associated with an authoritative figure, demonstrate as much as he hopes. For 2 Timothy or 2 Peter are not, like Isaiah 40—66, additions to an earlier document by someone long dead. They are independent documents written, even on Meade's assumptions, within a few years of the apostles' death.

The notion of the 'therapeutic lie', as we have already hinted, is problematic. There was not, as is often assumed, a widespread practice of writing 'real' letters (as distinct from philosophical treatises dressed up as letters) in the name of a revered figure. But this might in principle allow for the possibility that a NT letter which seems to be of a *general* nature without application to a specific audience is pseudonymous. For this would have a precedent in the pseudonymous 'letters' attributed to writers such as Plato and Apollonius.

237

So the debate has made progress, but it is not yet settled. In any discussion of the detailed arguments for or against the traditional authorship of a particular letter, we shall need to bear in mind the still unresolved question: to what extent did the first-century church accept pseudonymous letter-writing as a legitimate practice?

What do you think?

Reflect briefly on, or discuss with others, your initial reactions to this debate about pseudonymity. Does it unsettle you, excite you, raise further questions, or . . . ?

Do these reflections make any difference to your reaction to the debate in previous chapters about the authorship of some Pauline letters?

Make a note of your responses to these questions, so that they may inform your engagement with discussions of authorship in some later chapters.

ESSAY TOPICS

INTRODUCTORY

● In the light of your study of pp. 221–32, show how you would work from understanding Paul's meaning in Romans 12:9–21 to expressing the significance of his teaching for today.

INTERMEDIATE

● Write an article for a 'thoughtful' religious magazine in which – using Paul's letter to Philemon as an example – you explain what is involved in 'understanding' a letter when we have only one side of the correspondence.

FURTHER READING

* denotes books assuming knowledge of Greek; most books can be used by all students.

INTRODUCTORY

*R. J. Bauckham *Jude, 2 Peter*. WBC 50. Waco: Word, 1983 (includes discussion on pseudonymity).

G. D. Fee and D. Stuart *How to Read the Bible for All its Worth*. London: Scripture Union, 1983/Grand Rapids: Zondervan, third edition 2003 (a brilliantly simple presentation of biblical hermeneutics).

G. D. Fee *New Testament Exegesis: a Handbook for Students and Pastors*. Leominster: Gracewing/Louisville: Westminster/John Knox, revised edition 1993 (a more technical study).

P. Gooder, *Searching for Meaning: an Introduction to Interpreting the New Testament*. London: SPCK, 2008; Louisville: Westminster/John Knox, 2009 (clear explanation of a wide range of modern approaches).

D. Guthrie *New Testament Introduction*. Leicester: Apollos/Downers Grove: IVP, 4th edition 1990 (excellent conservative appendix on epistolary pseudepigraphy).

G. W. Hansen 'Rhetorical Criticism' *DPL*, pp. 822–6.

G. R. Osborne 'Hermeneutics/Interpreting Paul' *DPL*, pp. 388–97.

G. R. Osborne 'Hermeneutics' *DLNTD*, pp. 471–84.

T. R. Schreiner *Interpreting the Pauline Epistles*. Grand Rapids: Baker, 1990 (guide to using scholarly tools for interpreting Paul's letters for today).

INTERMEDIATE

R. J. Bauckham 'Pseudo-Apostolic Letters' *JBL* 107, 1988, pp. 469–494 (significant study of the possibility of pseudonymous NT letters).

W. C. Kaiser and M. de Silva *An Introduction to Biblical Hermeneutics: the Search for Meaning*. Grand Rapids: Zondervan, 1994, especially pp. 121–37 (readable traditional approach).

G. A. Kennedy *New Testament Interpretation through Rhetorical Criticism*. Chapel Hill: University of North Carolina, 1984 (the classical treatment of this topic).

W. W. Klein, C. L. Blomberg and R. L. Hubbard Jr *Introduction to Biblical Interpretation*. Dallas: Word, 1993 pp. 352–66 (full study from a conservative angle).

D. G. Meade *Pseudonymity and Canon*. Grand Rapids: Eerdmans, 1986 (argues that pseudonymity represents not deception but transmission of authoritative tradition for a later generation).

R. Morgan and J. Barton *Biblical Interpretation*. Oxford/New York: Oxford University Press, 1988 (historical approach to the topic as a whole; sets the theme in its wider context).

B. Witherington III *Letters and Homilies for Hellenized Christians, vol. 1: A Socio-Rhetorical Commentary on Titus, 1-2 Timothy and 1-3 John*. Downers Grove: IVP/Nottingham: Apollos, 2006 (on pp. 23–38 challenges several grounds on which pseudonymity is often advocated for later NT letters).

Section C

LETTERS BY OTHER CHURCH LEADERS

Chapter 16

THE LETTER TO THE HEBREWS

In this chapter we shall explore:

● what hints the author gives about the situation of his readers;
● the nature of the document;
● its structure and argument;
● its main theological themes;
● some special issues;
● issues of authorship and the location and of the readers.

The letter to the Hebrews poses more than its fair share of puzzles and questions. Yet it is a strikingly creative document offering vital insights into Christ's work and Christian discipleship.

The puzzles are of two kinds. First, there are so many things about it of which we cannot be sure. The document does not name its author or the location of its recipients. Is it really a letter? And what is meant by 'the Hebrews'?

The other kind of puzzle arises from the world of thought which pervades the document. Not many of us spend our leisure time discussing angels, a mysterious figure from Genesis named Melchizedek, or the

furniture of the portable shrine which the Israelites carried about the wilderness on their journey from Egypt to the Promised Land. Yet these are key elements in the writer's argument. And at its heart is a comparison between what Christ achieved on the cross and the practice of animal sacrifice. Though totally alien to most modern 'Western' people, sacrifice was a natural part of life for both Jews and Gentiles in the ancient Mediterranean world. It takes patience and empathy to appreciate the argument. In this chapter we shall refer to the document as 'Hebrews' and its writer as 'the author'.

CLUES ABOUT THE RECIPIENTS

Paul's letters, like other ancient letters, begin by identifying the author and his readers. From the start we know that we are dealing with a document sent to a particular group of people on a particular occasion. The opening of Hebrews (1:1–4) is quite different, opening up the possibility that it is not a letter at all. Nevertheless, there are clear clues within it that the writer has a particular audience in mind. If we scan through Hebrews we can begin to get a picture of them.

mirror reading

Romans?

1:1–14   The heavy reliance on Scripture, here and through most of Hebrews, makes it extremely likely that they are Jews, familiar with the Scriptures and with Jewish customs. Paul's letters to mainly Gentile churches, despite their frequent reference to Scripture, have nothing as sustained and complex as this.

2:3   Like the writer himself, they have not witnessed the events of Jesus' life, death and resurrection but have received the gospel from eyewitnesses. This means that they are separated from the earliest Christians in Palestine either by time (they are 'second generation') or by space (they do not live in Palestine) or by both.

10:32–34   They have existed as a community for some time. In those 'earlier days' they experienced serious persecution. Some of this may well have involved intimidation and physical abuse by hostile neighbours, but the reference to imprisonment implies also some kind of official action against them by governing authorities.

12:4   But their sufferings have not gone as far as martyrdom (though 13:7 may imply that fate for some leaders of an earlier generation).

6:10; 10:34   They have a record of generous support of fellow-Christians in need.

13:7, 17   Yet there is something wrong. The appeal to imitate former leaders and the strong exhortation to comply with the present leadership ('obey . . . and submit') suggests that they are inclined to go their own way – including following 'strange teachings' (13:9) and absenting themselves from meeting together (10:25).

5:11–12   Even more seriously, they have stopped growing as Christians. The writer warns them against lazy discipleship (6:12). He urges them to persevere (10:36), to hold on to hope (10:23), not to abandon meeting for mutual encouragement (10:25), and not to drift away (2:1) or shrink back (10:37–39). They need to take care that none of them has 'an evil, unbelieving heart that turns away from the living God' (3:12). They are a community in crisis.

Where was this community located? We cannot address that question without first exploring the main argument of Hebrews. Only then can we attempt to put the pieces of the jigsaw together.

WHAT KIND OF A DOCUMENT?

We call it 'the letter to the Hebrews'. The oldest surviving manuscript, the Chester Beatty papyrus P46 (early third century) identifies it as a letter by calling it 'To the Hebrews' and placing it between 'To the Romans' and 'To the Corinthians'. Certainly it ends like a letter, with a few brief instructions, prayer for God's blessing and final greetings (Heb. 13; cf. 1 Thess. 5:12–28). And, like other NT letters, it is clearly written by someone who knows his readers and their circumstances (10:32–34; 12:4; 13:19). But there are none of the usual opening greetings of a letter. The carefully phrased introduction, heavy with theological meaning, suggests something different (1:1–4).

The author himself calls his work 'a word of exhortation [or encouragement]' (13:22). The same phrase is used of Paul's synagogue sermon in Acts 13:15, and it is best to think of Hebrews as a sermon or homily. It reflects the style of sermon you might have heard in a Hellenistic Jewish synagogue (see Lane, pp. lxx–lxxi). As such it conveys instruction and exhortation based on exposition of Scripture. And it includes typical features of a *spoken* message:

- the author uses alliteration (five Greek words in Heb. 1:1 begin with the letter *p*);
- he repeats phrases to build towards a climax ('by faith' eighteen times in Heb. 11);
- he refers to his 'speaking' rather than 'writing' (2:5; 5:11; 8:1; 11:32);
- he identifies with his audience ('we' in 2:1; 3:19; 10:39).

Maybe the author had earlier preached parts of it as independent sermons, and now shapes his material into a single whole. Certainly some sections make sense as distinct homilies with a recognizable pattern:

What do you think?

Read 3:1—4:13 and see how it fits the pattern of a sermon. The basic outline is:

Introduction	3:1–6
Announcement of text	3:7–11
	(Ps. 95:7–11)
Expository comments on text	3:12—4:11
Concluding affirmation	4:12–13

Whether the homily was composed specifically for the situation which the recipients now face, or drew on earlier material, the author pours his heart and all his theological and rhetorical skill into creating his 'word of exhortation' to the community he cares for. Being distant from them he has to write it. But he imagines himself preaching to them personally.

Most scholars today describe Hebrews as a homily rather than a letter. But we should beware of distinguishing the two genres too sharply. Even if composed like a sermon it was sent like a letter (Heb. 13:22–25). In the Greco-Roman world most literary works were written with public oral presentation rather than private reading in mind. And we know that Paul's letters were read to the receiving church as they met for worship (1 Thess. 5:26–27).

THE STRUCTURE AND ARGUMENT OF HEBREWS

Two aspects of the document are fundamental for understanding its structure:

- It consists of alternating blocks of *teaching* about Christ and *exhortation*. In this alternating pattern the exhortation is not simply tacked on to the teaching. Rather it is the exhortation which drives the argument. The teaching gives grounds and motivation for the exhortation.
- The argument is developed around key quotations from Scripture. Apart from the string of citations in Hebrews 1, these do not merely illustrate the argument but are texts which the argument expounds.

The outline on p. 246, adapted from Vanhoye, draws attention to these two features.

Let us now read through Hebrews. Although the author dares to call it a 'short letter' (13:22), we shall not have space to consider it all in detail, but will give more attention to certain passages.

THE STRUCTURE OF HEBREWS

1:1–4	INTRODUCTION: GOD HAS SPOKEN		
1:5—2:18	JESUS THE SON OF GOD		
	1:5–14 *Teaching:*	Jesus superior to angels	*Text:* various (mostly Pss.)
	2:1–4 *Exhortation:*	Take the message seriously	
	2:5–18 *Teaching:*	Jesus made lower than angels	*Text:* Ps. 8
3:1—4:13	JESUS THE FAITHFUL HIGH PRIEST		
	3:1–6 *Teaching:*	Jesus faithful, superior to Moses	
	3:7—4:13 *Exhortation:*	Be faithful to him, enter his rest	*Text:* Ps. 95
4:14—5:10	JESUS THE SYMPATHETIC HIGH PRIEST		
	4:14–16 *Exhortation:*	Let us approach him for mercy	
	5:1–10 *Teaching:*	He has shared our suffering	*Text:* Ps. 110
5:11—6:20	THE DANGER OF SPIRITUAL IMMATURITY		
	5:11—6:3 *Exhortation:*	Press on to maturity	
	6:4–8 *Teaching:*	The danger of turning back	
	6:9–20 *Exhortation:*	Hope in God's promises	
7:1–28	JESUS, HIGH PRIEST LIKE MELCHIZEDEK		
	7:1–12 *Teaching:*	Melchizedek, the royal priest	
	7:13–28 *Teaching:*	Jesus, priest like Melchizedek	*Text:* Ps. 110 again
8:1—9:28	JESUS, HIGH PRIEST MADE PERFECT BY SACRIFICE		
	8:1—9:10 *Teaching:*	The first covenant, provisional and inadequate	*Text:* Jer. 31
	9:11–28 *Teaching:*	The new covenant and its sacrifice bring access to heaven	
10:1–18	CHRIST'S PERFECT SACRIFICE		
	10:1–10 *Teaching:*	Christ offers himself for us	*Text:* Ps. 40
	10:11–18 *Teaching:*	and thus brings full forgiveness	*Text:* Jer. 31 again
10:19–39	THE NEED FOR FAITH, LOVE AND ENDURANCE		
	10:1–25 *Exhortation:*	Come to God with faith, hope, love	
	10:26–31 *Teaching:*	The danger of turning back	
	10:32–39 *Exhortation:*	Endure till the promised salvation comes	*Text:* Hab. 2
11:1—12:13	FAITH AND ENDURANCE		
	11:1–40 *Teaching:*	The faith of our ancestors	
	12:1–13 *Exhortation:*	Like Jesus, endure testing	*Text:* Prov. 3
12:14—13:19	LIVING AS CHRISTIANS IN A HOSTILE WORLD		
	12:14–29 *Exhortation:*	Do not turn back from the living God	
	13:1–17 *Exhortation:*	Serve God in the true community	
13:18–25	CONCLUSION: PRAYER AND GREETINGS		

1:1–4 Introduction: God has spoken God has spoken through Israel's prophets, but nothing compares with how he has now addressed humanity through his pre-existent Son. Like Wisdom as portrayed in Jewish thought (Prov. 8:22–31; Wisd. 7:22, 25–27; 9:2, 9), the Son is involved in the creation and sustaining of the world, and is the imprint of God's being. But the Son embodies those characteristics in a human person, who 'made purification for sins' and was therefore exalted to God's presence, supreme over all. The homily will expound particularly the significance of Jesus as 'Son of God' and as the one who has 'made purification for sins'. And it will urge the readers to allow their faith and discipleship to be transformed by these truths.

1:5—2:18 Jesus the Son of God A string of seven OT quotations demonstrates the Son's superiority over angels. Despite the high status of angels in Jewish thought, God attributes higher status to the Son. And then comes our author's first exhortation, expressing his concern that his readers may 'drift away' like a ship drifting from its moorings (2:1–4). Heb. 2:5–18 returns to the comparison between Jesus and angels. Its key text, Ps. 8:4–6, speaks of humanity destined for universal authority – a hope now being fulfilled in the exalted Jesus. But the Son of God has attained glory only through sharing in humanity and in the suffering of humanity. He thereby becomes the 'pioneer' (2:10) who opens the way to heaven for them to follow. Meanwhile he is able to help those whose faith is under pressure now (2:18). The author's confidence about this rests on his view of Jesus as the 'merciful and faithful high priest' (2:17), which will dominate the central part of his homily.

3:1—4:13 Jesus the faithful high priest Jesus and Moses are both examples of faithfulness to God's call, but Jesus' faithfulness is superior, as a builder is greater than a house, a son than a servant. This introduction leads (3:6) to a summons to faithfulness by the readers, and a challenge to learn the lesson of Ps. 95:7–11, not to rebel against God but to strive to enter into his promised 'rest'. The image of rest is derived from God's sabbath rest at creation and ancient Israel's arrival in the promised land. Here it points not to a future hoped-for rest in heaven, but to a secure relationship with God available now to those who listen to his voice (see 4:3, 7).

4:14—5:10 Jesus the sympathetic high priest This section begins with an exhortation to come to the exalted Jesus for the help and strength we need, since he sympathizes with our weakness (4:14–16). 5:1–10 then reflects on his sharing in human suffering. We shall draw together later significant aspects of the author's presentation of Jesus as high priest. But we should note here not only his vivid description of Jesus' prayerful struggle with suffering (5:7–8), but also his introduction of Ps. 110 as a key text. Though Ps. 110:1 is cited by other NT writers (e.g., Acts 2:34; 1 Cor. 15:25), only our author makes the link with Ps. 110:4, with its reference to the mysterious character Melchizedek (5:6).

5:11—6:20 The danger of spiritual immaturity This is a long exhortatory section, punctuated by an explanation (6:4–8) of why responding to the exhortation is so vital. The readers have got stuck in their Christian growth and need to move on from an elementary faith towards maturity (5:11—6:3). For if any fall away after experiencing the saving power of God, 'it is impossible to restore them again to repentance' (6:4–8). So they should press on with patience, placing their hope in God's secure promises (6:9–20). For Jesus the forerunner has led the way to heaven, 'having become a high priest for ever according to the order of Melchizedek' (6:20).

As we reach the passage where the author develops his theme of Jesus as high priest, we should note how strange this is. Jesus of Nazareth did not come from the right tribe (Levi) to be a priest, he performed no cultic act such as a priest would perform, his death was certainly not a sacrifice conforming to the law of Moses. How did the title 'high priest' come to be attached to him? No other NT writer uses the title, so it is impossible to be sure whether the author of Hebrews picked up the term from earlier Christian discussion or whether it was his own distinctive contribution to Christology. (For discussion of possible origins of the author's use of the title see Attridge, pp. 97–103.)

7:1–28 Jesus, high priest like Melchizedek

We know from one of the Qumran Scrolls (a document known as 11QMelchizedek) that Melchizedek, mentioned in the OT only in Genesis 14 and Psalm 110, was a subject of speculation in contemporary Judaism. But what attracts our author to him is that the information – and silences – in the OT texts enables him to describe a different kind of priesthood from the familiar levitical priesthood of Judaism. Using methods of biblical interpretation familiar in his time, he plays on the name Melchizedek (7:1–2). He takes the fact that Scripture does not record his genealogy or his death to signify a priesthood which lasts for ever (7:3; compare Ps. 110:4). And he finds scriptural reason for seeing his kind of priesthood as superior to

the levitical priesthood (7:4–10). In 7:13–28 he works out the contrast between Jesus, as high priest according to the order of Melchizedek, and the levitical priests. In particular, he is a priest for ever, always living to make intercession for his people (7:24–25).

8:1—9:28 Jesus, high priest made perfect by sacrifice

Jesus as high priest in heaven performs his ministry in the 'true tabernacle', the heavenly sanctuary of which the earthly sanctuary is only a copy. According to Ex. 25:9, 40, Moses was instructed by God to design the tabernacle (the portable tent which was the Israelites' place of worship in the wilderness) according to the model shown to him from heaven. Our author uses this to develop a contrast between the earthly sanctuary, where the levitical priests function, and the heavenly sanctuary where Christ is. He does not refer to the Jerusalem temple rituals of his own day, but works out his argument entirely with reference to the wilderness sanctuary, the tabernacle described in Exodus, Leviticus and Numbers. The earthly sanctuary is a 'sketch and shadow' of the heavenly one, a mere copy of the ultimate reality. It forms part of God's provision under the 'first covenant', which was temporary and incomplete. For Jer. 31:31–34, quoted in 8:8–12, shows that God had something better in mind, a new covenant which would render the old obsolete (8:13).

9:1–14 The annual ritual of the Day of Atonement (Lev. 26, esp. 26:11–19) is contrasted with Christ's sacrifice and entry into the heavenly Holy Place. The sacrifices of the old covenant dealt only with unintentional sins and external matters; they did not cleanse the conscience (9:6–10). But Jesus has brought a totally adequate sacrifice into the heavenly sanctuary. Paradoxically, as high priest he has offered not the blood of an involuntary animal but his own blood.

9:15–28 Whereas the levitical sacrifices had to be endlessly repeated, Jesus has sacrificed himself once and for all, and therefore remains permanently in God's presence. From there he will one day return to save those who await his coming.

10:1–18 Christ's perfect sacrifice The contrast between old and new covenants continues, with one important new point made. Ps. 40:6–8 is introduced to make the point that the distinctive thing about Christ's sacrifice is that it was not a matter of ritual killing but of personal self-offering (10:5–10). The 'sacrifice of Christ' is not literally a sacrifice in the sense of conforming to OT ritual. It is an act of personal obedience to God which makes all animal sacrifice obsolete and brings into relationship with God all who are united with Christ. As 'the sacrifice to end all sacrifices' it is on a quite different plane from the levitical sacrifices. 'Sacrifice' is a metaphor, not a literal description, when applied to the death of Christ. His death is the real, completely effective means of forgiveness, which the literal animal sacrifices foreshadowed.

10:19–39 The need for faith, love and endurance Like 5:11—6:20, this is an exhortatory section, punctuated by an explanation (10:26–31) of why responding to the exhortation is so vital. In view of all that Christ has achieved for them, the readers are urged to come close to God, holding on to faith, love and meeting together for worship (10:19–25). Wilful persistence in sin will bring divine judgement (10:26–31). But their past experience of endurance in suffering encourages confidence that they will not fall away now but will press on to the end (10:32–39).

11:1—12:13 Faith and endurance To undergird his exhortation the author now describes faith (11:1) and offers examples of figures from the OT and the inter-testamental period who have lived by such faith. In speaking of 'faith', our author's emphasis is rather different from Paul's. It includes living in consciousness of unseen realities (11:1b, 27) and steadfastly holding on until hope is realized (11:1a, 8–16, 24–26). All these heroes of faith 'did not receive what was promised' because in God's purpose they were waiting for Christ's faithful people to join them (11:39–40).

Digging deeper

Explore the different ways in which Paul (esp. in Rom. 4), James (esp. in 2:14–26) and Hebrews (Heb. 11) understand 'faith' and use Abraham as an example of faith.

Do you find it problematic or helpful that they each have a different emphasis?

In view of this the readers are urged to look to Jesus, the supreme example of faithful obedience in face of hostility. They are to take courage from him and accept the discipline of suffering as a sign of God's fatherly care (12:1–13).

12:14—13:19 Living as Christians in a hostile world A final series of exhortations warns once more how serious it is to turn deaf ears to the living God, to whom Jesus has brought us close (12:15–29), and then offers ethical instructions on a variety of issues (13:1–17). Notable here is the way in which memorable statements about Jesus are included to motivate the readers' response (13:7–8, 12–13).

13:18–25 Conclusion: prayer and greetings
The author concludes with a blessing, a final plea to take to heart his 'short word of exhortation', a promise to visit his readers, and a generous supply of greetings.

THEOLOGICAL THEMES OF HEBREWS

We shall here briefly draw attention to some of the more distinctive theological contributions which Hebrews makes to the NT.

THE HIGH PRIEST AND HIS SACRFICE

No other NT author calls Jesus high priest; no other provides such an extensive exposition of his death as sacrifice. His comparison of Jesus' priesthood and sacrifice with the levitical priesthood and sacrifices is in two stages.

First, he establishes the analogy by stressing the *similarities* between them:

2:17   Every high priest, including Jesus, is fully human
5:1, 5–6   Every high priest, including Jesus, is appointed by God
8:3   Every high priest, including Jesus, has a sacrifice to offer

Second, he stresses the distinctiveness of what Jesus is and does by stressing the *differences*:

Digging deeper:
JESUS' HIGH PRIESTHOOD AND SACRIFICE CONTRASTED WITH OT HIGH PRIESTS AND SACRIFICES

Study Heb. 5:1–10 and 7:1—10:18 and make a list of the ways in which, according to Hebrews, Jesus as 'high priest' *differs* from the levitical high priests of the OT and his sacrifice *differs* from that which they offered.

(Remember that Melchizedek is not one of the standard levitical high priests; the author uses this mysterious figure from Gen. 14:17–20 and Ps. 110:4 as a picture of the superior kind of high priesthood embodied in Jesus.)

All these contrasts between Jesus' high priesthood and sacrifice and those of the Jewish tabernacle or temple underline the author's conviction that the suffering and exaltation of Christ have made possible a 'better hope', 'a better covenant' (7:19, 22). The real has replaced the shadow, the permanent has replaced the temporary (8:2, 5, 13; 9:24; 10:1). The old order was there only 'until the time comes to set things right' (9:10).

The language of sacrifice is problematic for people far removed from any contact with animal sacrifice. But essentially it addresses the awareness of sin, guilt, shame, failure and alienation which lie deep in human consciousness. We are made aware that we owe to God a total offering of ourselves – and that we cannot make it on our own. The OT sacrificial rituals symbolize this through the conviction that God himself provides the offering for his people to bring to him (Lev. 17:11). And the letter to the Hebrews argues that the sacrifice of Jesus is the one truly complete self-offering, into whose benefits people of faith may enter.

OTHER PERSPECTIVES ON JESUS

● The author shares with Paul (1 Cor. 1:24, 30; 8:6; Col. 1:15–20) and John's Gospel (1:1–18) the use of Jewish Wisdom motifs to describe the pre-existent Christ (Heb. 1:1–3).

● From the first announcement in 1:2, 'Son of God' is a prominent title of Jesus. He is the humiliated and exalted Son of God, rather in the manner of the hymn in Phil. 2:6–11. Particularly striking is his description of the Son's solidarity with humanity and his approach to suffering and death (2:5–18; 5:7–8).

● Two unusual titles of Jesus are 'pioneer' (or 'champion', 2:10; 12:2; elsewhere only in Acts 3:15; 5:31) and 'forerunner' (6:20; unique to Hebrews). Both speak of Jesus blazing the trail for his people to follow into the presence of God.

● Christ fulfils the OT which, without him, would be an unfinished story. Jesus and the salvation which he brings are constantly described in terms of biblical texts and images.

● The author's presentation of his Christology is shaped not merely by dogmatic concerns but by his exhortations about discipleship (see on 'Discipleship' below).

What do you think?

Imagine you are the recipients of Hebrews. Given your situation, how might the titles and descriptions of Jesus in this document encourage your faith?

SALVATION AND THE CHRISTIAN HOPE

In common with other NT writers, the author believes that Christ's coming marked the beginning of the 'last days', the climax of God's activity in the world (1:2; 9:26). and he expects a future coming of Christ in glory (9:28; 10:25). This will be a time of judgement, which is a serious matter for all, including the recipients of Hebrews (6:2; 10:26–31; 12:25–29). But it will also mark the entry of believers into their ultimate salvation (9:28). The final goal of salvation is entry into the eternal presence of God, the heavenly sanctuary (2:10; 5:9; 6:29; 11:16).

Though salvation is an object of future hope (6:19–20) it is also realized in the present because of Christ's death and exaltation in the past. Believers are forgiven, their conscience purified (9:14), they have shared in the Holy Spirit and the powers of the age to come (6:4–5), and have open access to God (10:19). A distinctive theme in this connection is 'perfection' (see Peterson 1982). This does not denote moral perfection, but rather the completion of a purpose, the reaching of a goal. Christ, having completed his saving work ('made perfect', 5:9; 7:28) has brought his people to God's intended goal ('made perfect', 10:14).

This salvation can be lost through turning away from Christ. Much controversy has surrounded the 'rigorist' passages 6:4–8 and 10:26–31. Some have argued that the biblical doctrine of predestination implies that genuine believers cannot ultimately fall away from Christ ('once saved, always saved'). They may therefore suggest that in these passages the author is alluding to merely 'nominal Christians' who turn away when the going gets tough. But it is surely inconceivable that the language of 6:4–5 and

10:29 refers to anything but genuine Christian experience.

If so, does the author really mean that 'it is impossible to restore again to repentance' those who abandon their faith (6:4–6)? From one perspective it is impossible because apostasy is the ultimate sin, a renunciation of all that Christ means, a rejection of the only Saviour. On the other hand, contemporary experience suggests that sometimes people who abandon their faith later return to genuine Christian discipleship. But our author's concern is not to speculate about theoretical possibilities. He faces the urgent need of particular readers who, under pressure of persecution, are tempted to turn away. This is not a time for dispassionate reflection on a theological problem, but for clear warning about their spiritual danger. So the writer warns them in the strongest language (6:4–8; 10:26–31), and then expresses confidence on the basis of their earlier experience (6:9–12; 10:32–39).

DISCIPLESHIP

What picture of discipleship does Hebrews offer to people whose commitment to Christ is sagging? His approach might be summed up in the three phrases 'hold fast', 'approach' and 'move on' – each of which is related to his presentation of the person and work of Christ.

- They are to *hold fast* to their confession of the one who has brought salvation, Jesus the High Priest and Son of God (4:14; cf. 3:14) and to the hope which already glimpses Christ in heaven (6:18–19; 10:23).
- This holding fast is to be nurtured by *approaching* God in worship (4:16; 7:25; 10:19–22; 12:22). The fact that Christ as high priest has entered the heavenly sanctuary before them gives confidence (or 'boldness', 4:16; 10:19) to draw near to God.
- They are to *move on*. Many of the verbs in the exhortations imply movement. Rather than 'drifting away', 'falling away' or 'shrinking back' (2:1; 6:6; 10:39) they must 'strive to enter that rest' (4:11), 'run the race' (12:2), 'go to Jesus outside the camp' (13:13). And Hebrews 11 pictures Abraham and others moving forward in response to God's call (11:8–16). In practical terms this means pressing on to spiritual maturity (6:1), resisting the temptation to cave in under pressure (12:4–13) and offering mutual support whilst practising a distinctive lifestyle (13:1–17).

But in a tough world the greatest inspiration to wholehearted discipleship is Jesus himself, who 'endured such hostility against himself from sinners' and so has taken his place at God's right hand (12:1–3). As their 'champion' and 'forerunner' he not only opens the way to God's presence but also shows them how to live whilst following him there.

SPECIAL ISSUES

THE AUTHOR'S THOUGHT-WORLD
Many answers have been given to the question, What influences shaped the distinctive theology and styles of argument found in Hebrews? Hurst has surveyed possible non-Christian backgrounds (including Philo of Alexandria, the Qumran community, Gnosticism) and Christian backgrounds (the tradition of radical Hellenistic Christianity stemming from Stephen, and possible links with Paul and 1 Peter). We shall consider here the suggested influence of Philo, the Jewish philosopher (c. 20 BC – c. AD 50), who was himself

influenced by the philosophical tradition stemming from Plato (c. 427–347 BC).

Certain similarities with Philo are not hard to find in Hebrews. We have already seen how our author describes the earthly sanctuary as a 'sketch and shadow' of the heavenly sanctuary, the 'true tabernacle' (8:2, 5; 9:2, 23). This echoes the Platonic belief (reflected in Philo's *Creation of the World* 15–25) that objects in the material world are copies of ideal realities in the invisible eternal world. The dualistic distinction between 'spirit' and 'soul' in Heb. 4:12 is reminiscent of Philo (*Who is the Heir of Divine Things?* 55; 130–1), as also is the treatment of Melchizedek's name and the argument from silence about his genealogy (Heb. 7:2–3).

THE WRITINGS OF PHILO

'When God wished to create the visible world he first fully formed the intelligible world, in order that he might use a non-material and God-like pattern in producing the material world . . .' (*Creation of the World* 16)

'The highest, and in the truest sense the holy, temple of God is, as we must believe, the whole universe, having for its sanctuary the most sacred part of all existence, even heaven . . . There is also the temple made by hands.' (*Special Laws* 1.66–67)

'God has made Melchizedek both king of peace – for that is the meaning of "Salem" – and his own priest. He has not fashioned beforehand any deed of his, but produces him to begin with as such a king, peaceable and worthy of his own priesthood . . . He is a priest, namely Reason, who has as his portion the One who is, and all his thought of God are high and vast and sublime.' (*Allegorical Interpretation of Genesis* 3.79, 82)

However, it is one thing to notice parallel words and phrases, but another to prove substantial influence of Philo's teaching on Hebrews. The notion that the earthly sanctuary is based on a divine design goes back to Ex. 25, which was hardly subject to Philo's influence. The word translated 'sketch' is very rare in Philo, and 'shadow' is used in a wide variety of authors to denote something transient and insubstantial (e.g., Job 8:9; Col. 2:17).

Spatial 'up and down' language is equally at home in apocalyptic and in Philonic thought. In Revelation, for instance, alongside all the temporal language about 'what must soon take place' (Rev. 1:1) we find the city of God coming down from heaven (Rev. 21:2). And however we evaluate the contrast between earth and heaven in Hebrews, we find there also a strong sense of past, present and future as the sphere of God's activity. 'Jesus Christ the same, yesterday and for ever' (13:8) is not, as might be assumed, a Philonic statement about the eternal unchangeableness of the divine. It reflects the shared conviction of early Christians that the same Jesus who died and was exalted ('yesterday') now lives 'to make intercession for us' (7:25) and continues his priestly ministry for ever (7:24). Philo, by contrast, shows little interest in eschatology.

In the treatment of Melchizedek we find similarities but also a crucial difference. In Philo Melchizedek is allegorized as Reason, whereas our author interprets him messianically (7:3). Philo sees him as an allegory of an eternal principle, our author preserves a temporal sense of 'before and after', anticipation and fulfilment.

We may conclude, therefore, that our author has picked up some popular ideas of his time and is closer to Philo's world of thought than any other NT writer. But the heart of his thought lies closer to the early Christian mainstream than to Alexandrian philosophy.

IS HEBREWS ANTI-JEWISH?

For the author the OT witnesses to its own incompleteness. By contrast, the new order brings a 'better hope' (7:19), a 'better covenant' (7:22), 'better promises' (8:6). It involves 'better sacrifices' (9:23) in 'the greater and more perfect tabernacle' (9:11). The whole structure of his argument seems designed to persuade his readers that they must move forward with Christ, resisting the temptation to find emotional and physical security in the ethos and institutions of the old order, which are now obsolete. There is something emphatic about the author's repeated use of the verb 'we have', as though he is countering the temptation to return to the more tangible institutions of Judaism:

'We have a great high priest' (4:14–15)
'We have freedom to enter the Most Holy Place by the blood of Jesus' (10:19)
'We have an altar' – and it is Christ's death on the cross (13:10)

All this raises questions: Is Hebrews hostile to Judaism? How might Christian readers of Hebrews view God's ongoing relationship with the Jewish people? It is important to recognize that the author affirms the OT as God's word and regards Moses, Abraham and others as prime examples of faithfulness to God. What he affirms about Jesus is the new thing which God promised in the Scriptures. So faithfulness to the God of Israel requires that his people move forward with the Messiah who has now inaugurated the new era.

Both the author and his readers are Jewish Christians. His concern is not with non-Christian Jews, but with Jewish Christians who are in danger of abandoning all that they have gained through Jesus. The call to faithfulness is all the more urgent now than it was under the old order. Greater covenant privilege entails greater covenant responsibility (12:18–25). Neither for his audience nor for Christians today does this mean deserting Israel as the people of God. But for him logic required abandonment of Judaism's sacrificial rites because of Jesus' ultimate sacrifice. Ironically, the Jews themselves had to face the same challenge after the temple's destruction in AD 70.

WHERE WERE THE READERS LOCATED?

A likely scenario is that this community formed a house-church, comparable to the several house-churches in Rome referred to by Paul (Rom. 16:5, 10, 11, 14, 15). Such groups met in homes and had a certain distinct identity, yet were thought of as together forming the church in the city where they were located. Part of the role of leaders may have been to ensure that links with other groups in the city were maintained. The exhortation to 'greet all your leaders and all the saints' (13:24) looks like a request to pass on greetings to other house-churches and leaders who are not among the primary recipients. There would be no point making this request if the documents were addressed to *all* the Christians in a city assembled together to hear it read.

An urban destination might also be inferred from the imagery of 13:14: 'Here we have no lasting city, but we are looking for the city that is to come.' But in which earthly city do these struggling Christians live? Various suggestions have been offered, ranging from Jerusalem to Spain. Three possibilities are considered here.

Alexandria in Egypt has been advocated as the destination of Hebrews on the grounds that it shares the thought-world of Alexandrian Jewish literature such as Wisdom, 4 Maccabees and especially the works of Philo. However, it was in Alexandria that belief in authorship by Paul first arose (Clement of Alexandria, late second century, according to Eusebius, *Hist. eccl.* 6.14.1–4), and it is hard to imagine that the people who first received Hebrews would forget who wrote it and attribute it to someone else.

Others have argued that Hebrews was addressed to **Jerusalem** at about the time of the outbreak of the war against Rome in AD 66. At that time 'intense political and psychological pressures must have been exerted on Jewish Christians to show their loyalty to their ancestral religion and their nation by sinking differences and helping to present a united front in the bitter struggle for existence'. In this crisis the author urges his radical message: 'To go back into Judaism . . . is to desert the Crucified and to join the ranks of the crucifiers. The only way to life is the way forward, not back: we must go outside the camp, bearing Christ's reproach.' (C. F. D. Moule *The Birth of the New Testament*. New York: Harper & Row, 3rd edition 1982 pp. 59–60.) This is an attractive interpretation of the text. But there are serious difficulties:

- It is hard to imagine the author writing Hebrews 2:3, since Jerusalem Christians in the sixties (if that is the correct date for Hebrews) would surely include some who *had* 'heard the Lord'.

- Allusions to the recipients' wealth and generosity (6:10; 10:34; 13:5, 16) sit uneasily alongside the NT's witness to the Jerusalem church's poverty (e.g., Acts 11:29; Rom 15:26).
- Hebrews 12:4 is incompatible with the fact that in Jerusalem Stephen had been martyred (AD 32–35, Acts 7), as had James the brother of John (AD 44, Acts 12:2) and James the brother of Jesus (AD 62, Josephus, *Ant.* 20.9.1 = 20.200).

These objections might be overcome if one sees the readers as a small group within the Jerusalem church. But a third proposed destination has much in its favour.

Evidence for **Rome** as the destination of Hebrews includes the following:

- The earliest external evidence for the existence of Hebrews is the allusions to Heb. 1:1–7 in 1 Clement 36.1–5, which was written in Rome probably in AD 96.
- There is a tantalizing piece of evidence in Heb. 13:24: 'Those from Italy send you greetings'. Does this mean, 'People with me in Italy send greetings to you (who are elsewhere)'? Or, 'People with me (elsewhere) who originate from Italy send you greetings'? Both explanations have their defendants, but the latter is a more natural reading of the Greek, as we can see from the similar use of 'from' in John 1:44; Acts 6:9; 10:23. Italian exiles or travellers who are with the writer send greetings back to their friends in Rome.
- Timothy (Heb. 13:23) was known to the church in Rome (Col. 1:1; Phlm. 1:1).
- The picture of the community's earlier sufferings in 10:32–34 fits with the known

history of the Roman church. In AD 49 the emperor Claudius expelled Jews from Rome (see p. 19). Public abuse and loss of property (Heb. 10:33–34) inevitably occurred at such a time.

That was in the 'earlier days' of Heb. 10:34. The author is writing at a later period when a new crisis has emerged. Though they 'have not yet resisted to the point of bloodshed' (12:4) this crisis is clearly more serious than the earlier one. The onset of persecution of Christians under the emperor Nero after the great fire in Rome in AD 64 would be a plausible occasion for writing. The author urges his readers to stand firm as Christians in these uncertain and dangerous times.

NERO'S PERSECUTION

The Roman historian Tacitus describes the devastating effects of the fire, which destroyed most of Rome, and then refers to the growth of rumours that Nero deliberately had the fire started in order to clear the ground for his own grand building schemes. He continues:

> To scotch the rumour, Nero substituted as culprits, and punished with the utmost refinements of cruelty, a class of people, loathed for their vices, whom the crowd styled Christians. Christus, the founder of the name, had undergone the death penalty in the reign of Tiberius, by sentence of the procurator Pontius Pilate, and the pernicious superstition was checked for a moment, only to break out once more, not merely in Judaea, the home of the disease, but in the capital itself, where all things horrible or shameful in the world collect and find a vogue.

He then gives details of the methods of persecution. (*Annals* 15.44)

As in the case of Jerusalem, we have here a collection of circumstantial evidence rather than knock-down argument. But, of the options available, the most plausible is that Hebrews was sent to a house-church of Jewish Christians in Rome at the time of Nero's persecution. Up to that time the Roman authorities had regarded Christians as a sect within Judaism. But by marking out Christians for persecution Nero was now clearly distinguishing them from Jews. This might well make them feel doubly vulnerable and tempt them to 'shrink back' into Judaism.

A date of writing in the sixties seems to be confirmed by two factors:

- An earlier date is unlikely in view of the author's comment that he and his readers were not among those who 'heard the Lord' (2:3) but have now been Christians for some time (5:12; 10:32).
- A date after the destruction of the temple in AD 70 is excluded by the author's comment that the regular sacrifices cannot make people perfect, 'otherwise would they not have ceased being offered?' (10:1–2).

Digging deeper

In view of your study of Hebrews, how would you now summarize the author's reasons for writing it?

WHO WROTE THE LETTER?

Origen (c. 185 – c. 254) famously remarked: 'Who wrote the letter is known to God

THE LETTER TO THE HEBREWS

alone.' But that did not stop him making intelligent guesses about the author's identity. In fact the history of study of Hebrews from ancient to modern times is littered with intelligent guesses. In Egypt Hebrews was regarded as Pauline before AD 200: it is included in the Chester Beatty Papyrus (P46, early third century) immediately after Romans, and Clement of Alexandria describes the letter as Paul's (Eusebius, *Hist. eccl.* 6.14.1–4). But authorship by Paul is ruled out by the clear theological differences: for instance, our author's description of Jesus as high priest, his focus on Jesus' exaltation rather than his resurrection, his perspective on 'faith' and his use of Alexandrian thought-forms.

In the Western church there was scepticism about Pauline authorship until Jerome (*Famous Men* 5.59) and Augustine (*City of God* 16.22; *Forgiveness of Sins* 1.50) put their weight behind it in the early fifth century. Meanwhile other suggestions were offered. Tertullian, for instance, proposed Barnabas (*Purity* 20) – perhaps because someone had thought it natural that this 'word of encouragement' (Heb. 13:22) should have been written by someone nicknamed 'son of encouragement' (Acts 4:36).

The list of more recent suggestions 'reads like a roster of the supporting actors on the stage of the NT' (Attridge 1989, pp. 4–5). Among them are Apollos (Acts 18:24–25), Priscilla (with help from Aquila?, Acts 18:2, 26), Silas or Silvanus (1 Thess. 1:1), and even the Virgin Mary.

Rather than try to fill the vacuum left by the the letter's author being unnamed, it is more useful to summarize what we can know about the kind of person who wrote it.

- He was a Hellenistic Jewish Christian.
- He was not an eyewitness of the ministry of Jesus (2:3).
- He was in touch with Paul's circle of influence, as we see from the reference to Timothy (13:23) and his use of certain Pauline letter-writing features (compare 13:22–25 with the endings of Phil., Col. and 1 Thess.).
- He writes in a refined Greek style and has some awareness of Greek philosophical thought.
- He is familiar with study and creative interpretation of the Greek OT.

The fact that we do not know his name reinforces the impression that the early church was richer in great characters and great minds than we often imagine.

SOME ISSUES FOR TODAY

Although Hebrews is not easy for modern readers, a 'word of encouragement' which unfolds such a vision of Jesus Christ and the way he has opened into God's presence, of faith and discipleship in a stressful world, will more than repay the effort.

How would you interpret for people today the following distinctive themes?

- Jesus as the high priest who sacrifices himself to bring people to God.
- Jesus as 'pioneer' and 'forerunner'.
- Christian discipleship as 'holding fast', 'approaching God', 'moving on'.
- Faith as 'living in consciousness of unseen realities and steadfastly holding on until hope is realized' (Heb. 11).

Focus on theology:
THE CHURCH AND ISRAEL

Hebrews addresses his readers in terms which in the OT designated historical Israel. They are 'the people (of God)' (2:17; 4:9; 8:10; 10:30; 11:25; 13:12), 'children (of God)' (2:10; 12:5–7), 'the saints' (6:10; 13:24), 'God's household' (see 3:6). In such ways he underlines the continuity of Jesus' followers with Israel. But does he go further? What conclusions might we draw from his insistence that the new order brings a 'better hope' (7:19), a 'better covenant' (7:22; 8:6), 'better promises' (8:6), 'better sacrifices' in 'the greater and more perfect tabernacle' (9:11 margin)? And what of the claim that, whereas 'the law has only a shadow of the good things to come', the new covenant renders the old 'obsolete' (10:1; 8:13)?

From evidence such as this many Christians have drawn the conclusion that the church of Jesus Christ has 'replaced' or 'superseded' the Jews as the people of God; Israel has failed in its responsibilities under the 'old' covenant and has rejected Jesus as Messiah and therefore 'Christianity has replaced Judaism'. This perspective is known as *replacement theology* or *supersessionism*. It goes back at least to the *Epistle of Barnabas* (early second century?), whose unknown author asserts that Israel forfeited their unique relationship with God through idolatry (*Barnabas* 4:8), disobedience (8:7; 9:4; 14:1–4) and ignorance of the law's true (spiritual) meaning (10:2, 9). Christians are the true heirs of God's covenant (4:8; 6:19; 13:6; 14:4–5), i.e., the covenant is 'ours', not 'theirs'. Since then, of course, this belief has been used to justify oppression of Jewish people and has been an embarrassment to many Christians since the Holocaust. But it would be wrong to imagine that those who adhere to supersessionism would *necessarily* be anti-Jewish or acquiesce in persecution.

Hebrews is certainly a source to which replacement theology has looked for evidence. But is this in fact the perspective of the author himself? He affirms plainly that through Jesus' life, death and exaltation God has introduced a new era which effectively replaces the old. The law and sacrifices of the old covenant have turned out to be a step along the journey, not God's final provision for his people. And Hebrews hangs his argument on the fact that in the Hebrew Scriptures *God himself promised* that he would one day establish a new covenant with his people (8:8–13, citing Jer. 31:31–34; see also Heb. 10:16–17). And by introducing OT quotations with phrases such as 'God says/said' (1:5; 4:3; 5:5; 8:8), and 'the Holy Spirit says' (3:7; 10:16–17) he insists that 'the word of God [in the OT] is [still] living and active' (4:12). He does not portray Abraham, Moses, Joshua and other saints of the past in a negative light, though Jesus has now brought what is 'better' (7:19, 22; 8:9; 9:23). And these heroes of Israel themselves *knew by faith* that God was planning this 'better' future (11:16, 35) which they would not experience 'apart from us' (11:40). Here clearly is a pattern not of simple replacement but of *fulfilment*. The new covenant does not replace the old as a new car might replace an old one. It is more like a permanent job succeeding a period of probation, or a marriage following an engagement.

Another significant factor is that the concerns and argument of Hebrews are expressed within a solely Jewish framework. There is no mention of Gentiles, and the author simply does not have in view the question whether the Jewish people has been replaced by a Gentile church. His message is that the story of Israel is not complete without the Messiah, that individual Jews find completion ('perfection') in him, and that it is therefore not an option for his Jewish-Christian readers to return to 'Judaism before Christ'. It is anachronistic to call the author of Hebrews 'supersessionist'. His disagreement with his fellow-Jews was not about whether Christianity was superior to Judaism, but about whether Jesus was in fact the Messiah.

What, then, are Christians to make of this for ourselves and for relations between Christians and Jews today? Our author leaves us with a dilemma. On the one hand, we know that Christianity owes its birth to Judaism, and we want to affirm that God has not abandoned his commitment to Israel as his people. On the other hand, it is fundamental to Christian faith that Jesus the Jewish Messiah is the decisive revelation of God for all human beings, so that we cannot say that it makes no difference whether a Jew believes in Jesus or not. For this reason, the idea often advocated today, that God has two covenants – one for Jews, based on Moses, and the other for Gentiles, based on Jesus – is unsatisfactory. It 'does not allow Jesus to be the decisive revelation for the people to whom the revelation was given in the first place' (Lincoln 2006, p. 118). If Jesus is not the Messiah for Jewish people, he cannot be the Saviour of the world.

A continued living with this tension may be the only way to handle it. Richard Hays suggests that it may be legitimate – on the basis of Hebrews' train of thought (though Hebrews does not himself go this far) – to propose that 'in some unforeseeable way God's eschatological salvation through Christ will include not only the great cloud of Israel's witnesses who lived before the time of Jesus but also "all Israel" in later times as well' (in Bauckham, Driver, Hart and MacDonald, eds, 2009, p. 167, n. 34). That is certainly Paul's conviction (Rom. 11), though the manner and the timing of it remain hidden.

See further chapters by Hays, Skausane, Nanos and Hooker in Bauckham, Driver, Hart and MacDonald, eds, 2009; K. Barth, *Church Dogmatics* II.2 (ET Edinburgh: T. & T. Clark/New York: Scribner's, 1957), pp. 195–305); Lincoln (2006), pp. 114–20; Witherington III (2007) 374–7.

Note
Nowhere in this discussion is 'Israel' meant to imply anything about the Israeli state since 1948. The focus is on Israel as a people in continuity with OT Israel.

See also the discussion in relation to 1 Peter on p. 283.

ESSAY TOPICS

INTRODUCTORY

- What contribution does Hebrews make to our understanding of the nature of Christian discipleship?

- Show how the author's use of the imagery of 'high priest' and 'sacrifice' (especially in 7:1—10:18) would appeal to his Jewish-Christian readers.

INTERMEDIATE

- Explore the distinctive approach to interpretation of the OT found in Hebrews.

- What contribution does Hebrews make to our understanding of the atonement? Is it still meaningful today to interpret Christ's death in terms of 'sacrifice'?

FURTHER READING

* denotes books assuming knowledge of Greek; most can be used by all students.

INTRODUCTORY

A. T. Lincoln *Hebrews: a Guide*. London/New York: T. & T. Clark, 2006 (excellent guide to understanding Hebrews).

B. Lindars *The Theology of the Letter to the Hebrews*. Cambridge/New York: Cambridge University Press, 1991 (valuable account of the theological message).

A. H. Trotter Jr *Interpreting the Epistle to the Hebrews*. Grand Rapids: Baker, 1997 (practical guide to making sense of the letter).

INTERMEDIATE

R. Bauckham, D. R. Driver, T. A. Hart and N. MacDonald *The Epistle to the Hebrews and Christian Theology*. Grand Rapids/Cambridge: Eerdmans, 2009 (offers careful reflection on many issues introduced in this chapter).

L. D. Hurst *The Epistle to the Hebrews: its Background of Thought*. Cambridge/New York: Cambridge University Press, 1990.

R. N. Longenecker *Biblical Exegesis in the Apostolic Period*. Grand Rapids: Eerdmans/ Exeter: Paternoster, 1975 (includes discussion of Hebrews' distinctive interpretation of the OT).

*D. G. Peterson *Hebrews and Perfection: an Examination of the Concept of Perfection in the "Epistle to the Hebrews"*. Cambridge: CUP, 1982.

*J. W. Thompson *The Beginnings of Christian Philosophy: the Epistle to the Hebrews*. Washington: Catholic Biblical Assn. of America, 1982 (sees Hebrews as significantly influenced by Philo).

*A. Vanhoye *Structure and Message of the Epistle to the Hebrews*. Rome: Pontifical Biblical Institute, 1989.

Commentaries

*W. Attridge *A Commentary on the Epistle to the Hebrews*. Herm. Philadelphia: Fortress, 1989 (detailed but readable and full of insight).

*F. F. Bruce *The Epistle to the Hebrews*. NICNT. Grand Rapids: Eerdmans, 2nd edn 1990.

*P. Ellingworth *Commentary on Hebrews*. NIGTC. Grand Rapids: Eerdmans, 1993 (includes huge bibliography).

R. P. Gordon *Hebrews*. Readings: a New Biblical Commentary. Sheffield: Sheffield Academic Press, 2000.

D. Guthrie *The Letter to the Hebrews*. TNTC. Leicester: IVP/Grand Rapids: Eerdmans, 1983 (this and the following are good shorter commentaries).

G. H. Guthrie *Hebrews*. NIVAC. Grand Rapids: Zondervan, 1998.

D. A. Hagner *Hebrews*. NIBC. Peabody: Hendrickson, 1990.

R. Jewett *Letter to Pilgrims: a Commentary on the Epistle to the Hebrews*. New York: Pilgrim Press, 1981 (highlights the theme of pilgrimage).

*L. T. Johnson *Hebrews: a Commentary*. NTL. Louisville: Westminster John Knox, 2006.

*C. R. Koester *Hebrews*. AB. New York: Doubleday, 2001.

*W. L. Lane *Hebrews*. WBC. 2 volumes. Dallas: Word, 1991 (strong both on critical issues and theological message).

*B. Witherington III *Letters and Homilies for Jewish Christians: a Socio-Rhetorical Commentary on Hebrews, James and Jude*. Downers Grove: IVP/Nottingham: Apollos, 2007.

Chapter 17

THE LETTER OF JAMES

In this chapter we shall:

● explore the unusual character of this letter;
● ask who wrote it, when and for whom;
● study its key themes;
● reflect on their significance for today.

To some readers, the letter of James is a breath of fresh air after the weighty theology of Paul and the complex argument of Hebrews. But to others it has seemed like the 'junk mail' of the New Testament. Martin Luther famously described it as 'an epistle of straw', because it contains no reference to the passion and resurrection of Christ or to the Holy Spirit, and in 2:14–26 appears to contradict Paul's doctrine of justification through faith (*Luther's Works*. ET Philadelphia: Fortress, 1960, vol. 35 p. 362).

THE CHARACTER OF THE LETTER OF JAMES

Every book, however strange or distinctive, shares some characteristics with literature that has preceded it. So, in exploring the nature of this document, we shall begin by noticing some of the influences that have

What do you think?

Here is an outline of James 1, giving the theme of each brief section. Read through the whole letter fairly quickly and make a list of the places in chapters 2—5 where the themes of chapter 1 recur. Do the contents remind you of any other books, within and outside the Bible, with which you are familiar?

1:1	Greeting
1:2–4	Face the testing of your faith with joy and endurance
1:5–8	Ask God for wisdom, in faith and without doubting
1:9–11	Let the lowly believer rejoice in being raised up, and the rich in being brought low
1:12–16	You are blessed if you endure testing – which comes not from God but from inner desires
1:17–18	God is a generous and faithful giver, who through his word has made us the beginning of his new creation
1:19–21	Be quick to listen, slow to speak, slow to anger
1:22–25	Be doers of God's word, and not merely hearers
1:26–27	The nature of false and true religion

shaped it. For brevity's sake, it will be referred to simply as James.

JAMES AS EXHORTATION OR 'PARENESIS'

About half of the verses in James contain verbs in the 'imperative' form, expressing commands or exhortations (e.g., 'consider' 1:2, 'be doers of the word' 1:22). This simple statistic gives James a distinctive flavour and focus among New Testament books, which Martin Dibelius identified as parenesis (Gk. *parainesis* means 'exhortation', 'advice'). This places James within a tradition of Greek and Jewish literature designed to offer 'admonitions of general ethical content' (Dibelius 1976, p. 3). Passages such as Col. 3:18—4:1 and 1 Pet. 2:13—3:12 also reflect this tradition (see further Dibelius and Greeven 1976, pp. 3–11; *DLNTD*, pp. 1156–9). But James is unique in the New Testament in that the whole document may be seen as parenesis.

Dibelius (whose commentary was originally published in 1921) claimed certain other characteristics for parenetic literature and believed James shared them. For example:

- The identity of the author is unimportant since he is merely a collector of unoriginal maxims and wisdom sayings.
- The presentation lacks continuity and development of thought.
- Where links do exist between passages, they are frequently based on repetition of catchwords (to aid memory) rather than real connection of thought (e.g., 'lack' in 1:4–5; 'fruits' and 'harvest' – the same word in Greek – in 3:17–18).
- Unlike Paul's letters, James was not addressed to a specific situation, but offers general exhortation. For instance, the rich people addressed in 5:1–6 and the merchants of 4:13–17 are not the same people as those referred to in 2:1–7. These

are unconnected examples, each designed to make a general ethical point. They do not relate to the actual circumstances of the original readers but are precepts to learn and store up for when they might be needed.

Though Dibelius' stress on James as parenesis has remained important, we shall see that James may not reflect all these supposed characteristics of parenetic literature.

JAMES AS WISDOM

James' religious and ethical perspectives are shaped by the Jewish wisdom tradition represented by Proverbs and Ecclesiasticus (ben Sirach). Features of James which are familiar from the wisdom tradition include:

- wisdom is a gift from God (1:5; 3:17) which produces righteous living (3:13–18);
- teaching about such themes as faith and perseverance in the face of trials and suffering (1:2–4, 12–16), anger (1:19–20), wealth and poverty (2:1–7; 4:13—5:6), patience (5:7–11), speech (3:1–12);
- literary units such as brief proverbs (1:20; 2:26; 3:16), comparisons with phenomena observed in the world (3:3–4; 4:14b), appeal to the example of Old Testament figures (2:21–25; 5:10–11, 17–18).

(For further discussion of James and Jewish wisdom see Martin 1988, pp. lxxxvii–xciii; Bauckham 1999, pp. 29–111.)

Yet James is not 'merely' wisdom literature. There is a greater stress on eschatology than in most Jewish wisdom literature. The radicalism of James' approach to wealth and poverty does not sit easily alongside the rather conservative ethos of Proverbs or Ecclesiasticus. It recalls the teaching of Jesus, who himself used wisdom categories and yet blended them with fresh and subversive elements.

JAMES AS A LETTER

James 1:1 uses the standard opening formula of a first-century letter: author, recipient, greeting. But from then on its resemblance to a letter seems to disappear. There is no thanksgiving, no personal greetings, no farewell. The description of the recipients – 'the twelve tribes in the Dispersion' is so general that the document could hardly be *sent* to them. Imagine yourself writing a letter 'to all British expatriates' or 'to all African Americans'!

Hence it has become common to dismiss the first verse as a merely conventional opening and to characterize the document as parenesis, wisdom literature or (more vaguely) sermon. However, it is impossible to define in detail what features a document must have in order to qualify as a letter (see Chapter 2). Though readers of the NT are liable to think that a 'proper' letter must always look like the letters of Paul, that is simply not the case.

Though lacking the familiar features of a Pauline letter (such as thanksgiving,

personal greetings and farewell), James does not 'lack continuity' as Dibelius claimed. Its basic 'shape' is:

1:1	Opening greeting
1:2–27	Introduction of themes
2:1—5:6	More extended treatment of various themes, many of them already announced in chapter 1
5:7–20	Closing exhortations

And such a shape is in fact found in some Hellenistic letters. 1 Maccabees 10:25–45 presents the text of a letter from the Syrian king Demetrius to the Jews. Here too we find:

- the standard greeting (10:25);
- introduction of the letter's main theme, the rewards of keeping agreements (10:26–28);
- a detailed statement of these rewards (10:29–45).

There is no farewell. If this is a letter, then James is a letter.

THE STRUCTURE OF THE LETTER

Though we can begin to see a shape to the letter, it is quite different from the carefully built up argument of Romans. It is as though James has a certain number of coloured balls in a bag which he keeps taking out, replacing and taking out again in a somewhat random order – yellow, green, blue, then yellow again, then red, then blue again . . . But he knows how many colours he has, and makes sure that they are all displayed sooner or later.

James 1 forms an introductory statement of main themes, mostly expressed in brief proverbial form ('aphorisms'). These themes are then taken up, often in more extended paragraphs, in subsequent chapters, and a few other themes are added in. The following outline simply states key themes of each section rather than attempting to find any subtle logic to the order in which James has placed his material. We shall explore some of these themes later.

1:1   GREETING

1:2–27   INTRODUCTORY SUMMARY OF EXHORTATIONS
For details see above, p. 261.

2:1—5:6 MORE EXTENDED EXHORTATIONS
2:1–13   Favouritism conflicts with the law of love
2:14–26 Faith without deeds is dead
3:1–12   The power and peril of speech
3:13–18 The nature of false and true wisdom
4:1–10   A call to turn from friendship with the world to friendship with God
4:11–12 Exhortation not to judge each other
4:13–17 The arrogance of businesspeople
5:1–6   The oppression of landowners

5:7–20   CONCLUDING APPEALS
5:7–11   Endure patiently the testing of your faith, because the Lord's coming is near
5:12   Speak the plain truth
5:13–18 Pray for the suffering, the sick, and all in need of forgiveness
5:19–20 Take responsibility for mutual correction

For a detailed survey of discussion of the structure and rhetorical character of James, see Taylor 2004; Witherington III 2007, pp. 388–93.

WHO WROTE THE LETTER?

The claimed author is 'James, a servant of God and of the Lord Jesus Christ' (1:1). Who is he? And even if we can identify him can we be sure that he is the real author, or might the letter be pseudonymous, attributed to James by a later writer?

WHAT DO WE KNOW ABOUT JAMES?

- His name is actually Jacob. It became James as it travelled through Italian and other European languages. But in the Greek of the New Testament he bears the name of Jacob, the patriarch.
- He was one of Jesus' brothers (Mark 6:3; Gal. 1:19).
- During Jesus' ministry James shared the family's scepticism about Jesus' significance (Mark 3:21; John 7:5), but was changed by an encounter with Jesus after his resurrection (1 Cor. 15:7).
- Acts 1:14 therefore records his presence with the eleven apostles in Jerusalem between the resurrection and Pentecost.
- He is first named as a significant leader in the Jerusalem church in Acts 12:17.
- He plays the key role in Luke's account of the discussion at the Council of Jerusalem over whether circumcision should be required of Gentile converts (Acts 15, AD 49).
- His associations (sometimes tricky!) with Paul are recorded in Acts 21:17–26; 1 Cor. 9:5; 15:7; Gal. 1:19; 2:9, 12.
- The Jewish historian Josephus records that the high priest Ananus had James stoned to death during the interregnum between the departure from Judea of the Roman governor Festus and the arrival of his successor in AD 62 (Josephus *Ant.* 20.9.1 = 20.197–203).
- The fourth-century church historian Eusebius gathered together numerous traditions about James. For instance, he draws on Hegesippus (second century), the first writer to call James 'the Just' (*Hist. eccl.* 2.23.4). Though some of the material gathered by Eusebius must be pious legend, this and other traditions found in extra-canonical documents such as the *Gospel of Thomas* and the two Apocalypses of James testify to his considerable reputation among succeeding generations of Christians.

Of the several Jameses mentioned in the New Testament, only one is a serious contender – James of Jerusalem, the brother of Jesus. The very simplicity of the introduction points to a James whose prestige in the church is so secure that he does not need to support it by claiming titles of authority.

But is the content of the letter consistent with authorship by James of Jerusalem? Authorship by him has been questioned on the following grounds:

● The fact that there are only two references to Jesus (1:1; 2:1) make it very unlikely that the author was James, the Lord's brother.
● The author's competence in the Greek language and rhetorical styles (examples in Davids 1982, p. 58; Johnson 1995, pp. 7–10) is incompatible with authorship by an Aramaic-speaking Palestinian Jew. The Bible he quotes is the Greek Old Testament (Septuagint) rather than the Hebrew text. For example, in 4:6 he cites the Septuagint version of Prov. 3:34, which differs significantly from the Hebrew text. All this suggests the writer is a Diaspora Jew, not James of Jerusalem.
● The passage about faith and works (2:14–26) appears to be a reaction against the message of Paul, and yet it shows little understanding of what Paul actually taught. But James of Jerusalem had ample opportunity in his meetings with Paul to understand him. So the views expressed in 2:14–26 can hardly be the views of James himself.
● Not until Origen do we find anyone referring to James as Scripture (*Commentary on John* 19.6, written around AD 235), and it was among the latest books to be accepted as canonical. This would not be the case if its genuineness and apostolic origin had been known from the start.

For reasons such as these some argue that an author of the late first or early second century attributed his writing to James of Jerusalem in order to gain acceptance for it (e.g., Dibelius 1976, pp. 11–21, 45–47; Laws 1980, pp. 38–42). In response to these arguments the following points have been made:

● There is more Christology in James than the two explicit references to Jesus might at first suggest (see below, p. 270). And the author is deeply influenced by the teaching of Jesus (see below, pp. 267–8). If we compare James with a parenetic section of Paul's letters, such as Rom. 12—13, we find a similar scarcity of explicit Christology alongside a significant debt to the teaching of Jesus.
● It is wrong to assume that a Palestinian Jew could not write fluent Greek or appreciate Greek rhetorical style. Studies such as Martin Hengel's *Judaism and Hellenism* (ET London: SCM/Philadelphia: Fortress, 1974) have shown the extent to which Greek language and culture permeated Palestine in the first century.

It is plausible that during his twenty years of leadership in the Jerusalem church James would frequently need to meet and talk with Diaspora Jewish Christians coming on pilgrimage to Jerusalem, and so would have plenty of opportunity to develop his fluency in Greek. In any case, when writing the letter he could easily have had assistance from someone more competent in Greek (a 'Hellenist', as in Acts 6:1), just as the Jewish historian Josephus had assistants to polish his Greek (*Against Apion* 1.9=1.50).

Though the quality of the Greek stands comparison with that of Hellenistic writers, the author's Palestinian origin is betrayed by the reference to 'the early and late rains' in 5:7 – a phenomenon peculiar to Palestine and not known elsewhere in the Mediterranean world.

- The argument that the author has misunderstood Paul – which can hardly be said of the historical James, who knew Paul quite well – falls to the ground if we recognize that James is not, after all, aiming in 2:14–26 to contradict Paul (see below, pp. 268–70).

- The church's slowness to use and affirm the authority of James might be due to the fact that its content offered nothing that would be of use in the great doctrinal disputes of the second to fourth centuries.

There is therefore no strong reason to question the tradition of authorship by James of Jerusalem. Perhaps the hardest argument to evaluate is the one about the author's familiarity with Greek language and rhetorical style. It is one thing to suggest that a man who (as far as we know) remained in Palestine all his life could learn to write good Greek. It is harder to judge the extent to which such a person could absorb the 'tricks' of Greek rhetorical style and write in a way that suggests parallels with a range of Greek parenetic literature. A possible solution to this dilemma will emerge in the next section.

TO WHOM WAS THE LETTER ADDRESSED? WHY, AND WHEN?

If we accept the plausibility of authorship by James the Lord's brother, the address 'to the twelve tribes in the Dispersion' (1:1) must also be weighed seriously. This description of the addressees may seem impossibly wide to be taken seriously as a real location of the

readers. How would one send a letter to all Jews, or all Jewish Christians, outside Palestine?

JEWISH CHRISTIANS IN PALESTINE?

Arguing that 'the Dispersion' is meant symbolically, Peter Davids has contended that the readers faced a quite specific situation in Palestine. He suggests that the reference to merchants (4:13–17), rich farmers (5:1–6) and the potential of the rich to persecute (2:6–7) rings true of Palestine in the decades before AD 70. The limited agricultural land could not support a growing population, and people deprived of land became hired labourers, rootless and vulnerable. Others saw how the influx of Hellenistic goods presented an opportunity to make money as traders, and in cities such as Jerusalem a class of wealthy merchants emerged.

Such a scenario affected the church in Palestine, whose poverty is attested by Paul in Gal. 2:10; 2 Cor. 8–9. Rich landowners would have 'robbed' some Christians of their land, and may have shown discrimination against Christians when hiring labour. So it would be natural for Christians in Palestine to resent the rich and to feel threatened by their power. Yet if a wealthy person visited or belonged to the church, they would be inclined to show favouritism and at all costs avoid offending him. Or they might be tempted to join the Zealots fighting for justice against the rich oppressors.

Against this background James denounces the rich (4:13–17; 5:1–6), and warns against showing special favours to the wealthy (2:1–7), but also urges his readers not to be over-concerned about financial security (1:9–11; 3:14–16; 4:4) and not to take the way of violence (4:1–3). He calls for unity and charity in the face of pressure and provocation, and patient waiting for the Lord's judgement (5:7–11).

Davids suggests that teaching material originating with James in the 40s and 50s was collected to form the letter in AD 55–65 (perhaps just after James' death in 62, when the tensions in Palestinian society were intensifying in the lead-up to the War against Rome). Such a view can explain why the letter seems to be assembled from many small parts, and can affirm that the content comes essentially from James the Lord's brother whilst attributing the high standard of Greek in the Letter to an editor (Davids 1982, pp. 28–34, 21–22; for a similar perspective see Martin 1988, pp. lxvii–lxxvii, though he suggests that the letter was edited for Christians in Antioch rather than in Palestine).

However, the diversity of material in the letter, and the fact that there is no sustained argument about the economic issues, create the suspicion that such a specific audience for the letter cannot be confidently identified. And the meaning of 'the twelve tribes in the Dispersion' must be revisited.

JEWISH CHRISTIANS IN THE DISPERSION?

Richard Bauckham proposes that James is not a personal letter written to a specific situation and specific readers, but 'an official letter or encyclical, in which James as head of the Jerusalem church addresses all of his compatriots and fellow-believers in the Jewish Diaspora' (Bauckham 1999, p. 13).

There was a tradition of letters sent from Jerusalem to the Diaspora, offering advice on cultic practice or on more general matters (examples in Jer. 29; 2 Macc. 1:1–9; Acts 15:23–29). And James in his letter 'communicates to the Diaspora the teaching of the revered head of the mother church in Jerusalem on how Messianic Jews should live' (Bauckham 1999, p. 20).

So we may see James as a letter of advice and exhortation addressed to any Jewish Christian community to whom it might be circulated. As such, it does not address specific readers in a specific situation, but addresses what James perceived to be *typical* situations and issues faced by Jewish Christians in the Diaspora.

So we find him imagining hypothetical situations such as might well occur from time to time (e.g. 2:2–3). And when denouncing the rich he envisages two familiar kinds of wealthy people, merchants and landowners, and condemns them for typical sins of those groups (4:13–17; 5:1–6). He is not addressing the challenge of a particular moment, but is preparing his readers for challenges that may come at any moment. An appropriate name for such a document is 'parenetic letter'.

As for the time of writing, it was most likely between AD 50 and 66. A date earlier than that makes it more difficult to account for the author's familiarity with Greek language and rhetorical styles. A later date is implausible because the War with Rome (66–70) would surely have left its mark on such a Jewish document; the churches are led simply by 'elders' (5:14), and there is no sign of a developed church structure; and the author is in close touch with early traditions of the sayings of Jesus.

JAMES AND THE TEACHING OF JESUS

Though James is rightly described as a teacher of wisdom, he has learnt that

What do you think?
ECHOES IN JAMES OF THE TEACHING OF JESUS

Compare these passages in James with those in the Synoptic Gospels. (It is not an exhaustive list of parallels.) Why do you think James never actually hints that he is alluding to sayings of Jesus? Is it simply a sign of how completely the words of Jesus have become part of his own thinking and teaching?

	James	Matthew	Luke
Joy when faith is tested	1:2	5:11–12	6:23
The call to perfection/maturity	1:4	5:48	
Asking and receiving	1:5, 17; 4:2–3	7:7–11	11:9–13
Endurance leads to salvation	1:12	10:22; 24:13	
Anger wipes out righteousness	1:20	5:22 (with 5:20)	
Be doers of the word	1:22–23	7:24, 26	6:47, 49
The poor inherit God's kingdom	2:5	5:3, 5	6:20
The law of liberty, love of neighbour	2:10–12	22:36–40	10:25–28
The merciless will be judged	2:13	7:1	
Practical care for the poor	2:14–16	25:34–35	
The fruit of good works	3:12	7:16–18	6:43–44
Warning against divided loyalties	4:4	6:24	16:13
Purity of heart	4:8	5:8	
Humility and exaltation	4:10	23:12	14:11; 18:14
The dangers of wealth	5:1–3	6:19–21	12:33–34
The prophets' example	5:10	5:11–12	6:23
Oaths forbidden	5:12	5:33–37	17:3
Restoring a sinner	5:19–20	18:15	

wisdom particularly from Jesus. Much of his teaching echoes sayings of Jesus (see box).

JAMES AND PAUL

James' apparent contradiction of Paul has loomed large in discussion of the letter. James 2:14–26 looks to many as though it sets out to undermine or to correct the emphasis on 'justification by faith', which is so significant in Paul's gospel. Four main ways of explaining the contradiction have been proposed:

1. Paul disagrees with James' teaching and sets out to correct it;

2. James disagrees with Paul's message and sets out to correct it;

3. James is correcting a misunderstanding of Paul by people who imagined that his gospel offered 'cheap grace' whereby salvation is gained by simple faith without any moral transformation;

4. Despite the overlap of language, they are addressing different issues without reference to each other.

What do you think?

Study the following passages where James and Paul write about faith, works and the law. Note the similarities and differences in language and perspective between them. What do these suggest about their different emphases and concerns?

Paul: Rom. 3:20, 28; Rom. 4, especially the use of Gen. 15:6 in vv. 3, 9

James: Jas. 2:14–26, including the use of Gen. 15:6 in v. 23

How are we to evaluate these possibilities?

1, 2. Both these views are difficult to accept in view of the evidence of Acts and Galatians that James and Paul knew and respected each other (Gal. 1:19; 2:9; Acts 15:13–29; 21:17–26). Though some interpreters have found in Gal. 2:1–15 a sharp clash of viewpoint between Paul and James, 2:9 suggests that Paul's disagreement was not so much with James himself as with others who claimed him as their mentor.

3. Paul himself admits the theoretical possibility that people may not take seriously the moral demands of his gospel of grace (Rom. 6:1). But the idea that James is opposing either Paul's teaching or a later development of it founders on the fact that James' letter shows little real engagement with the issues which actually concerned Paul.

4. This is the most likely explanation. Despite the impression that James 2:14–26 is directly reacting to the perspective of Rom. 3—4, James does not conduct his argument as though he has any close knowledge of, or interest in, what Paul is concerned about.

- The kind of faith that James says is 'dead' (that is, mere intellectual assent, 2:14–17) is not what Paul would have recognized as real faith (that is, 'faith working through love', Gal. 5:6).
- Paul's treatment of 'faith and works' is related to the question of whether Gentile Christians must do 'the works of the law' – mainly circumcision, sabbath and food laws. James' argument does not have Gentiles or such 'works of the law' in view at all.
- The coincidence of their reference to Abraham is not surprising. Any Jew would if possible appeal to him as their trump card in an argument. But they are in fact engaged in argument not with each other but with different opponents – Paul with those who would impose 'works of the law' on Gentiles, James with people who have become sluggish in their Christian living. (For fuller discussion, and variant views, on the whole issue of the tension between James and Paul – hinted at in Gal. 2:12 – see Bauckham 1999, pp. 113–40; Davids on 'James and Paul', *DPL* pp. 457–61; Johnson 1995, pp. 58–64).

Whichever explanation of the apparent conflict between James and Paul we prefer, how do we handle their very different perspectives? For many Christian readers, the temptation is to say, 'Well, they are both really saying the same thing. Paul stresses that salvation is through faith, while James adds – in agreement with Gal. 5:6 – that faith must be worked out in loving action.' If we are content to say this we are likely to miss the radical and uncomfortable challenge of both James and Paul. For Paul, the wonder of the gospel is that through Christ God, out of sheer generosity, welcomes human beings into relationship with himself. We can do nothing to earn or achieve it; by faith we receive it as a gift. For James, faith is not true faith unless it produces generous, radical, godly living.

It was perfectly possible for a Christian a generation later to use both Paul's and James' language without seeing a contradiction. I Clement (written in Rome about AD 95) says in chapter 30: 'Let us clothe ourselves with concord and humility, always exercising self-control, keeping our distance from all whispering and evil talk, being justified by our works, and not our words.' And two chapters further on he writes: 'We, being called by his will in Christ Jesus, are not justified by ourselves, nor by our own wisdom, or understanding, or godliness, or works which we have done in holiness of heart; but by that faith through which, from the beginning, almighty God has justified all people.'

THEMES IN JAMES

Here we draw together themes that are significant for James.

GOD

James affirms the Jewish conviction that God is one (2:19, cf. Deut. 6:4). God is the faithful and generous Creator (1:17; 3:9), who promises a new world order (1:18). He is the Saviour and Judge of all (4:12), worthy of worship (4:7–10) and generous obedience (1:22–27). He is the merciful Father (1:17, 27; 3:9; 5:11), whose gifts include wisdom (1:5; 3:17) and grace (4:6). He answers prayer (4:3), particularly for wisdom (1:5) and healing (5:13–18). He has a particular care for the humble poor and oppressed

(1:27; 4:6–10; 5:4). God's involvement with the story of humanity moves from creation through his care for Israel, which is established through Abraham the 'friend of God' (2:23), towards its completion in final judgement and the coming of God's kingdom (2:5; 5:7–9).

JESUS

This story is centred on 'our glorious Lord Jesus Christ' (2:1). Jesus has more significance for James than first impressions might suggest. His use of the title 'Lord' interchangeably for God (1:8, 12) and Christ (1:1; 2:1; 5:7–8) assumes an important status for Jesus. His final coming (*parousia*) will mark the completion of God's purposes in history (5:7). As exalted leader of the messianic community he is the authoritative teacher whose message and spirit permeates the whole letter. On his limited attention to Christology, we might listen to Calvin, who commented with a greater sense of balance than Luther: 'It is surely not required of all to handle the same arguments . . . This diversity should not make us to approve of one, and to condemn the other.' (*Commentary on the Catholic Epistles*. ET Grand Rapids: Eerdmans, 1948, p. 276.)

LIVING WITH INTEGRITY

A significant word introduced in 1:4 is 'mature' or 'perfect' (Gk. *teleios*). James longs for his readers to be 'mature and complete', and his development of this theme comes close to what we might call 'integrity' – wholehearted, consistent dedication to God's will for human living.

He develops this, for example in his contrast between friendship with God and friendship with the world. Faced with the stark choice between these alternatives, which will I choose (2:23; 4:4)?

For James 'world' is a negative word, denoting not God's creation but (as often in John's Gospel and 1 John) the value-system of humanity in resistance to God (as in 1:27; 2:5). There is no room for 'double-mindedness' (1:8; 4:8). But James does not adopt the comfortable position which affirms that 'we' are friends of God, while 'they' – those who are different from us, or do not belong to our group – are friends of the world. More disturbingly, he warns those within his communities that the temptation to compromise and divided loyalties is within each one of us (1:8; 2:1–5; 3:9; 4:3). At the heart of his message is a call for purity of heart, and single-minded devotion to God's will (4:8).

Alert to the dangers of formal religion and empty faith, James urges the importance of being 'doers of the word' (1:22–25; 2:14–26). 'Religion that is pure and undefiled before God' is not only to 'keep oneself unstained from the world' but positively to care for those in need (1:27; 2:15–17), to control the tongue (1:26; 3:2–12; 4:11), to be 'quick to listen, slow to speak, slow to anger' (1:19), to reflect the mercy of God in relationships with others (2:13), to practise just labour-relations (5:1–6). Faith without works such as these is lifeless (2:26).

But the inner life is also important. The wisdom that comes from God is the key to a life of integrity, which reflects the character of God and yields a 'harvest of righteousness' (3:13–18). Humility, purity of heart, openness to God and resistance to the forces of evil are essential qualities of those who would express friendship with God (4:4–10). Through prayer one may gain wisdom (1:5), healing (5:13–15), and perhaps material goods – but only if they are asked for out of need rather than self-indulgence (4:2–3).

THE LAW

James speaks in a consistently positive way about the law. It is 'the perfect law, the law of liberty' (1:25), 'the royal law' (2:8). This last phrase might be better translated 'the law of the king', or 'the law of the kingdom'. In 2:8 it is specifically related to the summary of the law, 'You shall love your neighbour as yourself' (cf. Mark 12:31; Rom. 13:9–10). This commandment comes originally, of course, from Lev. 19:18. Since allusions to Lev. 19:11–17 are found in 2:1, 9; 4:11; 5:4, 9,12, 20 this is clearly a crucial passage for the author (Johnson 1995, p. 31; Bauckham 1999, pp. 142–5).

Digging deeper

With the help of commentaries, study James' teaching about 'speech ethics' (1:26; 3:2–12; 4:11). What does he say about the potential of speech for good or evil, and how the tongue can be controlled? How might such teaching be applied among friends, in the workplace or in public life today?

THE TESTING OF FAITH

Introduced at 1:2, this theme runs like a thread through the letter. The 'trials' to which he refers are not necessarily open

Digging deeper

Study James 5.13–18.

What guidelines for healing ministry might you draw from this passage? What theological or pastoral questions does it raise for you? Might verses 7–11 also provide helpful guidance on this topic?

persecution, but any kind of pressure which tempts a believer to give up on faith, for example illness or tragedy, harassment from non-Christian neighbours, the difficulty of maintaining Christian values in a hostile world. Such trials are not traps set for us by God, but may come from our sinful human nature or from the devil (1:13–16; 4:7). But to endure such testing promotes growth towards maturity and in the final reckoning wins 'the crown of life' (1:4, 12; 5:7–11). The eschatological framework of James' convictions shapes his teaching about Christian living.

POVERTY AND WEALTH

Often the 'righteous sufferer' is also poor. James has striking words of reassurance for

Focus on theology:
ESCHATOLOGY

Though often played down by interpreters, eschatology is a vital theme for James. It comes to the fore in 5:7–9, where 'the coming of the Lord' *might* refer to the coming of God himself to bring in the final judgement and the age to come (as in OT prophetic expectation, e.g. Mal. 2:17). But more probably the reference is to the final coming of Christ, which is how most NT writers 'translate' or reshape OT expectation of the coming of God. His coming is 'near' (5:8) and it will involve a universal judgement, at which some will receive 'the crown of life' (1:12; cf. Rev. 2:10), while others will be condemned (2:13). Like other NT writers, James uses 'judge' and 'judgement' both in the negative sense of 'condemn' and in the neutral sense of 'express a verdict' on someone. In 5:9 'so that you may not be judged' means 'so that you may not be condemned', whereas 'the Judge' is one who may declare either the acquittal or the condemnation of those who come before him.

Though James offers no other details on how the future will unfold, his thinking is profoundly shaped by the eschatological perspective. It forms the framework within which his exhortation is expressed. For example, his argument about actions and faith (2:14–26) focuses on what God requires of people if he is to accept them as righteous ('justify'

them). And 'justification' is an eschatological term, expressing the verdict of the final judgement. James offers specific examples of actions and attitudes that will determine that verdict, for example, acts of mercy or the lack of them (2:13–17). Those who endure faithfully in face of all the pressures that confront them will receive from God the crown of life (1:12; 5:7–8). But self-confident and self-satisfied wealth will reap condemnation. When the day of reckoning comes the upside-down values of this age will be exposed for what they really are and injustice will be overthrown. Those who imagine they have everything will wither away like a wild flower (1:9–11; 2:1–5; 4:13–17; 5:1–6).

James shows very clearly that Christian hope is not simply a matter of holding certain beliefs about the destiny of the world and of humanity. Still less is it a matter of passively waiting, or of calculating from Scripture or from historical events when 'The End' will come. Hope is a motivation for a life of radical discipleship. Both James' social ethic (on wealth and poverty) and his personal ethic (on endurance, acts of mercy) are shaped by his eschatological convictions. It was Martin Luther King's 'dream' – his hope, his God-given vision of what ultimately *will be* – that shaped his view of how people should live now and inspired him to radical and costly action.

the poor and denunciations of the rich. In the spirit of Amos or Micah he condemns the abuse of power and the exploitation of the poor by wealthy landowners (5:1–6). He warns that the clock is ticking towards divine judgement upon them (5:3–4, 9). He does not suggest that all wealth is gained through oppression of the poor, but he challenges the arrogance of the merchant who imagines that nothing can stop him building his financial empire, warning of the transience of wealth (4:13–17). And he exposes the tendency for a church to show favour to wealthy visitors in the hope of receiving benefits from them, while showing contempt for the poor who have nothing to offer (2:1–7). A community that acts like this has forgotten that it has turned God's values upside-down, and that it is the poor who are closest to his heart (2:5; 1:9–11, 27).

James' attack on the rich and powerful 'may not be theologically sophisticated, but it is not naïve either . . . It lays bare the power interests involved in human relationships, actions and words, and calls the bluff of falsely motivated action. Against this, it calls for genuine faith and concrete, practical action' (Chester in Chester and Martin 1994, p. 58).

SOME ISSUES FOR TODAY

- **Radical lifestyle** Though originally addressed to Jewish Christians in the first-century Diaspora, James' letter can speak to twenty-first century Gentiles because it addresses common human needs, temptations and aspirations. The real difficulty presented by the letter is not one of understanding it or reconciling its message with that of Paul, but of taking seriously its challenge to a godly and radical lifestyle.

- **Wealth and poverty** The material on wealth and poverty reflect different social patterns from today's Western societies, yet it carries the urgent challenge that our idolization of wealth clashes violently with God's values. The spiritual malaise of Western society cannot be cured without confronting the wealthy with their responsibility towards the poor and the powerless.

- **Individualism** James confronts our individualism by advocating a community that depends on God's generosity (1:17; 4:6); resists favouritism, envy, selfish ambition, malicious talk, boasting and grumbling (2:1–9; 3:14–16; 4:2, 11, 16; 5:9); and engages in practical love for the neighbour, especially the poor and despised, and mutual pastoral care (1:27; 2:5–6, 15–17; 5:13–20).

- **Relating to the ethics and values of others** One final challenge emerges from James' readiness to make use of both Jewish and Greco-Roman ethical traditions and to minimize the use of an explicit Christology. It invites Christians into constructive exploration of ethical values with other religious believers, such as Jews or Muslims, on the basis of our common belief in God. And it encourages us to explore ethical issues with unbelievers too in the conviction that our shared humanity provides a solid basis on which to develop mutual understanding and co-operative action.

ESSAY TOPICS

INTRODUCTORY

- If the letter of James were not in the New Testament how much would this matter for Christians today?

- Take two of the themes in the section on 'Themes in James' and produce the outline of two group Bible studies on those themes. For each study, include the full text of a leader's introduction to the topic; a statement of what you hope participants would learn from the study; a set of discussion questions designed to help a group explore the issues; and a summary response to any particularly difficult question that you think might come up.

INTERMEDIATE

- What is James' teaching about wealth and poverty, and to what extent is it applicable in today's very different economic context? (See bibliography, including Bauckham 1999, pp. 185–203.)

- Was the author of this letter in the mainstream or on the edge of the development of the early church and its teaching? Discuss with particular reference to the relationship between the teaching of James and that of either Jesus or Paul.

FURTHER READING

* denotes books assuming knowledge of Greek; most can be used by all students.

INTRODUCTORY
R. Bauckham *James*. NT Readings. London/New York: Routledge, 1999 (stimulating study of the form, content and contemporary significance of James).

A. Chester and R. P. Martin *The Theology of the Letters of James, Peter, and Jude*. NT Theology. Cambridge: Cambridge University Press, 1994.

C. Blomberg *Neither Poverty nor Riches: a Biblical Theology of Possessions*. Leicester: Apollos, 1999 (contains valuable insight on this theme in James, as do the following books by Johnson and Maynard-Reid).

INTERMEDIATE
L. T. Johnson *Sharing Possessions: Mandate and Symbol of Faith*. Philadelphia: Fortress, 1981.

P. U. Maynard-Reid *Poverty and Wealth in James*. Eugene: Wipf & Stock, 2004.

J. Painter *Just James: the Brother of Jesus in History and Tradition*. Philadelphia: Fortress/Edinburgh: T. & T. Clark, 1999 (comprehensive study of traditions about James from the NT to the fourth century).

T. C. Penner *The Epistle of James and Eschatology: Re-Reading an Ancient Christian Letter*. Sheffield: Sheffield Academic Press, 1996 (detailed study of how eschatology shapes the perspective of the whole document).

M. E. Taylor 'Recent Scholarship on the Structure of James', *Currents in Biblical Research* 3.1, Oct. 2004, pp. 86–115.

Commentaries
W. F. Brosend II *James and Jude*. NCBC. Cambridge/New York: Cambridge University Press, 2004 (uses insights of historical, narrative and socio-scientific criticism in an accessible way).

*P. H. Davids *The Epistle of James*. NIGTC. Grand Rapids: Eerdmans/Exeter: Paternoster, 1982).

*M. Dibelius and H. Greeven *James*. Herm. ET Philadelphia: Fortress, 1976 (the most influential twentieth-century commentary, of which Dibelius' first German edition appeared in 1921).

*L. T. Johnson *The Letter of James*. AB. New York: Doubleday, 1995 (especially good on backgrounds of thought and rhetorical style, and on putting the James–Paul debate in proper perspective).

S. Laws *A Commentary on the Epistle of James*. BNTC. London: Black/New York: Harper & Row, 1980 (suggests the letter was written, using James as a pseudonym, in Rome some time between James' death and the early second century).

*R. P. Martin *James*. WBC 48. Waco: Word, 1988.

C. L. Mitton *The Epistle of James*. London: Marshall, Morgan & Scott/Grand Rapids: Eerdmans, 1966 (stresses James' practical message).

D. J. Moo *The Letter of James*. PNTC. Grand Rapids: Eerdmans/Leicester: Apollos, 2000 (expository study building on his 1985 Tyndale NT Commentary).

M. J. Townsend *The Epistle of James*. EC. London: Epworth Press/Valley Forge: Trinity Press International, 1994 (excellent shorter commentary).

R. W. Wall *Community of the Wise: the Letter of James*. Valley Forge: Trinity Press International, 1997 (stresses the wisdom element in James, and reflects on tensions between it and other books in the NT canon).

*B. Witherington III *Letters and Homilies for Jewish Christians: a Socio-Rhetorical Commentary on Hebrews, James and Jude*. Downers Grove: IVP/Nottingham: Apollos, 2007.

Chapter 18

THE FIRST LETTER OF PETER

In this chapter we shall study:

- the shape of 1 Peter;
- the situation of the recipients and the nature of their suffering;
- the letter's theological message and its significance today;
- the authorship of the letter;
- the nature and purpose of the 'household code'.

In a mere five chapters 1 Peter provides a wealth of teaching about the life of Christians in God and in society, and about facing opposition in God's strength. It points vividly to the significance of the sufferings of Christ and to the hope generated through faith in him.

When we receive a letter we often look first at the beginning and ending to find out who it is from and why they have sent it. The beginning and end of 1 Peter produce the following answers to such questions:

- it is from Peter, apostle of Jesus Christ (1:1);
- he has written from 'Babylon' – a code-name for Rome – and has sent his associate Silvanus to convey it to its destination (5:12–13);

- his purpose in writing is 'to encourage you and to bear witness that this is the true grace of God; stand firm in it' (5:12);
- his intended readers are spread across a wide area of Turkey (1:1).

With these bare facts in mind, we shall read through the letter to gain a sense of its overall shape and message.

What do you think?

As you read through 1 Peter with the outline that follows, note clues that may help answer the questions listed here.

- Were the recipients Jewish or Gentile, or a mixture of both?
- What was the social make-up of the churches addressed?
- What specific pressures are they facing?
- What main themes does the writer express to help them face these pressures?

OUTLINE OF THE LETTER

The letter follows a similar pattern to Paul's letters:

277

1:1–2	OPENING GREETING

1:3–12 PRAISE TO GOD FOR HIS MERCY
Like 2 Cor. 1 and Eph. 1, the main body of the letter begins with an expression of praise to God modelled on the Jewish *berakah* (benediction), beginning with 'Blessed is . . .' (Hebrew *barak*).

1:13—5:11 BODY OF THE LETTER
  1:13—2:10 Respond to God's grace shown in Christ
  2:11—3:12 Live positively in a non-Christian society
  3.13—4:11 Do what is right even if it brings suffering
  4:12—5:11 In your sufferings be joyful, maintain the unity of the church and resist the forces of evil, confident in the love and power of God

5:12–14 CLOSING GREETINGS

THE SITUATION OF THE RECIPIENTS

The writer identifies his intended readers in 1:1–2 as 'chosen exiles of the Dispersion' scattered across four Roman provinces. Pontus-Bithynia formed a single province, but they are separated in the list probably because they represent the beginning and end of the route that Silvanus, travelling from Rome, would have to follow in bringing the letter to churches in each of the provinces (see Hemer).

The term 'exiles in the Dispersion' suggests that the addressees were Jewish people, the Greek *diaspora* being a standard term for Jews living outside Palestine (compare Jas. 1:1). But 1:18 and 4:3–4 speak of their former way of life in terms that a Jew would typically apply to Gentiles and never to

What do you think?

'Honour everyone. Love the family of believers. Fear God. Honour the emperor.' (2:17)

This simple set of exhortations has more implications than may appear at first sight.

● In a hierarchical society such as the Roman empire, honour was accorded to people of power and influence. The command to 'honour everyone' is radical in its emphasis that no one is unworthy of honour.
● 'The family of believers' (Greek *adelphotes*, as in 5:9) echoes the description of the church as a 'spiritual household' (2:5), and is the context for the mutual love urged in 1:22; 3:8; 4:8.

● The contrast between '*fear* God' and '*honour* the emperor' is probably not accidental. It may reflect the growth of emperor worship in Asia Minor (see pp. 16–17) – a background against which the author relativizes the emperor's status in comparison with God's. Jesus differentiated between what is owed to God and what is owed to the emperor (Mark 12:17) and told his followers to fear (reverence) only God (Matt. 10:28).

These commands thus imply a set of values that were in tension with the prevailing values of that time. In what ways might Christians today find that taking such values seriously could bring them into conflict with the society around them?

Digging deeper

'Wives, accept the authority of your husbands' (1 Pet. 3:1)

1 Peter 3:1–7 is part of a 'household code' (1 Pet. 2:13—3:7, or perhaps 2:11—3:12), a type of literature familiar in the Greco-Roman and Hellenistic Jewish worlds and adapted for Christian use (compare Col. 3:18—4:1; Eph. 5:22–33; Titus 2:1—3:8; see pp. 165–6). These 'codes' were instructions for relationships and behaviour in typical life-situations such as those within a family, those between masters and slaves, and attitudes towards civil authorities. They tended to follow a standard form, frequently including the instruction to 'submit to' or 'recognize the authority of' superior persons.

3:1–6 is problematic for readers today who wish to use the Bible for guidance in matters of faith and behaviour.

- Do we take it to imply a lower status for a wife in comparison with her husband?
- Do we dismiss it as an ancient text, which has played a part in promoting the oppression of women over the centuries?
- Do we take seriously the context of its original composition and allow that to help us distinguish between what is permanent because it genuinely reflects God's purpose for humanity, and what does not apply today because it reflects the particular circumstances of a particular culture?
- Think through how you would argue for one or other of these three perspectives, and what understanding of the relationship between wife and husband it leads you to.

In developing your thought you may find helpful Elliott 2000, pp. 585–99.

fellow-Jews (compare 'futile' in 1:18 with Eph. 4:17). Hence 'Dispersion' must be seen as a metaphorical description of God's messianic people, both Jews and Gentiles, in churches scattered across the pagan world.

'Exiles' (1:1) and 'aliens and exiles' (Gk. *paroikoi kai parepidemoi*, 2:11; cf. *paroikia*, 'exile' in 1:17) have been the subject of much discussion in recent years. J. H. Elliott has proposed a sociological interpretation (Elliott 1981/1990, 1992, 2000 and *ABD* vol. 5, pp. 273–4). Recognizing that 1 Peter has much to say about the situation of the recipients over against society, he argues that these terms refer to the addressees' insecure social status as resident aliens. In the Greek OT these words are applied literally to Abraham in Canaan (Gen. 23:4; 26:3), Israel in Egypt (Gen. 15:13), Judah in Babylon (1 Esdras 5:7), and the later Jewish settlement in Egypt (3 Macc. 7:19).

In the Greco-Roman world 'aliens and exiles' (more precisely, 'permanently resident aliens and transient strangers') designated a class of resident aliens ranked below full citizens but above complete foreigners and slaves. They would include, for example, tenant farmers and travelling merchants, craftsmen and teachers. Without local roots or political loyalties, they were often regarded with suspicion. In Elliott's view, the Christian movement in Asia Minor enlisted many who belonged to this class. Almost inevitably, therefore, the movement as a whole felt the hostility of the local population, which was the typical experience of their social class.

Though Elliott makes his case powerfully, it can be challenged.

- If these technical terms are so significant, why is only one of them introduced in 1:1 and the other not used until 2:11, and neither term used again? If Peter wanted to refer literally to the readers' political status as aliens before their conversion, he could have used other more common terms (Achtemeier 1996, p. 174).

- The assumption underlying 4:3–4 is that the readers were previously acceptable to pagan society but lost that acceptance through transforming their lifestyle. It does not suggest that they belonged already to a despised class before becoming Christians.
- Hence it is better to see the use of these terms as one of the many examples of Peter's application to Christians (both Jewish and Gentile) of terms that originally referred to Israel. Abraham's *literal* experience as 'a stranger and alien' in Canaan (Gen. 23:4) is echoed in the *metaphorical* experience of churches in Asia Minor of feeling foreigners in the land where they live. But Peter is not using the image to convey the message, 'This world is not my home, I'm just a-passing through'. Rather he is recognizing the severe social pressures, which his readers now experience as Christians. Because of their conversion they have become like foreigners in their own land, shunned and abused by their neighbours. Like Israel of old, they know how uncomfortable it can be to be marked out as different from the surrounding culture.

B. Witherington III has recently argued that Elliott is right to understand 'aliens and exiles' in a sociological rather than metaphorical sense: they are *real* exiles, but *Jewish* ones rather than Gentiles. They are diaspora Jews in Asia Minor – probably evangelized by Peter in the 40s and 50s AD according to his commission to go 'to the circumcised' (Gal. 2:9). But they are *Hellenized* Jews who, until they became

Christians, may have practised those aspects of a Greco-Roman lifestyle which would merit Peter's warning in 4:3–4 (Witherington III 2007, pp. 23–34). This Jewish perspective makes coherent sense of much of the language and imagery of the letter, and deserves to be taken seriously. However, though there were certainly many Jews in Asia Minor in the mid-first century, it is intrinsically unlikely that the churches addressed were *exclusively* Jewish. If so, the language of 'dispersion' and 'exiles' and the OT quotations are being applied (metaphorically) to Gentiles as well as (more literally) to Jewish believers in Jesus.

Digging deeper

Study the arguments for and against Elliott's sociological interpretation of 'aliens and exiles'. If you are able, read his own discussion of 2:11, and the response to him by other commentators (e.g., Achtemeier 1996, Marshall 1991, Michaels 1988). Whose view do you think fits best the evidence of 1 Peter?

WHAT WAS THE NATURE OF THEIR SUFFERING?

Pliny, governor of Pontus-Bithynia, wrote to the Emperor Trajan in AD 111–12, reporting specific actions he had taken against Christians and seeking advice.

Some of the language he uses reminds one of 1 Peter. If we decide that 1 Peter must have been written in the light of the situation described by Pliny, this of course has a bearing on the date and hence on the authorship of 1 Peter. Notice the following comparisons:

- Pliny appears to have punished people simply for being Christians, not for committing a particular crime. Cf. 1 Pet. 4:15–16.
- Pliny says that in laying charges against Christians he is responding to accusations made by informers. Compare the comment about those who 'malign' or 'slander' Christians in 1 Pet. 2:12; 3:16; 4:4.
- 'Make your defence' (3:15) is legal language used in the context of a trial (Acts 22:1; 25:16). Thus it presupposes that Christians were being brought to court, as in Pliny's letter.

However, the references to suffering in 1 Peter as a whole (1:6; 2:12; 3:13–17; 4:12–19; 5:9) do not support the theory that 1 Peter reflects the situation described by Pliny.

- 1 Peter 5:9 makes clear that the kind of suffering endured by the Christians of Asia Minor was shared by Christians everywhere. But there is no evidence that suffering such as that imposed by Pliny was being inflicted at that time in other provinces of the empire.
- Under Pliny those found guilty of being Christians were routinely put to death. 1 Peter carries no hint of this.
- The word 'defence' (Greek _apologia_) in 3:15 was also used, as in modern English, in non-legal contexts (1 Cor. 9:3; Phil. 1:7). It refers to explaining one's faith whenever anyone asks about it.
- 1 Peter often uses the general Greek word for 'suffer' (_pascho_), 12 times – more than in any other NT document). He does not use _dioko_, _diogmos_ (normally translated 'persecute', 'persecution'): terms often denoting persecution instigated by official authorities.

All this shows that the suffering of 1 Peter's recipients was not state-inflicted persecution such as that which occurred under Pliny, but general abuse and harassment at the hands of a suspicious or hostile public. Ignorance, incredulity at what Christians claimed to believe, resentment that Christians no longer shared their lifestyle and thus were 'anti-social' – reactions such as these led to reviling and intimidation (2:12; 3:14, 16) of Christian communities.

THE LETTER'S MESSAGE TO THE CHURCHES

Peter's theology is a practical theology geared to encourage his readers. Here is a sketch of his message, drawing together key themes from the letter.

CHRISTIAN EXISTENCE IN A HOSTILE ENVIRONMENT

Theology must first be realistic about the situation that it addresses. Peter does not actually begin his letter with this, but it underlies everything he says. He acknowledges the reality of his readers' suffering. It should come as no surprise (4:12) because it is part of the ongoing battle between God and the forces of evil (5:8–9) and heralds the final judgement (4:17–18). It is unjust (1:19; 3:14), it puts their faith to the test (1:6–7), it involves experiencing verbal abuse (3:16; 4:4), intimidation (3:14) and sometimes formal accusations of crimes against society (2:12).

How, then, does the letter address this situation?

THE GRACE OF GOD IN CHRIST

Peter's aim is to encourage his suffering readers to stand firm in the grace of God (5:12). So his first thought is to remind his readers in trinitarian language. He affirms that God's activity is focused on their wellbeing and salvation (1:2). In 1:3–11 he stresses the hope and security derived from Jesus' resurrection.

Elsewhere he underlines the liberation made possible through Christ's saving death (1:18–19; 2:24–25; 3:18), his present exaltation and victory over evil (3:18–22), and the promise of eternal glory at Christ's future coming (1:7; 4:13; 5:4, 10). In fact, the work of Christ in past, present and future reverses the Christian's past life of ignorance and futility (1:14, 18), provides a secure hope in their present suffering (1:5–7) and brings the promise of future glory (1:4).

THE DEATH OF CHRIST IN I PETER

As part of his strategy for encouraging his readers to face suffering, Peter writes vividly of the significance of the sufferings of Christ. The key passages are 1:18–19; 2:21–24; 3:18. For discussion of this theme see Chester and Martin, pp. 107–117.

THE HOUSEHOLD OF GOD

In contrast with their 'homelessness' in society, Peter affirms the dignity and status of his readers by describing them as 'the household of God' (2:5; 4:17). Thus he stresses their solidarity with each other in a way designed to encourage people who could otherwise feel isolated and vulnerable. 'Family' language conveys the same message. They are reborn (1:2, 23; 2:2) into the family of which God is father (1:3, 17), a great family of brothers and sisters (2:17; 5:9).

GOD'S PEOPLE

Though his readers are 'nobodies' in society, Peter confers on his readers a new identity by addressing them in language that the OT applies to Israel. The key passage is 2:9–10, where familiar descriptions of Israel (Ex. 19:5–6; Isa. 43:20–21; Hos. 2:23) become words of reassurance and redefinition for embattled Christians in Asia Minor. It is no accident that these words are immediately followed by 2:11, for it is the assurance conveyed by them that will enable 'aliens and exiles' to handle their situation.

1:16 similarly takes up the fundamental calling of Israel – 'You shall be holy, for I am holy' (Lev. 11:44–45; 19:2; 20:7, 26) – and makes it a key theme of the letter's appeal to its readers. Other examples of 'Israel'

Digging deeper:
THE CHURCH AND ISRAEL

Peter's application of 'Israel' language to the church raises questions about how the relationship between Christianity and Judaism is to be understood. Christians must think about this sensitively in the light of a long history of anti-semitism.

Drawing on different strands in NT teaching, Christians have proposed several different perspectives on how this relationship should be understood. For example:

● **Replacement theology** The church has replaced ethnic Israel as 'the people of God'. Having rejected Jesus as Messiah, Jewish people no longer have any distinctive relationship with God or any special claim on the promises given to OT Israel. This view draws on passages such as Matt. 21:43; the claims that Jesus supersedes Jewish institutions such as law and temple in John 1:17; 2:19–22; the argument of Hebrews that the new covenant renders the old obsolete (Heb. 8).

● **One covenant** God made a single covenant with his people the Jews, into which Christians are able to share through Christ. There is no question of God giving up on the promises he originally made to Israel. This view draws on Rom. 11:13–32, esp. v. 29.

● **Two covenants** God has made two parallel covenants with Jews and Christians. While Christians find salvation through faith in Jesus, Jews continue to be in relationship to God through the original covenant. On this view the NT does not fulfil or supersede the OT; rather, the Old and New Testaments (or Hebrew Scriptures and Christian Scriptures) are seen as parallel testimonies to God's actions. Rom. 9—11 is interpreted as affirming the integrity of God's separate dealings with Jews and Gentiles.

● **Two different religions** Judaism and Christianity are two different religions with quite different characters and focuses of concern. They have no more in common than does either of them with other faiths. If a Jew converts to Christian faith, or a Christian to Judaism, that has no different significance from the conversion of a Buddhist or a secular agnostic.

Reflect on these different approaches in the light of your reading of 1 Peter. Does the letter's angle on the church as Israel provide evidence for one or other of these perspectives?

What further light might be shed on the issue by Paul's stance in Rom. 2:28–29 – which he drew from passages such as Deut. 10:16; Jer. 4:4; 9:25–26?

Two British church reports on this issue are: *Christians and Jews: a New Way of Thinking.* London: Council of Churches for Britain and Ireland, 1994; *Sharing One Hope? The Church of England and Christian–Jewish Relations.* London: Church House Publishing, 2001.

language may be found in 1:4; 2:4–8; 3:10–12; 5:2. 1 Pet. 1:10–12 provides the basis for such use of the OT: the prophetic writings were in fact inspired by the Spirit of Christ to foresee the sufferings and glory of Christ.

The surprising thing in all this is that Peter makes no reference at all to a continuing Israel separate from the Christian community. 'Israel' language has apparently been transferred without remainder to the followers of Jesus.

CHRIST'S 'DESCENT INTO HELL' AND HIS VICTORY OVER EVIL

Two very difficult verses (1 Pet. 3:19; 4:6) have sometimes been linked with the belief that after his death Jesus 'descended into hell' to offer salvation to people who had already died. This belief emerged in the second century and is expressed in the statement 'He descended into hell', which began to be added to the Apostles' Creed in the fourth century. However, it is now agreed, by many scholars from various church traditions, that 1 Peter does not support this belief. The following interpretation has widespread support.

3:19 After his resurrection (after he was 'made alive', v. 18), Christ went to the place where disobedient supernatural powers are imprisoned, to proclaim to them his victory and God's judgement. 'The spirits in prison' are evil supernatural powers held captive to await the final judgement. The Jewish tradition that the 'fallen angels' ('sons of God' in Gen. 6:1–4), who seduced women on earth in the period before the Flood, were imprisoned to await judgement was familiar in NT times, and is reflected also in 2 Pet. 2:4; Jude 6.

Although the word translated 'proclaimed' normally means 'preach the gospel', it can mean simply 'make proclamation' (Rev. 5:2). It seems best here to translate 'proclaimed victory', in view of the emphasis in v. 22 that the ascended Christ is victorious over 'angels, authorities and power'. Through this vivid – but difficult! – imagery or mythology Peter is assuring his readers that they have nothing to fear from those who threaten and oppress them. Christ has defeated the forces of evil, both supernatural and human, and will ultimately bring them to judgement.

4:6 'The gospel was proclaimed even to the dead' refers to the evangelization of those who are *now* dead (at the time of writing) but who received the gospel before they died. Though this meaning may seem strange, it follows appropriately from the reference to 'the dead' in v. 5. The thrust of Peter's argument is that those who presumed to condemn others in their lifetime will ultimately be brought to judgement themselves. Those who were condemned by society in their lifetime will be vindicated by God at the final judgement.

See further Elliott 2000, pp. 647–662, 731–740; Marshall 1991, pp. 122–9, 136–9. The standard detailed study is W. J. Dalton, *Christ's Proclamation to the Spirits: a Study of 1 Peter 3:18—4:6*. Rome: Pontifical Biblical Institute, 2nd edition 1989.

FACING SUFFERING

In the light of these perspectives, suffering can be viewed in a different way. It may be God's will, in that it can contribute as Christ's suffering did to the outworking of God's purpose (3:17–18). Those who suffer through being identified with Christ experience the blessing that comes from the presence of his Spirit and the assurance of his ultimate victory (4:13–14; 5:10). In this confidence they can hold their heads high despite everything that is thrown at them (4:16, 19).

CHRISTIAN RESPONSIBILITIES

Now that he has shown his readers how to find their identity and security in Christ, what strategy does Peter urge for living in a non-Christian society?

● **A mutually supportive community** The logic of his emphasis on household, family and people of God is his exhortations to mutual love (1:22; 2:17; 3:8; 4:8) and rejection of attitudes which would undermine this (2:1), hospitality (4:9), mutual service through spiritual gifts

(4:10–11), and awareness of the sufferings of others (5:9). Elders are to care gently for their flock, and all are to relate humbly to their leaders and to each other (5:1–5).

- **A distinctive community** While forming a close-knit supportive community they are to be marked off from the surrounding society by their distinctive lifestyle. To be 'holy' or 'sanctified' or 'purified' (1:2, 15–16, 22; the Greek root is the same) involves leaving aside the former way of life and becoming obedient to God (1:2, 14; 4:1–4).
- **Engagement with society** One could forgive Peter and his readers if their reaction to a hostile society was to pull up the drawbridge and hide behind the battlements. But Peter urges a more positive approach.
- **Live the good life** The letter advocates that Christians conduct themselves 'among the Gentiles' (2:12) in such transparently good and honourable ways that society cannot but notice (2:15, 20; 3:13–17; 4:19). It will mean repaying evil not with evil but with a blessing (3:9–12). Such living is difficult because it is counter-cultural and may therefore provoke resentment and the infliction of suffering. But it is the right course simply because it is God's will (2:15; 4:19).
- **Contribute positively to society** Most of these references to 'doing good' seem to refer to good conduct in the most general sense, since they include what is possible for slaves (2:20) and wives with limited scope for influence (3:1–2, 6). But 2:14–15 at least may refer to acts of public benefaction, such as financing improvements in a water supply or subsidizing the price of grain during a famine. It was the role of government to commend such acts of public service (2:14). Far from withdrawing from society they are to contribute to the public good, to

'seek the welfare of the city' as Jeremiah urged the Jews exiled to Babylon (Jer. 29:7).
- **Bear witness to Christ** The church's purpose is to 'proclaim the mighty acts of him who called you . . .' (2:9). By the quality of her life a Christian woman may win to faith her unbelieving husband (3:1). But all must be ready, when the opportunity is presented, to explain the reason for their hope in Christ (3:15).

WHO WROTE 1 PETER?

Questions have been raised about the authorship of this letter on the following grounds:

- The references to suffering reflect the persecution under Pliny in AD 111–12. We have already seen that this argument carries little weight.
- It would take time for the church to establish itself in the large area addressed, which included two provinces not evangelized by Paul (Pontus-Bithynia and Cappadocia). Hence a date before Peter's death (about AD 65) is implausible.
- There is minimal reference to Jesus' teaching or to his life, apart from the crucifixion and resurrection – which is surprising from one who was close to him.
- The use of Babylon as a symbol for Rome (5:13) is known from other Christian and Jewish sources only after the destruction of Jerusalem in AD 70 (e.g., Rev. 18:2, 10, 21; 2 *Baruch* 11:1; 67:7; 2 Esdras 3:1, 28, 31; the latter two books are Jewish apocalypses written around AD 100). Only after Rome had destroyed Jerusalem and its temple and had exiled its inhabitants would they draw the parallel with OT Babylon, the destroyer of Jerusalem and its first temple.
- The refined literary style, with a high proportion of words familiar in classical

Greek, rather than the 'Koine' Greek of popular communication, presupposes a level of formal education higher than Peter had (cf. Acts 4:13).

● No writer before Irenaeus (*Against Heresies* 4.9.2, c. AD 185) names Peter as the author.

These arguments have been countered as follows:

● The self-designation of the author as Peter must be taken seriously unless there are overwhelming arguments against Petrine authorship. And the letter was sent from Rome, where ancient Christian tradition firmly locates him (along with Mark, as in 5:13) in the last part of his life.

● If Jews from Pontus and Cappadocia as well as from Asia, Phrygia and Pamphylia (all in Asia Minor) were present at Pentecost (Acts 2:8–10) churches could have been formed in those areas from earliest times.

● There are in fact numerous allusions to the teaching of Jesus, though the letter does not attribute them explicitly to Jesus (see Davids 1990, pp. 26–27). In any case, it is a misguided modern assumption that someone who knew Jesus would keep quoting him. The early church seems to have kept a clear distinction between traditions about Jesus' life and teaching (which it eventually recorded in the Gospels) and instruction given to guide its own life (expressed orally or in letters). Thus we find that John the apostle (or the Johannine community) used traditions about Jesus' life and teaching in writing the Gospel, but made minimal reference to Jesus' life and teaching in 1–3 John.

● Though surviving texts equating Rome with Babylon are generally later than AD 70, there is no reason in principle why a Jewish or Christian writer before that should not make the connection, on the grounds that Roman society, like sixth-century Babylon, was marginalizing God's people. 'Babylon' is a natural part of the letter's 'exile' imagery. The commentary on Habakkuk found among the Dead Sea Scrolls (certainly earlier than AD 70) interprets Habakkuk's prophecies about Babylon as being fulfilled in the aggression of Rome. Interestingly, the Roman writer Petronius compares Roman decadence with that of Babylon (*Satyricon* 55, written in the 60s).

● On whether Peter could write Greek of the quality found in this letter, the same arguments as are set out in the discussion of the letter of James apply (see pp. 265–6). Acts 4:13 means that Peter had no formal rabbinic training, not that he had no fluency in Greek. Indeed, we would expect a man running a fishing business, who came from a Hellenized town (Bethsaida, John 1:44) and had a brother with a Greek name (Andrew), to be able to converse well enough in Greek. But the question remains what competence in literary style he could have achieved. K. H. Jobes has set the debate about the quality of 1 Peter's Greek on a more objective basis in her careful demonstration that it is unlikely to be the work of a native Greek speaker, because it is too full of Semitic (Hebrew or Aramaic) idioms (Jobes 2005, pp. 7–8, 325–38). This reduces the force of the argument that Peter *could not* have written it, but it does not in itself show that Peter was the author since he was not of course the only speaker of 'Semitic Greek'. (See also Grudem 1988, pp. 25–31, for a robust defence against the assault on Petrine authorship.)

● Whether or not 2 Peter is a genuine letter of the apostle, it attests Petrine authorship of this letter (2 Pet. 3:1) at a much earlier date than Irenaeus.

ASSESSING THE ARGUMENTS

Though many arguments against Petrine authorship are relatively weak, the issue of language is not easily resolved. A number of scholars have proposed that the quality of Greek is to be attributed to Silvanus (5:12). As Paul's companion on his second missionary journey (Acts 15:40; 2 Cor. 1:19; 1 Thess. 1:1; 2 Thess. 1:1) Silvanus (= Silas) had spent time speaking and preaching to Greeks and would need a level of fluency to gain acceptance with them. So now Peter could ask him to help in drafting his letter. While Peter was responsible for the content, Silvanus had freedom to shape the language and style.

Some object that '(I have written) through Silvanus' in 5:12 must refer, in line with ancient idiom, to Silvanus' role in *carrying* the letter to the readers, not in writing it (e.g. Elliott 2000, pp. 872–4). But such language could equally refer to the *writing* of a letter, as in 2 Thess. 2:2, where the reference to a 'letter as though from us' uses the same Greek word for 'from' as is here used for 'through (Silvanus)' (Witherington III, pp. 246–7). This is certainly about the writing of a letter, not merely the carrying of it to the recipients. Most likely, 1 Pet. 5:12 is both identifying Silvanus as the scribe and commending him as the carrier of the letter to its recipients.

There is one further possibility. Those who are persuaded by the arguments against authorship by Peter speak of the letter as pseudonymous (see the general discussion of pseudonymity on pp. 234–8). They insist that this is not a matter of deception, but that the aim of the writer, or writers, was sincerely to communicate what Peter would say to a new generation, or to convey 'a contemporary application of traditional Petrine material to the new situation of

persecution' (D. G. Meade *Pseudonymity and Canon*. Grand Rapids: Eerdmans, 1986, p. 177).

A number of these scholars attribute the document to a 'Petrine group' in Rome. Among them is Elliott, who argues that this group included Silvanus and Mark (1 Pet. 5:12–13; Elliott 2000, pp. 127–30). Others, in the absence of any clear evidence for the existence of this group, are sceptical about its existence. Horrell, for example, believes 1 Peter is the product of Christians in Rome concerned not simply to express the 'voice' of Peter, but to synthesize Petrine, Pauline and other traditions for a post-apostolic generation (Horrell 2002). Both Horrell and Elliott date the document in the period 70–95 AD.

The main choices, then, are the following:

- 1 Peter is a genuine letter by the apostle, written not long before his martyrdom in Rome in the 60s.
- Silvanus played a significant part in its production, under Peter's instruction, or perhaps immediately after his death.

Digging deeper

Evaluate the arguments for and against authorship by Peter and by a 'Petrine group'.

I have deliberately not offered my own conclusion here in order to encourage you to weigh up the evidence for yourself. If possible, look for more detailed argument in commentaries. This might be done as a group, with different people consulting one commentary each. If you have not already done a similar exercise on Ephesians (see p. 179) you may like to present your findings in the form of a debate.

● It is pseudonymous – the work of a 'Petrine group' or of some other individual or group concerned to draw together diverse traditions of Christian thought known to the church in Rome and to communicate them to the wider Christian world. The most favoured date on this view is the 80s. One argument for this date relies on Pliny's comment that some of those accused of being Christians claimed to have abandoned Christian faith 'as much as twenty years ago' (*Letters* 10.96). This might suggest an intense period of suffering around AD 85.

SOME ISSUES FOR TODAY

Themes of contemporary significance in 1 Peter include the following:

● **The significance of suffering for one's faith** Like other forms of suffering, it provokes the questions: Why does God allow it? Where is he in it all? Peter offers no slick explanations, but suggests positive significance can be found in such suffering.

● **The meaning of hope** Peter speaks not of hoping *for* something to turn up, but of hope rooted *in* God (1:21; 3:5). Hope is grounded in the resurrection of Christ (1:3), because of which they need not fear the forces of evil (3:22). It looks to his coming victory when all that is wrong in the world will be set right (2:12; 4:7–19; 5:10–11). Such hope is worth bearing witness to (3:15).

● **Engagement with society** Peter's exhortation to positive involvement in society – *both* showing respect for what is positive in society *and* living

---

Focus on theology:
LIVING IN SOCIETY

From a twenty-first-century perspective it is easy to dismiss 1 Peter as a document that

● regards women ('the weaker sex', 3:7) and slaves ('submit to your masters', 2:18) as inferior human beings;
● recommends a totally submissive attitude to governing authorities ('submit to . . . the emperor as the supreme authority', 2:13);
● upholds a conservative, hierarchical view of society.

But it is not so simple as this, as is illustrated by a significant debate between D. L. Balch and J. H. Elliott (written up in their essays in Talbert 1986).

Balch, an expert on the household code of 1 Pet. 2:13—3:12 (see Balch 1981), argued that the aim of this teaching is to encourage the Christians to conform to Hellenistic social norms so as to reduce the risk of slander and persecution. Thus it represents a 'paganization of Christianity', a move away from the values of the Jewish law and of Jesus' teaching. Elliott, however, saw the author as an advocate of cohesion and 'holy nonconformity' within the Christian community. He wrote to strengthen his readers' sense of their communal identity so that they could remain faithful to their Christian commitments in a hostile environment and so avoid precisely the kind of compromise which Balch sees in 1 Peter.

Probably the truth is more complex than either of these summary statements suggest. In some respects there is accommodation to society's norms in relation to family (including household slaves) and governing authorities. But this is only to be expected where most Christians had very limited rights and powers – just as one might find today in countries where there is totalitarian government or a dominant

counter-culturally in the midst of it – can provide a vision for committed living in society today. For Christians in the context of persecution it means not turning one's back on society but contributing to it. The Protestant Church in China today has caught this mood by showing support for the government wherever it judges that this is not in conflict with Christian principles. It teaches its members that 'being a good Christian is being a good citizen', and issues slogans such as 'Love your country, love the church'.

For Christians among the 'me-generation' of western societies engagement may mean demonstrating life-in-community, challenging the economic assumptions and goals of global capitalism, following the way of Jesus which consists in self-giving rather than self-interest.

ESSAY TOPICS

INTRODUCTORY

● Explain how the author of 1 Peter seeks to encourage and advise his readers in the light of their suffering.

INTERMEDIATE

● Compare the teaching in 1 Pet. 2:13–17 with that in Rom. 13:1–7 on how Christians are to relate to the state and civil authorities. How much do they have in common and what is distinctive about each? How, if at all, is it appropriate to follow their teaching in the country where you live?

religious culture hostile to Christianity. On the other hand, the differences between Peter's household code and many Greco-Roman ones are subtle and striking.

In the latter the standard form is to address the male head of the household, advising him how to organize it. Peter pays his wife and slaves the respect of addressing *them*. The husband is to honour his wife (rather than dominate her) as his equal in the eyes of God (3:7). In the public sphere, Christians are to 'live as free people' as God's servants (2:16). This involves not only honouring the emperor and his representatives (a traditional expectation) but honouring *everyone* (2:17). Thus is the emperor's claim to supremacy subtly relativized in favour of a valuing of all people, whatever their status. Though the household code calls slaves to 'accept the authority' of their masters, and wives of their husbands (2:18; 3:1), it begins with a call for all Christians to 'accept the authority of every human being' (2:13; *not* 'every human institution' – see Marshall 1991, pp. 82–3). In 2:14–15 those who have the means are urged to make positive contributions to public life by acts of benefaction. This is an example of conformity to society's norms, but with the intention not simply of enabling Christians to creep along unnoticed by society, but instead to put themselves on the map as people who are committed to the common good for God's sake.

In its historical context, all this is remarkable. Rather than judging the letter as less enlightened than we are, we should recognize the directions in which it points, and draw on it in building a positive, wide-ranging approach to Christian engagement in society.

See further Green 2007, pp. 279–88.

AT EITHER LEVEL

- Write a sermon to be preached in church, or a talk to be given to a student audience, on 'Living as Resident Aliens in Today's World'. Base it on texts or themes from 1 Peter.

FURTHER READING

* denotes books assuming knowledge of Greek; most can be used by all students.

INTRODUCTORY

A. Chester and R. P. Martin *The Theology of the Letters of James, Peter, and Jude*. NT Theology. Cambridge/New York: Cambridge University Press, 1994.

J. H. Elliott 'Peter, First Epistle of', in *ABD* vol. 5, ed. D. N. Freedman. New York: Doubleday, 1992, pp. 269–78 (valuable introduction to Elliott's sociological perspective on 1 Peter).

D. G. Horrell *1 Peter*. NT Guides. London/New York: T. & T. Clark, 2008.

INTERMEDIATE

D. L. Balch *Let Wives be Submissive: the Domestic Code in 1 Peter*. Chico, California: Scholars Press, 1981.

*J. H. Elliott *A Home for the Homeless: a Sociological Exegesis of 1 Peter, its Situation and Strategy*. Philadelphia: Fortress/London: SCM Press, 1981. Revised and expanded edition: *A Home for the Homeless: A Social-Scientific Criticism of 1 Peter, its Situation and Strategy*. Minneapolis: Fortress, 1990 (this sociological interpretation marked a major development in study of the letter).

C. J. Hemer 'The Address of 1 Peter', *ExpT* 89, 1977–78, pp. 239–43.

D. G. Horrell 'The Product of a Petrine Circle? A Reassessment of the Origin and Character of 1 Peter', *JSNT* 24.4 (June 2002), pp. 29–60.

C. H. Talbert, ed *Perspectives in First Peter*. Macon: Mercer, 1986.

*B. W. Winter *Seek the Welfare of the City: Christians as Benefactors and Citizens*. Grand Rapids: Eerdmans/Carlisle: Paternoster, 1994 (argues that 1 Peter and other NT letters commend positive commitment to society rather than withdrawal from it).

Commentaries

*P. J. Achtemeier *1 Peter*. Herm. Philadelphia: Fortress, 1996 (detailed commentary, including good assessment of the use made in the letter of early Christian liturgical and ethical traditions).

*F. W. Beare *The First Epistle of Peter*. Oxford: Blackwell, 3rd edition 1970 (dates the letter at the time of Pliny's persecution, AD 111–12).

P. H. Davids *The First Epistle of Peter*. NIC. Grand Rapids: Eerdmans, 1990 (includes a valuable essay on suffering in the NT).

*J. H. Elliott *1 Peter*. AB. New York: Doubleday, 2000 (totally comprehensive commentary presenting a sociological perspective on the letter).

J. B. Green *1 Peter*. THNTC. Grand Rapids/Cambridge: Eerdmans, 2007.

W. Grudem *1 Peter*. TNTC. Leicester: IVP/Grand Rapids: Eerdmans, 1988 (good shorter commentary).

K. H. Jobes *1 Peter*. BECNT. Grand Rapids: Eerdmans, 2005.

S. McKnight *1 Peter*. NIVAC. Grand Rapids: Zondervan, 1996.

I. H. Marshall *1 Peter*. IVPNTC. Downers Grove, IL: IVP/Leicester: IVP, 1991 (exposition of the text pointing to the message of 1 Peter for today).

*J. R. Michaels *1 Peter*. WBC. Waco: Word, 1988.

D. P. Senior and D. J. Harrington *1 Peter, Jude and 2 Peter*. SP. Collegeville: Liturgical Press, 2007.

B. Witherington III *Letters and Homilies for Hellenized Christians, Volume 2: a Socio-Rhetorical Commentary on 1–2 Peter*. Downers Grove: IVP, 2007.

Chapter 19

THE SECOND LETTER OF PETER AND THE LETTER OF JUDE

In this chapter we shall study:

- the relationship between the two letters;
- Jude's strategy for helping his readers deal with false teachers;
- the authorship of the letter;
- the genre and authorship of 2 Peter;
- the false teachers in 2 Peter;
- 2 Peter's purpose and theology.

These two letters may seem to many to be the 'also rans' of the New Testament. Jude's letter has been called 'the most neglected book in the NT', even 'Jude the obscure' (with apologies to Thomas Hardy!). Ernst Käsemann, in a famous lecture, labelled 2 Peter 'perhaps the most dubious writing in the canon' (Käsemann 1964, p. 169) – by which he apparently meant that it should not have been included. By the end of this chapter we should be able to assess whether such neglect is justified.

WHAT DO THESE LETTERS HAVE IN COMMON?

Why do we study these two letters together? We do so because they have similar aims,

and there is a substantial overlap of material between them. Only a few verses in Jude are not paralleled in 2 Peter (see the table on p. 292). So we have a small-scale version of the questions that confront us when reading the Synoptic Gospels. Who copied whom, and what did they intend by doing so? How do we account for the differences of wording between them even when they are obviously expressing parallel themes? Out of all the parallels listed in the table, only Jude 13 and 2 Pet. 2:17 are really close in wording – 'for whom the deepest darkness has been reserved'.

As with the Synoptic Gospels explanations of the similarities can in principle be:

- Jude is copying 2 Peter;
- 2 Peter is copying Jude;
- both draw on a common oral tradition;
- both draw on a common written source.

Nearly all modern investigators of this question conclude that 2 Peter used Jude as a source. Many of the arguments are quite technical, depending on detailed comparison of the Greek wording of the two letters. But arguments leading to this conclusion include:

● Dependence on a common *written* source is problematic since more than half of Jude consists of this supposed source. If the source already existed, it is hard to see why Jude would bother to write his letter since he had so little to add to it.

● If Jude were copying from 2 Peter, why did he not make more use of it? As with the Synoptics, it is in principle more likely that the shorter document is a source for the longer.

● Careful study of the parallel passages can consistently suggest reasons why Peter might have adapted the wording of Jude, whereas changes in the opposite direction are less plausible. (For detailed arguments see Bauckham 1983, pp. 141–3.)

While the view that 2 Peter used Jude is the usual explanation of the parallels, M. Green maintains that both used a common written source (M. Green 1987, pp. 58–64). He

Jude (NRSV)		2 Peter (NRSV)	
4	people who long ago were designated for this condemnation . . . licentiousness and deny our only Master and Lord, Jesus Christ	2:1 2:2 2:3	deny the Master who bought them licentious ways condemnation, pronounced against them long ago
6	the angels . . . he has kept in eternal chains in deepest darkness for the judgement	2:4	the angels . . . cast them into hell and committed them to chains of deepest darkness to be kept until the judgement
7	Sodom and Gomorrah . . . an example	2:6	Sodom and Gomorrah . . . an example
8	defile the flesh, reject authority, and slander the glorious ones	2:10	indulge their flesh in depraved lust, and who despise authority . . . slander the glorious ones
9	the archangel Michael . . . did not dare to bring a condemnation of slander against him, but said, "The Lord rebuke you!"	2:11	angels . . . do not bring against them a slanderous judgement from the Lord
10	these people slander whatever they do not understand . . . like irrational animals	2:12	these people . . . like irrational animals . . . slander what they do not understand
11	abandon themselves to Balaam's error for the sake of gain	2:15	following the road of Balaam . . . who loved the wages of doing wrong
12	blemishes on your love-feasts, while they feast with you without fear, feeding themselves	2:13	blemishes, revelling in their dissipation while they feast with you
12	waterless clouds carried along by the winds	2:17	waterless springs and mists driven by a storm
13	for whom the deepest darkness has been reserved	2:17	for them the deepest darkness has been reserved
16	they indulge their own lusts; they are bombastic in speech	2:18	they speak bombastic nonsense . . . licentious desires
17	beloved, remember the predictions of the apostles of our Lord Jesus Christ	3:1 3:2	beloved . . . remember the words spoken in the past . . . the commandment of the Lord and Saviour spoken through your apostles
18	"In the last time there will be scoffers indulging their own ungodly lusts"	3:3	in the last days scoffers will come, scoffing and indulging their own lusts

argues that Jude would think it worthwhile to take the source (the denunciation of false teachers) and add vv. 3, 20–23, which provide very significant advice and encouragement to the faithful.

What do you think?

Read through Jude, noting your response to the following questions.

What clues does he give about why he is writing? What characteristics of the 'intruders' make him so concerned?

THE LETTER OF JUDE – ITS PURPOSE

Writing to a church rocked by the influence of false teachers, Jude's declared purpose is to 'appeal to you to contend for the faith that was once for all entrusted to the saints' (Jude 3). Since the writer assumes a quite specific situation, we should assume that he wrote to one particular church, or a group of churches in a locality. Suggestions about their location have included Palestine, Syria, Alexandria and 'address unknown'.

Perhaps the most plausible proposal, in light of the nature of the false teaching, is that they were located in or near Hellenistic cities in Galilee (Sepphoris, Tiberias) or around the borders of Galilee (the cities of the Decapolis), where they would be open to the influence of a more libertine lifestyle.

THE FALSE TEACHERS

The teachers who have disturbed Jude's readers are not some hated group 'out there'. They are infiltrators who 'have stolen in among you' (v. 4) and are threatening the heart of this church community. We can deduce some of their characteristics from Jude's references to them:

- They are distorting the gospel of God's grace by advocating sexual licence ('defile the flesh', v. 8). In this way they are contradicting the lordship of Christ over their lives (v. 4).
- They are 'these dreamers' (v. 8). This probably alludes to the description of the false prophet as 'a dreamer of dreams' in Deut. 13:1, and identifies the opponents as prophets who claimed divine inspiration for their visions. As prophets they would initially have been accepted with respect by the church, and thus have 'stolen in among you' (v. 4).
- They 'slander the glorious ones', i.e. angels (v. 8). This might mean that they despise the Law which according to Jewish tradition was given through angels (cf. Gal. 3:19), or that because of their spiritual experiences they are claiming a superior status.
- While taking part in the fellowship meals they indulge their own needs (v. 12).
- They are 'grumblers and malcontents' (v. 16) – like Israel complaining against God in the wilderness (Num. 14:2–3, 27). This refers to their disregard of God's law. They pursue their own will (not specifically 'lusts', as NRSV has it) rather than God's.
- They are 'scoffers' (v. 18), laughing at moral purity and warnings of divine judgement as they pursue their own desires.
- Being worldly and – contrary to their own great claims – devoid of the Spirit, they provoke division (v. 19). Jude's complaint that they are without the Spirit may well be an ironic reference to their own extravagant claims to superior spiritual experience.

All this suggests they were antinomians (Greek *anti* = against, *nomos* = law) who

293

rejected traditional Jewish and Christian teaching about morality, including sexual morality. They had inflated ideas about the level of spiritual experience on which they operated. They claimed prophetic insight ('dreamers') and on this ticket had 'stolen in among' the community to which Jude writes (v. 4). To call them Gnostics, as some have done, is to appeal to a movement that did not clearly emerge until the second century. More probably, like some whom Paul encountered in Corinth, they claim 'super-spiritual' experiences while dismissing the ethical demands of the gospel. Accepting the church's hospitality, they took greedy advantage of the fellowship meal, bringing division to the very place where the church's unity was most vividly expressed.

THE WARNING AGAINST THE FALSE PROPHETS (vv. 5–19)

The midrashic style of the central part of the letter gives it the mood of a sermon (compare the synagogue sermon in Acts 13:16–41) built around various texts. It is not simply an outburst of animosity, but a scriptural argument explaining how the false teachers 'long ago were designated for this condemnation as ungodly' (v. 4). Its structure can be teased out as follows (details in Bauckham 1990a, pp. 7–8, 13–18; cf. pp. 221–6):

5–7	Three OT examples
8–10	Application of these examples to the false teachers
11	Three more OT examples
12–13	Application of these examples to the false teachers
14–15	A prophecy from 1 Enoch 1:9
16	Application of this prophecy to the false teachers
17–18	A prophecy from the apostles
19	Application of this prophecy to the false teachers

What do you think?

Look up the following passages, which seem to refer to real or potential danger from itinerant prophets. How do the writers suggest that the dangers can be spotted, and what safeguards do they try to establish against being seduced by false teaching?

Matt. 7:15; 24:11–12; 1 John 4:1; 2 John 10; Col. 2:18; Rev. 2:20.

Look at the extract from the *Didache* on p. 315. What evidence can you see that the situation presupposed there is comparable to the situation envisaged in Jude?

They sound like an extreme version of the kind of itinerant prophets whose disturbing effect is evident elsewhere in the NT and in the *Didache* (see p. 315). Prophets in principle were honoured as people who could bring special insight from God. But as itinerants not subject to the disciplines of a local community some could be 'loose cannons' causing havoc to a church unprepared for their arrival.

JUDE'S STRATEGY FOR ADVISING HIS READERS

The author distinguishes sharply between those whom he addresses as 'beloved' (vv. 3, 17, 20) and the ones whom he refers to scornfully as 'these' (vv. 8, 10, 12, 14, 16, 19).

In v. 3 he plunges into the urgency of the situation by suggesting that he intended to write on a general theme – salvation – but was diverted by the need to respond to the immediate crisis. The essence of his appeal, apart from warning about the nature and fate of the false prophets, is:

- to assure his readers of the reliability of the original apostolic message and to urge them to fight for it against the current threat (v. 3);
- to remind them that the apostles themselves had predicted the emergence of false teachers such as these (v. 17);
- to show them *how* to 'fight for the faith' (vv. 20–23). It is by:
  - building each other up on the foundation of the gospel;
  - praying under the inspiration of the Holy Spirit;
  - remaining in the love of God;
  - waiting for the eternal life which Christ in his forgiving mercy will grant at his final coming (vv. 20–21 – note the trinitarian structure here);
  - reflecting Christ's mercy in their own attitude;
  - showing mercy to those wavering under the false teachers' influence, rescuing others from the fire of judgement;
  - showing mercy to others whilst acknowledging the peril of their situation ('with fear');
  - being careful not to be infected by their sin (vv. 22–23).

What do you think?

Imagine a situation where the life of a local church is severely disturbed because some of its members have come under the influence of a sectarian group that advocates casual sex in the name of 'Christian freedom'. (Yes, there are such sects today!)

How helpful do you think Jude's advice would be in stabilizing their faith? What other advice might you want to give to those who are trying to maintain the church's Christian integrity?

All this he frames between the reassurance offered in the opening address and the closing doxology (vv. 1, 24–25).

WHO WROTE THIS LETTER?

The author is identified as 'Jude, a servant of Jesus Christ and brother of James' (1:1). The name in Greek is *Ioudas*, which occurs over 40 times in the NT, but English versions curiously translate this as Jude, Judas or Judah depending on the person being referred to. Though several people with this name are mentioned in the NT, there can be little doubt which of them is in view here.

It was very unusual to identify oneself as someone's brother (rather than as someone's son). The only plausible reason for this designation is that it would readily identify him as brother of the famous James, the brother of Jesus (see Mark 6:3). Like James, he was not a disciple during Jesus' ministry (John 7:5) but became one after the resurrection and took part in Christian mission (1 Cor. 9:5). Why is he not called 'brother of Jesus Christ'? Presumably because, like James (Jas. 1:1) he thought it disrespectful to claim for himself this relationship with one whom he now regarded as 'our only Master and Lord' (v. 4).

But is this Jude the actual author, or is a later writer using his name as a pseudonym to add authority to his document? This latter view has been argued on grounds such as the following:

- There is evidence in the letter that it comes from a later period, by which time Jude must have already died. 'The predictions of the apostles' (v. 17) looks back to the apostolic age as a past era.

EARLY CATHOLICISM

This term has been used by scholars to describe the transition from the first-century apostolic church to the Catholic orthodoxy of the following centuries. James Dunn (2006) summarizes its key distinguishing features as:

- the fading of the expectation of the imminent return of Christ.
- increasing institutionalization, including the development of specific 'offices' of leadership, and the belief that God's grace is channelled through the sacraments.
- crystallization of the faith into set forms, with the goal of creating a defence against charismatic enthusiasm and false teaching (particularly Gnosticism). (Dunn, pp. 372–6)

'The faith that was once for all entrusted to the saints' (v. 3) conveys a similar impression.

- The author speaks of 'the faith' (v. 3) as a fixed body of doctrine, a usage not found in the earliest period of the church. It is a sign of the 'early catholicism' that was developing at the end of the first century.
- The quality of the Greek is too good for a Galilean villager. The letter displays a wide vocabulary and some rhetorical turns of phrase.

But the strength of such arguments has been greatly exaggerated.

- Verses 3 and 17 are not referring back to a previous age, but *reminding* the readers of what they themselves heard from apostles when their church was first established.
- The letter does not reflect early catholicism since it retains a vivid eschatological expectation (vv. 14, 18, 21, 24) and shows no sign of church offices or

sacramentalism. The use of 'the faith' in v. 3 is no different from Paul's use in Gal. 1:23, meaning 'the gospel', and there is no need to attribute it to a later period.

- Study in recent decades has shown the widespread use of Greek in Palestine (see pp. 265–6). Though the vocabulary used in the letter is wide, much of it echoes Jewish sources. So the author did not necessarily have full command of such a wide range of words. Maybe he was like student essay-writers who use impressive words from books they have read without quite understanding them all! The literary style is no more impressive than could have been picked up over time by someone listening to and delivering Jewish and Christian sermons.
- Additionally, the character of the letter – its use of Scripture and Palestinian Jewish literature, its eschatological perspective – is consistent with an early Palestinian Jewish-Christian leader such as Jude. Interestingly, there are several structural, rhetorical and linguistic similarities between this document and the letter of James (summarized in Witherington III 2007, pp. 567–9). There is every reason to see the document as a genuine letter by him. There is no evidence which would help us pin the date down, and we do not know when he died. But the 50s is a plausible date of writing. (Witherington III 2007, p. 577).

2 PETER – GENRE AND OUTLINE

2 Peter has the usual letter-opening (1:1–2), in which the author identifies himself as 'Simeon Peter, a servant and apostle of Jesus Christ' (Simeon represents the Hebrew form of the name, which elsewhere in the NT is adapted to the Greek form Simon). It is

addressed to a specific audience who have previously received 1 Peter (3:1) and are aware of one or more letters of Paul (3:15). Like Jude, the letter ends not with closing greetings but with a doxology (3:18).

However, the author combines with the letter a genre found in Jewish literature known as the 'farewell speech' or 'testament'. Between 200 BC and AD 100 several Jewish works appeared recording what purport to be the final words of OT heroes, e.g. *Testament of the Twelve Patriarchs, Testament of Moses, Testament of Job*. In some cases the testament occurs within a larger work, e.g., 2 Esdras 14:28–36; *2 Baruch* 57–86. Biblical examples are in Gen. 47:29—49:32; 2 Sam. 23; John 14—16; Acts 20:18–35; 2 Tim. 4:1–8.

The Jewish and NT examples normally have three main features:

● announcement of the speaker that he expects to die soon;
● a summary of his ethical and religious instruction;
● revelations about the future.

These are represented in 2 Peter as follows:

● **1:12–15** In view of his impending death, Peter wishes his teaching to be remembered.
● **1:3–11** Definitive summary of Peter's ethical and religious teaching.
● **2:1–3; 3:1–4** Prediction of the rise of false teachers.

The rest of 2 Peter builds around these elements material that focuses particularly on the link between the second and third elements, offering a defence against false teachers and instruction about faith and behaviour in view of the threat they pose.

Digging deeper

Read through 2 Peter with an eye on the following outline, and write your own summary of the contents of each section.

Notice the parallels with Jude in 2:1—3:3.

Make a note of 'issues to follow up later', e.g., particular passages to explore with a commentary or to use in a context of teaching or preaching.

If you are working with a group, compare your notes on 'issues to follow up later', and investigate some of them together.

The document may be outlined as follows, using Bauckham's way of highlighting different types of material (Bauckham 1990a, pp. 41–42).

T = passages belonging to the genre of testament
A = passages which are apologetic in character (defence against false teachers)
E = passages of exhortation

	1:1–2	ADDRESS AND GREETING
T1	1:3–11	SUMMARY OF THE LETTER'S MESSAGE
T2	1:12–15	THE REASON FOR WRITING: LEAVING A REMINDER
A1	1:16–21	FIRST APOLOGETIC SECTION
	1:16–19	Response to objection 1, that the apostles based their teaching about Christ's future coming on invented myths
	1:20–21	Response to objection 2, that OT prophecies were merely inventions of human minds
T3	2:1–3a	PREDICTION OF FALSE TEACHERS
A2	2:3b–10a	SECOND APOLOGETIC SECTION Response to objection 3, that divine judgement never happens
E1	2:10b–22	DENUNCIATION OF THE FALSE TEACHERS

(Though not strictly a passage of
exhortation, it is classed as such because
it sets up a contrast with the holy living
to which the readers are exhorted in
3:11–16)

T4 3:1–4   PREDICTION OF SCOFFERS
A3 3:5–10   THIRD APOLOGETIC SECTION
       3:5–7   First response to objection 4
                     (cited in v. 4), that the
                     expectation of Christ's coming
                     is falsified by its delay
       3:8–10   Second response to
                     objection 4
E2 3:11–18a   EXHORTATION TO HOLY LIVING
       3:18b   CONCLUDING DOXOLOGY

2 PETER – THE PROBLEM OF AUTHORSHIP

The author is identified as the apostle
Peter (1:1). He is an eyewitness of the
transfiguration (1:16–18; see Mark 9:2–8),
has written an earlier letter, presumably 1
Peter (3:1), and is a colleague of Paul (3:15).
Despite the obvious claims of the letter to
be by Peter, many questions have been
raised against the presumption that Peter
was the real author. The most important
are:

1. The style is different from 1 Peter. There
are many unusual words, and much
striving for rhetorical effect (Bauckham
1983, pp. 135–8).
2. The author shows a knowledge of
Hellenistic religious and philosophical
culture which would be surprising in a
Galilean fisherman. (Once again we find
that comment on the limitations of the
poor old Galileans, which is regularly
used also in relation to the authorship of
1 Peter, James and Jude!) Examples are
'participants of the divine nature' (1:4)
and the sequence of virtues in 1:5–7. The

letter looks like the product of someone
with a Hellenistic Jewish background.
3. There is much which reflects a late date
(80–120?), including evidence of early
catholicism (see p. 296). The first
Christian generation has died without the
expected parousia of Christ taking place
(3:4), the apostolic tradition is something
handed down from the past (3:2), and a
collection of Paul's letters has been made
(3:15–16).
4. Would the real Peter not have appealed
to his own apostolic authority rather than
making substantial use of a document not
by an apostle (Jude)?
5. 2 Peter was the slowest of all NT
documents to gain acceptance as
canonical. Eusebius classed it among
'those that are disputed, yet familiar to
most', and also commented that of works
attributed to Peter 'I have recognized
only one epistle as authentic and accepted
by the early fathers' (*Hist. eccl.* 3.25.3;
3.3.4).
6. The literary genre of 'testament' in
Judaism was always fictional and
pseudonymous. For instance, the
Testaments of the Twelve Patriarchs, which
professes to be the final words of the sons
of Jacob, is a work of the second century
BC. Hence there is no ethical problem
about 2 Peter being pseudonymous.
Readers would regard the attribution to
the apostle as an acceptable literary
convention.
7. One particular feature, which betrays the
post-apostolic date, concerns the shifting
between present and future verbs in the
letter. The 'testament' parts of the
document predict the activities of false
teachers in the future, after Peter's death
(2:1–3a; 3:1–4, 17). But then he slips into
describing them as already present and
advising his readers how to deal with

them now (2:3b–22; 3:5–10, 16b). This is a sure sign that the author is writing about a crisis in his own time *as if* he were a writer of a previous generation looking forward.

Michael Green, in a vigorous defence of authenticity – very much a minority view among scholars – includes the following responses (M. Green 1987, pp. 13–39):

1. The difference of style between 1 and 2 Peter may be due to Peter's use of different secretaries (Jerome, *Epistles* 120.11). He may have given them considerable freedom in composing the letter.

2. Since Jews such as Philo and Josephus used language similar to 1:4, there is no reason why Peter should not have used it just as a modern preacher might refer to the quantum theory without understanding all its implications. Here and elsewhere Peter is putting his message into Greek dress for the sake of his audience.

3. The letter does not reflect a late date. The most natural meaning of 'your apostles' (3:2) is 'the apostles who preached to you and founded your church'. 'Our ancestors' (literally, 'fathers', 3:4) are not the first Christian generation but the OT 'patriarchs' (Rom. 9:5) or 'ancestors' (Heb. 1:1). As for Paul's letters, Peter does not necessarily refer to a *collection* of letters. But there is no reason why he might not have known some of Paul's letters, given the overlap of their ministries in Asia Minor (if Peter's presence there can be deduced from 1 Peter) and Rome. The supposed crisis about the delay of Christ's coming is reflected in 1 and 2 Thessalonians, so it would be no great surprise to find sceptics laughing at the idea in the 60s when Peter must have

written. (For a fuller critique of the labelling of 2 Pet. and other NT documents as 'early catholic' see Elliott 1969.)

4. If 2 Peter used Jude as a source, this does not rule out authorship by the apostle, any more than does 1 Peter's use of a variety of traditional materials.

5. Although evidence for acceptance of 2 Peter by the church fathers is weaker than for other NT books, it is much stronger than for the best attested of books that were excluded from the canon. Hesitation about accepting 2 Peter may have been due to the use of Peter's name to gain approval for unorthodox second-century literature such as the *Gospel of Peter*.

6. Might not Peter himself have cast his material into the combined form of letter and testament? It is not necessarily the case that all testaments in Judaism were fictional or pseudonymous. The final words of Moses (Deut. 31—34) or David (2 Sam. 23) need not be fictional.

7. Green does not comment specifically on the issue of the shift between future and present. But he asks why, if 2 Peter conforms to the genre of 'testament', this fact has eluded commentators until recent years. 1:13–15, the starting-point for the 'testament' theory, is better understood simply as expressing the concern of an apostle who knows he may die soon and is anxious for the church's next generation. (In support of Green see further Ellis 1999, pp. 120–133, 293–303.)

Authorship by Peter himself should certainly not be dismissed as readily as it has been by most scholars. But puzzles remain, particularly about the style and language. Though the distinctive style of 2 Peter might be explained by appealing to the

299

contribution of a secretary, the more weight one puts on the secretary's contribution the more one distances the actual content of the letter from Peter himself.

If the letter is authentic, it was probably written shortly before Peter's martyrdom in Rome in the 60s (1:15). Roman origin is supported by its affinities with the Roman works *1 Clement* and the *Shepherd* of Hermas (around AD 100) who seem to have drawn on its language and thought.

If, on the other hand, the 'pseudonymous letter-testament' theory is correct, the author was someone of the next generation after Peter, who perhaps belonged to a 'Petrine circle' in Rome. The dilemma over whether Christians would have regarded the writing of a pseudonymous *letter* as acceptable (see the discussion on pp. 234–8) is resolved by the recognition that the *testament* was a familiar pseudonymous genre. (However, whereas Bauckham proposes that, because 2 Pet. embodies the testament genre as well as being a letter, its pseudonymous attribution to Peter would be acceptable in the late first-century church, G. L. Green argues that it lacks several standard features of testaments and therefore the issue of pseudonymity remains problematic. See G. L. Green 2008, pp. 164–7.)

That the attribution to Peter is a *transparent* rather than deceptive fiction is shown by the author's shifts between future and present (paragraph 7 above of the arguments against Petrine authorship). The author is recalling genuine prophecies of the apostles (such as may be found in Acts 20:29–30; 2 Tim. 3:1–9) and placing alongside them present-day instances of what they prophesied. He thus shows how those warnings are now being fulfilled.

Though a date as late as AD 150 has occasionally been proposed, 80–90 is the most likely range. It fits between the apostolic period and the date of *1 Clement* and Hermas. The absence of early catholicism makes a later date implausible.

THE FALSE TEACHERS IN 2 PETER

Because of the parallels between 2 Peter and Jude it has often been supposed that the false teachers are the same in both cases. But what does the letter itself indicate?

In concentrating on his objections to them, 2 Peter does not tell us whether the false teachers had any positive religious teaching. But he makes clear that they were sceptics about the eschatology embodied in the apostles' teaching. This scepticism is related to and expressed in two key aspects of their teaching. First, there is scepticism about *theodicy*, the attempt to justify the purpose of God in the world in view of his failure to intervene to remove evil. Since the world continues on its way without divine intervention, and the expected parousia has not occurred, they have concluded that belief in such interventions is an illusion (3:4).

Secondly, the non-arrival of God's judgement fuels the promotion of *freedom* for sexual and sensual pleasure (2:2, 10, 12–14, 18).

This call for ethical 'liberation' parallels the similar evidence in Jude. But whereas from Jude's perspective it arises from the antinomian perversion of grace, here it results from scepticism about divine activity in the world and eschatology. Also absent from 2 Peter, in comparison with Jude, is the false teachers' claim to possess the Spirit and receive prophetic revelations. The false teachers whom 2 Peter sees as a threat to the church are essentially sceptics, not unbridled charismatics.

As such, they are best seen as Christians who compromised with popular contemporary ideas, particularly the philosophy of Epicurus, whose influence was widespread in the first century (see pp. 17–18). Epicureans denied divine involvement in the world and divine judgement, calling belief in rewards and punishments after death a 'myth' created for purposes of social control. Thus they were often thought of as encouraging immorality.

The false teachers picked up elements of the Epicurean worldview and used them to challenge the eschatological and ethical perspectives of apostolic teaching. Perhaps they saw themselves as bold radicals, liberating Gentile Christianity from the limitations of unnecessary traditions drawn from a Jewish eschatological framework. Or perhaps they were simply so influenced by Hellenistic culture that they did not see clearly the crucial distinctions between that culture and their Christian faith. (On the Epicurean background to 2 Peter see Neyrey 1993, pp. 122–8.)

THE PURPOSE AND THEOLOGY OF 2 PETER

The letter's aim is to remind his readers of the apostolic message which is threatened by the false teachers (1:12–15), particularly to assure them that God will keep his promise to pass judgement on evil and renew the world through the final coming of Christ (3:1–13); to defend this message against the scoffers' criticisms (2:1—3:13); and to urge his readers to live godly lives in the light of this hope (1:10–11; 3:11–15).

A striking feature of the author's thought is his combination of Hellenistic thought-patterns with the apocalyptic eschatology of primitive Christianity. Confronted by teachers who, in his judgement, have given up the apostolic gospel in their compromise with Hellenistic culture, he makes a bold move. Rather than simply repeating the old formulas and denouncing the new, he tries to develop a way of expressing the apostolic truths in a form appropriate for his readers' cultural context.

So, for example, he expresses Christian holiness in the Hellenistic terminology of becoming 'participants in the divine nature', while making it clear that this involves distancing oneself from 'the corruption that is in the world' (1:4). He borrows a list of virtues from the popular philosophers, but gives them a Christian 'spin' by giving the prominent first and last places in the list to 'faith' and 'love' (1:5–7).

THE HOPE OF CHRIST'S COMING

In response to the false teachers' questioning of the Christian hope, the author tries to engage with the objections (3:1–10):

- The expectation of Christ's powerful coming is no human invention because it is based on eyewitness testimony of Jesus' transfiguration (1:16–18. The event described in Mark 9:2–8 is here understood as God's appointment of Jesus as Messiah). And OT prophecy is not merely human dreams and visions but a product of divine inspiration (1:19–20).
- 'Scoffers' may ridicule the message by saying that the world has gone on its course for a long time without divine intervention and God shows no sign of fulfilling his supposed 'promise' of Christ's

coming (3:3–4). But they are reckoning without the fact that God *did* act to create the world and to judge it through the Flood, and he can act again to bring judgement and renewal of the world (3:5–7, 10, 12–13). They ignore the fact that God's perspective on time is different from ours (3:8–9), so that Christians can live in hopeful anticipation and yet not be distressed by delay. If only they would realize that God allows the delay to give time for repentance (3:9).

● He warns of the dangers of abandoning the Christian way as it has been received from the apostles. Promising freedom, the false teachers have become enslaved to corruption (2:19). Though made clean through baptism, they have returned to the 'pollutions of the world' (2:20), like the dog and the pig who show their true nature by returning to their filth (2:22).

● Since the goal of God's creative purpose for the universe is to establish a new order 'where righteousness is at home' (3:13), the link between human behaviour and divine judgement is indispensable. Judgement is a necessary part of God's overcoming evil in the world (2:3–10a).

● But righteousness cannot be promoted merely or mainly through warnings of judgement. The author sets before his readers the vision of God's kingdom as an incentive for wholehearted Christian living (1:11; 3:11–15). In 2:5–10 he presents Noah and Lot as models of righteous living in a corrupt and hostile society. And he reminds them that their ability to live such a demanding lifestyle derives from God's grace, calling and enabling (1:2–4, 10).

SOME ISSUES FOR TODAY

● Both 2 Peter and Jude raise sharp questions about the challenge posed

---

Focus on theology:
GODLY LIVING

One significant link between 1 Pet. and 2 Pet. is their shared stress on how important it is that God's people should reflect the character of God as it is expressed in Christ. So 1 Pet. appeals to the readers, 'As he who called you is holy, be holy yourselves in all your conduct' (1:15), in contrast with the way of life which often characterized the world around them. Similarly 2 Pet. stresses the importance of 'leading lives of holiness and godliness' and being 'found . . . without spot or blemish' (3:11, 14).

The exhortation in 2 Pet. 3 is set in the context of future hope and divine judgement. The motivation for this demanding lifestyle is the promise that the Lord

will surely come to assess people's lives and to establish a new world 'where righteousness is at home' (3:9–10, 13). At the beginning of the letter a more extended exhortation (1:3–11) is framed within a narrative which touches on the past, present and future of God's engagement with humanity. God has already called us, he has given us 'everything needed for life and godliness', he assures us of entry into 'the eternal kingdom of our Lord and Saviour Jesus Christ' (1:3, 11).

A key word is 'knowledge' (Greek *gnosis or epignosis*, verses 2, 3, 5, 6, 8). In verses 2, 3 and 8 it is specifically knowledge of God and Christ – a personal awareness of God and relationship with

by deviant teaching. Where are the boundaries between 'orthodoxy' and 'heresy'? How should the church deal with those who promote unorthodox teaching among its members? Or is it inappropriate to ask such questions in today's culture where a high value is attached to pluralism and tolerance?

- Jude touches on the question: How can we be open to the work of the Holy Spirit in charismatic gifts without being uncritical of claims which people may make that they have received special revelations from God? What criteria for judging such claims might be derived from Jude 3, 17, 19?

- In combining traditional expressions of Christian hope with Hellenistic language and themes, 2 Peter provides a model of relating the gospel to an alien culture.

- The hope of the coming of God's kingdom remains a crucial theme in a society that has lost personal hope and meaning even while it tries to renew itself with new gadgets and new experiences. 2 Peter stresses that God's promise concerns not merely individuals and their personal destinies, but the renewal of his whole creation.

ESSAY TOPICS

INTRODUCTORY

- Someone in your study group has asked why 2 Peter and Jude are in the Bible, since no one seems to read or preach from them. Explain what you think Christians would lose if these books were not part of Scripture.

INTERMEDIATE

- Assess the strength of Käsemann's attack on 2 Peter as expressing early catholicism. Does early catholicism represent a decline or a necessary development from the faith of the first generation of Christians?

---

him that develops in one who gives attention to him and responds in obedience. But in verses 5 and 6 it appears in a list of qualities which believers are called to pursue in working out their trust in God – faith (or, more likely, faithfulness), goodness, knowledge, self-control, endurance, godliness, mutual affection, love (see the comparable lists in Rom. 5:3–5; Gal. 5:22–23; Jas. 1:3–4). Here 'knowledge' probably means the practical wisdom and discernment which gives shape and direction to godly living.

God's purpose in all this is that 'you may become partakers of the divine nature' (1:4). In contemporary Hellenistic thought this striking phrase often referred to the attainment of divine qualities such as immortality or detachment from the world through mystical experience or ascetic lifestyle. But 2 Peter boldly adopts the Hellenistic language to speak of *moral* transformation: believers may reflect the holy character of God as they depend on God's power and promises (vv. 3–4). This process may only be completed on 'entry into the eternal kingdom' of Christ (v. 11), but we are left in no doubt that it begins now. Essentially 'participating in the divine nature' is expressing the same theme as Paul's language about being 'in Christ' or John's reference to the mutual indwelling of Christ and the believer (see John 14:20)

FURTHER READING

* denotes books assuming knowledge of Greek; most can be used by all students.

INTRODUCTORY

R. J. Bauckham *Jude, 2 Peter*. Word Biblical Themes. Dallas: Word, 1990a (expounds the message of the letters).

J. Knight *2 Peter and Jude*. NT Guides. Sheffield: Sheffield Academic Press, 1995.

A. Chester and R. P. Martin *The Theology of the Letters of James, Peter and Jude*. Cambridge/ New York: Cambridge University Press, 1994.

INTERMEDIATE

R. J. Bauckham *Jude and the Relatives of Jesus in the Early Church*. Edinburgh: T. & T. Clark, 1990b (comprehensive study of Jude, the man and the letter).

J. D. G. Dunn *Unity and Diversity in the New Testament: an Inquiry into the Character of Earliest Christianity*. London: SCM Press, third edition 2006 (includes a chapter on early catholicism).

J. H. Elliott, 'A Catholic Gospel: Reflections on "Early Catholicism" in the New Testament', *CBQ* 31, 1969, pp. 213–23.

E. E. Ellis *Prophecy and Hermeneutic*. Tübingen: J. C. B. Mohr (Paul Siebeck), 1978 (includes a study of Jude's interpretation of Scripture).

E. E. Ellis *The Making of the New Testament Documents*. Leiden: Brill, 1999.

E. Käsemann 'An Apologia for Primitive Christian Eschatology' in *Essays on New Testament Themes*, pp. 169–195. London: SCM Press/Philadelphia: Fortress, 1964 (criticizes 2 Peter as expressing 'early catholicism').

Commentaries

*R. J. Bauckham *Jude, 2 Peter*. WBC. Waco: Word, 1983 (overall, the best commentary on these books).

W. F. Brosend II *James and Jude*. NCBC. Cambridge/New York: Cambridge University Press, 2004 (uses insights of historical, narrative and socio-scientific criticism in an accessible way).

P. H. Davids *The Letters of 2 Peter and Jude*. PNTC. Grand Rapids: IVP/Nottingham: Apollos, 2006.

G. L. Green *Jude and 2 Peter*. BECNT. Grand Rapids: Baker, 2008.

M. Green *2 Peter and Jude*. TNTC. Leicester: IVP/Grand Rapids: Eerdmans, 2nd edition 1987 (includes detailed defence of authorship by Peter).

D. Horrell *The Epistles of Peter and Jude*. EC. Peterborough: Epworth/Valley Forge: Trinity Press International, 1998 (excellent short commentary).

J. H. Neyrey *2 Peter, Jude*. AB. New York: Doubleday, 1993 (focuses especially on the social and cultural setting of the letters).

R. A. Reese *2 Peter and Jude*. THNTC. Grand Rapids/Cambridge: Eerdmans, 2007.

D. P. Senior and D. J. Harrington *1 Peter, Jude and 2 Peter*. SP. Collegeville: Liturgical Press, 2007.

B. Witherington III *Letters and Homilies for Hellenized Christians, Volume 2: a Socio-Rhetorical Commentary on 1–2 Peter*. Downers Grove: IVP, 2007.

Chapter 20

THE LETTERS OF JOHN

In this chapter we shall look at:

- the background and authorship of 1 John;
- the circumstances addressed and the response offered in 1 John;
- the purpose and genre of 1 John;
- the relationship of 2 and 3 John to 1 John;
- the context and content of 2 and 3 John;
- some issues about theology and church raised by the three letters.

Ancient tradition and common themes link these three letters with the Fourth Gospel. Hence they are called 'letters of John'. The text of 1 John does not name the author, and the writer of 2 and 3 John identifies himself only as 'the elder'. Yet, in view of the close relationship between writer and readers, which is evident from the letters, his identity must have been clear to the original recipients.

2 John and 3 John are, like many ancient letters, brief personal messages from someone who hopes to see his friends soon. But what are we to make of 1 John, which has none of the normal marks of a letter – except the author's frequent comment that he is *writing* (rather than 'speaking': 1 John 1:4; 2:1, 12–14; 5:13)? To that document we now turn.

What do you think?

Read through 1 John. Do not dwell on details, but note your initial reaction to the questions listed here.

- If it is not a letter, what is it? A sermon, a tract, or . . . ?
- What connections with the thought and language of the Fourth Gospel do you notice?
- What clues can you pick up about why the situation of the readers is causing concern to the author?
- Do you notice particular issues or themes that have not come up in other NT documents which you have studied?

1 JOHN – BACKGROUND AND AUTHORSHIP

Irenaeus (late second century) is the earliest writer known to us who identifies the author of 1 John with the Fourth Evangelist, naming him 'John, the disciple of the Lord' (*Against Heresies* 3.16.5, 8). Any who are familiar with the Fourth Gospel will quickly sense that they are on familiar ground when they read 1 John. Examples of common themes and language include:

	John's Gospel	I John
life	1:4; 10:10; 20:31	1:2; 4:9; 5:11–12, 16
eternal life	3:15–16, 36; 5:24	1:2; 2:25; 3:15; 5:11, 13, 20
truth	3:21; 4:23–24; 8:32; 14:6	2:21; 3:18–19; 4:6; 5:6
light	1:4–9; 3:19–21; 8:12	1:5, 7; 2:8–10
Jesus as God's Son	3:16; 5:23; 20:31	1:7; 3:23; 4:9–10
Father/Son relationship	3:35; 5:19; 14:10–13	1:3; 2:22–24; 4:14
Jesus lays down his life	10:15–18; 13:37–38	3:16
salvation as 'knowing God'	17:3, 25	2:3; 4:8; 5:20
abiding/remaining in Christ	15:4–7	2:24, 27–28; 3:24
new commandment	13:34	2:7–8
'the world' as hostile	7:7; 15:18–19; 17:14	2:15–17; 3:13; 5:19

IS THE AUTHOR OF I JOHN THE SAME AS THE AUTHOR OF THE FOURTH GOSPEL?

Although these striking similarities of thought and language have persuaded numerous scholars that the same author was responsible for both documents, others have been less convinced. C. H. Dodd was influential with his argument that three key differences in theology show different authors at work:

- **Eschatology** 1 John expects the coming of Christ in the near future and focuses on that event as the moment of accountability for Christian life (2:18–19; 2:28—3:3;

4:17) – in contrast with the Gospel's famous emphasis on 'realized eschatology'.

- **Atonement** 1 John's description of Christ's death as 'atoning sacrifice' (2:2; 4:10; traditionally translated 'propitiation' or 'expiation') represents a quite different model of atonement from the Fourth Gospel's portrayal of the Son of God's 'descent' and 'lifting up' on the cross (John 3:13–17; 12:23–24, 31–33).

- **Holy Spirit** 1 John's references to God's Spirit (3:24; 4:6, 13; 5:6–8) differ from the highly personal description of the Spirit as 'Paraclete' in John 14:15–17, 25–26; 15:26; 16:7–15.

On each of these themes Dodd saw 1 John as expressing a more primitive perspective (i.e., closer to 'ordinary' early Christian belief) than the more sophisticated Fourth Gospel (Dodd 1946, pp. liii–lvi).

Against these points it can be argued that:

- there is futurist eschatology in the Gospel (5:20–29; 6:39–40; 12:48), and the letter shares the Evangelist's conviction that through the incarnation God's ultimate work of salvation is already present and the Evil One is already conquered (2:8, 13–14; 3:8, 14; 5:12–13);

- although the Gospel lacks the description of Christ's death as 'atoning sacrifice', it does have sacrificial imagery in the phrase 'the Lamb of God who takes away the sin of the world' (1:29). And both documents share the theme that Christ 'laid down his life for us' (1 John 3:16; cf. John 10:11, 15; 11:50–52; 15:13);

- in 1 John 3:24; 4:13 the Spirit is recognized as an indwelling presence in a manner reminiscent of the Fourth Gospel. And although 1 John does not refer to the Spirit as 'Paraclete', the 'anointing' in 1

John 2:20, 27 performs a similar role to the Paraclete in John 16:13.

Although the language and emphasis is not always exactly the same, there is more than enough overlap between the two documents to suggest that a single author wrote them both. (See Marshall 1978, pp. 31–41; Schnackenburg 1992, pp. 34–41, who present strongly the case for a common author, though in the end they leave the issue undecided.) And the differences between them may be accounted for by their different genres and by the different situations addressed. At least we can say with confidence that the author of 1 John belonged to the circle of people responsible for the Gospel and – if he did not write the Gospel – was deeply influenced by it.

A further complication in the authorship question arises from words of Papias (early second century), which seem to refer to two men named John. This evidence has sometimes been used to support the view that two distinct people, both named John, were responsible for the Gospel and the letters.

> If, then, anyone came who had been a follower of the elders, I inquired into the sayings of the elders – what Andrew or Peter said, or Philip, or Thomas, or James, or John or Matthew, or what any other of the disciples of the Lord said – and the things which Aristion and the elder John, the disciples of the Lord, were saying . . . (Papias, quoted in Eusebius, *Hist. eccl.* 3.39.3–4.)

Are the people named John here in fact distinct persons (as C. K. Barrett argues, *The Gospel according to St John*. London: SPCK, 2nd edition 1977, pp. 105–9, 133–4), or is Papias referring in a slightly muddled way

to the same John (D. Guthrie, *New Testament Introduction*. Leicester: Apollos/Downers Grove: IVP, 4th edition 1990, pp. 862–3)? Papias' reference to 'the elder John', of course, reminds us that the author of 2 and 3 John identified himself as 'the elder'. The style and language of 2 and 3 John is close to that of 1 John (see below on those letters). So, depending on whether we think Papias was referring to one or two Johns, we might adopt one of the following viewpoints:

- John the apostle wrote the Gospel and the three letters;
- John the apostle wrote the Gospel, John the elder wrote the three letters.

Or perhaps, since the author of 1 John does not call himself 'the elder':

- John the apostle wrote the Gospel and 1 John, John the elder wrote 2 and 3 John.

Each of those options, of course, assumes that John the apostle was the author of (or the authority behind) the Fourth Gospel. If, however, we conclude that the identity of the fourth evangelist cannot be established with any certainty, all we can say is that all four documents show signs of similar style and thought-patterns, and therefore can be attributed to the same Johannine 'school' or 'circle'. J. Lieu has recently maintained that arguments about the authorship of the letters (and by implication of the Gospel too) are inconclusive, and that 1 John is likely to have some dependence on an earlier 'Johannine' tradition rather than on the Gospel as we know it (Lieu 2008, pp. 6–9, 17–18).

THE LOCATION OF THE AUTHOR AND HIS READERS

Where was this group of Christians located? Irenaeus is the first writer definitely to place John the apostle, to whom he attributes the letters, in the province of Asia. He refers to 'the church in Ephesus, founded by Paul and having John continuing with them until the times of [the emperor] Trajan' (*Against Heresies* 3.1.1, in Eusebius, *Hist. eccl.* 3.23.3. Trajan ruled AD 98–117). John probably moved from Palestine to Ephesus about the time of the Jewish revolt (AD 66). Intriguingly, Irenaeus reports how as a youth he had listened to Polycarp, who himself had been a pupil of John. (E. E. Ellis cites other ancient evidence for the document's origins in Asia, *The Making of the New Testament Documents*. Leiden: Brill, 1999, pp. 200–2.)

THE CIRCUMSTANCES ADDRESSED IN 1 JOHN

What was the situation that demanded this kind of document? The author – whom for convenience we shall call John – gives some clues. A group of people offering some kind of 're-statement' of the Christian message has arisen and disrupted the church.

- These people are 'antichrists' who have been part of John's community but have now separated from it (2:18–19).
- But they are still in touch with members of John's community, since – from John's perspective – their intention is to deceive the church (2:26).

- They are 'false prophets' expressing 'the spirit of the antichrist' (4:1–3).
- They have had some success in attracting people outside the church to their message: 'the world listens to them' (4:5).

So false teaching is the background to the document. Like other Christian groups in Asia in the second half of the first century, John's readers were subject to the kind of syncretistic pressures that arose when Jewish or Christian faith encountered pagan religion or Greek philosophy. (Compare the false teaching addressed in Colossians; Acts 20:30; 2 Tim. 3:1–9; 4:3–4; Rev. 2–3.)

THE NATURE OF THE FALSE TEACHING

Can we say more about the nature of the false teaching? Many scholars have pointed out that sentences beginning with phrases like 'if we say . . .', 'those who deny . . .'

Gnostics stressed salvation through 'knowledge' (Greek *gnosis*). They saw themselves as privileged individuals who, unlike others, had been granted divine insight into their heavenly origin and hoped at death to be released from the prison of their bodies and to be reunited with God in heaven. They affirmed a sharp dualism between spirit and matter. The origins of the movement are disputed and there is no evidence of clearly defined Gnostic systems of thought in the first century. (Gnostic texts, as well as critiques by Christian writers such as Irenaeus, survive from the second century.) But the tendencies that emerged more clearly in the second century may have already influenced people in the first. Characteristic implications of Gnostic dualism included the ideas that:

- the divine Christ could not possibly get himself entangled with human flesh, which is inherently evil.
- since salvation means deliverance from the material world – including the body – it makes no difference how people behave in their earthly lives.

look like allusions to the teaching which John is combating. These can be gathered under two main headings so as to provide a summary of their message:

● Christological error

2:22–23 They 'deny that Jesus is the Christ', they 'deny the Father and the Son'.

4:1–3 They do not confess Jesus, that he is the Christ come in the flesh (cf. 2 John 7).

Denial that 'Jesus is the Christ' (2:22), if taken on its own, might simply mean refusal to believe that Jesus is the expected Messiah. But it would be odd for people who held that view to be associated with Christians at all. And the explanatory statements in 2:22 and 4:1–3 point in another direction. The heart of their error is their denial that the divine Christ – the eternal 'Word' of God described in the Prologue of John's Gospel – is embodied ('incarnate') in the human Jesus. Such a view has been compared with the *docetism* which Ignatius, bishop of Antioch in the early second century, combats in his letters. Docetism is the belief that the divine Christ could not possibly dwell in a genuinely human body: his body must have only seemed (Greek *dokeô*) to be human. More generally, the view of John's opponents has been seen as part of a *gnostic* interpretation of Christian belief.

● Ethical distortion

1:8, 10 They claim to be without sin, or they do not recognize 'sin' as a category which applies to them.

1:6; 2:4, 6 They claim to be close to God, yet their lives do not reflect the commandments or character of Christ

2:9; 4:20 They claim to love God, yet do not love their Christian brothers and sisters.

Such attitudes appear to reflect the kind of ethical indifference that characterized some later gnostic groups.

Drawing on further hints in 1 John, we can suggest a third strand of deviant teaching:

● The claim to special spiritual insight

We have just seen how John's opponents claimed to have fellowship with God, to know him, to 'abide in Christ', and to be 'in the light' (1:6; 2:4, 6, 9). And 4:1 suggests that the teaching was based on prophetic revelation, which they attributed to God's Spirit. Note also John's frequent and emphatic use of the word 'know' (40 times in 1 John). It is as if he is deliberately fighting his opponents with their own weapons, but giving a very different content to the 'knowledge' that it is appropriate for Christians to seek. His stress on the spiritual 'anointing' which *all* Christians have received, so that *all* have knowledge of God (2:20, 27), seems designed to combat a claim of the false teachers that they have a deeper experience of God denied to ordinary Christians.

Lieu acknowledges that the emergence of false teachers has disturbed the recipients. But she criticizes attempts such as this one to infer from 1 John by 'mirror-reading' (on which see p. 229) the nature of the opposition to which the author alludes. She stresses that 1 John's concern is not with the false teachers but with the internal commitment of its recipients. The author explores the implications of beliefs which he shares with his readers. The use of phrases like 'If we say . . .' is a rhetorical technique designed to engage them and 'draw them inevitably towards the position that he holds' (Lieu 2008, pp. 11–12; see also Lieu 1991, pp. 5–6, 13–16; Edwards in Lindars, Edwards and Court 2000, pp. 153–4, 159–61).

J. Painter, while agreeing that the letter is not directed *at* the opponents, argues that the 'If we say . . .' statements imply too serious a situation to be merely rhetorical, and that they do provide an indication of significant claims of the opponents (Painter 2002, pp. 87–93).

JOHN'S RESPONSE TO THE FALSE TEACHING

John's purpose is to encourage and stabilize his readers, not to refute the opponents' views specifically. But against the background of the false teaching we can see the significance of certain points emphasized in the letter. Drawing on traditions already familiar to his readers from the Fourth Gospel, he affirms fundamental truths that will both correct the false teaching and guide his readers in authentic discipleship.

- **'Jesus is the Christ'** (2:22; 4:2)
  As so often in the Gospel (e.g., John 20:31), John asserts the identity of the man Jesus with the Christ, the Son of God. And at the very beginning of his letter, he underlines that certain people can testify to the true nature of Jesus because they had personal experience of him (1:1–4).
- **'God is light'** (1:5)
  In the OT light is often a picture of knowledge of God's will (Ps. 27:1; 119:105). So here the idea is that God is holy and makes moral demands on his people (cf. John 3:21; 8:12; 12:46). In contrast with the false teaching, 1 John 2:7–11 shows how 'living in the light' of God inevitably implies living in love towards others.
- **'God is love'** (4:8)
  Living in obedience to God means reflecting his character of love (3:10–24; 4:16—5:5), just as Jesus did (3:16–18; cf. 2:6). Whatever the false teachers may suggest, there is no room for manoeuvre on this (4:20).

- **'You all have knowledge'** (2:20, 27)
  God's revelation has not come secretly to a privileged few. It is proclaimed openly to

all God's people. And assurance of this knowledge of God is not a matter of feeling super-spiritual. The test is fundamentally an ethical one (2:3; cf. 2:5–6; 3:14, 18–19; 4:12). There is also a spiritual test, our conscious experience of the Spirit (4:13), but claims to experience the Spirit are invalid if coupled with denial of the incarnation (4:1–6).

If, as seems likely, 1 John reflects the situation in the author's community a few years after the writing of the Fourth Gospel, and if we take seriously Irenaeus' comment that John lived in Ephesus until the time when Trajan became emperor (AD 98), the document should be dated in the 90s. This is consistent with other evidence we have observed, such as the emerging threats of docetism and gnosticism.

THE PURPOSE AND SHAPE OF I JOHN

The particular allusions to the false teaching outlined above now need to be set in a broader context. For the warnings about deviant belief and practice belong to a document whose general tone is one of encouragement, reassurance and exhortation. John's purpose is to recall his readers to fundamental convictions about what God has done through Jesus Christ and to urge them to live in the light of those convictions. He calls them to maintain the apostolic gospel, and reassures them about their own security in God's love. As he himself writes, echoing the language of John 20:31: 'I write these things to you who believe in the name of the Son of God, so that you may know that you have eternal life' (5:13).

We should probably imagine the readers as members of several house-churches in and

around Ephesus. (2 John 10 probably refers to one such house-church.) Aware of a crisis developing because of the activity of false teachers, John writes to guide and encourage them.

Although the document does not have the usual beginning and ending of a letter, it is not simply a transcript of an oral address, since the author frequently says, 'I am writing . . .' He knows his readers intimately, writes with affection and assumes their confidence in him. Perhaps he writes in order to get his message round to the different groups as quickly as possible. Perhaps there is no greeting because he sends short personal notes to individual house-church leaders. His letter is designed, like Paul's, to be read out when the churches are gathered for worship (cf. Col. 4:16).

The structure, however, is quite unlike a Pauline letter. Rather than displaying the tight, logical structure of Romans or Galatians, 1 John has a shape that has been described as spiral or (less kindly) repetitious. As in a piece of music, the same themes keep recurring, with variations. The letter's contents may be summarized as follows:

1:1–4 Prologue In language that echoes the Prologue of the Gospel, John focuses on Jesus as Son of God who draws us into fellowship with God and with each other. John and others have heard, seen and touched him.
1:5—2:2 Because God is light, walk in the light Often, as we shall see, John makes a statement about God, from which he draws out the implications for our attitudes and behaviour. Jesus has shown that God is light (a symbol of God's gift of revelation and salvation, and of his holiness). Therefore, those who claim to be in fellowship with him must reflect that holiness. If they do sin,

311

they can be confident of God's willingness to forgive through Jesus' atoning sacrifice.

2:3–11 Because the light is already shining, obey God's commandments Scattered through the letter is a series of signs or tests by which we may find assurance that we really are in communion with God. *The first sign* is in 2:3: 'By this we may be sure that we know him, if we obey his commandments.' Those who know God through Jesus will follow the pattern of life exemplified in Jesus (2:6). His commandment is essentially the commandment to love.

2:12–17 Because you belong to God, avoid the false values of the world John urges his communities to remain true to Christ rather than being shaped by the distorted values of contemporary society (vv. 15–17).

2:18–27 Because you know the truth, renounce those who teach a lie While the false teachers show their true colours by 'going out from us' (2:19), John's readers are to remain true to the faith which they have received, and thus keep their life in God secure (vv. 24–25). Because God has 'anointed' them with his Spirit they are assured of God's truth and need not be led astray (vv. 20, 26–27).

2:28—3:10 Because God is your Father, live like God's children *The second sign* that we are in relationship to God is doing what is right. God's true children will reflect his character (2:29), motivated by the hope of being with Christ and like Christ in the future (3:2–3). In 3:4–10 a contrast is drawn between the lifestyles of God's children and devil's children: both groups show themselves to be their parents' true children!

3:11–24 Because Jesus has shown what love is, love one another Here comes *the third sign* that God has given eternal life: practical love for Christian brothers and sisters (v. 14). Verses 23–24 provide a link from the theme

of love to the theme of 'spirit' found in the next passage, and include *the fourth sign* of relationship to God: experience of his Spirit (repeated in 4:13).

4:1–6 Because you listen to the Spirit of God, beware of false prophets who would deceive you John develops the theme of 2:18–19. The church must test their teaching in the light of the tradition they have received.

4:7–21 Because God is love, love one another Christians' love is a response to the love that God has already shown, especially through the death of Christ, and will bear witness to the reality of God's love (vv. 7–12). Communion with the God of love banishes fear at the prospect of divine judgement (vv. 16–19). No one can genuinely love God without at the same time loving their brothers and sisters (vv. 20–21).

5:1–5 Faith, love and the commandments John now weaves together these three themes, because they cannot be separated in Christian experience. As in 3:23, believers are commanded both to express authentic faith in Jesus and to express authentic love towards God's children.

5:6–12 The testimony which leads to faith and life It is crucial for John, in opposition to the false teachers, that the union of God and humanity in Jesus Christ was no mere temporary phase beginning with his baptism and ending before his crucifixion. Otherwise, his death could not be God's means of atoning for the sins of the world (2:2). So John stresses (rather obscurely!) that the true nature of Jesus is evidenced in both his baptism and his death, and God's Spirit brings home the truth of this (vv. 6–9).

5:13–21 Conclusion: Christian certainties Echoing John 20:31, the writer states that this letter is written 'so that you may know that you have eternal life' (v. 13). The confidence thus instilled leads to boldness in prayer (vv. 14–17).

The letter reaches its climax with three 'we know' statements, which underline the sharp distinction between those who are born of God and those who are in the grasp of the Evil One. Finally comes not the usual letter-ending, but a passionate appeal. With an eye to the false Christology of his opponents he urges: Because Jesus is the true God, 'keep yourselves from idols' (v. 21).

SOME ISSUES FOR TODAY

● **The balance between truth and love**
1 John insists on the importance *both* of holding to a true understanding of Jesus *and* of love for one another. His exposition of love is rooted in his conviction that the truth about Jesus lies in his embodying the love of God (4:9). How is it possible for people of faith to avoid stressing truth at the expense of love, or vice versa?

● **Inward-looking love?**
Why does John speak exclusively about 'loving one another' within the community, and never about 'loving your neighbour' or 'loving your enemy'? Does he not describe a community that is narrow and sectarian rather than open to the world and concerned to win back those who have gone astray?

What do you think?

Look up 1 John 2:15–17; 3:13–14; 4:5–6; 5:19–20. Do you think that, by the way John contrasts 'us' and 'them', he is expressing too narrow a view of church? Would you call his community 'sectarian'?

Certainly John's teaching, both here and in the Gospel, can be described as 'dualistic'. Yet he continues to affirm the gospel that 'the Father has sent his Son as the Saviour of the world' (4:14). Although John's approach may carry within it the *risk* of becoming sectarian, we know that the *reality* was different. For his perspective on Jesus – stressing his pre-existence and incarnation – became established as Christian orthodoxy, shared by churches in different places. For example, in the early second century Ignatius of Antioch wrote that Christ was 'born and unborn, God in man' and 'God revealed in human form' (*Ephesians* 7:2; 19:3; compare also *Smyrnaeans*. 2–3; 5.2).

2 AND 3 JOHN – THEIR RELATION TO 1 JOHN

Several phrases in 1 John are paralleled in 2 and 3 John, suggesting identity of author. Note especially how 2 John 5–7 echoes the language of 1 John 2:7–8, 18–19, 26; 3:7; 4:1–2; and the emphatic concern for truth in 2 John 1–4; 3 John 3–4, 8, 12 (compare 1 John 1:6, 8; 2:4–5, 21, 27; 3:18; 4:6; 5:6, 20). And, as we shall see in a moment, the situations addressed in these two short letters (particularly 2 John) are plausibly linked with the situation we have found in 1 John.

Thus it is likely that all three letters were written by a leader whose status among his readers was secure enough for him to identify himself simply as 'the elder'. He is familiar with, and very likely the author of, the Fourth Gospel. The three letters most probably all belong to the last decade of the first century.

THE CONTEXT AND CONTENT OF 2 JOHN

What do you think?

Read through 2 John and note what clues it gives about the situation addressed and the writer's purpose. Use the questions below as a guide.

- Who are 'the elect lady and her children' (v. 1) and 'the children of your elect sister' (v. 13)?
- What echoes of themes from 1 John are there?
- What do you think vv. 10–11 refer to?

'The elect lady' is probably a personification of a local church and 'her children' are its members. It is one of the house-churches within the author's sphere of influence. Possibly it was the same church, or one of several churches, which received 1 John. If so, 2 John might be an earlier, less developed form of the instruction that was later set down in 1 John. Or it was written a little later to a different church that was now beginning to feel the impact of the false teachers as their circle of influence grew.

The elder has had news that 'some of your children [are] walking in the truth' (v. 4). Does he mean 'some but not all', implying that others have come under the spell of the false teachers? More likely, the elder is saying that some whom he has met, or some of whom he has specific news, are remaining faithful – without implying anything negative about others. But he is aware that the false teachers are on their way to spread their deviant message (vv. 10–11). So he writes a brief message, to 'hold the line' until he is able to make a visit (v. 12).

The elder's letter, which follows the normal letter-pattern of his time, can be analysed as follows:

Opening (vv. 1–3) The sender and addressee are identified and greetings expressed. The much shorter form normally found in letters of this period is expanded by the addition of Christian themes.

Expression of joy (v. 4) 2 and 3 John are the only NT letters which share this common feature of a Greek personal letter.

Body of the letter (vv. 5–11) The author reaffirms his familiar themes of mutual love, obedience to God's commandments and the true incarnation of Jesus Christ.

The recipients are to beware of those who advocate a distorted Christology by 'going beyond' the traditions about Christ received from the beginning. They should refuse even to welcome into the house-church anyone who is suspected of bringing deviant teaching.

Conclusion (vv. 12–13) The elder expresses the hope that he may visit his readers soon in order to deal more fully with the issues. His final greeting includes the church from which he writes. He is writing not merely as an individual but as leader of a community who share the task of maintaining the tradition that they have received 'from the beginning'.

HOSPITALITY TO MISSIONARIES

Modern readers may think the elder's attitude in vv. 10–11 harsh. Does it not lead to a sectarian mentality, whereby each little group maintains its own traditions and repeats its own doctrinal formulas in an increasingly sterile way? And what has happened to Christian generosity and love?

It is helpful to recognize that the attitude taken here is not peculiar to the Johannine letters. The *Didache* includes similar

> The *Didache* (in full, *The Teaching of the Lord to the Gentiles through the Twelve Apostles* – *didache* is Greek for 'teaching') is a compilation of teaching about Christian morality and church life. It was probably compiled a little later than 1–3 John, in the early second century – perhaps in Syria or Egypt. Its guidelines for dealing with travelling missionaries and prophets instruct that their genuineness should be evaluated in the light of the orthodoxy of their teaching, their motivation and their manner of life. Here are some extracts from *Didache* 11–12:
>
> Let every apostle [i.e., missionary] who comes to you be received as the Lord, but let him not stay more than one day, or if need be a second as well; but if he stay three days, he is a false prophet. And when an apostle goes forth let him accept nothing but bread till he reach his night's lodging; but if he asks for money, he is a false prophet . . .
>
> Not everyone who speaks in a spirit is a prophet, except he have the behaviour of the Lord. From his behaviour, then, the false prophet and the true prophet shall be known. And no prophet who orders a meal in a spirit shall eat of it: otherwise he is a false prophet. And every prophet who teaches the truth, if he do not what he teaches, is a false prophet . . . But whosoever shall say in a spirit, 'Give me money, or something else', you shall not listen to him . . .
>
> Let everyone who 'comes in the name of the Lord' be received; but when you have tested him you shall know him, for you shall have understanding of true and false. If he who comes is a traveller, help him as much as you can, but he shall not remain with you more than two days or, if need be, three.

guidance about how to react to travelling preachers and prophets (see box). Within the NT we find Paul's exhortation not to associate with professing Christians who persist in serious sin (1 Cor. 5:11) or in destructive doctrinal arguments (Titus 3:10–11).

Though the elder emphasizes love, he will not do so in a way that is indifferent to the truth as he perceives it. In the affirmation or denial of Christ's real incarnation a fundamental truth is at stake, and he believes it would be misguided for his churches to offer a platform to the false teachers. Christian communities throughout history have had to make difficult judgements about when doctrinal flexibility is important, and when standing firm for an unpopular truth is necessary for the church's integrity and survival.

THE CONTEXT AND CONTENT OF 3 JOHN

The elder writes to an individual named Gaius. He is a Christian leader held in affection by John (vv. 1, 2, 5, 11), who shares John's commitment to the received tradition of faith (vv. 3–4), is influential (v. 5) and commands respect (v. 6).

The theme of this letter is quite different from 1 and 2 John. It hints at a newly developing type of church organization, as we shall discover on reading it through.

Opening (vv. 1–2) Sender and addressee are identified very briefly, in the format of most secular letters. The health wish (v. 2) is a further feature typical of the opening of contemporary Greek letters, though the writer adds a comment on Gaius' spiritual health.

315

Expression of joy (vv. 3–4) The elder rejoices at Gaius' Christian orthodoxy and integrity as reported to him by some travelling Christians. These are probably missionaries commissioned, or at least approved, by the elder, who are able as they travel about to keep him informed about the state of the churches in Asia.

Body of the letter (vv. 5–12) The elder commends Gaius for welcoming the travelling missionaries, even though they were strangers to him. They in turn have reported to John's church his loving hospitality (vv. 5–6. Notice the word 'church' here and in vv. 9, 10; it occurs nowhere else in John's Gospel or letters). Now John urges Gaius to provide financial sponsorship for the missionaries' ongoing work (vv. 6–7. 'Send them on' – Greek *propempo* – in v. 6 is a technical term, e.g. in Acts 15:3 and Romans 15:24 for financial support of a missionary journey). Those who provide such sponsorship become 'fellow-workers in the truth' (v. 8).

Suddenly in v. 9 a new factor emerges, which explains why the elder is so anxious for Gaius to take responsibility for missionary support. Diotrephes, 'who likes to put himself first', has ignored a letter which the elder has written to the church, rejects the elder's authority and spreads malicious gossip about him. He refuses to provide hospitality for the travelling missionaries and even expels from the church others who wish to do so. When the elder can make a visit there he will take these issues up with Diotrephes (vv. 9–10). Significantly, the author does not call Diotrephes 'antichrist' or criticize his Christology. The problem is not that he is a false teacher, but that he has too big a view of his own importance.

The simple reference to 'the church' naturally suggests that Diotrephes was prominent in the same church to which Gaius also belonged. But if that were so, why does John explain to Gaius the disruption that Diotrephes is causing? So perhaps we should think of two neighbouring churches. Clearly Diotrephes in his desire for power and control is determined to challenge what he sees as the interference of the elder and his representatives there. And John, for his part, does not have the kind of authority that would enable him to discipline Diotrephes.

So John urges Gaius not to imitate evil (i.e., to behave differently from Diotrephes!) but to follow good examples – such as that of Demetrius, presumably a missionary not yet known to Gaius (vv. 11–12). Demetrius is no doubt the bearer of this letter, and the words of commendation here show that 3 John serves as a letter of introduction for him to Gaius (see p. 28 on letters of introduction).

Conclusion (vv. 13–15) The writer expresses the hope of visiting the readers and sends greetings.

3 JOHN – EVIDENCE OF AN EMERGING PATTERN OF CHURCH LEADERSHIP?

Diotrephes was dismissing the elder's influence and authority. His power in his local church was sufficient to persuade most other members to support his policy of refusing hospitality to the missionaries. The elder was clearly unhappy at the way Diotrephes was throwing his weight around, yet had no guaranteed strategy for bringing him under control. How had this situation come about?

It has been argued that Diotrephes was an 'elder-bishop' of the type that was emerging about the turn of the first century and is best known to us from the example of Ignatius of Antioch. (Ignatius reminded the church at Philadelphia that God had commanded them through him 'never to act independently of the bishop', *Philadelphians* 7.) As such, he would resent John's efforts to exercise what he regarded as illegitimate influence over a church where he himself had rightful authority. But it is risky to propose such a scenario on the basis of the brief and ambiguous evidence of 3 John. (For detailed discussion of this and other explanations of the antagonism between the elder and Diotrephes, see Smalley 2007, pp. 340–2.)

Perhaps it is more realistic to see Diotrephes as a strong individual in his church with 'an egocentric lust for power, which he had confused with zeal for the gospel' (Smalley 2007, p. 342). As such, he resented the influence and prestige of John and went to considerable lengths to frustrate it. The nature of the elder's authority, on the other hand, was not coercive, but was based on love and respect and years of pastoral leadership.

Digging deeper

Read Raymond Brown's discussion of the different possible meanings of the word 'elder' in the early church and in 2 and 3 John (Brown 1982, pp. 647–651; or see the summary discussion in his *Introduction to the New Testament*. New York: Doubleday 1997, pp. 398–9).

Do you agree with his conclusion about what kind of 'elder' the author of these letters is?
What light does this discussion throw on the use of the term 'elder' in other parts of the NT?

Hence he was relatively powerless when that authority was seriously challenged – especially if Diotrephes' church lay near the edge of his geographical area of influence.

However, this was the kind of situation which made the emerging pattern of

Focus on theology:
SPIRIT AND TRADITION

Churches today are often divided between those that stress a continuity of tradition derived from the past and those that focus on a vivid contemporary experience of God's Spirit. John, however, suggests that to choose between the two is misguided. He constantly draws attention to the tradition of faith and discipleship that has been handed down in the Christian community right from the time of Jesus' ministry (1:1–4; 'from the beginning' in 1:1; 2:7, 24; 3:11; and see the table on p. 306, showing echoes in 1 John of material from the Fourth Gospel).

But alongside this is evidence of personal experience of the Spirit. His readers have each been 'anointed' by the Spirit, giving them access to knowledge of God and insight into his truth (2:20). So they are not merely passive recipients of teaching from those who pass on the tradition (2:27). Awareness of the Spirit brings confidence that they truly belong to Christ (3:24; 4:13). The Spirit enables a community to discern when the truth about Christ is being taught (4:1–6), for it is the Spirit who bears witness to the reality of Christ's incarnation (5:6).

How might John's insight help Christians today to be both faithful to the tradition and open to the Spirit? How might a church express in its life and worship the importance of both the tradition and the fresh impetus of the Spirit?

'elder-bishops' or 'monarchical episcopate' attractive. Now that the age of the apostles had drawn to a close, and the growing church was challenged by seriously deviant doctrine, the idea of having in each locality a clearly recognized authoritative leader who represented the church and safeguarded its teaching must have been very attractive to many. The style of church pictured by the Johannine Gospel and letters – a community of brothers and sisters, apparently without any hierarchy of leaders apart from the benevolent figure of the now aged John himself – might have seemed a romantic ideal, impractical in the face of forces which threatened the church's existence.

There are always both gains and losses when Christian movements and churches develop from one style and structure into another.

The Johannine pattern of church is perhaps one-sided and inadequate as a pattern for churches in all times and places. Yet a church is missing something vital if it knows little of the intimacy and shared responsibility for each other's Christian growth that is John's vision for God's people.

ESSAY TOPICS

INTRODUCTORY

● 'I write these things to you who believe in the name of the Son of God, so that you may know that you have eternal life' (1 John 5:13). Show how the contents of 1 John are designed to achieve this purpose.

● You have been asked to give a talk on 'How to maintain a healthy church life'. Explain what insights and emphases from 1–3 John you could draw on for this purpose, and why.

INTERMEDIATE

● What is the nature of the false teaching which forms the background of 1 John? Evaluate the specific proposals of Brown (1979, 1982), Lieu (1991, pp. 13–16), Smalley (xxi–xxiii), and Stott (pp. 48–55).

● Explore the various uses of the term 'elder' in the NT. In what ways do you think their function might be best expressed in churches today?

FURTHER READING

* denotes books assuming knowledge of Greek; most can be used by all students.

INTRODUCTORY
R. E. Brown *The Community of the Beloved Disciple*. New York: Paulist Press, 1979 (significant study of the nature of John's community and the relationship between the Gospel and letters of John).
R. A. Culpepper *The Gospel and Letters of John*. Nashville: Abingdon, 1998 (interprets the letters in close relation to the Fourth Gospel).
J. Lieu *The Theology of the Johannine Epistles*. Cambridge: CUP, 1991.
B. Lindars, R. B. Edwards and J. M. Court *The Johannine Literature*. Sheffield: Sheffield Academic Press, 2000 (includes Edwards' excellent survey of contents and issues in 1—3 John).

INTERMEDIATE
A. R. Campbell *The Elders: Seniority within Earliest Christianity*. Edinburgh: T. & T. Clark, 1994.
J. Lieu *The Second and Third Epistles of John*. Edinburgh: T. & T. Clark, 1986 (detailed study of the background and purpose of these letters).

Commentaries

*R. E. Brown *The Epistles of John*. AB. Garden City, NY: Doubleday, 1982.

G. Burge *The Letters of John*. NIVAC. Grand Rapids: Zondervan, 1996.

C. H. Dodd *The Johannine Epistles*. London: Hodder & Stoughton, 1946.

J. L. Houlden *A Commentary on the Johannine Epistles*. BNTC. London: Black/New York: Harper & Row, 2nd edition 1994.

C. G. Kruse *The Letters of John*. Leicester: Apollos/Grand Rapids: Eerdmans, 2000.

J. Lieu *I, II & III John*. Louisville: Westminster/John Knox, 2008 (thorough treatment, suggesting new approaches to many issues of interpretation).

I. H. Marshall *The Epistles of John*. NICNT. Grand Rapids: Eerdmans, 1978.

J. Painter *1, 2 and 3 John*. SP. Collegeville: Liturgical Press, 2002.

R. Schnackenberg *The Johannine Epistles*. ET New York: Crossroad, 1992.

*S. S. Smalley *1, 2, 3 John*. WBC. Nashville: Nelson, revised 2007.

J. R. W. Stott *The Letters of John*. TNTC. Leicester: IVP/Grand Rapids: Eerdmans, 2nd edition 1988 (excellent shorter commentary).

*R. W. Yarborough *1–3 John*. BECNT. Grand Rapids: Baker, 2008 (very thorough).

APOCALYPTIC
LITERATURE

Chapter 21

THE REVELATION TO JOHN

In this chapter we will look at:

- the origins of apocalyptic and the kind of writing Revelation is;
- the historical context of Revelation and how this affects our reading;
- some theological perspectives of the book;
- the mythological world of its readers and how that has shaped Revelation;
- Revelation's use of the OT;
- an overview of its structure and composition;
- some key interpretative issues;
- its relevance for today.

Without doubt, Revelation is the most intriguing and fascinating of NT books. As we turn its pages, a cascade of images – some thrilling, some frightening, all gripping – come tumbling forth, a bewildering kaleidoscope of colour, number and shape. Over the years, it has inspired an enormous range of art and initiated some of the most extraordinary and powerful theological ideas. Its influence, for good or ill, is disproportionate to its place on the fringes of the biblical canon.

As literature, it is perhaps the most complex and sophisticated piece of writing the world has ever seen. As theology, it has been the inspiration of a wide range of ideologies, from fundamentalists to libertarians. Through it all, it has been a source of strength for millions of believers as an assurance that 'the Almighty reigns'.

The drama of its imagery both attracts and repels. Since the second generation of followers of Jesus, its meaning has been shrouded in mystery. This vacuum of understanding has sucked into it all manner of explanations, and there are not a few times when a dominant leader has based his influence on a group on his ability to explain or 'decode' this most opaque of texts.

What do you think?

How have you encountered this book up till now? What impressions do you have of it, both positive and negative? How does this shape the way you will read it and perhaps approach it as an object of study?

You will need to read through the whole book before going any further. In what ways does the text confirm or undermine your preconceptions of it? Is there anything that surprises you about it?

Revelation is classified as 'apocalyptic' literature. The term comes from the Greek word of self-description in Rev. 1:1 'The revelation (*apokalypsis*) of Jesus Christ . . .' but interestingly this is the only place within 'apocalyptic' literature where the term occurs.

The origins of this kind of writing lie in the OT prophets. Revelation has been called 'the climax of prophecy', and apocalyptic stands at the end point of two trends evident within OT prophetic literature. The first is the move from the oral to visual. The earliest pre-exilic writings of Hosea and Amos are mostly verbal, though they include short visions and visual illustrations. But Isaiah is able to introduce his oracles as something he 'saw' (Isa. 1:1; 2:1; 6:1; 13:1 and so on). By the time of the exile, Ezekiel largely writes of things he has seen, and the second half of Daniel (which most scholars date to the second century BC in the form we have it) contains fully-fledged apocalyptic visions.

The second trend is the development of increasingly cosmic imagery to depict God's intervention in judgement and salvation. In Isaiah 11, the coming of the anointed one transforms the natural order ('the wolf shall lie down with the lamb' v. 6). In Isaiah 13 the hoped-for judgement of Babylon on the day of the Lord (vv. 6, 9) is described in cosmic terms (v. 10), even though we might describe it as a military or political event. By the end of Isaiah, nothing less than a total transformation of the cosmos can express God's deliverance of his people from exile ('new heavens and a new earth', Isa. 65:17), though the life of the restored people is expressed in quite ordinary terms (vv. 21–23).

From the second century BC until the second or third century AD, apocalyptic literature became quite widespread. Subsequently this gave way to a different genre of mystical writing, associated with *merkabah* mysticism, which derives its name from the throne chariot (*merkabah* in Hebrew) of Ezekiel's vision of God (Ezek. 1).

When learning a foreign language, it can feel rather technical until a certain level of fluency is reached. Likewise, studying Revelation can seem rather technical at times – we will be looking at three different ways that numbers have significance in the text. But it is important to remember that, as with a language, the purpose of the technical study is to facilitate understanding.

Digging deeper

Look at Ezekiel 1, 37 and 40, and Daniel 7—9. What similarities and differences do you see compared with Revelation in terms of style, imagery and literary context?

You may also like to compare Revelation with two first-century Jewish apocalypses, 4 Ezra (= 2 Esdras 3–14 which can be found in the NRSV Apocrypha) and 2 Baruch (which can be found in *OTP* vol. 1).

A discussion of Revelation's relation to other apocalyptic works can be found in Bauckham 1993a, pp. 5–12.

LANGUAGE AND GENRE

There has been considerable debate in recent years about the nature of Revelation's genre. 'Genre' simply means 'kind of writing', but it is important to the interpretation of a text. This is because

Interpret literally

genre is defined by the conventions that a writer uses and that a reader needs to follow in order to make sense of a text in the way the writer intended. This may include the nature of the vocabulary and grammar used, sentence structure, even the medium of writing originally employed – think of the difference in presentation between a letter from a lover and a bank manager! The important thing about genre is that different genres require different approaches to interpretation. We would normally expect to interpret a car maintenance manual or a letter from a bank manager fairly 'literally', but the same is not true of a love letter or a poem. Understanding something of Revelation's genre will give us clues as to how to read it aright. Perhaps the main reason why most people find Revelation difficult to read and make sense of is that they are unfamiliar with the apocalyptic genre, and so do not understand the conventions used within it.

John J. Collins led a team of scholars in thinking about apocalyptic genre, and published this definition:

> 'Apocalypse' is a genre of revelatory literature with a narrative framework, in which a revelation is mediated by an other-worldly being to a human recipient, disclosing a transcendent reality which is both temporal, insofar as it envisages eschatological salvation, and spatial, insofar as it involves another, supernatural world. (J. J. Collins 'Introduction: Towards the Morphology of a Genre' in *Semeia* 14, 1979 p. 9)

Although it makes a number of technical points, the difficulty with this definition is that it aims to encompass a wide range of apocalyptic texts, some of which appear to function quite differently from Revelation.

As a result, it does not give sufficient prominence to the visual nature of the text; most readers would say that Revelation's most striking feature is its imagery, and yet this only appears as a sub-point within this definition. Although there are points in the text of Revelation when the author does appear to move from one place to another (as at 4:1 and 17:3), it is not clear that the 'heavenly journey' motif is as important in Revelation as it is in other apocalyptic texts.

What do you think?

Read the following text:

The stars will fall from heaven,
   the sun will cease its shining;
the moon will be turned to blood,
   and fire and hail will fall from heaven.
The rest of the country will have sunny intervals
   with scattered showers.

Why is this funny? Notice that superficially the grammar and vocabulary of the two sections are very similar. Why is it that changes in genre affect the way we interpret texts?

If the genre of a text gives us clues to how we should read it, then continuity of genre makes a text consistent and easy to read. Where there are rapid changes of genre within a text (changes in 'microgenre' within the 'macrogenre') then this can be disorienting for the reader. Revelation does just this, which is another thing that can make it difficult to read.

The changes in genre here reflect Revelation's mixed 'pedigree', claiming as it does to be a 'revelation', a 'prophecy' and a letter. The changes in genre continue

325

Revelation 1	Genre
1 The revelation of Jesus Christ, which God gave to show his servants what must soon take place …	Apocalypse
3 Blessed is the one who reads aloud the words of this prophecy …	Benediction
4 John to the seven churches that are in Asia …	Letter
5 … To him who loves us and freed us from our sins by his blood …	Doxology
7 Look! He is coming with the clouds, and every eye will see him …	Apocalyptic
8 'I am the Alpha and the Omega,' says the Lord God …	Prophecy
9 I, John, your brother …	Letter

throughout the book, mainly moving between vision report (most of chapters 4 and 5), narrative (most of chapters 12 and 13), doxology (4:11; 5:9 and so on) and instruction (e.g. 22:18).

The genre of a text is closely related to the purpose of that text as an act of communication. We employ different genres when we wish to do different things. The mixed genre of Revelation corresponds to the fact that there is continuing debate about what the original purpose of the book was.

What do you think?

What do these different genres within Revelation suggest about its purpose? (This will involve reflecting on what you think is the purpose of letters, prophecy and visions.) How might this affect the way we read it?

HISTORICAL CONTEXT AND DATING

Why bother thinking about the historical context of Revelation?

First, carefully locating a text within its historical context offers a control on the possible meanings of a text. This has been

seen as important since the Reformation with its concern to avoid the more extreme speculation of some mediaeval interpretations of the Bible.

Second, Revelation claims to be (among other things) a letter, that is, it is addressed to particular people in a particular place. This means that precision about its date and location might be of greater significance than for a text that claims to set out generalities.

Third, Revelation speaks of people and events in a way that invites some reflection on specific historical events that it might be referring to.

DATING
There are two main contenders for dating the book in current debate: an earlier date towards the end of Nero's reign as emperor (54–68); and a later date towards the end of Domitian's reign (81–96).

External evidence
● **Irenaeus**
The second-generation Christian leader Irenaeus comments that Revelation was written 'no long time ago, but almost in our own day, towards the end of Domitian's reign' (*Against Heresies* 5.30.3). Irenaeus was a disciple of Polycarp of Smyrna, and so is likely to be a reliable

witness, though he believes John the apostle wrote Revelation (which many commentators think unlikely) and he can only guess at the meaning of 666 in Revelation 13:18.

● **Churches at Smyrna and Thyatira**
Evidence from Polycarp (*Philippians* 11) and Epiphanius (*Heresies* 51.33.1) suggests that the churches in Smyrna and Thyatira were only founded late in the first century.

● **Persecution**
References to martyrdom within the book (see, for example, Rev. 2:13; 6:9; 20:4) have made readers over many generations assume Revelation was written at a time of persecution. However, some recent scholars (particularly Thompson 1990, and Collins 1984, pp. 84–110) have argued

that the text is *creating* a crisis rather than *responding* to one. The historical evidence for persecution of Christians in the first century, and especially under the reign of Domitian, is now much disputed.

Internal Evidence

● **The King List in Revelation 17:9–12**
Using this list to work out the reigning Emperor appears to be straightforward, but is actually beset with problems. Which Emperor should we start with? Should we count them all, or omit some (no other ancient list does so)? The most straight-forward reckoning takes us to the 'year of three emperors' in 68–9, but then the prediction here would quickly have been shown to be untrue. Is this likely? The text itself appears to be more symbolic, with the seven kings also being seven hills. Does this list tell us anything about date – and why would John need to communicate the date of his writing to his readers?

Digging deeper

'Our life as professors is too remote from prison to allow us to understand John.' (Paul Minear, 'Ontology and Ecclesiology in the Apocalypse' *NTS* 12, 1966, p. 92.)

'What mattered is that they suffered ... We read history not in terms of the relative difference between oppressors but in terms of the reality of suffering and oppression, the joys and hopes of the little people of God. We see and understand the events of history from the underside.' (Boesak 1987, p. 25.)

Look through Revelation again, making a note of any texts that suggest pressure or persecution. What difference might it make to your reading if you were (or are) feeling persecuted for your faith? How does the text speak to those who are quite comfortable in their situation within society?

ROMAN LEADERS/EMPERORS

BC
49 Julius Caesar
44 Antony and Octavian (Augustus)
31 Augustus (first emperor)

AD
14 Tiberius
37 Gaius Caligula
41 Claudius
54 Nero
68 Galba
69 Otto, Vitellius, Vespasian
79 Titus
81 Domitian
96 Nerva
98 Trajan
117 Hadrian

● **Measuring the Temple in Revelation 11**
Revelation 11:1–2 speaks of measuring the temple (but not the outer court); whether it has any bearing on dating the book depends on whether this is to be taken literally (which would imply the temple is still standing, and so lead to a pre-70 date), or is metaphorical (symbolic). The text does have close parallels with Jesus' words in Luke 21:24 ('trampled' and 'Gentiles' = 'nations', Greek *ethne*). But there are stronger parallels with Ezekiel's vision of measuring the temple in Ezekiel 40 and the apocalyptic passage about the temple's restoration in Zechariah 4, and Rev. 11 focuses on the symbolic period of 'forty-two months' (also described as '1,260 days' and 'time, times and half a time'). This suggests it should not be taken as a literal reference to the temple.

● **The use of the term 'Babylon' to refer to Rome**
In Rev. 14, 16, 17 and 18 a great city called Babylon is celebrated as having fallen. This is very widely understood as referring to Rome; it is the 'great city who rules over the kings of the earth' (17:18), is fabulously wealthy and is an international centre of trade (18:11–17). This identification occurs in other literature (4 Ezra = 2 Esdras 3, the Apocalypse of Baruch 10, the Sibylline Oracles 5 and 1 Peter 1) and would have become widespread after AD 70 and the destruction of Jerusalem by Rome, as Babylon was the other great destroyer of the city.

● **The nature of the church communities**
It has been suggested that the internal situation of the churches is very different from that depicted in the Pauline correspondence, and therefore that Revelation must be considerably later than the 50s–60s. But it is often difficult to use a text as a 'window' on its context in this way. For example, the group called the 'Nicolaitans' (Rev. 2:6, 15) appears to be unknown to Paul and does not feature in his writings. But how do we know that the term refers to an established social group in Revelation? It is quite possible that John is coining the term in order to give a label to a compromising tendency within the churches.

David Aune puts forward a theory of 'diachronic composition' for the book's construction: it was originally a series of more-or-less independent visions from an earlier date that was later brought together into one work. Although this raises considerable questions about how we read the text, it may explain the apparently contradictory evidence for date. It is also worth noting that (often complex) arguments about date usually affect actual exegesis less than many commentators suggest.

AUTHORSHIP

Related to the question of date is the question of authorship. All the early (second century) testimony is that the author was John the Apostle. Dionysius of Alexandria in the third century was the first to point out that the style was very different from that of the Gospel or Letters of John, and concluded that Revelation could not have been written by the same author (Eusebius, *Hist. eccl.*, 7.25). Most modern commentators take this view, though the evidence one way or the other is thin. All the text itself claims is that 'John' is a servant of God (1:1), brother of his readers (1:9) and a prophet (22:8). Most important is that he knows the Christians he is writing to and he understands their situation because he shares in it.

CONTEXT

In the last one hundred years, a lot of work has been done to connect the text of

Revelation with local features of the churches to which it was written. Some major work was done on this by Ramsay (1904), but the most extensive recent study is that of Colin Hemer (1986).

One of the best illustrations of the importance of local context on the meaning of the text relates to the 'Laodicean lukewarmness' in Rev. 3:15–16. This had long been a problem for

commentators – what kind of coldness could be preferable to being lukewarm? The natural reading – of 'hot' as signifying faithful commitment, 'cold' as indifference, and 'lukewarm' as somewhere in between – does not make sense. What would these terms mean to local people at the time?

Laodicea is situated in the Lycus Valley. The river itself dries up in the summer, but the

The seven churches of Asia

area has a number of springs. The best known of these are the hot springs at Pammukale (ancient Hierapolis) with its striking calcified terraces, six miles across the valley from the site of Laodicea. (You can find pictures of Pammukale in just about any brochure advertising tourism in Turkey.) Not far away, Colossae was renowned for its cold water springs. But Laodicea had neither. The remains of an aqueduct, recently obliterated by farming, showed that the city relied on water from hot springs some five miles away which would cool on its journey; the pipes in the aqueduct were encrusted with deposits. The lukewarm water on its arrival no longer had any medicinal value, yet it was not fit to drink, and most likely had to be left in jars to cool and settle before it could be used.

The reference to 'hot', 'cold' and 'lukewarm' is not then a description of the Laodiceans' lack of faith, but of their ineffectiveness. In the same way that drinking the lukewarm water as it arrived in the city would make a person throw up, the Laodiceans' lack of fruitfulness made God sick.

Digging deeper

This aspect of the message to Laodicea is explored in M. J. S. Rudwick and E. M. B. Green, 'The Laodicean Lukewarmness' *Expository Times* 69, 1957, pp. 176–178, and is commented on by Hemer 1986, pp. 186–191. The majority of ordinary readers of Revelation do not have ready access to this kind of information. What does this imply for our reading and interpretation of the book?

The order in which the churches are addressed follows the order one would visit them in travelling a circular route from Ephesus clockwise. There are numerous aspects of the messages to the churches that appear to relate to their local situations:

- **Smyrna** To this church, Christ is described as the one 'who was dead and came to life' (Rev. 2:8). The city itself was destroyed in 600 BC and refounded in 300 BC, and its name means 'myrrh' which was used in burials (see John 19:39). Before the closing formula of the message is a promise of 'the crown of life' to the faithful (Rev. 2:10). Smyrna was famous for its games, in which the winners would be awarded a 'crown' in the form of a laurel wreath. As a city it was also known as 'the crown of Asia' and featured a crown on its coins. Along with Philadelphia, it receives no rebuke; it is the only city where the church has survived into modern times.

- **Pergamum** The threat to the church here is expressed as their living 'where Satan's throne is' (Rev. 2:13); the city is dominated by an acropolis that appears throne-shaped as you approach from the previous city, Smyrna. Part of the promise to those who conquer is a 'white stone, and on the white stone is written a new name' (Rev. 2:17). The natural stone in the area was black, and for inscriptions on buildings slabs of white stone were specially transported there for carving.

- **Sardis** The challenge to the church here is to 'wake up' (3:2–3). Twice in its history, attackers had taken the city during the night, when the defenders thought they were safe.

- **Laodicea** The church here is accused of arrogant self-sufficiency: 'I am rich, I have prospered, I need nothing' (3:17). After a devastating earthquake in AD 61 the city had taken the unusual step of refusing imperial aid in the rebuilding process. The church is charged with being 'poor, blind and naked' (3:17); the city was a centre of banking, ophthalmology, and a clothes industry producing black wool.

The parallels and contrasts between the messages to the churches and the situation of the cities demonstrate the importance of reading the text in its first-century context. In some places the impact of the message is amplified; at others the actual meaning of the text is at stake.

What do you think?

What do these references to the churches' local settings suggest about the importance of the local context for church leadership and teaching?

THEOLOGICAL PERSPECTIVES

Before looking more closely at the way Revelation communicates its message, we will look at the main features of its theological orientation.

GOD

A large part of Revelation's theology is embedded in the titles it uses for God. 'Alpha and Omega/first and the last/ beginning and the end' has its biblical origins in later prophetic pronouncements of God's uniqueness amongst the nations (see Isa. 41:4; 44:6; 48:12). But in this form the title makes strong connections with Greek philosophy and mysticism and its speculations about the divine name. 'The one who is, who was, and who is to come' (1:4; 1:8; 4:8; 11:17; 16:5) develops the understanding of the divine name (Ex. 3:14) in line with Jewish interpretation. But it

prioritizes the present reality of God, and expresses his future reality in terms of his coming to judge and save. 'Lord God Almighty' (1:8; 4:8; 11:17; 15:3; 16:7; 19:6; 21:22) is a translation of the biblical phrase, 'Yhwh, God of hosts' and emphasizes God's actual control over events, in spite of appearances. 'The one who sits on the throne' draws on another prophetic image of sovereignty (Isa. 6, Ezek. 1), which relates God's rule to its recognition in worship.

Strikingly (in the light of Revelation's use of the OT) there is no language attributing human characteristics to God (anthropomorphism). Only twice does God speak (in 1:8 and 21:6); elsewhere others speak on God's behalf (e.g. in 6:1) or the voice is disembodied (as in 16:17). Revelation's language about God is primarily the language of transcendence. But this does not mean God is unconcerned with creation. God is worshipped as creator (4:11) with a rainbow around his throne (4:3; cf. Gen. 9:13–17). God's judgement will involve 'destroying the destroyers of the earth (11:18, cf. Gen. 6:11f.) and the final vision (Rev. 21) is of a renewed creation that is beyond the threat of evil.

JESUS

In the context of God's transcendence and uniqueness, Jesus shares the language God uses for self-designation. Whereas the titles connected with 'first and last' are used separately by God and Jesus in chapter 1 (1:8 and 1:17), by the end they merge together and appear to be uttered by Jesus himself (21:6; 22:13). 'As a way of stating unambiguously that Jesus Christ belongs to the fullness of the eternal being of God, this surpasses anything in the NT' (Bauckham 1993a, p. 57). The language of worship reinforces this. In contrast to the angel who refuses worship (in Rev. 19 and 21) Jesus accepts it. And the language of worship of the lamb echoes the language of worship of God (Rev. 4 and 5) so that worship of the lamb leads to worship of God and the lamb together (5:13). Jesus and God are so closely identified that the future of God for humankind is the coming of Jesus.

The primary designation of Jesus is as witness. Although the lamb wages war and brings judgement, the high point of his victory is his faithful witness to the point of death (Rev. 12:10–11). If God is transcendent and at something of a distance, then Jesus is present as the one among the lampstands (1:12–20), the lamb who conquers by suffering (2:9–10).

THE SPIRIT
Two phrases are used in Revelation – the simple title 'the Spirit' and the puzzling phrase 'the seven Spirits'. This second expression is closely connected with the lamb that has been slain and with the churches themselves. The seven Spirits are seven lamps (4:5, not 'torches', NRSV), presumably placed on the seven lampstands (1:12, 20). But they are also the eyes of the lamb that roam throughout the earth (5:6, cf. Zech. 4:5). The phrase comes four times, corresponding to the 7 x 4 = 28 occurrences of the word 'lamb'. 'The seven Spirits as the divine power released into the whole world by the victory of Christ's sacrifice are the power of divine truth' (Bauckham 1993a, p. 114).

'The Spirit' occurs fourteen times, seven of these in the messages to the churches. It is the Spirit who makes the voice of Jesus known to his people. And it is the Spirit who equips them for faithful witness after the pattern of Jesus (11:11; 19:10). This witness is manifest both within the churches and to the world at large.

THE FOLLOWERS OF THE LAMB
The followers of the lamb are soldiers fighting a holy war (Rev. 7; see under 'Use of the OT'). They are to conquer, as the lamb conquers, through faithful endurance in times of suffering. However they will be conquered as well as conquering (13:7), but final victory belongs to the lamb and to the lamb's followers. This victory came first through Jesus' death and resurrection; it belongs to his followers during the end times of conflict, and it will be complete on Jesus' return.

The followers of the lamb are also participants in an end-times Exodus. They follow the Passover lamb that has been slaughtered (5:6) to purchase their freedom as a kingdom of priests (1:5–6, Exodus 19:6). They have passed through a Red Sea of resistance to the beast (15:3–4), and the Exodus plagues fall on those who follow the beast (Rev. 16). But this vision is inclusive rather than exclusive – the fourfold phrase 'tribes, nations, tongues and peoples' combines Ex. 19:5 with Gen. 10:31. The people of God come from every nation, not in the sense of being separated out of them, but in the sense of comprising people from all nations.

Thirdly, the followers of the lamb are to be witnesses like Jesus to the truth about God. Jesus is the faithful and true witness (3:14) and his followers conquer by their testimony (12:11). The world is pictured as a courtroom, where the truth about God is on trial; the faithful and true witness finally becomes the faithful and true judge (19:11) who vindicates his faithful people.

MYTHOLOGICAL CONTEXT AND EMPEROR WORSHIP

Part of reading a text with an awareness of its original context involves engaging with what we can discover about the thought-world of the author and first hearers. For Revelation's first audience, the ideology of emperor 'worship' (the imperial cult) would have formed an important part of the way they viewed the world.

There has been some debate over the significance of emperor 'worship' – was it truly a 'religious' phenomenon, or was it really just political? Such a debate assumes a modern separation between the 'religious' and the 'political', which would have been quite unknown in the ancient world. What was clear was that there was perceived to be a serious conflict of loyalty. The Roman Emperor claimed in various ways to be the source of peace and prosperity within the empire and therefore deserving of a distinct loyalty – something both Jews and Christians had difficulty with. We see evidence of this conflict sporadically in the gospels (as in the debate about paying taxes, Matt. 22:15–16 and parallels).

In Asia Minor, the issue of allegiance to the Emperor was doubly important. On the one hand, its distance from Rome meant that it was essential to ensure the loyalty of its inhabitants. The clearest way of demonstrating this was the offering of a pinch of incense to the Emperor at one of the public shrines. On the other hand, although Rome ruled Asia through its own appointed governor, it left the traditional patterns of city government intact, so long as they stayed loyal to Rome. Thus local leaders had their position reinforced as long as they could 'deliver' the local population's loyalty. This combination of circumstances meant that there was more enthusiasm for the imperial cult here than perhaps in any other part of the empire. The Emperor was more closely associated with the pantheon of gods than could ever be the case back in Rome.

Digging deeper

Read Revelation 4.

- What can you learn from the text alone about the nature of worship, without considering anything about its original context (for example, the importance of the Spirit in accessing God's presence, God's ruling from a throne, both from v. 2)?
- What images and ideas do you recognize from the OT (for example, thunder and lightning as signalling God's presence, as in Ex. 19:18)?
- What images and ideas appear novel, and do not reflect earlier aspects of worship elsewhere in the Bible?

While we can read the text perfectly well as it stands, a new dimension of meaning opens up when we know something of the cultural context in which it was written – much in the same way that watching television in colour offers us more than watching in black-and-white. Many of the features of the worship scene in Revelation 4 derive from pagan worship and the imperial cult.

- When on his travels around the empire, the Emperor would be accompanied by various officials and advisers. On arriving at a city, he would take his seat in a (moveable) throne room surrounded by these officials. Domitian changed the number of officials (*lictors*) from twelve to twenty-four.

● In the OT, entering into God's presence was the province of the priesthood alone, yet in Revelation it is 'elders' who surround the throne. This follows the pattern of imperial visits, where the Emperor would be greeted first by elders from the city he was visiting.

● White was the normal ritual apparel in Greek culture, in contrast with the coloured garments of OT priests (see Ex. 28).

● The wearing of gold crowns and the casting of these crowns before the ruler was a feature of Greek worship since Alexander. In other places in the NT the use of 'crown' probably refers to the victor's wreath in the games (e.g. 2 Tim. 4:8; 1 Pet. 5:4).

● The choruses sung to God here and elsewhere in Revelation are simpler and more repetitive than either the Psalms or texts that appear to have functioned as hymns in the early church (such as Phil. 2:6–11 or perhaps Col. 1:15–20). In form they more closely resemble the acclamations that were repeatedly sung or shouted to the Emperor as he approached a city.

So Revelation 4—5 combines a great variety of OT imagery with contemporary practices of pagan worship and obeisance to the Emperor. In doing this, it is claiming for God alone all expressions of worship, and so offers a powerful critique of the acknowledged sources and structures of power in the first-century world.

The single most significant contact with pagan mythology and the imperial cult comes in Revelation 12. This chapter is of great importance in Revelation as a whole; almost every commentator notes its significance within the structure of the book.

The characters in the story (the woman, the dragon, the child, Michael) are familiar enough from the OT (see below). But the shape of the story is unfamiliar, and interpretations diverge widely here. The closest resemblance to the plot is found in a myth of combat between Python and Apollo that circulated (probably in two main forms) in Egypt and Asia Minor from the first century BC to the second century AD.

THE PYTHON MYTH

This form of the Python myth was written down by Hyginus (*Fabulae* 140) some time prior to AD 207. His works can be found in M. Grant *The Myths of Hyginus* (Lawrence: University of Kansas, 1960).

Python, son of Terra, was a huge dragon. He was accustomed to giving oracles on Mount Parnassus before the time of Apollo. He was informed by an oracle that he would be destroyed by the offspring of Leto. At that time Zeus was living with Leto. When [Zeus' wife] Hera learned of this, she decreed that Leto should give birth at a place where the sun does not reach. When Python perceived that Leto was pregnant by Zeus, he began to pursue (her) in order to kill her. But, by order of Zeus, the North Wind (Aquilo) lifted Leto up and carried her to Poseidon; Poseidon protected her, but in order not to rescind Hera's decree, he carried her to the island Ortygia and covered the island with waves. When Python did not find Leto, he returned to Parnassus. But Poseidon returned the island Ortygia to the upper region, and it was later called the island of Delos. There, holding on to an olive tree, Leto gave birth to Apollo and Artemis, to whom Hephaestus gave arrows as a gift. Four days after they were born, Apollo avenged his mother. He went to Parnassus and killed Python with arrows.

The significance of this parallel is that the myth was used by Domitian (and other emperors) as imperial propaganda (see J. W. van Henten, 'Dragon Myth and Imperial Ideology in Revelation 12—13' *SBL Seminar Papers* 33, 1994, pp. 496–515). The Emperor takes the role of Apollo, defeating the forces of chaos which are pushed back beyond the boundaries of the empire and becoming the guarantor of peace and prosperity. But in Revelation 12, the roles are reversed. Imperial power (the beast from the sea in Rev. 13) is actually an agent of the primeval chaos monster, the opponent of both God and God's people, and this force of chaos has been defeated by the true Prince of Peace in the person of Christ.

This sharp critique of imperial power has made Revelation 12 and 13 the theological counterpoint to Romans 13 with its positive view of the state and its role under God.

USE OF THE OLD TESTAMENT

The text of Revelation is soaked in the OT; it is hardly possible to read a single verse without finding some echo or allusion to the OT. If the modern Western reader is baffled by this text because of ignorance of its first-century context, he or she stumbles as much on ignorance of the earlier Scripture.

Certain Greek editions of the NT (such as the United Bible Societies Third Edition, usually known as UBS 3) include a table of citations and allusions. In this listing, there are reckoned to be 676 distinct allusions to OT verses (some of them to the same OT verse), and this within a book of just 405 verses! The allusions are most frequently to Isaiah (128 times), Psalms (99), Ezekiel (92), Daniel (82) and Exodus (53). The number of allusions does not, of course, necessarily determine the relative importance of the texts, but does at least give some indication.

Three questions immediately arise in considering the place of the OT in Revelation.

● **Detection** How do we know that a given word or phrase is actually an echo of or allusion to a passage or verse in the OT? This may seem like a straightforward question, until you realise how much disagreement there is. In the passage on the seven trumpets (Rev. 8:7—9:21 and 11:15–18) ten different commentators between them propose that there are allusions to 288 OT passages – and yet agree on only one (that Rev. 9:5 alludes to Job 3:21)!
● **Intention** Is the occurrence of OT words and phrases a product of 'a memory so charged with OT words and thoughts

that they arrange themselves … without conscious effort on [the author's] part' (Swete 1917, p. cliv). Or is Revelation 'a book *designed* to be read in constant intertextual relationship with the OT' (Bauckham 1993b, pp. x–xi, emphasis mine).

It may be argued that it makes little difference whether an allusion was 'intended' or not – after all, we can often say and write things ourselves, and only later realize the true implications of what we have said.

● **Interpretation** To what extent does the meaning and context of the phrase alluded to *in its original OT context* shape its meaning in the new context of Revelation? At one extreme, Elisabeth Schüssler Fiorenza describes Revelation as using the OT as a 'language arsenal' to make its own theological statement, paying no attention at all to the meaning of the original (1985 p. 135). At the other end of the spectrum, Greg Beale (*The Book of Revelation*. NIGTC, Grand Rapids: Eerdmans/Carlisle: Paternoster, 1999) believes that meanings do not change, and so we must assume that an OT text carries its full meaning into its new place in Revelation. Steve Moyise (1995) plots an intermediate course.

SOME EXAMPLES
Revelation 7 and the numbering of the tribes
In chapter 7 the servants of God are sealed to protect them from harm. This is probably derived from the marking of the faithful in Ezekiel 9, and forms a counterpoint to the later marking of the followers of the beast in Revelation 13. But those who are sealed are listed according to their tribes. The form of this is strongly reminiscent of the census of Israel in the desert in Numbers 1. The

theme of desert as interim place occurs elsewhere in Revelation (most notably in the woman in the desert in Revelation 12). The purpose of such a census was to determine the fighting strength in preparation for conflict, and this too fits in with the overall theme of cosmic conflict in Revelation.

What do you think?

Whilst Ephesians 6 pictures each believer as a soldier, Revelation 7 offers an image of the people of God as an army, and as such is the only picture in the NT of corporate 'spiritual warfare'. What aspects of this idea might be helpful pastorally in the local church context? What aspects of it might be unhelpful, and in what situations? Have you experienced this idea being either used well or misused?

Revelation 12 and the characters of the drama
The plot of Revelation 12 derives from the Python myth, but the characters are unmistakably biblical. The woman in the pain of childbirth represents the longing of the people of God for deliverance in Isaiah 26:17; 66:7 and Micah 4:10; 5:3. The dragon is the opponent of God (Ezek. 29:3), the primeval serpent (Gen. 3:13) and accuser of God's people (Job 1:6, Zech. 3:1). The male child is the expected Messiah, the king to come (Ps. 2:9), whose victory is the victory of the champion of Israel (Michael, Dan. 10:13).

Revelation 21 and the new Jerusalem
Revelation makes extensive use of Ezekiel, and a number of key passages derive from it – the vision of God's throne in chapter 4 (Ezek. 1), the sealing of the saints in chapter. 7 (Ezek. 9), the eating of the scroll in

chapter 10 (Ezek. 3), the measuring of the temple in chapter 11 (Ezek. 40). The climax of the whole book is the vision of the temple, and yet at the climax of Revelation, there is no temple (Rev. 21:22).

From these examples we can see that the OT meaning of these ideas is important, but that Revelation uses them with freedom and to its own theological ends.

STRUCTURE AND COMPOSITION

Discussion of the structure of Revelation is rather different from such a discussion of other books of the NT, as Revelation presents itself so clearly as structured. Moreover, it further suggests that its structure gives significant clues to its meaning – much in the way that the meaning of a work of art is often contained in the arrangement of its different elements and their relation to one another. As Revelation has such a wide range of

interpretations, there are almost as many schemes for the structure of Revelation as there are commentators!

Revelation was designed for oral performance ('the one who reads aloud', Rev. 1:3 NRSV) and so we should start by focusing on things that would be noticed by the hearer, such as explicitly numbered series.

Though our concern might be to divide the text up, John's was surely to hold the text together. A clear part of this is the technique sometimes called 'intercalation' or overlapping, where a clearly structured section is interrupted by something different, or when the end of one part overlaps with what appears to be the beginning of another. Thus the series of seven seals in chapter 6 appears to be 'put on hold' and the visions of chapter 7 inserted before the seventh seal is reached in 8:1. A similar thing happens between the

THE STRUCTURE OF REVELATION

1:1–8	PROLOGUE	
1:9—3:22	VISION OF CHRIST AND THE SEVEN CHURCHES	
	2:1–3:22	The seven messages
4:1—5:14	WORSHIP IN HEAVEN	
	6:1–8:1 and 8:3–5	Seven seals
		7:1–17 The sealing of God's people
	8:2 and 8:6—11:19	Seven trumpets
		10:1–11 The call to prophesy
		11:1–13 The temple and the two witnesses
12:1—14:20 and 15:2-4	GOD'S PEOPLE IN CONFLICT WITH THE FORCES OF EVIL	
	15:1 and 15:5—16:21	Seven bowls
17:1—19:10	FINAL JUDGEMENT: THE VISION OF THE HARLOT BABYLON	
19:11—20:15	THE RIDER ON THE WHITE HORSE AND THE 1000 YEARS	
21:1—22:5	FINAL VICTORY: THE NEW JERUSALEM	
22:6–21	EPILOGUE	

sixth trumpet in chapter 9 and the seventh in 11:15, in between which is inserted the vision of 'another mighty angel', the episode of the scroll, and the vision of the temple and witnesses. Note too that the seven trumpets are introduced before the completion of the seventh seal (8:2), and likewise the seven plagues are introduced before the 'song of the Lamb' in chapter 15.

John also connects different parts of the book by means of verbal parallels and echoes.

- The intercalations in the first two series of seven judgements are both linked back to the vision of the lamb in chapter 5. The worship in 7:11f. echoes that of 5:8f. and 'another mighty angel' in 10:1 recalls the 'mighty angel' of 5:2.
- The intercalations are also linked with the later section of Rev. 12—14. The 144,000 of 7:4 reappear in 14:1; the apocalyptic period of suffering and witness in 11:2–3 reappears in 12:6 and 14; and the beast hinted at in 11:7 comes into full view in chapter 13.
- The phrase 'there appeared a great sign' introduces the new section of chapters 12—14, but also introduces the third series of seven (the plagues) in 15:1, thus integrating the new section into what had gone before.

Digging deeper

Read carefully through Rev. 1 and Rev. 21—22 using a more literal translation, and list any literary connections you find. What effect does noticing these connections have on reading what comes in between?

- The angel who introduces the vision of the harlot (Rev. 17) is one of the seven holding the bowls of plague (17:1; 15:1) thus connecting this vision with the end of the three series of sevens.

NUMBERS AND THEIR MEANING

PHRASE REPETITION AND WORD FREQUENCIES

The repetition of words and phrases in Revelation appears to have been carefully organized, and the patterns of repetition have a good deal of theological significance. This is an area that has only recently been studied in much depth, and there is more to be discovered.

Digging deeper

Read Bauckham 1993b, pp. 22–29 where he lists four phrases that are repeated exactly, but 26 that are repeated with variations. See also his special study of the sevenfold repetition of the four-fold phrase 'tribes, nations, tongues and peoples' and its variants, used to describe the people of the earth (pp. 326–337).

What does this apparently careful use of phraseology suggest about Revelation's composition? What light does it shed on the theory that Revelation is an editorial combination of earlier works?

Word frequencies can now be checked and explored comparatively easily, using computer-based Bible texts such as *Online Bible* or *Accordance*. Care needs to be taken using English-language texts, as translations differ from one another in the consistency with which they translate Greek words and

WORD REPETITIONS

Number	Possible Significance	Words
Four	Natural number for the world (four winds, four corners)	'seven Spirits' 'in the Spirit' 'Serpent' (Rev. 12) 'lightning, rumblings and thunder'
Seven	Completeness (days in the week, known planets, seas) rather than divinity	'blessed' 'sickle' (Rev. 14) 'Lord God Almighty' 'one sitting on the throne' 'Alpha and Omega/first and last/beginning and end' 'Christ' 'testimony/witness to Jesus' 'prophecy' 'I am coming'
Ten	Another natural number	'inhabitants of the earth'
Fourteen	Completeness (as twice seven) and witness (since true testimony needs two witnesses, Deut. 17:6, Rev. 11)	'Jesus' 'Spirit' 'saints'
Twenty-eight	Complete in the whole world (7 x 4)	[judgements, including the thunders of Rev. 10:3–4] [cargoes in Rev. 18:12–13] 'tribes (multitudes, kings)'/ 'languages'/'peoples'/'nations' 'lamb'

Digging deeper

Take one group of these word frequencies and look up where the particular words or phrases occur. What is the theological significance of the frequency for these words? How does it relate to the contexts in which the terms occur and to wider themes in the book?

phrases. For example, the NRSV translates *Christos* as 'Messiah' in 11:15 and 12:10; 'I am coming' is translated as 'I will come' in 2:5 and 2:16 in most versions.

Note that terms associated with the forces of evil consistently avoid this patterning. 'Dragon' occurs 13 times, 'Satan' eight times, 'devil' five times, 'beast' 38 times (excluding 6:8) and 'Babylon' six times.

NUMEROLOGY

We have already noted the symbolic significance of the numbers four and seven, and these occur explicitly in the text as well as implicitly in word frequencies. Understanding seven as signifying completeness suggests that each of the series of judgements is one way of understanding the whole of God's judgement, rather than being one in a sequence that follow on from one another. Noting that each series is completed by something signifying the end supports this. Again, the seven kings of Revelation 17 are most likely to be representative of the whole sequence of imperial rulers, rather than an enumerated historical list. The number 12 is closely associated with God's people by virtue of there being 12 tribes, and features strongly in the description of the new Jerusalem.

Digging deeper

Bauckham 1993b, pp. 390–404, explores the significance of the numbers 144, 666, 42 and 1,260 in relation to Pythagorean understandings of square, 'triangular' and 'rectangular' numbers.

What are the strengths and weaknesses of this argument as a contribution to the exegesis of the text? If Bauckham is correct, what are the implications for our interpretation of Revelation?

WORDS AND THEIR NUMBERS

Hebrew, Greek and Latin were all without separate number systems in the ancient world (our numbers derive from Arabic) and letters were used to represent numbers (see J.-P. Prévost 1993, p. 37). This meant that potentially any word could be given a value.

The calculation of the value of words was called *gematria* (Hebrew) or *isopsephism*

(Greek). It took a number of different forms, and was used in different ways.

- In Pompeii, there is an inscription: 'I love her whose number is 545.'
- The Roman historian Suetonius quotes a popular saying: 'A new calculation: Nero killed his own mother.' In Greek the value of 'Nero' and 'killed his own mother' both came to 1005, and this was supposed to confirm the rumour that Nero had done just that (Suetonius *Nero*, p. 39).
- Some rabbis taught that the Messiah would be called Menachem (meaning 'Comforter'), since in the messianic title 'branch of David' (see Jer. 23:5) the word 'branch' in Hebrew has the value 138, the same as the value of Menachem.
- One rabbinical reading sees a reference to the angel Gabriel in Ezekiel 43:2, since the phrase 'many waters' and 'Gabriel' both have the value 342.
- Within Revelation, the word 'angel', when transliterated from Greek to Hebrew, has the value 144. An angel measures the new Jerusalem in Rev. 21:15f. and finds it is 144 million stadia in area and the walls are 144 cubits (thick?).
- In the Christianized apocalyptic work the Sibylline Oracles, it is 'predicted' that the Messiah will have a name whose value is 888, and several hints are given that this must be Jesus (*Syb Or*. 1.323–331). 'Jesus' in Greek does indeed have this value, and the number 8 was associated with the Messiah and the beginning of the age to come.

To a certain extent, this use of numbers reflects a belief in the ancient world that numbers had a strange and mysterious power. Greek thinkers puzzled long and hard over aspects of mathematics that we take for granted, and the Romans' mastery of calculation in their engineering was an important plank in the maintenance of the empire. But perhaps there is a lighter side to believing that something's number 'revealed' something about the subject, much as we might think an anagram revealed something true about its subject (so 'Flit on, cheering angel' is an anagram of 'Florence Nightingale'). As with anagrams, the most common use of this numerology was in equating two things, in this case those with the same number. This is in fact the derivation of the word 'iso-' (same) '–psephism' (calculation).

THE DECODING OF 666 (Rev. 13:18)

This is perhaps one of the most intriguing and talked-about features of Revelation. Irenaeus puzzled on it in the second century, but could not find a solution that really worked. It is not uncommon today to hear all sorts of solutions, usually referring to contemporary people or things (Hitler, the Pope, barcodes, Bill Gates (!)). What are we to do with these?

Some commentators argue that it is mistaken to look for a 'solution' at all. The point is to be found in the number itself, a three-fold repetition of falling short of perfection, as represented by the number 7. Some also note that 666 is a 'triangular' number (see Bauckham 1993b, pp. 390–404). Against this, the text itself does invite us to solve a puzzle, and one that involves calculation (the Greek word in 13.18 is *psephizo*, as in *isopsephism*).

Normal considerations for understanding the Bible suggest that any solution should:

- be something that could have been understood by the author and his audience;
- make sense of the text as we have it;
- also account for any variant readings in different manuscripts (in this case, '616');
- be consistent with the use of language elsewhere in the book;
- cohere with the larger theological context.

The solution now most widely accepted in academic circles was proposed in the early nineteenth century, apparently independently, by four German scholars. If you take the phrase 'Nero Caesar', write it in Greek and then transliterate it into Hebrew, its value is 666. The text of Revelation 13:18 does in fact suggest that we should calculate the number of 'the beast' and equate it with the number of a man. 'Beast' in Greek (*therion*), transliterated into Hebrew, also has the value 666. Nero Caesar is the beast.

This form of isopsephism, identifying two things by means of their numbers, would have been familiar to a first-century audience. It does require that the name 'Nero' has an additional 'n' added on the end, but we know from inscriptional evidence that this variant was used. Removing the 'n' gives the value 616, which also corresponds to the value of the phrase '*of* the beast' in Greek (*theriou*), thus accounting for the variant. This use of numbers appears to be present also in Revelation 21:15 in the word 'angel' whose value is 144 (the measurement of the city).

One of the consistent themes of Revelation is that the power of the Roman empire is fundamentally opposed to the power of God. The identification of Nero and the beast is not primarily about an individual. Rather, it reveals the true nature of imperial power: the spirit of empire is the spirit of Nero, the arch-persecutor and opponent of God's people.

INTERPRETATIVE ISSUES

TRADITIONAL APPROACHES

There are generally agreed to be four ways of understanding the text of Revelation and its interpretation:

- **Idealist** This sees the text as describing timeless spiritual truths about the nature and purposes of God, and the relationship between the church and the world. Some of the earliest allegorical interpretations of Revelation were of this sort, but this approach has more recent exponents too.
- **Futurist** A rival school of early interpreters saw in Revelation the prediction of an imminent end and the advent of the millennial age. Joachim of Fiore in the twelfth century understood it as predicting the end in his time, and there has been a strong revival of this approach in the twentieth century.
- **Church historical** As the centuries passed, it became increasingly attractive to see Revelation as having some historical references, but not to the 'end times' only. Berengaud in the ninth century was the first to suggest that Revelation described events through history to the writer's day.
- **Contemporary historical** (or **preterist**) The rise of biblical criticism and the rediscovery of the historical context of Revelation's writing has made it possible to argue that Revelation is primarily speaking to its own day, and only secondarily (and derivatively) to later readers.

Some comment on the approach taken is usually featured at the beginning of works on Revelation, and these four are not necessarily mutually exclusive. But the most important thing to notice about these 'approaches' is that they are actually conclusions from reading the text, not assumptions made on approaching the text. Whether Revelation is primarily concerned about the past, present or future, and in what way, must be decided on the basis of engagement with the text, not assumed as a tool with which to *approach* it. Why should we treat Revelation any differently from other NT texts in asking questions about its author, first readers and literary shape?

IMAGE, SYMBOL AND METAPHOR

The most pervasive characteristic of Revelation is its imagery and symbolism. This is one of its distinctive features in comparison with other apocalyptic literature; Revelation offers a far more thoroughgoing depiction of an alternative 'symbolic universe' in which it invites its readers to participate.

Although this aspect of the text is described as 'imagery' or 'symbolism', these terms strictly belong to the extra-textual world, and it is more correctly called 'metaphor'. Part of the reason why Revelation has been difficult to read is that, in the development of Western thought, we have not been very good at understanding metaphor. This has been part of a wider intellectual movement, which, since the Enlightenment, has consistently prioritized literal language over the metaphorical.

Linguistically, metaphor involves bringing together two things that are unlike, that do not belong together. When I describe a friend as 'eating like a horse' I am bringing together two things that are different – a person and a horse – and making some identification between them. But the identification is only partial; I am suggesting that my friend is like a horse only in some respects (in this case, in eating large quantities) but not in others. How do we know which aspects are brought together, and which are not? First, by knowing something of the context – how much horses eat, and what my friend is like. But we also need to understand conventions, and the previous use of this kind of language. We all understand what it means to 'sleep like a baby', but the strange thing is that babies rarely do it! The meaning of this metaphor (which has become a figure of speech) has been shaped by its use elsewhere. So to read Revelation, we need to understand both its historical and wider literary context.

The partial nature of the metaphorical identification holds the key to understanding how Revelation continues to speak powerfully to modern readers. In chapters 12 and 13, Roman imperial power is identified with the beast from the sea, acting alongside the beast from the land, and with the power of the dragon. As such it is characterized by repressive violence, conflict with the true people of God, control of economic systems, and the maintenance of respect for its image. In characterizing it this way, Revelation is shearing off many of the historical particularities of the empire – it is creating a caricature, in which certain aspects of reality are focused on and others ignored. Such a caricature is then easily seen to apply to other contexts, wherever there

are regimes marked by repression, persecution, economic control and maintenance of image. The metaphorical nature of the language makes it widely applicable beyond its original context, and in fact appears to invite us to similarly re-imagine our world using biblical categories in the way Revelation itself does.

The openness and applicability of Revelation's metaphors means that there is a constant temptation to make a direct connection between the text and our own world – to think that the referent of the text is the world of our day (dotted line). But the historically conditioned nature of the metaphors means that we have to read Revelation in its historical context, and only then find a 'correspondence of relations' (Elisabeth Schüssler Fiorenza) with our own situation (solid lines).

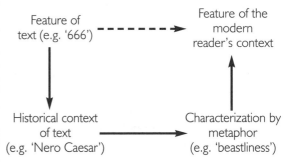

According to Revelation's theological scheme, we continue to live in the 'in-between' time before the return of Christ, when God's rule has only partially broken in and Satan's defeat is yet to be made complete. God continues to call his saints to faithful witness in the face of suffering, and the final destiny of all powers opposed to God will be the same as the judgement prophesied for the Roman empire. To this extent, a contemporary historical approach allows for elements of both idealist and futurist readings.

SOME ISSUES FOR TODAY

1. Looking to the future

In many parts of the church in the West, this future orientation has been lost. The problems and challenges of the present appear so overwhelming that many are unable to put them into a wider context. We are also living in a society that has lost confidence in its past, and has correspondingly lost any sense of vision for the future. Against this, Revelation is thoroughly eschatological; it is looking forwards (in both senses) to 'the end' and is re-imagining its world in the light of that end.

2. A sense of God's involvement with history

Some Christian traditions see God as involved in the minutiae of the believer's life. On its own, this can lapse into a concern with the trivial. Others minimize any sense of God being actively involved with the world. Yet others see this involvement as fatalist, and treat Revelation much as they would the predictions of Nostradamus. Rightly understood, Revelation sees God's involvement with his people as expressed by his involvement with history. This involvement is not fatalistic but is concerned with issues of power, freedom, and faithfulness in suffering. It holds together the paradoxes of the sovereignty of God and the reality of evil.

3. Ecology

Revelation has a positive view of the created world. The creation suffers under God's judgement along with humanity, but also has a place within God's ultimate purposes. The destiny of a redeemed humanity is to enjoy a renewed creation that will include the fruit of human creativity – its goal is a heavenly city, not a garden. This has implications for the way we treat the world, how we view our bodies, and the place we give to human creativity.

4. Apocalyptic language and the imagination

Apocalyptic language is the language of crisis, whether that is a crisis that is already felt or one that the language itself aims to precipitate. We therefore have to be careful how we deploy it in the pastoral context. But it is also a language of imagination, and Revelation challenges the reader to consider the pastoral task of enabling the church to re-imagine its own world in biblical terms.

ESSAY TOPICS

INTRODUCTORY

● Prepare an outline study course on the book of Revelation for use in small groups. This should include material giving some background and comment on the text together with appropriate questions for discussion.

● How does Revelation relate to its social context? What does this tell us about its pastoral function?

● 'Revelation comforts the discomforted and unsettles the comfortable.' Which of these do you see as the more important within the book?

INTERMEDIATE

● 'Revelation does not interpret the OT but uses its words, images, phrases and patterns as a language arsenal in order to make its own theological statements.' Do you agree with this statement on Revelation's use of the OT? Answer with reference to one passage of Revelation, or one book of the OT that is alluded to in Revelation.

● What language does Revelation use to describe God? How does this relate to other NT language and to debate in the church in the following centuries?

● 'The St John who gave us the last words of the Bible was an apocalyptic pastor. To be like him, I must submit my imagination to his apocalypse, and let its energies define and shape me' (Eugene Peterson *The Contemplative Pastor*. Grand Rapids: Eerdmans, 1993, pp. 40–2). What might it mean to be an 'apocalyptic pastor'? Does Revelation offer us an appropriate language with which to re-imagine our world?

FURTHER READING

*denotes books assuming knowledge of Greek; most can be used by all students.

INTRODUCTORY
R. Bauckham *The Theology of the Book of Revelation*. Cambridge: CUP, 1993a (excellent overview of Revelation's theological themes).

A. Boesak *Comfort and Protest*. Edinburgh: St Andrew Press, 1987 (a gripping read from apartheid South Africa).

M. Gilbertson *The Meaning of the Millennium*. Cambridge: Grove Books Ltd, 1997 (clear exploration of the millennium in Revelation 20).

G. Goldsworthy *The Gospel in Revelation*. Carlisle: Paternoster, 1994 (a simple way in to Revelation's message).

C. Koester *Revelation and the End of All Things*. Grand Rapids/Cambridge: Eerdmans, 2001 (a readable and innovative introduction, combining comment on themes and comment on text).

C. Le Moignan *Following the Lamb*. London: SCM Press, 2000 (a stimulating attempt to relate Revelation to today).

J.-P. Prévost *How to Read the Apocalypse*. London: SCM Press, 1993 (helpful introduction, though with some omissions).

S. Woodman *The Book of Revelation*. SCM Core Text. London: SCM Press, 2008 (quite a good introduction to some of the central issues).

INTERMEDIATE
* R. Bauckham *The Climax of Prophecy*. Edinburgh: T. & T. Clark, 1993b (outstanding series of in-depth studies on Revelation).

A. Y. Collins *Crisis and Catharsis: The Power of the Apocalypse*. Philadelphia: Westminster, 1984.

S. J. Friesen *Imperial Cults and the Apocalypse of John*. Oxford/New York: Oxford University Press, 2001 (a detailed exploration of archaeological issues, combined with reflection on the interpretative and theological significance of the findings).

C. J. Hemer *The Letters to the Seven Churches of Asia in Their Local Setting*. Sheffield: JSOT Press, 1986.

W. Howard-Brook and A. Gwyther *Unveiling Empire*. New York: Orbis Books, 1999 (connects the original political context of Revelation with its political implications for today).

H. O. Maier *Apocalypse Recalled*. Minneapolis: Fortress Press, 2002 (a sophisticated reading of Revelation in the post-modern context).

J. R. Michaels *Interpreting the Book of Revelation*. Grand Rapids: Baker, 1992 (helpful introduction to the exegetical issues).

*S. Moyise *The Old Testament in the Book of Revelation*. Sheffield: Sheffield Academic Press, 1995 (a balanced assessment of the subject).

*S. Moyise (ed.) *Studies in Revelation*. Edinburgh: T. & T. Clark, 2001 (some key essays on a range of subjects by leading scholars).

I. B. Paul 'Ebbing and Flowing: Scholarly Developments in the Study of the Book of Revelation' *Expository Times* 119.11 2008, pp. 523–31 (a review of scholarship in the last twenty years).

W. M. Ramsay *The Letters to the Seven Churches of Asia*. London/New York: Hodder & Stoughton, 1904 (and several subsequent editions).

E. Schüssler Fiorenza *The Book of Revelation: Justice and Judgement*. Philadelphia: Fortress Press, 1985 (combines literary and sociological analysis from a feminist perspective).

L. Thompson *The Book of Revelation: Apocalypse and Empire*. Oxford: Oxford University Press, 1990 (important study arguing that Revelation is more precipitating a crisis than responding to one).

Commentaries

* D. E. Aune *Revelation*. WBC. 3 volumes. Dallas, Texas: Word, 1997–2000 (very detailed and technical without really offering a reading of the text, but cites a vast range of secondary literature).

G. R. Beasley-Murray *The Book of Revelation*. NCB. London: Marshall, Morgan and Scott, 1974 (out of print, but something of a classic).

I. Boxall *The Revelation of John*. Black's New Testament Commentary. Peabody: Hendrickson/London: Continuum, 2006 (good, clear commentary, the successor to Caird in the Black's series).

R. H. Mounce *Revelation*. NICNT. Grand Rapids: Eerdmans, 1977/1998 (reliable, and now revised, commentary).

C. Rowland *Revelation*. EC. London: Epworth, 1993 (brief narrative commentary especially aware of the political dimensions of the text).

*H. B. Swete *The Apocalypse of St John. The Greek text with introduction, notes and indices*. London: Macmillan, 1917 (assumes knowledge of Hebrew, Greek and Latin, but the 200-page introduction contains a wealth of historical information, much of it still useful).

M. Wilcock *I Saw Heaven Opened: The Message of Revelation*. BST. Leicester: IVP, 2nd edition 1991 (a useful short introduction).

B. Witherington III *Revelation*. NCBC. Cambridge: CUP, 2003 (excellent medium-length commentary, including consideration of socio-rhetorical issues though with quite traditional conclusions).

GLOSSARY

This gives brief definitions of terms used in the book and a reference in square brackets to the main discussion(s) of this topic in the book.

Amanuensis A person who assists an author by performing the physical act of writing at their dictation or following their instructions.

Apocalyptic Literature or ideas associated with God revealing unknown things or events, often in the form of a dream or a visit by an angel. Sometimes used of the belief that God will act to destroy the present universe and replace it.

Apostle A term used to refer to people specially commissioned by God as his messengers and missionaries. Usually it refers to people who were so commissioned in a personal revelation by the risen Jesus Christ, but it is also used of people commissioned by Christian congregations.

Asceticism The practice of denying oneself material or bodily pleasures, usually out of religious conviction.

Authenticity A term applied to documents or statements that are genuinely the compositions of the persons to whom they are attributed.

Catchword A word introduced at the end of a statement to form the bridge to the content of the next statement.

Charisma (pl. *charismata*) A Greek word meaning 'gift' used especially by Paul in 1 Corinthians 12 to refer to various manifestations of the power of the Holy Spirit in people's lives, including the ability to convey divine truth, teach, be generous, prophesy, perform healings,

show compassion, speak in tongues, and so on. The adjective 'charismatic' is used to refer to such gifts of the Spirit [pp. 83, 91].

Circumcision A surgical operation involving the removal of the foreskin of males, usually carried out on Jewish children at birth and serving as a physical sign that they belonged to the people of God.

Colony A settlement of veteran or demobilized Roman soldiers and their families to form a small town with various privileges. In practice many such towns also had a substantial population of non-Romans.

Conversion The process by which a person undergoes a significant shift in their religious views, usually from one religion to another.

Covenantal nomism A term created by E. P. Sanders to characterize the Judaism of New Testament times as a religion based on God's covenant with the Jews to which they were expected to respond by keeping his law (Gk. *nomos*). Keeping the law was not required to 'get in' but rather to 'stay in' [pp. 53–4, 204–5].

Diatribe A form of rhetoric in the Greco-Roman world that adopted a lively dialogical style, including the posing of questions attributed to imaginary opponents and answers to them.

Dispensationalism A theological and interpretative perspective which distinguishes between successive periods of human history or 'dispensations', in each of which God reveals a particular purpose to be accomplished during that period. Particular emphasis is generally placed on eschatology and on the nature of the future 'millennium' (Rev. 20).

Dispersion The term used for Jews living outside Judea; the area in which they lived.

Docetism A heresy that emerged in the early second century, according to which Jesus was a divine figure who only seemed (Gk. *dokei*) to be human, but wasn't really.

Doxology An expression of praise to God.

Early catholicism A term describing the character of the church when it had gradually evolved from the comparatively simple structures attested in the New Testament to the more institutionalized form, with elaborate structures of leadership and discipline, that culminated in the Roman Catholic Church [p. 296].

Eschatology Beliefs about how God will bring to fulfilment his purposes for his creation, whether in the near or distant future [p. 272].

Exegesis The process of trying to understand what a text would have meant to its original readers.

Exposition The process of trying to explain the significance that a text might have for readers today.

Flesh The material of which human beings are made; it came to refer to their human nature in its perishability, weakness and tendency to sin [pp. 50, 203].

Genre The literary type or category of a book or piece of writing [pp. 324–6].

Gentile A term used by Jews to refer to all non-Jews.

Gnosticism A term used to describe a variety of dualistic movements that flourished in the second century AD and later. They believed in a heavenly redeemer, who came into the world to save people from bondage to the material world by giving them divine knowledge (Gk. *gnosis*) [pp. 83–4, 308].

Hellenistic A term used to refer to the period from the time of Alexander the Great onwards during which the language and culture of 'Classical Greece' (the period of the great dramatists, historians and philosophers) broadly influenced the eastern Mediterranean world.

Hermeneutics The 'science' of interpretation, dealing particularly with theories of how we understand texts [pp. 221–32].

Integrity In New Testament scholarship a term applied to documents which are single compositions rather than artificial combinations of several originally separate documents.

Intercalation Author's insertion of material which interrupts the flow of a larger unit of text.

Interlocutor Partner in a conversation or debate.

Interpolation A passage inserted into a document by a later writer.

Judaizing A term applied to people who tried to impose Jewish practices, such as circumcision, Jewish festivals and food laws, on Gentile converts to Christianity.

Justification The process whereby God declares sinners to be in a right relationship with himself and does not hold their sins any longer against them [pp. 50, 205–6].

Kosher A term used for foods that satisfied the Jewish law, e.g. meat from which the blood had been drained.

Law In Paul's writings 'law' normally means the Jewish law, traditionally understood as contained in the books of Moses (Genesis – Deuteronomy) but continually being elaborated in Jewish traditions that came to be regarded as equally authoritative [pp. 50, 216–7].

Lectionary A set of passages from Scripture for consecutive reading over a period of time in a synagogue or Christian congregation.

Manumission The release of a slave by his/her owner to become a freedman, often on payment of a price but sometimes unconditionally. Note the distinction between a 'freedman' (a former slave) and a 'free man' [p. 152].

Midrash A Hebrew word, meaning something like 'searching', used to describe Jewish traditions that grew up interpreting and commenting on the OT; hence applied to Christian reflection on the OT in a similar style.

Mirror-reading An attempt to understand the situation underlying a document, such as a letter, by reconstructing what must have been happening to evoke the contents of the document [p. 229].

Pantheon A collection of gods, e.g., the chief gods of the Greeks.

Parousia The 'coming' of Jesus again to earth, expected by the early Christians in line with Acts 1:11.

Pauline letters Letters written by, or attributed to, Paul.

Persecution Hostile activity, whether social, economic or physical, directed against persons because of their religious views.

Pogrom Organized persecution of a group (originally of Jews in Russia).

Prophet A person who receives messages from God and communicates them to other people.

Proselyte A convert to Judaism. In the case of males this involved acceptance of circumcision and the other requirements of the Jewish law.

Pseudonymity The composition of a document by a person other than the person named as the author, usually involving an element of deception. *Pseudepigraphy* is an alternative term for the composition of such documents.

Rhetoric The art of persuasion by the spoken word and, by extension, by written accounts of the spoken word. It was a major element in ancient education [p. 143].

Sacramentalism Belief in or special emphasis upon the efficacy of the sacraments for conferring grace. Negatively, it can refer to excessive *reliance* on the sacraments to be effective, irrespective of the faith and obedience of the recipient [p. 296].

Septuagint The Greek translation of the OT, which was familiar to Greek-speaking Jews and Christians of the NT period.

Slave A person who was owned by another person ('master/mistress') and had to work for them, often as a household servant.

Soteriology (Gk. *soteria*) The doctrine of salvation.

Syncretism The attempt to combine the beliefs of two different systems or religions.

INDEX

Abraham 51, 118, 213, 254, 269

Achtemeier, P. J. 236, 280

Acts of Paul and Thecla 31, 194

Acts of the Apostles, reliability of 32–4

Adam 119–20, 203

Aeschylus 84

Alexander, L. C. A. 44

Alexander the Great 334

allegorical use of Scripture 51, 342

amanuensis 24, 128, 180, 184, 287, 299–300

amphitheatre 13

Antiochus Epiphanes 70

Antony *see* Mark Antony

apocalyptic 70–2, 253, 342–4

Apollodorus 12

Apollonius of Tyana 235–7

apostle, apostleship 98, 101–2, 115, 127, 201–2, 214, 299, 315, 318

Apuleius 15

archaeology 4, 133

Aretas 43

Aristotle 17, 165

Arnold, C. E. 161–2

asceticism 80, 87, 190, 193–4

astrology 16

athletics 13

Attridge, W. 257

Augustine 257

Augustus 3, 5, 6, 8, 9, 10, 16, 18, 20, 23, 137

Aune, D. E. 328

authority 155, 163–4, 316–17

authorship of letters 24, 34–6, 72–4, 167–8, 177–80, 183–7, 197–9, 234–8, 256–7, 264–7, 285–8, 295–6, 298–300, 305–7, 328

Babylon 277, 279, 285–6, 328, 339

Balch, D. L. 288

baptism 114, 164, 210

Barrett, C. K. 12, 18, 101, 105, 108, 146, 152, 197, 307

Barth, K. 111, 134, 230

baths 14

Bauckham, R. J. 236–7, 262, 267, 269, 271, 292, 294, 297–8, 318, 324, 331–2, 338, 340–1

Beale, G. K. 336

Beare, F. W. 235

Beck, J. R. 189

Berengaud 342

Betz, H. D. 49, 104

bishops *see* overseers

Blocher, H. 119

Blomberg, C. L. 189

Bloomquist, L. G. 143–5

body 203, 213–14

Boesak, A. 327

Bornkamm, G. 113

Botham, I. 224

Brown, R. E. 317

Bruce, F. F. 57, 139

Brunner, E. 68

Brutus 5, 137

Bultmann, R. 68

Butterfield, H. 169

Cadbury, H. J. 181

Caligula *see* Gaius Caligula

Calvin, J. 270

canonical criticism 233

Carson, D. 35

Cassius 5, 137

Chae, D. S.-J. 114

chariot races 6, 13–14

charisma *see* spiritual gifts

Chester, A. 273, 282

Christian living 66–8, 126–7, 164–6, 188, 195, 207–11, 210–11, 215–17, 247–50, 252, 270–3, 284–5, 294–5, 301–3, 311–12, 332

Christology 146, 148–9, 163, 176, 211–12, 247–52, 270, 309–10, 310, 312, 331–2

chronology of Paul's life 42–4

Chrysostom, John 225

church 90–2, 145–7, 173–4, 176–7, 189–90, 194–6, 212–15, 282–4, 310–11, 316–18, 330–2

Cicero 24, 41

circumcision 19, 48, 117, 142, 162

circus 19

citizenship 10, 40

Claudius 6, 10–11, 16, 43, 112, 133, 256

Clement of Alexandria 257

Clement of Rome 42, 255, 270, 300

Cleopatra 5

client kingdoms 9

collection, Paul's for Jerusalem 57–8, 93, 95–6, 103, 130, 138, 217

Collins, A. Y. 327

Collins, J. J. 325

Collins, R. F. 197

colonies 9, 137

'covenantal nomism' 52, 204–5

co-workers of Paul 26, 40, 63–4, 73, 102–3, 137, 154–5, 183, 185

Cranfield, C. E. B. 113–14

Crassus 5

creation 123, 163, 202, 211–12, 270, 331

Cynic philosophers 17

Dalton, W. J. 284

Davids, P. H. 265–7, 269, 286

Davies, M. 197

deacons 190, 195, 214

Dead Sea Scrolls *see* Qumran

death 102, 145, 148, 218

Dibelius, M. 230, 262, 265

Didache 294, 315

Dionysius of Alexandria 328

discipleship *see* Christian living

Dispersion, *diaspora* 19, 263, 266–7, 278–9

divisions in church 80–1, 85–6, 141, 146–7

docetism 309

Dodd, C. H. 306

Domitian 7, 16, 326–7, 333, 335

Donfried, K. P. 113

Doty, W. G. 27

doxology 28, 129, 295, 297, 326

Dunn, J. D. G. 35, 52–3, 114, 130, 204–5, 296

early catholicism 178–9, 296, 298–9

ecology 134, 344

Edwards, R. B. 310

elders 187, 195, 214, 267, 285, 307, 313–17, 334

elemental spirits 50–1, 160–1

Elliott, J. H. 279, 284, 287–8, 299

Elliott, J. K. 32

Ellis, E. E. 74, 198, 299, 308

emperor worship *see* imperial cult

emperors *see* Roman emperors

entertainment 13

Epictetus 17

Epicurus, Epicurean philosophy 17–18, 235–6, 301

Epiphanius 327

eschatology 67–72, 84, 87, 102, 119, 215, 217–18, 251–2, 272, 284, 288, 296, 301–2, 290, 331–2, 344

ethics 15, 71, 80, 86–8, 126–7, 164–6, 176, 188, 211, 215–17, 248, 251, 272, 302–3, 306, 309–12

Eusebius 138, 186, 235, 257, 264, 298, 307–8, 328

evangelism *see* mission

faith 51, 116, 118–19, 206–7, 210, 249, 268–70, 296, 312

false teaching, heresy 70–2, 141–2, 160–4, 190, 192–6, 293–5, 297, 300–2, 308–11, 314

fate 16, 161–2

Fee, G. 198

Felix 9, 11

Ferguson, E. 18

Festus 9, 43

flesh 50–1, 121–2, 203, 210–11

food offered to idols 82–3, 88–9

form criticism 232

freedmen 11, 24, 82

freedom in Christ 51, 163, 216, 282

Frör, H. 80

Gaius Caligula 6, 16, 18, 70

Gallio 43, 64, 77

Gates, B. 341

Gnosticism 83–4, 104, 161, 168, 194, 252, 294, 308–11

God, character and activity of 110–13, 116–19, 207–8, 211–12, 256, 310, 331

gods, Greek and Roman 14–15

grace of God 52–5, 205, 282

Grant, M. 334

Greek language 9, 13, 34, 257, 265–6, 285–6, 296

Green, G. L. 300

Green, J. B. 289

Green, M. 140, 292, 299, 330

Groothuis, R. M. 189

Grudem, W. 189, 286

Guthrie, D. 198, 307

gymnasium 14

Hanson, A. T. 197

Hardy, T. 291

Harnack, A. 173

Harrison, P. N. 186, 197

healing cults 15

Hemer, C. J. 33, 57, 278, 329–30

Hengel, M. 265

Henten, J. W. van 335

heresy *see* false teaching

Hermas 300

hermeneutics 221–32, 342–3

Herod Agrippa I 9, 43

Herod the Great 9, 18

historical criticism 232

Hitler, A. 341

holiness, sanctification 66, 211, 216, 217, 282, 285, 311–12

Holy Spirit *see* Spirit (of God)

Horace 3, 13

Horrell, D. G. 287

household codes 165–6, 279, 288–9

humanity 202–3

Hurd, J. C. 80

Hurst, L. D. 252

Hurtado, L. 146

Hyginus 334

hymn 146, 334

ideology criticism 233

idolatry 82–3, 88–9, 313

Ignatius of Antioch 155, 179, 195, 309, 313, 317

immorality 66–7, 78, 80, 86–7, 277, 300

imperial cult 16, 20, 73, 80, 333–4

'in Christ' 176, 208–9, 215

interpolation 36, 79, 92, 100, 103–4

Irenaeus 286, 289, 307–8, 311, 326

Israel, church's relation with 123–5, 254, 258–9, 282–3

Jerome 225, 257, 299, 310

Jervell, J. 113

Jesus Christ: death of 51–2, 117–20, 205, 248–9, 282, 306, 312; teaching of 68, 267–8, 286

Jew–Gentile relations in Christ 113, 123–7, 134–5, 174, 176, 207

Jewish revolt 6, 10

Jews, Judaism 6–7, 13, 15, 17–19, 52–4, 129, 162

Joachim of Fiore 342

Jobes, K. H. 286

Johnson, L. T. 198, 265, 269, 271

Josephus 9, 43, 71, 255, 264–5, 299

judaizing 47–9, 51–3, 104–5, 141–2

judgement 70, 91, 102, 116–17, 203–5, 207, 215, 217–18, 251–2, 267, 272–3, 282, 301–2, 331, 340

Julius Caesar 5, 24, 137

justification 50–5, 117–20, 204–6

Juvenal 3, 13–14, 19

Käsemann, E. 291

Kim, S. 38

Lactantius 18

Latin language 9, 13, 34

law of Moses 47–55, 64, 117, 120–2, 204, 207, 216, 269, 271, 293–4

Laws, S. 265

lectionary 128

Lepidus 5

letter, types of in NT 23, 172–3, 244–5, 263, 305, 311, 314–15, 326

letter-writing, ancient 23–5

letters, format of Paul's 25–8

letters of introduction/ recommendation 28, 160, 316

Lietzmann, H. 107

Lieu, J. 25, 307, 309

literary criticism 233

litigation 80, 86

liturgical material 28, 146, 179

Livy 3

Lohse, E. 167

Longenecker, R. N. 228

Lord's supper 90–1

love 51, 88, 91, 126, 207, 249, 284–5, 312–15

Lucretius 18

Luther, M. 111, 206, 261, 270

McDonald, J. I. H. 133

magic 16

Manson, T. W. 113

manumission 152

manuscripts see textual variations

Marcion 129, 173

Marius 4

Mark Antony 5, 137

marriage and singleness 87–8, 176, 217

Marshall, C. D. 204

Marshall, I. H. 74, 198, 280, 284, 307

Martin, R. P. 103, 262, 267, 282

Meade, D. G. 236–7, 287

Menken, M. J. J. 73

metaphor 249, 342–3

midrash 27, 294

Minear, P. S. 113, 327

miracles 105, 213

mirror-reading 143, 159, 229

mission, missionaries, evangelism 5, 34, 63–4, 66, 77, 111–12, 138, 148, 202, 219, 314–16

money see rich and poor

Moo, D. J. 121

Moule, C. F. D. 255

Mounce, W. D. 198

Moyise, S. 336

Muddiman, J. 180

Murphy-O'Connor, J. 27, 37, 82

mystery religions 15–16

mysticism 324

mythology 333–5

narrative criticism 233

Nero 6, 11, 16–17, 19, 43, 217, 256, 326, 340–1, 343

'New Perspective' on Paul 52–3

Neyrey, J. H. 301

Nostradamus 344

numbers 338–41

Oakes, P. 137, 141

Octavian (Augustus) 5, 137

Old Testament, use of 51, 101, 114, 123–5, 193, 213, 244–6, 247–51, 282–3, 294, 335–7

Ollrog, W.-H. 154

opponents of Paul 50–1, 96, 98, 104–6, 141–2, 193–4

Origen 256, 265

overseers 187, 190, 194–5, 214, 316–17

Ovid 122

Painter, J. 310

Papias 307

papyrus 23–4, 151, 244

parenesis 27, 262, 267

parousia 67–70, 72, 177, 218, 270, 300–2

party spirit see divisions in church

patrons and clients 12–13, 71, 82

Paul: background of 36–8; call and conversion 38–9, 57; as captive 41–2, 137, 151–2, 159, 166–7, 186; gospel 65, 113, 116; life and chronology of 36–44; as missionary 39–42, 111–12, 115, 127, 219; sources for 32–4

Pax Romana 5

perfection 217, 251, 270

persecution 6, 17, 19–20, 41–2, 66, 69–70, 126, 133, 192–3, 244, 255–6, 280–2, 284, 327, 332, 343

Peterlin, D. 141

Peterson, D. G. 251

Petronius 3, 286

Pharisees 37, 54

Phillips, J. B. 231

Philo 18, 122, 154, 164, 252–4, 299

philosophers, philosophy 3, 6–7, 11, 14–15, 17–18, 65

Pierce, R. W. 189

Piper, J. 189

Plato 16, 222, 235–7, 253

Pliny the elder 24

Pliny the younger 17, 280–1, 285

Plutarch 15

Polycarp 308, 326–7

Pompey 5

poor see rich and poor

praetorian guard, praetorium 6, 10–11, 138–9

prayer, prayer report 26, 65, 69, 115, 137, 162–3, 190, 192, 207–8, 211

Prévost, J.-P. 340

principalities and powers 161–2, 164, 174–7

prophet, prophecy 66, 91–2, 294, 301, 308–9, 315, 324–5

provinces *see* Roman provinces

pseudonymity 34–6, 72–3, 167–8, 183–7, 197–9, 221, 234–8, 264–6, 285–8, 295–6, 298–300

Python myth 334–6

Qumran 54, 86, 248, 252, 286

Ramsay, W. M. 33, 329

Rapske, B. M. 40

reader-response criticism 233

reception history 233

reconciliation 102, 153, 163, 206

redaction criticism 232

redemption 206

religions 12, 14–16, 18, 161

resurrection: of believers 67–8, 84, 92, 102, 194, 218; of Christ 92, 146, 163, 284; *see also* Christology

rhetoric, rhetorical style 27, 49, 106, 115, 143–5, 227–8, 233, 296, 298

rich and poor 71, 81–2, 191, 217, 266–7, 272–3

Richard, E. J. 73–4

righteousness of God 116, 205–6

Robinson, J. A. T. 186

Roman army 4–6, 8–11, 18

Roman classes 10–13

Roman emperors 5–8, 327

Roman government 4, 8–9, 126, 217, 327

Roman history 4–7

Roman propaganda 9–10, 335

Roman provinces 4–6, 8–10

Rudwick, M. J. S. 330

sacrifice 118, 205, 247–51, 306, 312

salvation 116, 119, 173, 175–6, 204–6, 248–9, 251–2, 308

sanctification *see* holiness

Sanders, E. P. 52–3, 204

Schmithals, W. 74

Schnackenburg, R. 307

Schneemelcher, W. 31–2

Schüssler Fiorenza, E. 336, 343

Schweizer, E. 74

secretary *see* amanuensis

Seneca 6, 11, 17, 23

Silva, M. 230

sin 51, 116–17, 119–22, 134, 175, 203

slavery (as metaphor) 51, 121

slaves 7, 9, 11–12, 17, 78, 88, 151–6, 217

Smalley, S. S. 317

social classes 10–13, 81–2

sophists 81

source criticism 232

Spirit (of God) 51–4, 105, 119, 122–3, 126, 188, 192, 210–11, 215, 218, 293, 306–7, 309–11, 317, 332

spiritual gifts 83–4, 91, 120, 174, 176, 213–15, 284, 303

state *see* Roman government

Stobaeus 190, 191

Stoic philosophers 17

'strong' and 'weak' believers 82–3, 127

Suetonius 3, 6–7, 16, 19, 112, 340

suffering *see* persecution

Swete, H. B. 336

syncretism 161–2, 292

Tacitus 3, 6–7, 10, 18, 19, 256

Tarsus 36

taxes 4, 7, 9

Taylor, M. E. 264

temple (in Jerusalem) 7, 71, 256

tent-making 37

Tertullian 236–7, 257

testament 191–2, 297–9

textual criticism 232

textual variations 92, 128–30, 132–4, 172, 224, 233

theatre 4, 13, 171

theodicy 300

Thiselton, A. C. 84, 87, 92

Thompson, L. L. 327

Thompson, M. B. 52–3

Thrall, M. E. 104–5

Tiberius 6, 13, 16

Titus 7

Tix, H. U. 222

tradition 317

Trajan 17, 281, 308, 311

travel 9, 63, 77–8, 95, 111–12, 138, 140, 186

Tübingen school 33

Vespasian 6, 10, 16

Virgil 3, 9

Wanamaker, C. A. 74

Watson, D. F. 143–5

Watson, F. B. 98–9

wealth *see* rich and poor

Wenham, D. 68

Wesley, J. 111

Westerholm, S. 53

White, J. L. 27

widows 191

Winter, B. W. 71, 83, 79, 84

wisdom 83, 85, 163, 247, 262–3, 267–8, 270–1

Witherington III, B. 45, 264, 280, 287, 296

witness 140, 145, 190, 192–3, 332, 338–9, 343

women 9–10, 12, 90–2, 189–90, 217, 224–7, 233

worship, worship meetings 83, 90–2, 189, 331–2, 333–4

wrath of God 203–4

Wright, N. T. 52–3, 114

writing materials 23–4

Zeno 17

Ziesler, J. 121